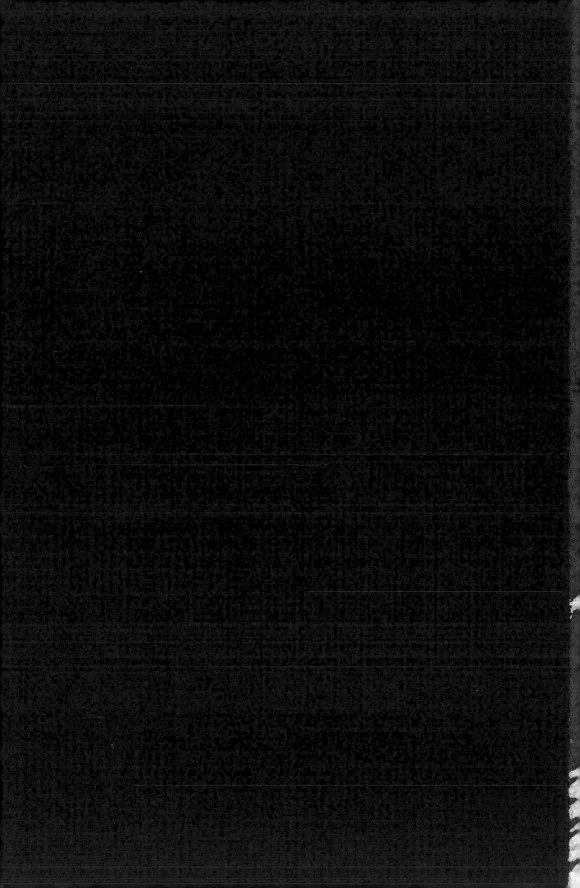

UNITIES

UNITIES

STUDIES IN THE ENGLISH NOVEL

H. M. DALESKI

THE UNIVERSITY OF GEORGIA PRESS   ATHENS

© 1985 by the University of Georgia Press
Athens, Georgia 30602
All rights reserved

Designed by Sandra Strother Hudson
Set in Mergenthaler Trump Medieval with Delphian display
The paper in this book meets the guidelines for
permanence and durability of the Committee on
Production Guidelines for Book Longevity of the
Council on Library Resources.

Printed in the United States of America

90 89 88 87 86 85   6 5 4 3 2 1

Library of Congress Cataloging in Publication Data

Daleski, H. M. (Hillel Matthew), 1926–
Unities: studies in the English novel.

1. English fiction—History and criticism—Addresses,
essays, lectures. I. Title.
PR823.D34 1985   823'.009   84–8842
ISBN 0–8203–0743–2 (alk. paper)

In Memoriam

T.P.D.   and   J.D.

1902–1957   1897–1980

One must not come to feel that he has
a thousand threads in his hands,
He must somehow see the one thing;
This is the level of art
There are other levels
But there is no other level of art

George Oppen, "Of Being Numerous"

CONTENTS

PREFACE

It comes as a pleasant surprise to find that there is a figure in one's own carpet, and that essays written under a variety of circumstances and over a number of years consort readily with those specially prepared for this book. Though about half the essays have been published previously or are currently in press, they are all related to the idea of unity that has specifically generated the new work; and so in grouping them, I have ignored differences in their dates of composition. In undertaking the new essays, I have been very much aware of the challenge posed by the tenets of Deconstruction to the unitary meanings I pursue. I do not directly confront this challenge in the essays themselves—only that on *The History of Henry Esmond* was written in immediate response to a deconstructionist analysis—but they are all presented in tacit affirmation of a more traditional critical method and as a practical demonstration that texts may continue to be seen as "readable." I realize that Deconstructionists would willingly undertake to show that the same texts are "unreadable," but then their assumptions and procedures seem to me to be open to radical objection. I leave the essays to speak for themselves, therefore, hoping that their univocality will not be found to be disabling, and in the Postscript briefly formulate some of the objections that deconstructionist criticism appears to invite. If we have to choose between univocal and equivocal readings of texts, we might do well to recognize that the former need not be as limiting nor the latter as liberating as is sometimes supposed these days.

I have grouped together those essays which use similar means in attempting to demonstrate the unity of the works they analyze. The four sections into which the book is divided point (among numerous other possibilities, no doubt) to some large contexts in which unitary meaning may be traced.

Unifying Narrative Designs

THE NOVELS discussed in part 1 all directly pose the problem of their unity. *Vanity Fair* is unusual among Victorian novels in dispensing with even the modicum of unity afforded by an encompassing plot, and its apparent failure to integrate its narrative elements is heightened by the double focus provided by its two protagonists, Becky Sharp and Amelia Sedley. The fact that *Daniel Deronda* has a unifying plot has not saved it from being widely held to fall into two separate and jarring parts—to a degree that F. R. Leavis was urged to advocate the drastic cure of surgery for one of them. Virginia Woolf saw the "break of unity" caused by the ten-year interval between parts 1 and 3 of *To the Lighthouse* as the particular technical problem she was required to solve in composing the novel. And *A Passage to India* may be viewed as challenging (on another level) the very notion of unity by declaring unequivocally that in human relations, at any rate, unity is unattainable.

I argue that all these works are in fact successfully unified. Unity is demonstrably achieved by means of the technique of narration and through the employment of core images in *Vanity Fair*; through the use of recurrent motifs in *Daniel Deronda*; through the establishment of structural balance and of metaphoric parallels in *To the Lighthouse*; and through the play of linked symbols in *A Passage to India* (though in this novel, as in those discussed in part 2, unity of form subserves the depiction of disunity).

Unity in Disunity: Structures of Self-Division

THE ESSAYS in part 2 evolved out of the writing of my book *The Divided Heroine*. In this book I trace the recurrence in a number of novels of a pattern in which the self-division of the heroine is both projected and contained in the configurations of a love-triangle. *The Mill on the Floss* and *The White Peacock* were two of the novels that I studied in this regard; and, struck by the persistent similarities between the two narratives—over and above the general lines of the pattern I was tracing—I realized that George Eliot, rather than Thomas Hardy, as is commonly supposed, was the major initial influence on D. H. Lawrence. In the essay on Lawrence and George Eliot, I show how Lawrence, in seeking to organize and unify the narrative materials of his first novel, turned for a model to *The Mill on the Floss*. In my discussion of the patterns of

self-division in the third section of the essay, I draw on my analyses of
the two novels in *The Divided Heroine*.

My interest in these patterns of self-division led me to see that the
main relationships in Conrad's *Victory* lent themselves to description
in similar terms, and that they too are held together by the unifying
configurations of a triangle (though not, in this case, a love-triangle).
Though *Howards End* culminates in triangular opposition when the
heroine is torn between her husband and her sister, self-division is primarily projected in the novel through the presentation of the contrasted qualities of two families; and the narrative is unified by posing
one family against the other in an elaborate balance, a point
counterpoint.

Generic Unity: The *Bildungsroman* Trajectory

A CHARACTERISTIC FEATURE of the English form of the *Bildungsroman*,
as distinct from its German counterpart, is that its point of departure is
the childhood of the protagonist. Since its natural termination is his
early maturity, the *Bildungsroman* form establishes a trajectory of development from childhood to maturity which serves both to delimit
and to bind the narrative. The child fathers the man, and the protagonist's development is perforce tied to his life as a child. Or, as Lawrence once put it, "One may seem very different from one's past, but
one is nevertheless the new child of one's yesterdays."[1] The
Bildungsroman traces the continuity within change in a process of
growth, and the narrative in this form is further unified by the predominant presence of a single protagonist, whose story subsumes
everything else.

It has been said that *The History of Henry Esmond* is "the first true
Bildungsroman in English fiction";[2] but I make the claim for *Mansfield Park*. The first two essays in part 3, accordingly, show how the
Bildungsroman form was effectively inaugurated in the English novel.
The essays on *A Portrait of the Artist* and *Free Fall* discuss two representative modern examples of the form, in which the protagonists' final achievement of self is much more uncertain than in the nineteenth-century novels, and even ambiguous.

Beyond the Single Text: Unifying Preoccupations

A WRITER'S recurrent preoccupations in various works establish a
frame and enable us to interpret one narrative in relation to another. In
part 4 I follow such an interpretative procedure in regard to three writ-

ers—and in respect of increasingly larger bodies of work. The three
tales which Lawrence published together in a volume which he called
The Ladybird are very different in milieu and mode, but they are unified by a common thematic concern. When the first story, moreover, is
read in the light of a later novel, a concealed significance is revealed—
and it then becomes apparent that this hidden meaning is even more
deviously present in the other two tales as well. Thomas Hardy is fairly
direct in his presentation of a sexual incapacity on the part of the heroine of *Far from the Madding Crowd*. Our understanding of her enables
us to follow the progressively more obscure depictions of a similar incapacity in the heroines of *The Woodlanders* and *Jude the Obscure*.
Finally, it is possible to show that Alan Sillitoe's whole oeuvre as a
novelist may be understood in terms of recurring preoccupations. The
essay on Sillitoe also brings the collection full circle, back to *Vanity
Fair*, that is, for the image of life as a battle dominates the work of the
modern novelist in much the same way that it does Thackeray's classic
more than a hundred years before.

ACKNOWLEDGMENTS

A number of essays in this book have been previously published, though in somewhat different form, in various collections of essays. I am grateful to the editors and publishers of these volumes for permission to reprint the following material: "Rhythmic and Symbolic Patterns in *A Passage to India*" in *Scripta Hierosolymitana*, ed. Alice Shalvi and A. A. Mendilow, vol. 17 (Jerusalem: Magnes Press, 1966); "Journeys to a Lighthouse" in *Scripta Hierosolymitana*, ed. A. A. Mendilow, vol. 25 (Jerusalem: Magnes Press, 1973); "Owning and Disowning: The Unity of *Daniel Deronda*" in *Daniel Deronda: A Centenary Symposium*, ed. Alice Shalvi (Jerusalem: Jerusalem Academic Press, 1976); "Aphrodite of the Foam and *The Ladybird* Tales" in *D. H. Lawrence: A Critical Study of the Major Novels and Other Writings*, ed. A. H. Gomme (Sussex: Harvester Press; New York: Barnes and Noble, 1978); and "*Howards End*: Goblins and Rainbows" in *Hebrew University Studies in Literature: Essays in Honour of A. A. Mendilow*, ed. Ruth Nevo (Jerusalem: Magnes Press, 1982).

Three other essays are currently in press, and I am grateful to the following editors and publishers for permission to reprint them: "D. H. Lawrence and George Eliot: The Genesis of *The White Peacock*" in *D. H. Lawrence and Tradition*, ed. Jeffrey Meyers (London: Athlone Press); "*Victory*: The Battle for Heyst," a shortened version of "*Victory* and Patterns of Self-Division" in *Conrad Revisited: Essays for the Eighties*, ed. Ross C. Murfin (University of Alabama Press); and "Alan Sillitoe: The Novelist as Map-Maker" in *The Contemporary British and Irish Novel*, ed. Hedwig Bock and Albert Wertheim (Max Hueber Verlag).

I wish to thank the Hebrew University for a grant toward the cost of typing; and Suzan Hamer for preparing the typescript with exemplary precision and cheerfulness.

I am most grateful to the Rockefeller Foundation for an invitation to spend a month at its Bellagio Study and Conference Center. I put the finishing touches to this book at the Center, amid the most congenial of surroundings.

The ideas in some of these essays were first tried out on various groups of students at the Hebrew University, and their responses were of great help to me. I am particularly indebted to two recent graduate students, Chen Gratz and Michael Goldman, for insights into *Mansfield Park* and *Free Fall*, respectively.

I am indebted also to a number of friends and colleagues who provided aid in the preparation of this book—to Dorothea Krook, who at a crucial moment gave invaluable advice in respect of its organization; to Shlomith Rimmon-Kenan and Robert Friend, whose astute comments helped me to improve the essays they read; and most of all to Ruth Nevo, whom I have thanked publicly so many times that I can now add only that I found her quite exceptional discernment in regard to all aspects of the book indispensable. To my wife, Shirley Kaufman Daleski, I owe much—and in equal measure—for constant support and continually challenging criticism.

PART ONE

UNIFYING
NARRATIVE DESIGNS

STRATEGIES IN *VANITY FAIR*

The opening sentence of *Vanity Fair* scarcely prepares us for the astonishing handling of point of view which characterizes the novel as a whole. It is not only "the famous little Becky Puppet" that may be said to be "uncommonly flexible in the joints" but the narrative method, and this results in the kind of virtuoso display that the "Manager of the Performance" could equally have taken pride in.[1] The opening sentence, however, accords comfortably enough with our sense of how stories are conventionally told in Victorian fiction: "While the present century was in its teens, and on one sunshiny morning in June, there drove up to the great iron gate of Miss Pinkerton's academy for young ladies, on Chiswick Mall, a large family coach, with two fat horses in blazing harness, driven by a fat coachman in a three-cornered hat and wig, at the rate of four miles an hour." That the narrator is omniscient is at once communicated by that precise "four miles an hour," and the rich particularity of time and place and circumstance seems designed to evoke a factual, "objective" view of the setting. The objectivity, a concomitant of this type of omniscience, seems also to be a function of the narrator's taking a god's-eye view of the scene, and thus of his having assumed a position outside the fictional world. He distances himself still further by locating his story at a point in time remote from that in which he is living. The narrative mode, therefore, appears to be that of a detached, impersonal omniscience; but before the end of the first short chapter there is a decided change of method.

Far from maintaining a posture of impersonality, the narrator speedily begins to refer to himself in the first person; and though, to judge by the opening sentence, he has been at pains to establish the existential

3

solidity of what he is depicting, he is soon insisting on its fictionality and on his own status as novelist:

> But as we are to see a great deal of Amelia, there is no harm in saying, at the outset of our acquaintance, that she was a dear little creature; and a great mercy it is, both in life and in novels, which (and the latter especially) abound in villains of the most sombre sort, that we are to have for a constant companion so guileless and good-natured a person. As she is not a heroine, there is no need to describe her person; indeed I am afraid that her nose was rather short than otherwise. (p. 43)

The posture of omniscience that the narrator adopts here may be described—in contradistinction to that referred to above—as both personal and self-conscious. Instances of such self-consciousness abound in the novel, but I shall quote only two further representative examples:

> If, a few pages back, the present writer claimed the privilege of peeping into Miss Amelia Sedley's bedroom, and understanding with the omniscience of the novelist all the gentle pains and passions which were tossing upon that innocent pillow, why should he not declare himself to be Rebecca's confidante too, master of her secrets, and seal-keeper of that young woman's conscience? (p. 192)

> As his hero and heroine pass the matrimonial barrier, the novelist generally drops the curtain, as if the drama were over then: the doubts and struggles of life ended: as if, once landed in the marriage country, all were green and pleasant there: and wife and husband had nothing to do but to link each other's arms together, and wander gently downwards towards old age in happy and perfect fruition. But our little Amelia was just on the bank of her new country, and was already looking anxiously back towards the sad friendly figures waving farewell to her across the stream, from the other distant shore. (p. 310)

It is not the practice of "the novelist" that we are enjoined to consider but that of other novelists; and it is not "our little Amelia" whom we are urged to identify as different but our novelist, as he pursues a new realism in the presentation of marriage.

The narrator, however, slides back as easily into a posture of impersonal objectivity; and so in the first chapter, for instance, his reflections about "life and . . . novels" and the sort of description that is appropriate to a non-heroine coexist happily with his vivid, scenic rendering of the confrontation between Miss Pinkerton and her sister over the question of a present for Becky Sharp or of the way the latter flings the dictionary back at the startled feet of Miss Jemima. As early as chapter 1, therefore, it seems that, if omniscience is the chosen narrative method, it is a particularly flexible kind of omniscience, modulating freely from the impersonal to the personal, from the dramatic to the confidential, and from the detached to the self-conscious. But in fact (as we shall see) omniscience turns out to be only one of the major narrative stances that the novelist adopts.

The narrator's omniscience, moreover, is itself put in question, though he is given to drawing attention to it. He declares his omniscience, for instance, in the passage already quoted in which he refers to the passions and secrets of the two young ladies whose story he is telling. And periodically he reminds us of the fact: apropos of his telling us that Joseph Sedley thinks "a great deal" about Becky, he remarks parenthetically that "novelists have the privilege of knowing everything" (p. 62); and he explains his being "in a situation to be able to tell the public how Crawley and his wife lived without any income," by remarking that "the novelist, it has been said before, knows everything" (p. 428). In fact, however, the narrator does not appear to know everything: "I wonder," he says, "whether [Miss Crawley] knew it was not only Becky who wrote the letters, but that Mrs. Rawdon actually took and sent home the trophies—which she bought for a few francs . . . The novelist, who knows everything, knows this also. Be this, however, as it may . . ." (p. 389). He may know that it is Becky who procures and sends the trophies, but he does not seem to know whether Miss Crawley knows this or not. Miss Crawley, indeed, seems to be altogether beyond him, for when she meets Rawdon at Brighton, the narrator says, "I don't know whether Miss Crawley had any private feeling of regard or emotion upon seeing her old favourite; but she held out a couple of fingers to him" (p. 304). On other occasions it is Amelia who seems to be beyond his ken, for he admits that he does not know what her thoughts are (p. 335), and that he "cannot explain the meaning" of a particularly striking act of hers (p. 466). The narrator's admission, in certain situations, of his own limited knowledge is thus also a recurrent feature of the narrative.[2] Accordingly, the most famous (or infamous) example of such an admission—the narrator's uncertainty about Becky's guilt when her husband finds her in compromising circumstances with Lord Steyne: "What *had* happened? Was she guilty or not? She said not; but who could tell what was truth which came from those lips; or if that corrupt heart was in this case pure?" (p. 622)— should not be viewed in isolation as an epitome of the novelist's cowardly evasiveness but seen as an integral part of a calculated narrative strategy, a consistent inconsistency.

Unlike the changes of role that the narrator adopts within the overall play of omniscience, a regular shift of focus (in Gérard Genette's sense) within the fictional world may be regarded as a conventional feature of most omniscient narrative, especially the massive Victorian variety such as *Vanity Fair* or *Our Mutual Friend* or *Middlemarch*, in which there are a large number of focal characters. This kind of shift, however, has by itself been found to be dizzy-making in *Vanity Fair:* "Thackeray," say Geoffrey and Kathleen Tillotson, "turns from one personage to another and sometimes so quickly that we grow giddy unless we keep pace by reading slowly."[3] It seems to me that we easily accept such shifts of focus because we are used to encountering them in other novels too, and in this novel we are anyway preoccupied with the narrator's own transformations. The combined effect of these variations of narrative mode and focus, however, is to establish a general fluidity that facilitates radical movements away from the fictional world itself. For in *Vanity Fair* there are, in addition, repeated shifts of dimension, shifts from the fictional to the real world.

We may distinguish, in this regard, five kinds of shift. First, there is the shift from the fictional world to the putative real world of the reader—and to his imagined response to fictional events. Sometimes the shift of dimension that is forced on us in such cases is so sharp that it is subversive of the dramatic action that is in progress, suddenly cutting it short, as in the following account of the events that lead to Dobbin's famous fight with Cuff: " 'Take that, you little devil!' cried Mr. Cuff, and down came the wicket again on the child's hand—Don't be horrified, ladies, every boy at a public school has done it. Your children will so do and be done by, in all probability—Down came the wicket again; and Dobbin started up" (p. 80). The narrator seems here to be at least as much concerned with his readers as his characters, and makes us shift our attention accordingly. Sometimes the shift is occasioned by the narrator's apparent wish to justify his fiction to an imagined critical reader, as when he tells us of the response Amelia evokes in those close to George Osborne:

After every one of her visits (and oh how glad she was when they were over!) Miss Osborne and Miss Maria Osborne, and Miss Wirt, the vestal governess, asked each other with increased wonder, "What *could* George find in that creature?"

How is this? some carping reader exclaims. How is it that Amelia, who had such a number of friends at school, and was so beloved there, comes out into the world and is spurned by her discriminating sex! My dear sir, there were no men at Miss Pinkerton's establishment except the old dancing-master; and you would not have had the girls fall out about *him*? (pp. 147–48)

And sometimes the narrator turns from the fiction to the reader in order (ironically) to defend something he has *not* done in the narrative:

a polite public will no more bear to read an authentic description of vice than a truly refined English or American female will permit the word breeches to be pronounced in her chaste hearing. And yet, Madam, both are walking the world before our faces every day, without much shocking us. If you were to blush every time they went by, what complexions you would have! It is only when their naughty names are called out that your modesty has any occasion to show alarm or sense of outrage, and it has been the wish of the present writer, all through this story, deferentially to submit to the fashion at present prevailing, and only to hint at the existence of wickedness in a light, easy, and agreeable manner, so that nobody's fine feelings may be offended. (pp. 737–38)

Second, there are shifts from the fictional world to the putative real world of the reader in which attention is directed not to his response to the fiction but to his own imagined conduct in the real world. Describing how the rich Miss Crawley exploits the people round her, the narrator first generalizes from her behavior, and then, in a sudden shift, turns the generalization on the reader:

Gratitude among certain rich folks is scarcely natural or to be thought of. They take needy people's services as their due. Nor have you, O poor parasite and humble hanger-on, much reason to complain! Your friendship for Dives is about as sincere as the return which it usually gets. It is money you love, and not the man; and were Croesus and his footman to change places, you know, you poor rogue, who would have the benefit of your allegiance. (p. 176)

Sometimes the narrator changes focus as well as dimension, includes himself as well as the reader in the criticism that is voiced, and (confounding confusion) details an imagined response in the supposed real world an event that is actually taking place in the fictional world— as when he remarks how everyone attends Lord Steyne's parties: "In a word, everybody went to wait upon this great man—everybody who was asked: as you the reader (do not say nay) or I the writer hereof would go if we had an invitation" (p. 553). The moralizing note in a number of these exhortations to the reader becomes frankly hortatory on occasion, as when Miss Crawley's illness is depicted: "Picture to yourself, O fair young reader, a worldly, selfish, graceless, thankless, religionless old woman, writhing in pain and fear, and without her wig. Picture her to yourself, and ere you be old, learn to love and pray" (p. 173).

Third, the narrator also generalizes from specific fictional incidents not in order to turn his satire on the reader but to establish universal principles of being, drawing us once again, however, from the fiction to life in the supposed real world. This, for instance, is how he moves from Becky to "the world" in which she figures in the fiction, and then to "the world" in which he and his readers live: "Miss Rebecca was not, then, in the least kind or placable. All the world used her ill, said this young misanthropist, and we may be pretty certain that persons whom all the world treats ill deserve entirely the treatment they get. The world is a looking-glass, and gives back to every man the reflection of his own face" (p. 47). The shifts in dimension become more complex when the general truth that is elicited from the fiction and applied to the real world is then subsequently disproved in the fiction. The narrator makes this comment, for instance, after he has described how Becky seeks to inveigle Jos Sedley into marriage when she first meets him: "And this I set down as a positive truth. A woman with fair opportunities, and without an absolute hump, may marry WHOM SHE LIKES" (p. 65)—but he thereafter proceeds to show how the attractive Becky loses her opportunity. Sometimes the narrator, moving from his specific fictional world to the world at large by means of a generalizing comment, contrives at the same time (through a deft use of parenthesis, which—as we shall see—is one of his most effective narrative weapons) to narrow the focus to the more restricted domain of the British reader and his foibles:

> There is little doubt that old Osborne believed all he said, and that the girls were quite earnest in their protestations of affection for Miss Swartz. People in Vanity Fair fasten on to rich folks quite naturally. If the simplest people are disposed to look not a little kindly on great Prosperity (for I defy any member of the British public to say that the notion of Wealth has not something awful and pleasing to him; and you, if you are told that the man next you at dinner has got a half a million, not to look at him with a certain interest); if the simple look benevolently on money, how much more do your old worldlings regard it! Their affections rush out to meet and welcome money. (pp. 247–48)

Fourth, there are a number of shifts from the fictional world to the real, real world—that is to say, not to a real world of imagined readers but of historic personages. Such a shift is made as early as chapter 2, following Becky's defiant rejection of the dictionary at the end of the previous chapter:

> Miss Sedley was almost as flurried at the act of defiance as Miss Jemima had been; for, consider, it was but one minute that she had left school, and the impressions of six years are not got over in that space of time. Nay, with some persons those awes and terrors of youth last for ever and ever. I know, for instance, an old gentleman of sixty-eight, who said to me one morning at breakfast, with a very agitated countenance, "I dreamed last night that I was flogged by Dr. Raine." Fancy had carried him back five-and-fifty years in the course of

that evening. Dr. Raine and his rod were just as awful to him in his heart, then, at sixty-eight, as they had been at thirteen. (p. 46)

With regard to the reference to Dr. Raine, J. I. M. Stewart tells us that Matthew Raine served as headmaster of Charterhouse from 1791 until 1811. Though Thackeray himself did not go to this school until 1822, the anecdote in the novel is based on a real-life experience, as an 1841 letter to Edward Fitzgerald, which describes the dream of the "old gentleman," indicates: "The old fellow is 65 years old, and told me that only that night he had a dream about being flogged at Charter-House— There is something touching in this I think about which Mr. William Wordsworth might make a poem if he chose" (p. 799). Was it forgetfulness, we wonder, that made Thackeray some six years after the letter (when he wrote the first monthly number of the novel) change the old fellow's age from 65 to 68—or a wish, for all his deliberate shifts of dimension, to assert the autonomy of his fiction? Certainly, in other instances the fiction absorbs the real world, as it were, when the shift is made in the course of a single sentence, and the back-and-forth movement between worlds is so quick it almost escapes the eye: "The curses to which the General gave a low utterance, as soon as Rebecca and her conqueror had quitted him, were so deep, that I am sure no compositor in Messrs. Bradbury and Evans's establishment would venture to print them were they written down. They came from the General's heart" (p. 337). Bradbury and Evans, of course, were Thackeray's publishers.

Fifth, some shifts to the real world are made by way of reference not to historic personages but to the narrator's projecting himself as the historic novelist, engaging, under the pressure of the fiction, in something very like personal reminiscence. When Dobbin is left alone at Vauxhall, for instance, we are told: "It wasn't very good fun for Dobbin—and, indeed, to be alone at Vauxhall, I have found, from my own experience, to be one of the most dismal sports ever entered into by a bachelor" (p. 92). Similarly, in deliberating on the effect of rack punch on the destinies of his characters, the narrator says: "To this truth I can vouch as a man; there is no headache in the world like that caused by Vauxhall punch. Through the lapse of twenty years, I can remember the consequence of two glasses!—two wine glasses!—but two, upon the honour of a gentleman; and Joseph Sedley, who had a liver complaint, had swallowed at least a quart of the abominable mixture" (p. 95). But the narrator's most audacious sleight of hand in this regard is a shift (signaled by a parenthesis) to the world of the historic novelist which draws with it the transformation of a character into something like a real-life personage, though this sudden life is speedily collapsed into the fiction. The narrator recounts how Jos Sedley presents "two handsome nosegays of flowers" to Amelia and Becky:

> "Thank you, dear Joseph," said Amelia, quite ready to kiss her brother, if he were so minded. (And I think for a kiss from such a dear creature as Amelia, I would purchase all Mr. Lee's conservatories out of hand.)
> "Oh heavenly, heavenly flowers!" exclaimed Miss Sharp. (p. 75)

No editor that I am aware of has established the identity of Mr. Lee, but it would seem to me not unreasonable to assume that his conservatories were well known in Thackeray's day—the more especially since we are almost at once informed by Jos that he has bought his flowers "at Nathan's" (p. 75).

What the narrative steadily encompasses, therefore, are changes of focus, as it moves from one focal character to another (as the Tillotsons remarked); transformations of the narrator, as he moves from one role to another; and shifts of dimension, as we are made to move from one world to another. But the novelist's most striking innovation is his threefold changing of the position from which the narrator views the fictional world. The method, in this respect, is far more revolutionary than that employed in Dickens's *Bleak House* (published a few years after *Vanity Fair*), in which there are two alternating narratives, for they are separate narratives (even though they overlap) and there are two separate narrators, the omniscient narrator and Esther Summerson, the first-person protagonist-narrator. In *Vanity Fair* there is only one narrative and only one narrator (for all his transformations), but the fictional world is viewed from three distinct and separate positions, not two, as in *Bleak House.* The first position that the narrator takes up is outside the fictional world; and all the examples of his procedures that I have referred to so far are variants of the flexible omniscience that characterizes this major stance. But he also takes up a position inside the fictional world.

The first instance of the narrator's change of position comes in chapter 22 after some two hundred pages of omniscient narrative, and it is signaled by a quietly deceptive parenthesis. The narrator is describing Amelia's marriage to George in a manner that we are by now thoroughly accustomed to:

> In a word, George had thrown the great cast. He was going to be married. Hence his pallor and nervousness—his sleepless night and agitation in the morning. I have heard people who have gone through the same thing own to the same emotion. After three or four ceremonies, you get accustomed to it, no doubt; but the first dip, everybody allows, is awful.

The bride was dressed in a brown silk pelisse (as Captain Dobbin has since informed me), and wore a straw bonnet with a pink ribbon . . . (p. 259)

The shift here is outrageous. If previously the validity of the narrative has been based on the narrator's privileged omniscience (though this, as we have seen, is on occasion unaccountably limited), it is now made a matter of information which the narrator directly amasses within the fictional world itself. No longer taking a god's-eye view, which enables him to penetrate into the thoughts of a Becky or Amelia, he is lending an all too human ear to what Dobbin tells him. And yet, though he is now a distinct presence in the fictional world, a man whom Dobbin can talk to, he is quite without substance, remaining the same un-named, unparticularized figure whom we have encountered in the om-niscient narrative. Though he is clearly not a Marlow recounting the story of Lord Jim and himself playing a part in it, technically he is here transformed into an observer-narrator. This transformation might be expected to split the novel in two; but since it does not, we are forced to conclude that all that has happened is that the narrator we have known to this point has merely changed his position, stealthily slip-ping (in that parenthesis) into the fictional world from outside it.

Nor is this a random occurrence. From here on the novel is steadily punctuated by illicit border crossings. The narrator is "told by Dr. Pestler (now a most flourishing lady's physician . . .), that [Amelia's] grief at weaning the child was a sight that would have unmanned a Herod" (pp. 457–58); he declares Dobbin was mistaken in seeing a re-semblance to Amelia in "a figure in a book of fashions": "I have seen it, and can vouch that it is but the picture of a high-waisted gown with an impossible doll's face simpering over it" (p. 510); he has a special "in-formant," who "knows everything" and is appropriately named Tom Eaves, and it is Tom who shows him Gaunt House: " 'The Prince and Perdita have been in and out of that door, sir,' he has often told me" (p. 545); and he relates that "the before-mentioned Tom Eaves (who has no part in this history, except that he knew all the great folks in London, and the stories and mysteries of each family) had further information regarding my Lady Steyne, which may or may not be true," but he pro-ceeds to provide it (in Tom Eaves's name, of course) (pp. 547–49). It is, however, at the very end of the novel, in the section which is set at Pumpernickel, that the narrator begins positively to obtrude his ob-server status on us: "Georgy was always present at the play, but it was the Major who put Emmy's shawl on after the entertainment . . . It was on this very tour that I, the present writer of a history of which every word is true, had the pleasure to see them first, and to make their acquaintance" (p. 721). This statement now challenges some major suppositions in the omniscient narrative. Though we, in keeping with the convention, have been ready to take the omniscient narrator's word for the truth of his narrative, he (as we have seen) has been at pains to insist over and over on its fictionality; now, though we may be inclined to believe that an observer-narrator may possibly be unreliable, and though he indeed on occasion purveys information which "may or may not be true," he here categorically asserts the absolute truth of his narrative. Further contradictions speedily materialize. It appears that, at Pumpernickel, it is the observer-narrator who will conduct the narrative, for he takes over at the point at which he first sees Dobbin and his party, and the rest of this chapter (pp. 721–25) is full of references to his direct observation of them at the opera, especially Amelia ("I suppose it was because it was predestined that I was to write this particular lady's memoirs that I remarked her" [p. 722]). The omniscient narrator, however, returns in the next chapter and maintains his presence to the end, though the observer-narrator intrudes into his narrative on a number of occasions. Furthermore, though the observer-narrator does a lot of watching at the opera, he seems in general to be more of a listener than an observer, and it becomes evident that his narrative ("of which every word is true")—*the* whole narrative of *Vanity Fair* if we accept his claims—is certainly second-hand and possibly unreliable. One half of it, that relating to Amelia and her circle, is based, we must assume, on what he is told by an interested party; for it is Dobbin (who, we remember, informed him what Amelia wore at her wedding) who presumably gives him that piece of information, together with other details of her history, at Pumpernickel, where they first make acquaintance. And the other half, that relating to Becky and her circle, is based on mere gossip:

William, in a state of great indignation, though still unaware of all the treason that was in store for him, walked about the town wildly until he fell upon the Secretary of Legation, Tapeworm, who invited him to dinner. As they were discussing that meal, he took occasion to ask the Secretary whether he knew anything about a certain Mrs. Rawdon Crawley, who had, he believed, made some noise in London; and then Tapeworm, who of course knew all the London gossip, and was besides a relative of Lady Gaunt, poured out into the astonished Major's ears such a history about Becky and her husband as astonished the querist, and supplied all the points of this narrative, for it was at that very table years ago that the present writer had the pleasure of hearing the tale. Tufto, Steyne, the Crawleys, and their history—everything connected with Becky and her previous life, passed under the record of the bitter diplomatist. (p. 772)

Nor is the novelist content with these maneuvers. A narrator, or-
dinarily speaking, may occupy one or other of two major positions in
relation to his narrative: he may be inside or outside the fictional
world. Thackeray not only shows how this choice may not necessarily
be exclusive but invents a third possibility:

> Sir Pitt had an unmarried half-sister who inherited her mother's large for-
> tune . . . She had signified . . . her intention of leaving her inheritance be-
> tween Sir Pitt's second son and the family at the Rectory . . . Miss Crawley
> was, in consequence, an object of great respect when she came to Queen's
> Crawley, for she had a balance at her banker's which would have made her
> beloved anywhere.
>   What a dignity it gives an old lady, that balance at the banker's! How tender-
> ly we look at her faults if she is a relative (and may every reader have a score of
> such), what a kind good-natured old creature we find her! How the junior part-
> ner of Hobbs and Dobbs leads her smiling to the carriage with the lozenge upon
> it . . . How, when she comes to pay us a visit, we generally find an opportunity
> to let our friends know her station in the world! We say (and with perfect truth)
> I wish I had Miss MacWhirter's signature to a cheque for five thousand pounds.
> She wouldn't miss it, says your wife. She is my aunt, say you, in an easy care-
> less way, when your friend asks if Miss MacWhirter is any relative. Your wife is
> perpetually sending her little testimonies of affection, your little girls work
> endless worsted baskets, cushions, and footstools for her. . . . Ah, gracious
> powers! I wish you would send me an old aunt—a maiden aunt—an aunt with
> a lozenge on her carriage, and a front of light coffee-coloured hair—how my
> children should work workbags for her, and my Julia and I would make her
> comfortable! Sweet—sweet vision! Foolish—foolish dream! (pp. 123–25)

The first paragraph of this passage is clearly part of the omniscient
narrative, and its satirical point is simple and concisely expressed in its
last sentence. What is puzzling is why the novelist elaborates the same
(simple) satirical point in the second paragraph, and at much greater
length (thirty-three lines as opposed to the first eleven lines in the full
printed text) in relation to characters we have not yet met; and we
therefore wonder too what sort of narrative this is. At first, when the
narrator turns to the reader and directly addresses him, it seems that
we have here yet another instance, familiar enough by this point in the
narrative, of a shift of dimension (from the fictional to the real world)
which is designed to force the reader to contemplate his own conduct.
It is the junior partner of Hobbs and Dobbs and Miss MacWhirter who
give us pause. Who exactly are they? If they make their appearance in
the same fictional dimension as the reader, namely, the putative real
world, are they then historic personages like Dr. Raine? Clearly not.
Are they then fictional characters, like Sir Pitt and Miss Crawley and

the family at the Rectory? Equally clearly not, for they make no further appearance in *Vanity Fair*, and even here have little existence apart from their names. And where is it, then—in what realm, as it were— that they do make their appearance? If it is neither the real world, for they are not real like Dr. Raine, nor the fictional world, for they have no part whatsoever in the story of Amelia and Becky (and Miss Crawley), we can only conclude that they have their being (such as it is) in an amorphous area that is insinuated in between the fictional and real worlds. They are not so much fictional characters (whom the om- niscient narrator sometimes refers to as puppets) as dummies, who are no more than their names, and whom the novelist places in a shadow (fictional) world that he creates to mediate between the real world and the (real) fictional world. It is as if the fictional world casts long shad- ows out to this world and so gains in solidity, for the way in which Miss Crawley is treated at Queen's Crawley is validated, so to speak, by the analogous treatment of Miss MacWhirter. At the same time the reader is satirized for being as ready to fawn on his rich aunt as Miss Crawley's relatives are on her. But if that is the case, then the reader, in this instance, is also not situated in the real world but coexists with Miss MacWhirter. And who, then, is the "I" who makes his appearance (with his Julia and his children) at the end of the passage? He is not the historic Thackeray, whose wife was not named Julia; he is not the om- niscient narrator, who has so often addressed the reader, for he has here taken up a position in the shadow world of Miss MacWhirter; for the same reason, he is not the observer-narrator who exists in the world of Amelia and Dobbin and Becky; he is not even an incarnation of the implied author, whom we may take to abhor the "I's" sycophantic val- ues. This "I" is a dummy-narrator, a nominal fictional projection of the novelist, whom he places in the shadow fictional world for satirical purposes: the satirical attack is pressed home (in a manner that recalls "A Modest Proposal") by having the dummy-narrator take the obnox- ious values for granted.[4] The novelist, we see, has contrived to invent a third narratorial position: neither inside the fictional world nor outside it in the ordinary omniscient sense, it is somewhere in between.

The novelist makes extensive use of the shadow world,[5] but one fur- ther example of this should suffice. I quote the following passage both because it is also charmingly exemplary of the humor with which Thackeray often camouflages his tactical narrative moves, and because it indicates in addition another dimension of the Vanity Fair image: Vanity Fair is the world in which Becky and Amelia live; it is also the world in which the novelist and his readers live; and it is amenable too, as here, to projection in the shadow world. This is how the novelist satirically emphasizes the extent of Becky's chagrin at being unable to marry Sir Pitt because she is already married to his son:

I remember one night being in the Fair myself, at an evening party. I observed Old Miss Toady . . . single out for her special attentions and flattery little Mrs. Briefless, the barrister's wife, who . . . is as poor as poor can be.

What, I asked in my own mind, can cause this obsequiousness on the part of Miss Toady . . . ? Miss Toady explained presently . . . "You know," she said, "Mrs. Briefless is granddaughter of Sir John Redhand, who is so ill . . . that he can't last six months. Mrs. Briefless's papa succeeds; so you see she *will* be a baronet's daughter." And Toady asked Briefless and his wife to dinner the very next week.

If the mere chance of becoming a baronet's daughter can procure a lady such homage in the world, surely, surely we may respect the agonies of a young woman who has lost the opportunity of becoming a baronet's wife. (p. 193)

THE FOREGOING ACCOUNT should give some idea of the richness of the narrative method in *Vanity Fair*, but the mixture of effects (insofar as these have been noted at all) is not to everyone's taste, and has in fact been the object of strong criticism by two well-known critics. Dorothy Van Ghent, for instance, refers first to the comment, "If Miss Rebecca can get the better of *him* [that is, Jos], and at her first entrance into life, she is a young person of no ordinary cleverness," and then to the passage (which I have previously quoted) in which the narrator, in what she calls an "unforgivable parenthesis," expresses a desire to kiss Amelia:

What we feel is that two orders of reality are clumsily getting in each other's way: the order of imaginative reality, where Becky lives, and the order of historical reality, where William Makepeace Thackeray lives. The fault becomes more striking in the . . . unforgivable parenthesis. . . . The picture of Thackeray himself kissing Amelia pulls Amelia quite out of the created world of *Vanity Fair* and drops her into some shapeless limbo of Thackerayan sentiment where she loses all aesthetic orientation.[6]

It seems to me, however, that the shifts from one order of reality to the other are so pervasive that we become quite habituated to them; and, moreover, as I have tried to show, that they are smoothly supportive of the imaginative reality by repeatedly offering a validation of it in other terms. As for that wished-for kiss, I have also argued that "the created world of *Vanity Fair*" consists steadily of three worlds, what I have called the real fictional world, the shadow fictional world, and the fictional real world; and consequently it seems to me more accurate to say that Amelia (in that offensive parenthesis), far from being left in some limbo, is pulled out of the fictional world into the real world for a moment—and then returned to her natural habitat with no apparent ill effects. Magicians, if they are skillful enough, get away with such things.

Another influential critic, Wolfgang Iser, objects to further aspects of the method:

[The narrator's] reliability is . . . reduced by the fact that he is continually donning new masks: at one moment he is an observer of the Fair, like the reader; then he is suddenly blessed with extraordinary knowledge, . . . "knowing everything"; and then, toward the end, he announces that . . . he overheard [the whole story] in a conversation.

The "Manager of the Performance" opens up a whole panorama of views on the reality described, which can be seen from practically every social and human standpoint. The reader is offered a host of different perspectives, and so is almost continually confronted with the problem of how to make them consistent.[7]

It seems to me, however, that what is at issue is not the narrator's change of masks (if he may indeed be thought of as "continually donning" new ones) but position, and that his changes of position do not affect the reliability of what he reports. The observer-narrator's presentation of Amelia and her party in Pumpernickel, for instance, is no less (and no more) reliable than the omniscient narrator's account of their journey to Pumpernickel. Furthermore, I think that Iser creates an unnecessary problem for the reader when he implies that his only recourse, in face of the "host of different perspectives" that confront him, is to try "to make them consistent." I trust it has become evident in the previous discussion that it is quite impossible to reconcile the contradictions thrown up by the narrative, to account satisfactorily, for example, for the narrator's being both omniscient and limited in his knowledge, or for his being able—quite against nature and the laws of fiction—to be both inside and outside the fictional world and in a third position as well. All we can do is accept the blatant inconsistencies. But we might do well to ask why it is that a novelist, who in this very work proves himself to be a master of his craft, should go out of his way to force inconsistencies on us.

I believe this question should be related to another aspect of the narrative. *Vanity Fair* is a revolutionary novel—for its times—in a further respect: it is a novel without a plot. In abandoning plot (in the sense of a single, encompassing, causally-connected action), Thackeray gave up the traditional (and conventional Victorian) mechanism for unifying his material; and he compounded his difficulty by deciding to have two major protagonists, Becky and Amelia, for this deprived him as well of a single, steady center. It is true that through a skillful use of a principle of contrast in his handling of Becky and Amelia (and of the characters who surround them), Thackeray manages to balance one part of the novel against the other and so achieve a modicum of unity; but, as J. Y. T. Greig has pointed out, the principle (which he describes earlier) is not maintained throughout: "*Vanity Fair* is unified and shapely up to . . . the Battle of Waterloo . . . It becomes unified and shapely again after Chapter XLIII (Pumpernickel) . . . But in between—roughly 300 pages—the plot of the first and last sections of the book is suspended, and the unity of the novel disappears. Two stories now occupy the author's attention alternately."[8] The unity of the novel, as this is established through the working of contrast, no doubt disappears in the way Greig claims it does; but this is not to say it lacks all unity. For, paradoxically enough, the narrative method ensures that it should be apprehended as a whole. We might expect that the various inconsistencies of the method would fragment the novel in chaotic disruptions of effect; but in fact they help to bind it together. In theory the observer-narrator should, as it were, cancel out the omniscient narrator, who anyway repeatedly undermines his own status both by denying his omniscience and by leading a surreptitious dummy existence. In practice, however, each merges into the other, for throughout we have only one speaker: we hear only one (immediately recognizable) voice; and we never doubt that all along we have only one narrator, whose solidity is increased, not diminished, by the successfully encompassed contradictions—and whose pervasive and dominating presence is a cohesive force.[9] Similarly, we know that what at times seems like three narratives is actually and throughout only one, and our awareness of its oneness, of a wholeness which successfully holds together and subsumes its three constituent parts, is productive of a greater sense of its unity than that lent it by even an effective use of contrast. Furthermore, the constant shifts from the fictional world to the real world and also to the shadow fictional world ensure that we perceive the fictional world as a separate entity, one that—for all its multifariousness—is apprehended as a unified whole when it is compared, in its own distinctness, with another order of existence. There is method, we come to see, in the narrative madness.

2

IT IS the novelist's imaginative sense of his subject, however, more even than his technical intuition, that produces the imagery which unifies

Vanity Fair at a more profound level. It might be thought that it is the image of Vanity Fair—which Thackeray, nicely exemplifying an awareness of the phenomenon of intertextuality that so enthralls us today, lifts straight out of Bunyan—that effectively binds the novel together. This, to a degree, is the case since the society that is depicted in the novel *is* the Fair, is located in it; and in all its varied manifestations it gives repeated embodiment to the values of the Fair, to the materialism and sensuality which are its most marked features in Bunyan, and to the "humbugs and falsenesses and pretensions" (p. 116) which Thackeray adds to Bunyan. The novel consequently has great thematic concentration, asserting over and over that, in a society whose only values are the world and the flesh, "all is vanity." But the Fair, even in Bunyan and more so in the novel, is an intellectual construct rather than an image; and its lack of concrete particularity reduces its force. As an image it was probably of more significance to the novelist than it is now to the reader. To the novelist, we may be inclined to believe, it may have served—during the process of composition—as a species of scaffolding, encompassing the structure that was slowly taking shape, and enabling it to be built. But, like scaffolding, it remains external, and once the structure exists may be dispensed with. As an image in the finished work it certainly is secondary, and a different image animates the whole from within and binds it together. Whereas the idea of Vanity Fair may be regarded as having shaped the novelist's sense of his subject, it is his imaginative conception of the subject which generates the binding image.

The image arises naturally out of the setting of the novel, though this has been taken to be merely incidental to its main concerns: "*Vanity Fair*," say Geoffrey and Kathleen Tillotson, "is not primarily a 'historical' novel . . . because, unlike a truly historical novel, it owes nothing essential to the time of its action . . . *Vanity Fair* deals first and foremost in human nature, and without essential loss, could be set in any time, past, present, or future."[10] We have only to compare *Vanity Fair* with *The History of Henry Esmond* to agree that it is not a historical novel; and it seems reasonable to believe that the society portrayed in it is, in essentials, that of Thackeray's own day.[11] But that is not to say that it "owes nothing essential" to its setting. The fact that Thackeray chose to set his novel at the time of the Battle of Waterloo (and its aftermath) even though it is the personal lives of his characters which are at its center and not the historical events in which they are caught up, suggests that his imagination seized on some essential connection between his idea of (the Victorian) Vanity Fair and the Napoleonic conflicts.

At one point in the novel the connection becomes explicit, though it is muted in a parenthesis; it is when Pitt Crawley and Lady Southdown concert a strategy for approaching (the rich) Miss Crawley:

> "And if I might suggest, my sweet lady," Pitt said in a bland tone, "it would be as well not to take our precious Emily, who is too enthusiastic; but rather that you should be accompanied by our sweet and dear Lady Jane."
>
> "Most certainly, Emily would ruin everything," Lady Southdown said: and this time agreed to forgo her usual practice, which was, as we have said, before she bore down personally upon any individual whom she proposed to subjugate, to fire in a quantity of tracts upon the menaced party (as a charge of the French was always preceded by a furious cannonade). Lady Southdown, we say, for the sake of the invalid's health, or for the sake of her soul's ultimate welfare, or for the sake of her money, agreed to temporize. (pp. 396–97)

The parenthesis, like a carefully laid mine, has an unexpected explosive effect. It is a means of comic, ironic deflation, and is so contrived as to hit two targets at once. On the one hand, Lady Southdown with her tracts, when compared to the French with their cannon, is made to appear a ridiculous (if determined) figure; on the other, the fierce French are conflated with an old woman, "tall and awful missionary of the truth" (p. 394) though she may be, and are reduced in turn. This kind of double deflationary effect is common to the host of military images that permeate the novel, for though it is only here that the novelist insinuates a direct analogy, the historical background is throughout so strongly rendered that any military image triggers an association with the Napoleonic wars. A special see-saw relation is thus established between activities at the Fair and the historic conflict: social battles, of whatever kind, are made absurd when compared to the real thing; historic battles, no matter how momentous, are implicitly reduced—amid a barrage of drawing-room war imagery—to an analogous scale. At the same time a major function of the Napoleonic setting becomes clear: the actual historic War becomes the ground for the metaphorical social war that is the novelist's subject. Life in Vanity Fair is more of a battle than a market. In this sense, as well as that advanced in the text, it may be said that "the French Emperor comes in to perform a part in this domestic comedy of Vanity Fair" (p. 221).[12]

The war imagery is so pervasive that examples must be limited to a few representative instances. The imagery is mainly directed, following the emphasis in Bunyan, to evoking struggles for gain and attempts at sexual conquest in the Fair. "These money transactions—" we are told, apropos of the relations that pertain between Sir Pitt Crawley and his brother Bute, "these speculations in life and death—these silent battles for reversionary spoil—make brothers very loving towards each other in Vanity Fair" (p. 132). Both war and Fair images are combined in this passage; it is only the striking phrase "reversionary spoil" that animates it, however, and the last three words could in effect have been omitted. The struggle for such spoil lends itself to considerable elaboration:

when Mrs. Bute took the command at Miss Crawley's house, the garrison there were charmed to act under such a leader, expecting all sorts of promotion from her promises, her generosity, and her kind words.

That [Rawdon] would consider himself beaten, after one defeat, and make no attempt to regain the position he had lost, Mrs. Bute Crawley never allowed herself to suppose. She knew Rebecca to be too clever and spirited and desperate a woman to submit without a struggle; and felt that she must prepare for that combat, and be incessantly watchful against assault, or mine, or surprise.

In the first place, though she held the town, was she sure of the principal inhabitant? Would Miss Crawley herself hold out . . . ? (p. 227)

Rawdon, who is ultimately deprived of his anticipated share of the said spoil, is forced to fight his wars by other means and becomes (among other skills that he develops) "a consummate master of billiards":

Like a great general, his genius used to rise with the danger, and when the luck had been unfavourable to him for a whole game, and the bets were consequently against him, he would, with consummate skill and boldness, make some prodigious hits which would restore the battle, and come in a victor at the end, to the astonishment of everybody—of everybody, that is, who was a stranger to his play. Those who were accustomed to see it were cautious how they staked their money against a man of such sudden resources, and brilliant and overpowering skill. (p. 429)

Sexual conquests follow the same pattern; and though Glorvina O'Dowd's intentions are no doubt more honorable than those of Lord Steyne, they take much the same form: "[Lady O'Dowd and Glorvina] agreed between themselves on this point, that Glorvina should marry Major Dobbin, and were determined that the Major should have no rest until the arrangement was brought about. Undismayed by forty or fifty previous defeats, Glorvina laid siege to him" (p. 509). In his pursuit of Becky, Lord Steyne decides she should be relieved of all unnecessary encumbrances, and so first disposes of her son and then of her companion: "it was clear that honest Briggs must not lose her chance of settlement for life; and so she and her bags were packed, and she set off on her journey. And so two of Rawdon's out-sentinels were in the hands of the enemy" (p. 611).[13]

The war imagery is seen most clearly as a controlling principle in the depiction of the lives of Becky and Amelia. The title of chapter 2 is "In which Miss Sharp and Miss Sedley prepare to open the Campaign" (p. 46); and though the particular campaign that the two young ladies are intent not only on opening but on bringing to a speedy conclusion is the capturing of a husband, the image—since the previous chapter details their departure from Miss Pinkerton's academy—refers as well to their embarking on the larger and more general battle of life. The way Becky and Amelia wage the more general war is in keeping with their characters, and follows the lines of two main alternatives open to combatants in such a struggle—to conquer or surrender. From an early stage in the narrative, therefore, the war imagery gives rise to two implicit but controlling metaphors that define the contrasted roles of the protagonists.

Thackeray himself seems, somewhat tentatively, to have thought of Becky as a Napoleon. Edgar F. Harden says that she is "in fact, a kind of female Napoleon, a clever leader who excites great interest and certain kinds of frantic devotion in the men around her. . . . The identification reaches its climax in Chapter LXIV . . . , where an original woodcut portrays Becky in exile, dressed like Napoleon, with spy-glass in hand."[14] Since Thackeray did his own illustrations to the text, that woodcut has considerable force. In the text itself, however, the novelist is more reserved: on one occasion Becky's admiring husband tells her she is "fit to be Commander-in-Chief, or Archbishop of Canterbury, by Jove" (p. 196); and on another is said to believe in her "as much as the French soldiers in Napoleon" (p. 412). Though Becky's career may be viewed as that of an upstart who rises to great heights before she meets her Waterloo, it seems to me that, on the mercenary and predatory field of the Fair, we are led to think of her, more appropriately, as a soldier of fortune. What we witness, as she sets out on that aforementioned campaign, is her attempt to forage where she can and by whatever means as she attempts to take society by storm. Amelia, by contrast, is a much more passive figure. She may be seen, again implicitly, as an unwilling conscript in the battles that engulf her, defeatist by temperament, wanting always to opt out of the fight, and ready to give in. In the opening description of her it is clearly suggested how easily she collapses, all fight knocked out of her: "even" Miss Pinkerton, we are told, "[ceases] scolding her after the first time," and gives orders to everyone "to treat Miss Sedley with the utmost gentleness, as harsh treatment [is] injurious to her" (p. 43).

Becky's campaign, with its attendant strategies, is her pilgrim's progress in the world of Vanity Fair; but, since the campaign is her whole life, I shall refer only to some of the main stages in her progress, indicating how these are informed by the military imagery. Becky starts with neither status nor possessions, being a penniless orphan, the

daughter of an artist and an opera girl. All she has are the natural resources with which she is endowed, her quick wits and her "famous
frontal development" (among other physical attractions) (p. 235). The
first stage in the campaign consists in the securing of a firm base from
which to conduct operations, and to that end Becky sets out to get a
husband. Jos ("this big beau") is the first man who presents himself,
and she determines "in her heart upon making the conquest" of him (p.
57). When he escapes her, she turns her attentions to Rawdon Crawley;
and the "skirmishes" which "[pass] perpetually [between them] during
the little campaign" are always "similar in result": "The Crawley
heavy cavalry [is] maddened by defeat, and routed every day" (p. 175)
until Becky becomes Mrs. Rawdon. Nor is Rawdon the only one who is
put to rout. In the face of enemies, Becky is even more devastating, as
she shows in the case of George Osborne, whom she intuitively knows
has come between Jos and herself. When she meets George at Miss
Crawley's and he tries to patronize her, Becky exhibits the "presence of
mind" which always characterizes her in the field (though she does lose
it on one occasion when Sir Pitt proposes to her); she at once goes over
to the attack and is so "cool and killing" as to cause "the Lieutenant's
entire discomfiture." Showing too that she knows how to follow up an
advantage, Becky presses home the attack until George is "utterly
routed" (pp. 181–82, 186).

   Becky makes her debut at the famous ball that "a noble Duchess"
gives at Brussels on the eve of the Battle of Waterloo. She arrives late:
"Her face was radiant; her dress perfection. In the midst of the great
persons assembled, and the eye-glasses directed to her, Rebecca seemed
to be as cool and collected as when she used to marshall Miss Pinkerton's little girls to church" (p. 342). The effect is subtle. To be "cool and
collected" is presented as a distinctively soldierly quality: when
Rawdon leaves for the battle next morning, it is said that "no man in
the British army which has marched away, not the great Duke himself,
could be more cool or collected in the presence of doubts and difficul-
ties, than the indomitable little aide-de-camp's wife" (p. 353). As the
eye-glasses are directed to Becky, therefore, it is neatly suggested how
she comes under fire. And the reference to the peaceful little girls going
to church sustains the implied image, for Becky's task then was to
"marshall" the girls. There is no doubt, at all events, about the view we
are intended to take of what she does next. Making her way through
"fifty would-be partners," Becky heads straight for where Amelia is
sitting "quite unnoticed, and dismally unhappy"; and in order "to
finish" her forthwith, proceeds "to patronize her," remaining with her
until she claims her husband George as a partner: "Women only know
how to wound so. There is a poison on the tips of their little shafts,

which stings a thousand times more than a man's blunter weapon. Our poor Emmy, who had never hated, never sneered all her life, was powerless in the hands of her remorseless little enemy" (pp. 342–43).

Moving from one victory to another, Becky goes from Brighton to Brussels and then to Paris "during [the] famous winter" after Waterloo: "Lady Bareacres and the chiefs of the English society, stupid and irreproachable females, writhed with anguish at the success of the little upstart Becky, whose poisoned jokes quivered and rankled in their chaste breasts. But she had all the men on her side. She fought the women with indomitable courage, and they could not talk scandal in any tongue but their own" (pp. 413–14). In London, however, though she quickly becomes "the vogue . . . among a certain class," the ladies shut their doors on her; and it is she who has to restrain her enraged husband: "You can't shoot me into society," she says to him "good-naturedly" (pp. 439–41). Instead she uses her talents to engineer a presentation at Court, and then to secure an invitation to Gaunt House. At Gaunt House the ladies are frigid, but Becky proceeds to attack Lady Bareacres with such spirit and malice that she is forced to "[retreat] to a table, where she [begins] to look at pictures with great energy." By the end of the evening, with the men "crowded round the piano" at which she is singing, and "the women, her enemies, . . . left quite alone," Becky has another "great triumph" (pp. 571–73). Thereafter Lady Steyne "succumbs" before Becky, and "the younger ladies of the House of Gaunt" are "also compelled into submission," though they occasionally still "set people at her":

Mr. Wagg, the celebrated wit, and a led captain and trencherman of my Lord Steyne, was caused by the ladies to charge her; and the worthy fellow, leering at his patroness, and giving them a wink, as much as to say, "Now look out for sport," one evening began an assault upon Becky, who was unsuspiciously eating her dinner. The little woman attacked on a sudden, but never without arms, lighted up in an instant, parried and riposted with a home-thrust, which made Wagg's face tingle with shame; then she returned to her soup with the most perfect calm and a quiet smile on her face. (p. 590)

If Becky is thus pictured as an intrepid fighter, it should be stressed that she is also repeatedly shown to use her weapons with the greatest ruthlessness and unscrupulousness. This characterizes her exploitation of all the men round her, including her husband and Lord Steyne. It is in relation to Steyne's pursuit of her that the novelist gives a fine turn to the line of military imagery. Steyne proceeds to lay siege to her, disposing methodically, as we have seen, of Rawdon's "out-sentinels," and then of the chief guard himself. Since the fortress does not in fact fall to Steyne's attack, however—for Rawdon returns home in time, it seems, to prevent an actual sexual misdemeanor and the question of Becky's guilt (as we have also seen) is left open—her defeat does not take place in the field, so to speak. But she loses everything she has so carefully amassed—husband, possessions, the bubble reputation she has meticulously guarded—and is said to have "come to this bankruptcy" (p. 622), an exhaustion of resources that even a campaigner as resourceful as she may be reduced to. She soldiers on, however, as best she can, and finally restores her fortunes, we are told, after she encounters Jos again and makes short shrift of him—the victim at whom she first directed her fire.

The war imagery is less direct in the case of Amelia, the unwilling conscript who avoids battle whenever she can, but it shapes her presentation too. The schoolgirl, who is said (in the opening description of her) to "cry over a dead canary-bird; or over a mouse, that the cat had haply seized upon" (not to mention over "the end of a novel, were it ever so stupid") (p. 43), is destined—when she is eventually dragged onto the battlefield—to be overwhelmed by the slaughter. The role that she then adopts is to bemoan the dead. She is drawn, willy-nilly, into the social war when her father is ruined and Mr. Osborne in "a brutal letter" announces the severing of relations between his family and hers (p. 218). Her response is to "[pine] silently," and to "[die] away day by day." When her father, in return, demands that she "banish George from her mind, and . . . return all the presents and letters" she has had from him, she is unable to part with the letters and places them "back in her bosom again—as you have seen a woman nurse a child that is dead." Where Becky collects trophies as she goes, Amelia is left to contemplate the relics of a past conquest: "It was over these few worthless papers that she brooded and brooded. She lived in her past life—every letter seemed to recall some circumstance of it. How well she remembered them all! His looks and tones, his dress, what he said and how—these relics and remembrances of dead affection were all that were left her in the world. And the business of her life, was—to watch the corpse of Love" (p. 219).

Amelia's making it the business of her life to watch the corpse of Love is one of the most powerful images in the novel. Since George's love for her seems, at this point, to have been killed by his father's prohibition (and in fact is only resuscitated by Dobbin's interventions and George's own instinctive resistance to his father), it is a love which has itself gone dead, and Amelia's making it the "business" of her life to mourn its demise suggests the emotional bankruptcy of her own position in the Fair, a bankruptcy as far-reaching as her father's financial crash. The metaphor of "the corpse of Love," moreover, has an astonishing proleptic force, and leads straight to an actual battlefield.

When George (married to Amelia, in the end, but having speedily proposed an elopement to Becky) is killed, "lying on his face, dead, with a
bullet through his heart" at Waterloo (p. 386), what Amelia precisely
proceeds to do is to make it the bankrupt business of her life to watch
his corpse. She hangs "her husband's miniature" over her bed, "the
same little bed from which the poor girl [went] to his; and to which she
[retires] now for many long, silent, tearful, but happy years" (p. 457).
She may be said to pass happy years in corpse-watching, but they are
years in which she defrauds both Dobbin and herself of life. Indeed, her
retirement to that little bed is not only a withdrawal into a self-imposed and self-restored virginity, though she has borne a son; it is also a
strategic retreat from the perils and challenges of life's battles.

For years Amelia devotes herself to the raising of her son. Where
Becky, the dashing soldier of fortune, lives off the pickings of the field,
lives, that is, off anyone and everyone available; Amelia, the victim of a
literal war, "made by nature for a victim" (p. 690), nursing her long
wound in private, "[lives] upon" her son, who is "her being" (p. 425).
Though she retreats from the field of battle, she takes her place in the
field of the Fair, where everyone tries to live on or off everyone else. Her
subtle emotional parasitism, as she lives on her son's substance, is no
better than Becky's blatant financial variety as she consumes the property of a Raggles—and perhaps no less ruinous in effect, though Georgy
is not shown to grow up into a son and a lover. Amelia, however, is
forced into one last unwilling battle over Georgy. Since it is "her
nature . . . to yield" (p. 465), the ultimate outcome is not unexpected,
but when she is cornered, she does make an initial stand and fight.
Georgy's grandfather makes a formal offer to take him "and make him
heir to the fortune which he . . . intended that his father should inherit," promises her a decent allowance, but stipulates that the child must
"live entirely with his grandfather" (pp. 540–41). Amelia at first rejects
the offer, but then is led by her mother to feel that in "her selfishness"
she is "sacrificing the boy" (p. 544). She nevertheless tries to fight back
by seeking to give lessons and so add to the income of her father's
struggling household, but that comes to nothing: "Poor simple lady,
tender and weak—how are you to battle with the struggling violent
world?" (p. 575). The "combat" lasts for weeks in her heart, but she
gives way daily "before the enemy with whom she [has] to battle":
"One truth after another was marshalling itself silently against her,
keeping its ground. Poverty and misery for all, want and degradation for
her parents, injustice to the boy—one by one the outworks of the little
citadel were taken, in which the poor soul passionately guarded her
only love and treasure" (p. 576). And in the end she admits defeat: "She
was conquered, and laying down her arms, as it were, she humbly sub-

mitted. That day [Miss Osborne and she] arranged together the pre-liminaries of the treaty of capitulation" (p. 580). The capitulation firmly locates the battle in the Fair, for it is to its mercenary values that Amelia capitulates here, accepting that financial advantage means more to a boy than a mother's love.[15] This capitulation precedes her ultimate surrender to Dobbin, who has lain in weary wait for her for years—and is rewarded with a boon (if not a booty) that he hardly wants by then.

IF THE NARRATIVE METHOD subtly compensates for the absence of a plot and holds the narrative together from without, the war imagery effec-tively unifies it from within. It binds together the manifold activities that are depicted in the narrative, for where these are not directly ren-dered in its terms, they implicitly fall within its encompassing frame of reference. It also firmly links the personal and historical conflicts which are the distinct and apparently disjunctive components of the narrative; and, furthermore, joins the stories of Becky and Amelia, the two protagonists, and holds them together in constantly contrasted balance even when they seem to strain apart in centrifugal disarray. *Vanity Fair*, despite its inconsistent narrator and seemingly divided worlds, is all of a piece.

OWNING AND DISOWNING:
THE UNITY OF
DANIEL DERONDA

Joan Bennett quotes George Eliot as complaining about "the lauda-
tion of readers who cut [*Daniel Deronda*] up into scraps, and talk
of nothing in it but Gwendolen," and as insisting that she "meant
everything in the book to be related to everything else there"; but
she herself maintains that what unity the novel has is "a deliberate
contrivance of [George Eliot's] craftsmanship rather than a necessary
consequence of her response to her subject. There is no inevitable connection between the perception of Gwendolen's predicament and of
Deronda's as there is between Lydgate's and Dorothea's."[1] It seems to
me that the apparent lack of unity—Joan Bennett's view in this regard
may be taken as representative of a widely held judgment—may be
attributable not to a fortuitousness of connection but to the striking
discrepancy in the quality of the two parts into which the novel falls:
what we may call the Gwendolen Harleth part, and the Jewish part,
with the eponymous hero acting as a bridge between the two. The
Gwendolen Harleth part must surely rank as among the best things
George Eliot ever did, while the Jewish part has no mean claim to being
among the worst. The result of this discrepancy is that the two parts do
not readily cohere in our imaginative response to the novel, but that is
not the same as saying that the novelist's imaginative conception of
her subject is not unified. I shall argue that George Eliot clearly did
conceive her subject in terms which relate "everything in the book
. . . to everything else there," even if she proved unable to realize the
various aspects of this conception with equally convincing force.

The question that arises is: how do we proceed critically to affirm
the existence of a unity of imaginative conception in a novel? To talk of
the unifying force of a given plot will presumably not be of much help

since a plot, by definition, unifies all it encompasses; and all we can do is to refer to the degree of skill or clumsiness with which it is contrived. The plot of *Daniel Deronda* so firmly involves the hero in both the Gwendolen Harleth and the Jewish parts that it would be quite impracticable to try to cut out the Jewish part in order to salvage a fine novel, as F. R. Leavis once suggested; but the existence of this unifying plot has manifestly not convinced large numbers of readers that there is an essential relation of parts. It seems to me that one sure indication of a unity of imaginative conception in a given work is the proliferation of analogous situations in it. I do not include under this head what is sometimes referred to as inverse analogy or contrast, for anything that is not like something else is obviously different from it. Accordingly, it does not seem to me to be useful to assert the evident "unity of design" of *Daniel Deronda*, as a critic has done, in terms of "a counterposing of 'bad' Gentile and 'good' Jewish worlds" (even if the adjectives are placed in inverted commas);[2] or, as another critic has claimed, in terms of a "central contrast of character—the contrast of Gwendolen Harleth and Daniel Deronda."[3] Instead, we should look for unity of design in direct analogies of situation. The novelist's imagination seizes on his material and organizes it in such a manner that it moves to the beat of an insistent inner rhythm (if we define rhythm in the novel, with E. M. Forster, as "repetition with variation")—in much the same way that Shakespeare's imaginative sense of his subject in, say, *Hamlet* expresses itself in a rhythmic recurrence of images of disease.

Another indication of an imaginative unity of conception may be the way in which an opening scene in a novel relates to what follows, serving as a springboard from which the novelist dives into what is still the amorphous fluidity of his design. The opening scenes of Dickens are particularly illuminating in this regard, for he often astonishingly seems to concentrate the essence of a long and complex novel in a vivid opening evocation of his subject—as in *Bleak House* and *Our Mutual Friend*, for instance. The opening of *Daniel Deronda* is also memorable, and the first view we get of Gwendolen Harleth playing roulette, a "problematic sylph" who has decided that since she is "not winning strikingly, the next best thing [is] to lose strikingly," does much to fix the image of the gamble that her life becomes. But I should like to draw attention to another figure in that opening scene:

Round two long tables were gathered two serried crowds of human beings, all save one having their faces and attention bent on the tables. The one exception was a melancholy little boy, with his knees and calves simply in their natural clothing of epidermis, but for the rest of his person in a fancy dress. He alone had his face turned towards the doorway, and fixing on it the blank gaze of a bedizened child stationed as a masquerading advertisement on the platform of an itinerant show, stood close behind a lady deeply engaged at the roulette-table. (pp. 35–36)[4]

George Eliot's touch here, with the wordy elaborations of the "natural clothing of epidermis" and the "masquerading advertisement," is a little heavy, but what is striking is that she should have chosen to include the little boy in the scene at all. This is his one and only appearance in the novel, and, unnamed and unknown, passing unlamented from it, he cannot be regarded as having any conceivable function in the narrative; yet he is unquestionably made into a focus of attention among the fifty or sixty gambling adults who are first assembled for our inspection. We can only conclude that, whether George Eliot was conscious of this or not, it was in some way important for her that the boy should be there, that her imagination had seized on him as necessary to the scene. What we register about him, apart from his fancy dress, is that he is ignored by all the adults, that he has been effectively forgotten by the lady whom he stands close behind, and that "the blank gaze" he turns on us is that of a child who not only looks like an advertisement but feels forsaken. And though this little boy forthwith disappears from the novel, it is thereafter pervaded by the motif of the forsaken child.

Perhaps the central feature of Gwendolen's involvement with Grandcourt is her discovery of his prior attachment to Mrs. Glasher. We are told that, some ten years before the beginning of the action, Mrs. Glasher was married to an Irish officer, and she is "understood to have forsaken her child along with her husband" when she elopes with Grandcourt—her three-year-old son dies two years afterward (p. 385). Mrs. Glasher has four children by Grandcourt, but he steadily refuses to marry her or to make the one boy among them his heir. She bitterly resents her boy's being "thrust out of sight for another," thus presenting him to Gwendolen as having been forsaken by his father (p. 189). Nor is Gwendolen's sense of what it feels like to be a forsaken child limited to the second-hand, adult though she is. When she first faces up to the implications of the loss of all the money her family possesses, she falters: "for the first time the conditions of this world seemed to her like a hurrying roaring crowd in which she had got astray, no more cared for and protected than a myriad of other girls, in spite of its being a peculiar hardship to her" (p. 278). And when Grandcourt drowns and she has to struggle with her sense of responsibility for his death, she begs Deronda not to "forsake" her: "Her quivering lips remained parted as she ceased speaking. Deronda could not answer; he was obliged to look away. He took one of her hands, and clasped it as if they were going to walk together like two children: it was the only way in which he could answer, 'I will not forsake you'" (p. 755). Though Deronda tries to reassure her as if she were a child, her dread of being forsaken becomes increasingly frantic: "'You must not forsake me,' said Gwendolen . . . 'I will bear any penance. I will lead any life you tell me. But you must not forsake me. You must be near. If you had been near me— if I could have said everything to you, I should have been different. You will not forsake me?'" (p. 765). In her protracted anguish Gwendolen becomes more and more dependent on Deronda, crying out to him "as the child cries whose little feet have fallen backward—[cries] to be taken by the hand, lest she should lose herself" (p. 842); and Deronda, knowing that he must part from her, feels "as if she [has] been stretching her arms towards him from a forsaken shore" (p. 839). When he finally tells her he is going to marry someone else, she answers: "I said I should be forsaken. I have been a cruel woman. And I am forsaken"; and she then submits "like a half-soothed child" to his attempt to comfort her (p. 878). Though she finally finds the strength to try to take up her life again, we are left feeling that her new life will have to grow painfully out of a sense of self not unlike that of the child who was a mute witness to the glory of her self-possession at the roulette table.

Deronda himself knows something of the feeling of desolation he tries to comfort in Gwendolen. He is thirteen when he first suspects he may be the illegitimate son of Sir Hugo Mallinger, the man who has brought him up as his nephew. This suspicion is strengthened when Sir Hugo asks him whether he would like to be a singer, for Daniel knows "a great deal" of what it is to be "a gentleman by inheritance," and is well aware that English gentlemen do not go in for a singing career. He has previously "never supposed he could be shut out" from the lot he has anticipated, but Sir Hugo's query seems to him "an unmistakable proof" that there is "something about his birth which [throws] him out from the class of gentlemen to which the baronet [belongs]" (p. 209). Daniel's fears prove to be justified, if inaccurate. As a grown man he finds out that his birth was legitimate, but he is shown to have been no less forsaken than when he felt shut out as a boy, for he also discovers that his mother abandoned him at the age of two to Sir Hugo. Deronda may thus be seen as the prototypical forsaken child in the novel; and in this respect too he serves as a bridge between the two parts of the book, for the motif recurs in the Jewish section.

We first see Mirah when Deronda saves her from committing suicide. The impression she agitatingly makes on him then is of a "forsaken girl" (p. 231); and thereafter she is constantly associated with this image: she informs Mrs. Meyrick that, when she was a child, she "played the part of a little girl who had been forsaken and did not know it" (p. 253); and we are told that her manners as an adult had probably "not much changed since she played the forsaken child at nine years of age" (p. 266). She thinks of herself, in a related image, as "a poor little bird, that was lost and could not fly," which has been put into "a warm nest" at the Meyricks' where there are "a mother and sisters" (p. 419); and Deronda is glad to have rescued "this child acquainted with sorrow" and to have placed "her little feet in protected paths": "The creature we help to save, though only a half-reared linnet, bruised and lost by the wayside—how we watch and fence it, and dote on its signs of recovery!" (p. 428).

The motif of the forsaken child begins to take on another dimension of meaning when Mirah is presented as thinking her unhappiness comes from her "being a Jewess," and as believing her suffering is "part of the affliction of [her] people, [her] part in the long song of mourning that has been going on through ages and ages" (p. 256). This analogy between her condition and that of the Jewish people emerges with greater force in the account Mirah gives Mrs. Meyrick of how she decided to take her life:

"The world about me seemed like a vision that was hurrying by while I stood still with my pain. My thoughts were stronger than I was: they rushed in and forced me to see all my life from the beginning; ever since I was carried away from my mother I had felt myself a lost child taken up and used by strangers, who did not care what my life was to me, but only what I could do for them. It seemed all a weary wandering and heart-loneliness . . . And I began to think that my despair was the voice of God telling me to die. But it would take me long to die of hunger. Then I thought of my People, how they had been driven from land to land and been afflicted, and multitudes had died of misery in their wandering—was I the first? . . . With these thoughts I wandered and wandered, inwardly crying to the Most High, from whom I should not flee in death more than in life—though I had no strong faith that He cared for me. The strength seemed departing from my soul: deep below all my cries was the feeling that I was alone and forsaken. . . . And a new strength came into me to will what I would do. You know what I did. I was going to die. You know what happened—did he not tell you? Faith came to me again: I was not forsaken. He told you how he found me?" (pp. 263–64)

Mirah becomes here the epitome of the wandering Jew, and if her life seems "all a weary wandering and heart-loneliness," it is an enactment in miniature of the fate of her People, "driven from land to land" in their affliction. By the same token her sense of herself as "a lost child," a creature "alone and forsaken," deserted by the Most High, who seems to have no special care for her, would seem to figure the lot of the children of Israel—the chosen but apparently forsaken people. And

Mirah is saved from despair and suicide by the active outside interven-
tion of Deronda, whose fortuitous presence at that moment serves to
restore her faith in the Most High. It is a fitting prelude to the Zionist
theme.

2

IN *Daniel Deronda* the forsaken child is typically a child that has been
disowned by one or the other of his parents. The disowning is seen
concretely in terms of a dispossession that results in the child's loss of
his inheritance. The impelling drive of the action is toward a restoration that enables the disowned child to come into his birthright. This
is the core situation that, repeated again and again, functions to relate
everything in the book to everything else.

A simple, vivid example of this process is provided by a group of
characters who are only of marginal importance. When Catherine Arrowpoint and Klesmer decide to marry, Catherine's parents respond by
disowning her. "It is useless to discuss the question," Mrs. Arrowpoint
says to Klesmer. "We shall never consent to the marriage. If Catherine
disobeys us we shall disinherit her. You will not marry her fortune. It is
right you should know that." And when her husband later asks her
"what the deuce" they are "to do with the property," she replies:
"There is Harry Brendall. He can take the name" (pp. 291–92). But in
the end the Arrowpoints come round and "condone the marriage," and
Sir Hugo for one views this as the sensible thing to do: "It shows the
Arrowpoints' good sense," he says. "And disowning your own child because of a *mésalliance* is something like disowning your one eye:
everybody knows it's yours, and you have no other to make an appearance with" (p. 460).

Grandcourt's disowning of the children he has had by Mrs.
Glasher—to whom he sometimes appears as the "friend of mamma's"
(p. 391)—extends on occasion into a tacit denial of their very existence.
Married to Gwendolen and riding with her in Rotten Row one morning,
he is waylaid by Mrs. Glasher, who has brought her son and one
daughter with her: "[Gwendolen] and Grandcourt had just slackened
their pace to a walk; he being on the outer side was the nearer to the
unwelcome vision, and Gwendolen had not presence of mind to do
anything but glance away from the dark eyes that met hers piercingly
towards Grandcourt, who wheeled past the group with an unmoved
face, giving no sign of recognition" (p. 667). The issue of Grandcourt's
disowning of his children is typically focused as his disinheriting of his
son: when Mrs. Glasher complains to Gwendolen that Grandcourt
"ought to marry" her and not Gwendolen, she adds in the same breath:

"He ought to make that boy his heir" (p. 189). Which is what he ultimately does in his will in the absence of a son as issue to his marriage
with Gwendolen, providing, moreover, that the boy take his name—
though he would appear to have been less concerned with the restoration of his son's rights than with putting "a finish to [Gwendolen's]
humiliations and . . . thraldom" (p. 663). It might be noted that, if
Grandcourt thus moves to an unexpected owning of his son, Gwendolen moves ineluctably to a disowning of her husband: when Grandcourt is drowning and calls to her to throw him the rope, he never
doubts that she will own to her connection with him and allow him to
cling to it. His death is thus the occasion of more than one surprise.

In the case of the Cohen-Lapidoth family there is an interesting reversal of the motif under discussion. It is a parent, not a child, who is
dispossessed: Mordecai tells Deronda that, when Lapidoth deserted his
wife and son, running off with the seven-year-old Mirah, Mrs. Cohen
cried out "from the depths of anguish and desolation—the cry of a
mother robbed of her little one" (p. 601). And it is a child who is driven
to a metaphorical disowning of a parent: Mirah, having discovered that
her father proposes, in effect, to sell her to a Gentile count, repudiates
him and flees to England. She insists, however, on owning to the parent
she has effectively disowned: "I was forced to fly from my father," she
says, "but if he came back in age and weakness and want, and needed
me, should I say, 'This is not my father'?" (p. 425). And when Lapidoth
does in fact turn up in London, his children unhesitatingly take him in.
Though Mirah says he is "like something that [has] grown in her flesh
with pain," she recognizes she could not cut him away "without worse
pain"; and Mordecai takes an uncompromising moral stand: "While
we have a home we will not shut you out from it," he says to his father.
"We will not cast you out to the mercy of your vices. For you are our
father, and though you have broken your bond, we acknowledge ours"
(p. 847).

Growing up in the belief that he is Sir Hugo's son, Deronda has to
live with the idea that he has been dispossessed. When Sir Hugo marries and Lady Mallinger begins to have her "fast-coming little ones,"
Deronda feels that "his own claim" to "the feelings and possessions of
the baronet" are "prior" (pp. 214–15); and when Sir Hugo's lady igno-
miniously produces only girls and so unwittingly establishes Grandcourt as the heir to the Mallinger estates, Deronda cannot but register
that "Grandcourt's prospect might have been his" (p. 323). Gwendolen,
indeed, is piercingly aware of this aspect of her relationship to Deronda: she reflects that "Deronda would probably some day see her mistress of the Abbey at Topping, see her bearing the title which would
have been his own wife's," and—in an explicit establishment of an

analogy of situation—this seems "to her imagination to throw him into one group with Mrs. Glasher and her children" (p. 380).

Deronda's sense of dispossession, however, is not most strongly inflamed by the contemplation of material loss, for while it is asserted that "many of us complain that half our birthright is sharp duty," we are told that he "was more inclined to complain that he was robbed of this half" (p. 526). That inheritance should not merely be regarded as a matter of material possession is again insisted on when reference is made to the "world-wide legends of youthful heroes going to seek the hidden tokens of their birth and its inheritance of tasks" (p. 573); and this idea of a nonmaterial inheritance is still further extended to that pertaining to the "historic life" of nations, which may sometimes be perceived only as "a pathetic inheritance in which all the grandeur and the glory have become a sorrowing memory" (p. 415). Though the revelation of the true circumstances of Deronda's birth confirms that he indeed has no claim to the Mallinger inheritance, it makes him heir to an unlooked-for national heritage. And he comes into his birthright through owning of kinship both with Mordecai and his mother.[5]

Mordecai, a man without progeny and slowly dying, seeking desperately to propagate his ideas, is said to have "an ideal life" that strains "to embody itself" (p. 531); and he yearns "for some young ear into which he [can] pour his mind as a testament, some soul kindred enough to accept the spiritual product of his own brief, painful life, as a mission to be executed" (p. 528). As I remarked earlier, there is a reversal of the nuclear situation in the Jewish part of the novel; and where there is elsewhere the repeated thrust toward the righting of a child by a parent's owning to it, here Mordecai seeks the vindication of a child's owning to his parentage, the child of his spirit. In a scene that rings loud and empty with its mystical insistences, Mordecai sees "the face of his visions" in the face of Deronda when he appears in a wherry under Blackfriars Bridge just as "the grey day [is] dying gloriously," and he promptly views Deronda as his "new life," his "new self—who will live when this breath is all breathed out" (pp. 549–51). We are told that Mordecai "claims" Deronda as "a long-expected friend," but that he is really claiming him as a son, though they are much of an age, is brought out in a curious passage. In Mordecai's "yearning consumptive glance" (shortly after the recognition scene at the bridge) there is "something of the slowly dying mother's look when her one loved son visits her bedside, and the flickering power of gladness leaps out as she says, 'My boy!'—for the sense of spiritual perpetuation in another resembles that maternal transference of self" (p. 553). The unexpected change of sex here is startling, for we feel that a father's look and a paternal transference of self would have done as well. But it suggests that Deronda is being called on to respond to the look of a mother as well as a father—and in fact it is only the discovery of his Jewish mother that finally enables him to own to the kinship Mordecai offers him.

The act of owning to kinship is shown to have vitalizing and restorative properties. Just before the Princess tells Deronda that she is his mother, she places both her hands on his shoulders, and her face gives out "a flash of admiration in which every worn line [disappears] and [seems] to leave a restored youth" (p. 687). In a sense the Princess's owning of Deronda as her son brings him back to life too, for she has previously declared him to be dead. She reveals to Deronda that, when Joseph Kalonymos (a close friend of her father who knew of Deronda's birth) came to inquire about him, she told him he was dead: "I meant you to be dead to all the world of my childhood. If I had said you were living, he would have interfered with my plans: he would have taken on him to represent my father, and have tried to make me recall what I had done" (p. 700). Her plans, apart from the wish to free herself of an encumbrance, were certainly to have Deronda die to his Jewishness (as she has done by being baptized before her second marriage), but she clearly conceived of this as a liberation. In asking Sir Hugo to take her son and "bring him up as an Englishman" with no knowledge of his parents (p. 697), she believed she was relieving Deronda "from the bondage of having been born a Jew" (p. 689). In bringing him back to life, she may thus be said in a double sense to restore his birthright. The birthright she consciously offers him, as the pattern of the novel might have led us to expect, takes the tangible form of an inheritance. Before he died, the Princess's father, a faithful Jew, had charged her to deliver a chest of his papers to her eldest son, and it is this that she now gives to Deronda, though he has to claim it from Joseph Kalonymos, who has had it in his safekeeping ever since the boy was pronounced dead. Kalonymos spells out the significance of the chest when he gives it to Deronda: "You come with thankfulness yourself to claim the kindred and heritage that wicked contrivance would have robbed you of," he says. "You come with a willing soul to declare, 'I am the grandson of Daniel Charisi'" (p. 788). The inheritance that Deronda ultimately comes into, that is to say, is the same that Mordecai offers him on the day that he claims him as a son: "You will take the inheritance," Mordecai says then, "which the base son refuses because of the tombs which the plough and harrow may not pass over or the gold-seeker disturb: you will take the sacred inheritance of the Jew" (p. 558).

3

WHEN DERONDA CLAIMS his grandfather's chest he in effect redeems his Jewish heritage—which his mother has, so to speak, placed in pawn. The motif of pawning and redeeming functions as a further uni-

fying principle in the novel; and, like so much else in it, is given its
first concrete embodiment in the opening description of the gambling
at Leubronn. Having lost at roulette and been made keenly aware of
how Deronda has beheld her "forsaken by luck" (p. 46), and then having
received news of the loss of the family fortune, Gwendolen is reduced
to pawning her necklace in order to get together some cash for her
journey. She pawns it, of course, at a Jewish pawnshop, and reflects on
how "Jew dealers" are "so unscrupulous in taking advantage of Chris-
tians unfortunate at play!" (p. 48). But Deronda redeems the necklace
and sends it to her, though he does not openly reveal it is he who has
done so. That the incident is of more than local significance is suggested by the fact that a pawning and a redeeming provide Deronda
with his first real point of contact not only with Gwendolen but also
with Mordecai. It is when he pawns his ring at Ezra Cohen's pawnshop
and again meets Mordecai, after their brief exchange at the second-
hand bookshop, that Deronda begins to think of him as "a remarkable
man" and determines to use the occasion of the redeeming of the ring
to try "to gain a little more insight into [his] character and history" (p.
452).

These literal instances of pawning point to other, metaphorical manifestations of it. I have already referred to the way in which the Princess
may be said to place her father's chest in pawn with Joseph Kalonymos.
He says to her then: "If you marry again, and if another grandson is
born to him who is departed, I will deliver up the chest to him" (p. 701).
What she disposes of to Kalonymos is the last vestige of her Jewishness; and what she comes away with is the pledge of her own freedom, the wherewithal to lead her own life unhindered since Kalonymos will not now "interfere with [her] plans" (p. 700).

Like Gwendolen, Grandcourt too is not averse to pawning, though of
a sophisticated and gentlemanly variety. Since Sir Hugo wishes to "secure Diplow as a future residence for Lady Mallinger and her daughters, and keep this pretty bit of the family inheritance for his own offspring" though Grandcourt is in fact due to inherit it (p. 197), he
dangles "the bait of ready money" with such seductive persistence before his heir that Grandcourt finally agrees in effect to pawn the property. He also might be said to place the diamonds he gives Mrs. Glasher
in pawn with her, pending his marriage to someone else. Mrs. Glasher
readily complies with his demand that she "[deliver] them" when he is
about to marry Gwendolen, maintaining she has always been ready to
"give them up to [his] wife" (p. 396). Lapidoth even pawns his
daughter—in order to redeem himself. Arrested for debt, he orders her
"to see a Count who [will] be able to get him released," and so begins
the "conspiracy with that man against [Mirah]" (p. 258).

The motif begins to gather further meaning when Gwendolen thinks of Deronda's redeeming of her necklace as a "rescue": " 'Don't sell the necklace, mamma,' she [says], a new feeling having come over her about that rescue of it which had formerly been so offensive" (p. 319). Other connotations of the idea of "redeeming" are present in a passage in which it is again associated with the notion of rescuing:

Persons attracted [Deronda], as Hans Meyrick had done, in proportion to the possibility of his defending them, rescuing them, telling upon their lives with some sort of redeeming influence; and he had to resist an inclination, easily accounted for, to withdraw coldly from the fortunate. But in the movement which had led him to redeem Gwendolen's necklace for her, and which was at work in him still, there was something beyond his habitual compassionate fervour—something due to the fascination of her womanhood. (pp. 369–70)

Deronda's character, it is apparent, casts him in the role of rescuer, but this passage suggests his role will not be confined to physical acts of rescue—such as the redeeming of Gwendolen's necklace, the aiding of Hans Meyrick (when his eyes are severely inflamed) which Hans declares to have been "the salvation of him" (p. 224), and the saving of Mirah from suicide. What he becomes engaged in pre eminently is the attempt to bring a "redeeming influence" to bear on Gwendolen's life.

Gwendolen first turns to Deronda for succor when she begins to dread she may be led to murder Grandcourt. Her dread expresses itself as a fear of herself—"When my blood is fired I can do daring things," she says, "take any leap; but that makes me frightened at myself"— and Deronda tries to persuade her to "turn [her] fear into a safeguard," feeling as if he is "seizing a faint chance of rescuing her from some indefinite danger." But he perceives that what he has been saying has been "thrown into the pallid distance of mere thought before the outburst of her habitual emotion," and—in an image which strikingly relates his relationship with Gwendolen to that with Mirah (while it also encompasses that between her and her husband)—he feels it is as if "he [has seen] her drowning while his limbs [are] bound" (pp. 508–9). The comparison between Gwendolen and Mirah later becomes explicit: "Easier now about 'the little Jewess,' Daniel relented towards poor Gwendolen in her splendour, and his memory went back, with some penitence for his momentary hardness, over all the signs and confessions that she too needed a rescue, and one much more difficult than that of the wanderer by the river—a rescue for which he felt himself helpless" (p. 620). When Gwendolen obviously becomes more and more dependent on him following Grandcourt's death, Deronda realizes that she is falling in love with him and recognizes that, if he were not involved with Mirah, "he would hardly have asked himself whether he loved her; the impetuous determining impulse which would have moved him would have been to save her from sorrow, to shelter her life for evermore from the dangers of loneliness, and carry out to the last the rescue he had begun in that monitory redemption of the necklace" (p. 835). As it is, he has to be content with helping her to see that she has been "saved from the worst evils that might have come from [her] marriage," making her gain, that is, out of another's loss (the central extension of the gambling image), and being driven, perhaps, to the act of violence she has dreaded. He helps her, moreover, to see that the best she can do is to accept the duty of being kind to those closest to her—and so to accept "looking at [her] life as a debt" (p. 839). Deronda, in a word, shows her how her life may be redeemed. And Gwendolen does finally experience "some of that peaceful melancholy which comes from the renunciation of demands for self, and from taking the ordinary good of existence, and especially kindness, even from a dog, as a gift above expectation" (p. 866).

Deronda performs one further act of rescue. He becomes the deliverer for whom Mordecai has anxiously waited, "the deliverer who [is] to rescue Mordecai's spiritual travail from oblivion" (p. 531); and once again the rescue is associated with the idea of redemption. This time it is a land that has to be redeemed, a land that the Jews have left in pawn, we might say, but which Mordecai, in an impassioned declaration at the *Hand and Banner*, proclaims they will be able "to redeem . . . from debauched and paupered conquerors" (p. 594). And Deronda, indeed, when he parts from Gwendolen, declares his personal dedication to this effort: "The idea that I am possessed with," he tells her, "is that of restoring a political existence to my people, making them a nation again, giving them a national centre" (p. 875).

JOURNEYS TO A LIGHTHOUSE

W hen novelists arrange for painters to talk about the technical problems of their art, we do well to keep at least one
ear open to noises coming from the writer's workshop. In
Sons and Lovers, for instance, Paul Morel declares that he
has tried to paint "the shimmering protoplasm in the leaves . . . and
not the stiffness of the shape," maintaining that "only this shim-
meriness is the real living. The shape is a dead crust." Paul's declaration points ahead to D. H. Lawrence's abandonment of conventional
methods of characterization in his next novel, *The Rainbow*, and to his
own attempt to render the shimmering protoplasm of character in his
presentation of it as a series of allotropic states. And in *To the Lighthouse*, Lily Briscoe's description of her painting provides us with what
is still today the most suggestive, if indirect, account of Virginia
Woolf's own preoccupations in the novel:

Nothing could be cooler and quieter. Taking out a penknife, Mr. Bankes
tapped the canvas with the bone handle. What did she wish to indicate by the
triangular purple shape, "just there?" he asked.
It was Mrs. Ramsay reading to James, she said. She knew his objection—that
no one could tell it for a human shape. But she had made no attempt at likeness, she said. For what reason had she introduced them then? he asked. Why
indeed?—except that if there, in that corner, it was bright, here, in this, she felt
the need of darkness. Simple, obvious, commonplace, as it was, Mr. Bankes was
interested. Mother and child then—objects of universal veneration, and in this
case the mother was famous for her beauty—might be reduced, he pondered, to
a purple shadow without irreverence.
But the picture was not of them, she said. Or, not in his sense. There were
other senses, too, in which one might reverence them. By a shadow here and a

light there, for instance. Her tribute took that form, if, as she vaguely supposed, a picture must be a tribute. A mother and child might be reduced to a shadow without irreverence. A light here required a shadow there. . . . She took up once more her old painting position with the dim eyes and the absent-minded manner, subduing all her impressions as a woman to something much more general; becoming once more under the power of that vision which she had seen clearly once and must now grope for among hedges and houses and mothers and children—her picture. It was a question, she remembered, how to connect this mass on the right hand with that on the left. She might do it by bringing the line of the branch across so; or break the vacancy in the foreground by an object (James perhaps) so. But the danger was that by doing that the unity of the whole might be broken. She stopped; she did not want to bore him; she took the canvas lightly off the easel. (pp. 84–86)[1]

Analogies between the procedures of Lily Briscoe and those of the novelist at once suggest themselves. Just as Lily has "made no attempt at likeness" in her rendering of Mrs. Ramsay and James, so Virginia Woolf in her presentation of her characters eschews "materialism," the kind of representational realism that she associates with the work of writers such as H. G. Wells, Arnold Bennett, and John Galsworthy, and derides as the attempt to provide "an air of probability embalming the whole so impeccable that if all [their] figures were to come to life they would find themselves dressed down to the last button of their coats in the fashion of the hour."[2] The painter's "reduction" of Mrs. Ramsay "to a purple shadow," moreover, adverts us to the novelist's brilliantly successful attempt in her portrayal of Mrs. Ramsay to reduce a lifetime to an evening, so to "boil down" character (as she phrases it in a diary entry)[3] as to reveal its essentials in the depiction of a woman sitting at a window knitting, strolling in a garden with her husband, dining with her family and guests, comforting sleepless children, and reading some poetry before going to bed. And Virginia Woolf's presentation of all her characters is of course directly related to her reduction of the space occupied in their lives by external events. Consequently, to view *To the Lighthouse* with the sort of preconceptions Mr. Bankes brings to Lily's painting would be to conclude that the novel is about nothing more significant than the eating of a dinner, the painting of a mediocre picture, and the undertaking of an excursion to a lighthouse.

In defending her reduction of mother and child to a triangular purple shape, Lily insists that anyway "the picture [is] not of them"; the novel, I think it should equally be insisted, is not primarily about Mr. and Mrs. Ramsay—despite Virginia Woolf's avowed intention to "do" the characters of her father and mother in the novel and to place her "father's character" at "the centre" of it, and despite her admission that she was impelled to write of her parents in order to purge herself of an unhealthy obsession with them.[4] That Lily's picture may provide us with a clue as to what the novel is ultimately about is suggested—given the close relation in achieved art between form and substance—by the striking similarity between the major formal problem that Lily has to contend with and that which confronted Virginia Woolf. Lily's problem is "how to connect" the two parts of her picture, the "mass" on the right with that on the left, without breaking "the unity of the whole"; similarly, Virginia Woolf saw her problem as being how to connect the two parts of her novel, parts 1 and 3, in such a way as to maintain the unity of her design despite a time-gap of what in the event turned out to be ten years:

[To the Lighthouse] might contain all characters boiled down; and childhood; and this impersonal thing, which I'm dared to do by my friends, the flight of time and the consequent break of unity in my design. That passage (I conceive the book in 3 parts. 1. at the drawing room window; 2. seven years passed; 3. the voyage) interests me very much. A new problem like that breaks fresh ground in one's mind; prevents the regular ruts.[5]

Part 2 of the novel ("Time Passes"), that is to say, corresponds to "the line of the branch" that Lily contemplates "bringing across" her picture; but, though it is no doubt intended to be as natural and delicate a link, part 2 is in fact both elaborate and heavy-handed. An adumbration of what was to come in *The Waves*, the writing in this part is precious and self-conscious, drawing attention to itself as "poetic" or coyly succumbing to parentheses of prose announcement. Moreover, the twenty-five-odd pages of this section do not succeed in evoking the passage of ten years—as Bennett, one of the whipping boys of "Modern Fiction," saw clearly in his review of the novel.[6] What is significant, therefore, is that *To the Lighthouse* does not disintegrate after part 2. It does not do so because part 3 is itself closely related to part 1, Virginia Woolf having solved her problem quite independently of the excrescence of part 2.

The aesthetically satisfying principle of unity that Virginia Woolf employs is that of balance, as is readily apparent in her handling of the two main "actions" of the novel. The Ramsays' abandonment of the proposed excursion to the lighthouse in part 1 is balanced, ten years later, by the trip made by Mr. Ramsay, Cam, and James; Lily Briscoe's failure to complete her picture is balanced in part 3 by her successful completion of a painting of the same scene. Round these events are grouped further manifestations of balance: James's rejection and hatred of his father as a boy of six (which are evoked in part 1 by Mr. Ramsay's smashing of his hopes of making the trip to the lighthouse) are bal-

anced ten years later by his sense of identification with his father and
his feeling of love for him when Mr. Ramsay praises his steering as they
reach the lighthouse. James's experience of disappointment as a child is
balanced by his painfully recovered memory of the circumstances as a
boy of sixteen. In part 3 Lily takes up her position to paint her picture
in precisely the spot where she stood ten years previously and finds
that someone in the house has thrown "an odd-shaped triangular shadow over the step" (p. 309) in much the same way that Mrs. Ramsay did
in part 1. This is only one instance of the manner in which Mrs. Ramsay's actual presence in the first part of the book is balanced by the
pervasiveness of her spiritual presence in the third section. Balance, in
a word, is the structural principle of the novel. And it is a vision of
balance, we recall, that Lily seeks to give body to in her picture, grop-
ing for it "among hedges and houses and mothers and children"; for, as
she explains to Mr. Bankes, she feels the need to balance brightness in
one corner with darkness in another, "a light here [requiring] a shadow
there," and a "mass on the right hand" necessitating a balancing mass
on the left. Lily's "vision" is a vision of harmony that springs from a
successful balancing or reconciliation of opposites; and this, it seems
to me, is the vision that Virginia Woolf pursues in her novel.[7] *To the
Lighthouse*, indeed, despite the novelist's sense of it as posing a temporal problem, is essentially spatial in its organization. It is best regarded as a vision, in that it is primarily concerned with the evocation
of timeless experience and not (as we might expect in a novel) with the
development of an action or a theme or of character. Virginia Woolf's
"tribute" to her characters, like that of Lily Briscoe's to mother and
child, also "takes the form" of incorporating the human within a larger
pattern.

   Given the structural principle of the novel, it is not surprising that in
its middle section there should appear a centrally important image of
scales:

For now had come that moment, that hesitation when dawn trembles and
night pauses, when if a feather alight in the scale it will be weighed down. One
feather, and the house, sinking, falling, would have turned and pitched downwards to the depths of darkness. . . .
If the feather had fallen, if it had tipped the scale downwards, the whole
house would have plunged to the depths to lie upon the sands of oblivion. But
there was a force working; something not highly conscious; something that
leered, something that lurched; something not inspired to go about its work
with dignified ritual or solemn chanting. Mrs. McNab groaned; Mrs. Bast
creaked. . . . Attended with the creaking of hinges and the screeching of bolts,
the slamming and banging of damp-swollen woodwork, some rusty laborious
birth seemed to be taking place, as the women, stooping, rising, groaning, sing-

ing, slapped and slammed, upstairs now now down in the cellars. Oh, they said, the work! (pp. 214–16)

As applied to the Ramsay house, left abandoned as "time passes," the image of the scales is representative of another aspect of the bad writing that characterizes this section of the novel, its fancifulness, its inexactness. What the image requires us to visualize is a "poetic" condition in which the house is poised in such precarious balance between "birth" and "oblivion" that the lightest feather-touch—let alone the "slapping and slamming" of the women or the continued blows of Time—will be sufficient to tip the scales in one direction or the other. Allowing for a metaphorical feather, we still cannot help feeling that a house in such a condition would perhaps best be left in the amorphous area of nonbeing between birth and oblivion in which the image of the scales places it. What is interesting in the passage is the relation of this moment in the history of the house to a moment in the diurnal cycle, the moment when "dawn trembles and night pauses"; for the cycle is thus also viewed in terms of balance (the regular rhythmic movement in the natural world to the attainment of a still point between night and day, a point of perfect balance), followed by repeated tippings of the scale. The precarious balance of opposites, it is implied, is a universal principle. It is certainly seen as the sine qua non of artistic creativity: "The disproportion . . . seemed to upset some harmony in [Lily's] mind. She felt an obscure distress. It was confirmed when she turned to her picture. She had been wasting her morning. For whatever reason she could not achieve that razor edge of balance between two opposite forces; Mr. Ramsay and the picture; which was necessary" (p. 296). The "razor edge of balance" is one that can be tipped by a feather; and it is evident that in order to be able to compose Lily has first to achieve an inner "harmony" that is dependent on her maintaining a difficult balance between the "opposite forces" of "Mr. Ramsay," whose progress to the lighthouse she is observing, and "the picture" she is working at— on her managing, that is, to reconcile the opposed demands of life and art. The moment at which she starts to paint is seen in analogous terms: experiencing "a curious physical sensation, as if she were urged forward and at the same time must hold herself back," she makes "her first quick decisive stroke" (p. 244), the stroke being a product, it would seem, of the tension between the creative drive that animates her and the artistic control she exercises over it.

The rhythmic movement of the diurnal cycle is matched by a human rhythm which suggests that life itself subsists between opposed motions: Mrs. McNab, a figure of life at its most elemental, sings as she works, and the sound is "like the voice of witlessness, humour, persistency itself, trodden down but springing up again," and she seems to say "how it [is] one long sorrow and trouble, how it [is] getting up and going to bed again, and bringing things out and putting them away again" (pp. 202–3). And the need for balance and the difficulty of attaining it constantly impinge, as Lily is made aware, not only on artistic endeavor but on ordinary, everyday life with its tacit but recurring demands for a reconciliation of opposed points of view:

Such was the complexity of things. For what happened to her, especially staying with the Ramsays, was to be made to feel violently two opposite things at the same time; that's what you feel, was one; that's what I feel was the other, and then they fought together in her mind, as now. It is so beautiful, so exciting, this love, that I tremble on the verge of it . . . ; also it is the stupidest, the most barbaric of human passions. (p. 159)[8]

Indeed, opposed or multiple points of view, as Mitchell Leaska has shown in detail,[9] are a characteristic mark of Virginia Woolf's handling of the "stream of consciousness" technique, consisting as it does of repeated shifts from one consciousness to another. (Part 2, though not very successful as a bridge between parts 1 and 3, is interesting for the major shift in point of view that it attempts, from the subjective and human to the objective and nonhuman.) In the end the sense of opposites poised against one another so pervades the novel that we realize, with James, that "nothing [is] simply one thing," that both the "silvery, misty-looking tower" which he remembers from his childhood and "the tower, stark and straight" which he confronts at the age of sixteen "are" the lighthouse (p. 286).

2

JAMES'S RECOGNITION that his childhood image of the tower is "also the lighthouse" seems to have constituted for critics implied authorial sanction to make of the lighthouse what they will. Certainly over the years this central symbol of the novel has become all things to all men. It seems to me, however, heretical though this may be thought to be,[10] that the lighthouse, as actually presented, does lend itself to a single view—though this not unexpectedly provides us with an image of the central opposition on which the book is based—and that the richness of the lighthouse as a symbol consists not in the infinite multiplication of "meanings" that may be attributed to it but in its free applicability as a paradigm. The actual journey to the lighthouse becomes symbolic of all the metaphoric journeys that are made to it in the course of the action; and disparate activities that are depicted in these terms are consequently unified in a rich metaphoric design.

What the lighthouse represents is perhaps best grappled with in respect of its immediate physical quidditas, as Stephen Dedalus might say, though it is notable that the novelist does not give us much to hang on to. After all the attention that has been focused on it, the description of the lighthouse that is finally offered us is, like the object itself, bare:

Indeed they were very close to the Lighthouse now. There it loomed up, stark and straight, glaring white and black, and one could see the waves breaking in white splinters like smashed glass upon the rocks. One could see lines and creases in the rocks. One could see the windows clearly; a dab of white on one of them, and a little tuft of green on the rock. A man had come out and looked at them through a glass and gone in again. So it was like that, James thought, the Lighthouse one had seen across the bay all these years; it was a stark tower on a bare rock. (pp. 311–12)

Whether the lighthouse is "stark and straight," as James now sees it, or whether it is "silvery" and "misty-looking," as he has previously thought of it, does not seem to me to be as important as the fact that it stands on its rock amid the engulfing sea, as it always has done. The dominant impression conveyed in the description is of the lighthouse's resistance to the sea: "a stark tower on a bare rock," made one with its rock, the lighthouse stands firmly resistant to the breaking waves that smash themselves "in white splinters" against it. Its firmness, indeed, is the quality most emphasized, the twice-repeated "stark" suggesting stiffness as well as bareness. The lighthouse on its rock in the sea, that is, projects an image of firmness or stability amid flux.[11]

Further support for this reading is to be found in one of the crucially important passages in the novel, which it is necessary to quote at length:

No, [Mrs. Ramsay] thought, putting together some of the pictures [James] had cut out . . . children never forget. For this reason, it was so important what one said, and what one did, and it was a relief when they went to bed. For now she need not think about anybody. She could be herself, by herself. And that was what now she often felt the need of—to think; well not even to think. To be silent; to be alone. All the being and the doing, expansive, glittering, vocal, evaporated; and one shrunk, with a sense of solemnity, to being oneself, a wedge-shaped core of darkness, something invisible to others. Although she continued to knit, and sat upright, it was thus that she felt herself; and this self having shed its attachments was free for the strangest adventures. When life sank down for a moment, the range of experience seemed limitless. And to everybody there was always this sense of unlimited resources, she supposed; one after another, she, Lily, Augustus Carmichael, must feel, our apparitions, the things you know us by, are simply childish. Beneath it is all dark, it is all spreading, it is unfathomably deep; but now and again we rise to the surface and that is what you see us by. Her horizon seemed to her limitless. There were all the places she had not seen; the Indian plains; she felt herself pushing aside the thick leather curtain of a church in Rome. This core of darkness could go anywhere, for no one saw it. They could not stop it, she thought, exulting. There was freedom, there was peace, there was, most welcome of all, a sum-moning together, a resting on a platform of stability. Not as oneself did one find rest ever, in her experience (she accomplished here something dexterous with her needles), but as a wedge of darkness. Losing personality, one lost the fret, the hurry, the stir; and there rose to her lips always some exclamation of tri-umph over life when things came together in this peace, this rest, this eternity; and pausing there she looked out to meet that stroke of the Lighthouse, the long steady stroke, the last of the three, which was her stroke, for watching them in this mood always at this hour one could not help attaching oneself to one thing especially of the things one saw; and this thing, the long steady stroke, was her stroke. Often she found herself sitting and looking, sitting and looking, with her work in her hands until she became the thing she looked at— that light for example. (pp. 99–101)

The passage suggests that Mrs. Ramsay's sense of her existence—as that of other people, of Lily and Augustus Carmichael, for instance—is of being immersed in a deep body of water from which she occasionally rises to the surface: "beneath it is all dark, it is all spreading, it is unfathomably deep; but now and again we rise to the surface and that is what you see us by." Mrs. Ramsay sees herself, that is to say, as having two selves: an outer self, the "personality" by which others know her; and an inner self, "invisible to others," which she thinks of as being her real self, the self in which she can "be herself." What char-acterizes the life of her outer self, her existence on the surface of being, is the degree to which it is subject to flux: it is a life that is given over to "the fret, the hurry, the stir"; and it is a life so utterly devoid of all solidity that she thinks of her outer self as an "apparition" and of its "evaporating" when she becomes herself. The movement to her inner self she figures as a "sinking down" from the surface to "a wedge-shaped core of darkness"—we remember the "triangular purple shape" that Lily reduces her to—a dropping down through the depths to "a platform of stability." In contradistinction to her outer self, therefore, her inner self is associated with something solid; and it is precisely when "things come together" and she is filled with a sense of stability amid the flux that she identifies herself with the lighthouse, "[becoming] the thing she [looks] at," the long "steady" stroke of the lighthouse. For her too, as for her son James, a "turn in the wheel of sensation has the power to crystallize and transfix the moment" (p. 11).

What a journey to the lighthouse images, therefore—the metaphoric journey of Mrs. Ramsay as well as the actual journey of Mr. Ramsay, James, and Cam—is, quite simply, a movement through flux to a point of fixity. Such a formulation, however, suggests the archetypal journey of life itself, a movement through the flux of being to a point of final rest; and indeed when Mrs. Ramsay sinks to her inner core, she feels she has won a "triumph over life" and is suffused with a sense of "this peace, this rest, this eternity." If her descent to her inner self is thus like a kind of death, there is nothing deathly about it, partly because she never loses connection with the self on the surface that "continues to knit" and is ready to respond to any demands that may be made on it. It seems to me quite misleading to assert, as William Troy does, that her experience represents "a dread of being and doing, an abdication of personality and a shrinking into the solitary darkness."[12] Mrs. Ramsay allows herself to drop into that solitary darkness only when she is no longer required by those who "[come] to her, naturally, since she [is] a woman, all day long with this and that; one wanting this, another that" until she often feels she is "nothing but a sponge sopped full of human emotions" (p. 54). Her dropping down to the dark platform should rather be viewed as an expression of her need for balance, of a need to balance exposure to flux with concealment in stability. And her sense of such exposure is certainly disturbing. Reminded during dinner of a day she spent with the Mannings, whom she has not seen for twenty years, she reflects that "while she [has] changed, that particular day, now become very still and beautiful, [has] remained there, all these years" (p. 137); and she expresses her sense of this contrast in a striking image: "life, which shot down even from this dining-room table in cascades, heaven knows where, was sealed up there [i.e., "in the Mannings' drawing-room at Marlow twenty years ago"], and lay, like a lake, placidly between its banks" (p. 145). For Mrs. Ramsay, life, as it is lived from moment to moment in perpetual flux, is a hapless experience of being shot down a waterfall; but once the moment is lived through and becomes part of the past, it is safely contained, like a lake, in placid fixity. Mrs. Ramsay's characteristic introspectiveness, her continual recalling of the past as she summons herself together, resting on the platform, is thus a means of anchoring her life.

The "need" to shed her outer self, which Mrs. Ramsay now often feels, is a need, then, for spiritual revitalization; and if her sinking to the "core of darkness" is a kind of death, it is followed by the rebirth of a return to the surface. The fact, moreover, that "this core of darkness

[can] go anywhere" suggests that essential being (for she "can be herself" only when she sinks to this core) is not bound by or limited to the body and so is independent of its death. Mrs. Ramsay's experience of "dying" and being "reborn" in the flesh, in other words, points to the possibility of continued life after death, a possibility that is reinforced by the abundance with which she continues to live in the lives of all those who return to the island after her death.

In another passage solidity is poised against fluidity in a way that interestingly extends the significance of the opposition:

> Now all the candles were lit, and the faces on both sides of the table were brought nearer by the candle light, and composed, as they had not been in the twilight, into a party round a table, for the night was now shut off by panes of glass, which, far from giving any accurate view of the outside world, rippled it so strangely that here, inside the room, seemed to be order and dry land; there, outside, a reflection in which things wavered and vanished, waterily.
>
> Some change at once went through them all, as if this had really happened, and they were all conscious of making a party together in a hollow, on an island; had their common cause against that fluidity out there. (pp. 151–52)

The dining room is described in terms which suggest that it is like a lighthouse or, at any rate, which make it an analogue of the lighthouse: all beyond its lit-up panes of glass is envisaged as rippling in a watery fluidity.[13] Significantly, however, the stability which is associated with the lighthouse and the sense of which leads the diners to make "common cause against that fluidity out there" is here equated with the conception of "order"; the flux against which the stability is set is here equated with dissolution, with a condition in which "things [waver] and [vanish], waterily." A gloss on the force of the word "order" in this passage is provided by the description (in an earlier work of Virginia Woolf's) of a room that is specifically compared to a lighthouse, the description in *Night and Day* of the Hilbery's drawing-room, as seen from the street by Ralph Denham:

> Lights burnt in the three long windows of the drawing-room. The space of the room behind became, in Ralph's vision, the centre of the dark, flying wilderness of the world; the justification for the welter of confusion surrounding it; the steady light which cast its beams, like those of a lighthouse, with searching composure over the trackless waste. In this little sanctuary were gathered together several different people, but their identity was dissolved in a general glory of something that might, perhaps, be called civilization; at any rate, all dryness, all safety, all that stood up above the surge and preserved a consciousness of its own, was centred in the drawing-room of the Hilberys.

What "might, perhaps, be called civilization," we note, is the "dryness" and the "safety," all that "stands up above the surge" in the lighted "sanctuary" and that is opposed to the "flying wilderness of the world," the "welter of confusion" and the "trackless waste" outside it; and this might equally be said of the "order and dry land" represented by the Ramsay dining room. Civilization is implicitly defined in *To the Lighthouse* as the achievement of stability amid flux, the successful balancing of the fluid by the fixed, and what the novel explores are dry pockets of firmness in a wet world.

3

ONE SUCH POCKET is art. Lily Briscoe thinks of her brush as "the one dependable thing in a world of strife, ruin, chaos" (p. 232); she also imagines that the poet Carmichael would explain what life means by saying that "nothing stays; all changes; but not words, not paint," and she believes that one may say even of her own imperfect work that it "[remains] for ever" (p. 276). Just as Mrs. Ramsay moors her life by keeping lines tied to what "remains" for her, the past, so Lily clings, as *she* is shot down the waterfall, to art. In other words, she too has a "platform of stability," though the nature of her activity makes her tenure of it more dangerous, more exposed, than that of Mrs. Ramsay: "It was an odd road to be walking, this of painting. Out and out one went, further and further, until at last one seemed to be on a narrow plank, perfectly alone, over the sea" (p. 265).

Analogies between Lily's ordeal of art and Mrs. Ramsay's experience of life are insistent:

Down in the hollow of one wave [Lily] saw the next wave towering higher and higher above her. For what could be more formidable than that space? Here she was again, she thought, stepping back to look at [her canvas], drawn out of gossip, out of living, out of community with people into the presence of this formidable ancient enemy of hers—this other thing, this truth, this reality, which suddenly laid hands on her, emerged stark at the back of appearances and commanded her attention. She was half unwilling, half reluctant. Why always be drawn out and haled away? Why not left in peace, to talk to Mr. Carmichael on the lawn? It was an exacting form of intercourse anyhow. Other worshipful objects were content with worship; men, women, God, all let one kneel prostrate; but this form, were it only the shape of a white lamp-shade looming on a wicker table, roused one to perpetual combat, challenged one to a fight in which one was bound to be worsted. Always . . . before she exchanged the fluidity of life for the concentration of painting she had a few moments of nakedness when she seemed like an unborn soul, a soul reft of body, hesitating on some windy pinnacle and exposed without protection to all the blasts of doubt. . . .

Can't paint, can't write, she murmured monotonously, anxiously considering what her plan of attack should be. For the mass loomed before her; it protruded; she felt it pressing on her eyeballs. Then, as if some juice necessary for the lubrication of her faculties were spontaneously squirted, she began precariously dipping among the blues and umbers, moving her brush hither and thither, but it was now heavier and went slower, as if it had fallen in with some rhythm which was dictated to her . . . by what she saw, so that while her hand quivered with life, this rhythm was strong enough to bear her along with it on its current. Certainly she was losing consciousness of outer things. And as she lost consciousness of outer things, and her name and her personality and her appearance, and whether Mr. Carmichael was there or not, her mind kept throwing up from its depths, scenes, and names, and sayings, and memories and ideas, like a fountain spurting over that glaring, hideously difficult white space, while she modelled it with greens and blues. (pp. 244–47)

Lily's exchanging of "the fluidity of life for the concentration of painting" is depicted as a movement through water. She abandons "gossip" and ordinary "living," and, "losing consciousness of outer things," shedding her "personality," as Mrs. Ramsay does, she plunges into the towering waves. If she is thus like a "swimmer" (p. 244), she makes her way underwater, for when her concentration slackens momentarily, she finds that "against her will she [has] come to the surface" and so is "half out of the picture" (p. 274). Where Mrs. Ramsay, however, effortlessly sinks to her core of darkness, Lily has to fight for her progress, engaged as she is in "perpetual combat" with her "formidable ancient enemy." Different though the descents into the depths of the two women are, the identity of Lily's enemy nevertheless suggests that their destinations are not dissimilar. The antagonist that Lily dives to meet is "this truth, this reality" which emerges "stark at the back of appearances"; it is analogous, therefore, to Mrs. Ramsay's core of being, her real or true self that is hidden behind the "apparition" she is known by—the self she identifies with the lighthouse. The word "stark," moreover, further recalls the stark tower on its bare rock and suggests that Lily's plunge is yet another journey to a lighthouse, that art, indeed, as Lily later reflects (in a passage to which I will refer) is the striking of flux into stability. Certainly it is more than a coincidence that Lily should successfully complete her painting just as the Ramsay party reaches the lighthouse.

If Mrs. Ramsay is revitalized by dropping down from the fretful surface of life, Lily lives most intensely in her art—may even be said only really to live then. Just before she begins to paint, she feels "like an unborn soul, a soul reft of body"; for her, art is a coming to life—her hand "[quivers] with life" as she paints—is life in the flesh. In a sense, therefore, it is also a compensatory activity. An "exacting form of intercourse," artistic creation is made possible for her by what the squirting of the vital juice suggests is a necessary prior consummation in the unborn soul; and though this is in accord with what Virginia Woolf elsewhere regards as the dependence of creativity on a "fusion" of male and female elements within the individual psyche, on a woman artist's having "intercourse with the man in her,"[14] it is strongly implied that in her art Lily also seeks to satisfy a sexual hunger. If she creates her picture out of the "fountain" that gushes up from the depths of her mind, Mrs. Ramsay, the lavish mother of eight children, is also (as we shall see) a fountain into which her husband plunges.

At dinner Mrs. Ramsay takes particular pleasure in looking at a dish of fruit, "putting a yellow against a purple, a curved shape against a round shape," without "knowing why" she does so or why, as she looks, she feels "more and more serene" (p. 168). Mrs. Ramsay, that is, instinctively lives what Lily has to fight for in her art—as Lily begins to understand ten years later:

When [Lily] thought of herself and Charles throwing ducks and drakes and of the whole scene on the beach, it seemed to depend somehow upon Mrs. Ramsay sitting under the rock, with a pad on her knee, writing letters. . . . But what a power was in the human soul! she thought. That woman sitting there, writing under the rock resolved everything into simplicity; made these angers, irritations fall off like old rags; she brought together this and that and then this, and so made out of that miserable silliness and spite (she and Charles squabbling, sparring, had been silly and spiteful) something—this scene on the beach for example, this moment of friendship and liking—which survived, after all these years, complete, so that she dipped into it to re-fashion her memory of him, and it stayed in the mind almost like a work of art.

. . . This, that, and the other; herself and Charles Tansley and the breaking wave; Mrs. Ramsay bringing them together; Mrs. Ramsay saying "Life stand still here"; Mrs. Ramsay making of the moment something permanent (as in another sphere Lily herself tried to make of the moment something permanent)—this was of the nature of a revelation. In the midst of chaos there was shape; this eternal passing and flowing (she looked at the clouds going and the leaves shaking) was struck into stability. (pp. 248–50)

The fact that Mrs. Ramsay has "made" something "complete," something which has "survived" her own death, suggests—as Lily now sees and has often been remarked—that she is in her own way an artist, an artist of life. What is worth noting is the way in which Lily implicitly defines the attributes of art, and what is implied therefore by Mrs. Ramsay's spontaneous artistry. Art, for Lily, is the "making of the moment something permanent," the discovery of "shape" in "the midst of chaos," and the striking of the "eternal passing and flowing" into "stability." What Mrs. Ramsay quietly enacts on the beach through the sheer force of her personality—of that which others know her by, as she "brings together" Lily and Tansley, who have been squabbling—is how in the "sphere" of life shape may be imposed on chaos by the creation of relations. Amid the "eternal flowing" she is thus a stabilizing force—everything, indeed, "depends" on her—and the way in which she shapes and stabilizes the liquid moment is to make of it something as "permanent" as life allows. The stabilizing, integrative force that she represents in ordinary life, in other words, is seen—as art is—as a mark of civilization.

It is Mrs. Ramsay, we remember, who binds the dinner party together in the dining room that suggests "order and dry land." The harmony that is finally achieved on that occasion is a product of her deliberate "creating"—as the diners "all [sit] separate," the "whole of the effort of merging and flowing and creating" rests on her (pp. 130–31)—and her creative effort is presented as yet another journey by water: she begins to work "as a sailor not without weariness sees the wind fill his sail and yet hardly wants to be off again and thinks how, had the ship sunk, he would have whirled round and round and found rest on the floor of the sea" (p. 131). As the diners initially resist her efforts, Lily responds to an unspoken appeal for help, understanding that Mrs. Ramsay is in effect saying to her: "I am drowning, my dear, in seas of fire. Unless you apply some balm to the anguish of this hour and say something nice to that young man there, life will run upon the rocks" (p. 143). Finally, when "everything [seems] right," when she at last feels she has "reached security" and that they are all held "safe together," Mrs. Ramsay directly connects her sense of well-being with that experienced earlier that afternoon when she rested on her platform of stability:

Nothing need be said; nothing could be said. There it was, all round them. It partook, she felt, carefully helping Mr. Bankes to a specially tender piece, of eternity; as she had already felt about something different once before that afternoon; there is a coherence in things, a stability; something, she meant, is immune from change, and shines out (she glanced at the window with its ripple of reflected lights) in the face of the flowing, the fleeting, the spectral, like a ruby; so that again to-night she had the feeling she had had once to-day already, of peace, of rest. Of such moments, she thought, the thing is made that remains for ever after. This would remain. (p. 163)

It is, we realize, the same kind of journey she has been making; and from the place at which she lands and can rest we see, with her, how things hang together: the "coherence" she registers is the "order," the "civilization," that has just before been achieved in the dining room; it is equated here with "stability," with what (like a work of art) is "immune from change" and "remains for ever after"; and it is compared to something that "shines out in the face of the flowing," like "a ruby"—or, we might add, perhaps more appropriately, like a lighthouse.

IT IS NOT ONLY Lily Briscoe who feels as if she has walked out on a narrow plank over the sea; Mr. Ramsay repeatedly has an analogous experience:

> It was his fate, his peculiarity, whether he wished it or not, to come out thus on a spit of land which the sea is slowly eating away, and there to stand, like a desolate sea-bird, alone. It was his power, his gift, suddenly to shed all superfluities, to shrink and diminish so that he looked barer and felt sparer, even physically, yet lost none of his intensity of mind, and so to stand on his little ledge facing the dark of human ignorance, how we know nothing and the sea eats away the ground we stand on—that was his fate, his gift. But having thrown away, when he dismounted, all gestures and fripperies, all trophies of nuts and roses, and shrunk so that not only fame but even his own name was forgotten by him, he kept even in that desolation a vigilance which spared no phantom and luxuriated in no vision, and it was in this guise that he inspired in William Bankes (intermittently) and in Charles Tansley (obsequiously) and in his wife now, when she looked up and saw him standing at the edge of the lawn, profound reverence, and pity, and gratitude too, as a stake driven into the bed of a channel upon which the gulls perch and the waves beat inspires in merry boat-loads a feeling of gratitude for the duty it has taken upon itself of marking the channel out there in the floods alone. (pp. 71–72)

The sea-land opposition in this passage, though it evokes the familiar notion of the flowing and the fixed, is somewhat puzzling in its application. The sea is apparently viewed as the swirling multifariousness of life, all that cannot be subdued to form or contained, and so makes Mr. Ramsay aware of "the dark of human ignorance"; and therefore it is viewed too as the irreducible force that is "slowly eating away" and undermining whatever stability man on his "spit of land" has achieved. Walking in his garden, Mr. Ramsay makes a journey, as it were, to that final point of fixity which he reaches "at the edge of the lawn." Unlike his wife and Lily Briscoe, who move in water, he imagines himself as ambling "at his ease" on horseback "through the lanes and fields of a country known to him from boyhood" (p. 71) (through the territory possessed by the scholarly mind, that is), until he reaches the unknown and dismounts for the final solitary confrontation, but he—like them at analogous moments of vision—at this point sheds his habitual self with its superfluities, forgetting "not only fame but even his own name." Standing alone at the edge of the lawn, Mr. Ramsay evokes in those who see him the same "feeling of gratitude" that travelers by water feel for a stake that stands amid the waves which beat on it and "[marks] the channel out there in the floods" for them, being for William Bankes and Charles Tansley and his wife a trusty guide who can be relied on for the firmness of his stand. For them, in a word, he is like a lighthouse—of which the stake is yet another analogue.[15] Though utterly dependent on his wife emotionally, intellectually Mr. Ramsay is ready both to stand alone and to admit how little he knows. His intellectual qualities (allowing for the ironies of the philosopher's self-dramatization) are of a heroic cast, being compared by the novelist to those that "would have saved a ship's company exposed on a broiling sea with six biscuits and a flask of water" or would have made him the indomitable leader of "a desolate expedition across the icy solitudes of the Polar region": "Yet he would not die lying down; he would find some crag of rock, and there, his eyes fixed on the storm, trying to the end to pierce the darkness, he would die standing" (pp. 57–59). On the lawn, however, Mr. Ramsay turns "from the sight of human ignorance and human fate and the sea eating the ground we stand on," and looks instead at his wife and child. We are told that "had he been able to contemplate [the sight] fixedly," it "might have led to something" (p. 73); the casual "something," of course, is meant to suggest the momentous—and the intellectual firmness figured by the fixity of such contemplation the kind of force that makes for civilization.

MARRIAGE is simultaneously seen as a journey by water and an area of stability amid the flux. Reflecting on the coming marriage of Paul Rayley and Minta Doyle, the unmarried Lily feels "inconspicuous" by Paul's side: "he, bound for adventure; she, moored to the shore; he, launched, incautious; she solitary, left out" (p. 158). But, watching Mr. Ramsay raise his wife from her chair, Lily also thinks of the Ramsay marriage as a stepping on shore, as it were: "It seemed . . . as if he had once bent in the same way and raised her from a boat which, lying a few inches off some island, had required that the ladies should thus be helped on shore by the gentlemen. . . . Letting herself be helped by him, Mrs. Ramsay had thought (Lily supposed) the time has come now; Yes, she would say it now. Yes, she would marry him. And she stepped slowly, quietly on shore" (pp. 304–5). On the one occasion, however, when our attention is overtly drawn to the symbolic significance of marriage, it is clearly viewed as a locus of stability:

So that is marriage, Lily thought, a man and a woman looking at a girl throwing a ball. That is what Mrs. Ramsay tried to tell me the other night, she thought.

For she was wearing a green shawl, and they were standing close together watching Prue and Jasper throwing catches. And suddenly the meaning which, for no reason at all . . . descends on people, making them symbolical, making them representative, came upon them, and made them in the dusk standing, looking, the symbols of marriage, husband and wife. Then, after an instant, the symbolical outline which transcended the real figures sank down again, and they became, as they met them, Mr. and Mrs. Ramsay watching the children throwing catches. But still for a moment . . . there was a sense of things having been blown apart, of space, of irresponsibility as the ball soared high, and they followed it and lost it . . . Then, darting backwards over the vast space (for it seemed as if solidity had vanished altogether), Prue ran full tilt into them and caught the ball brilliantly high up in her left hand, and her mother said, "Haven't they come back yet?" whereupon the spell was broken. (pp. 114–16)

If Mr. and Mrs. Ramsay are here explicitly seen as "the symbols of marriage," as the "representative" husband and wife, it is by way of reminding us that *To the Lighthouse* is also concerned with another kind of balance, that which may be attained by a man and a woman in marriage. "Standing close together," watching their children playing in a moment of achieved equilibrium, it is notable that Mr. and Mrs. Ramsay provide the one point of stability in a scene which evokes the "flying wilderness" that lies outside the Hilbery drawing-room or the "fluidity" that ripples outside the Ramsay dining room: with Prue running and the ball soaring high, it seems as if things have "been blown apart," as if "solidity [has] vanished altogether"—until Prue runs "full tilt" into her parents.

How a feather can tip the scales of married equilibrium, the razor edge of balance that is the customary condition of married bliss, is vividly shown in an early scene between the Ramsays:

Not for the world would she have spoken to him, realising, from the familiar signs, his eyes averted, and some curious gathering together of his person, as if he wrapped himself about and needed privacy into which to regain his equilibrium, that he was outraged and anguished. She stroked James's head; she transferred to him what she felt for her husband . . . when stopping deliberately, as his turn came round again, at the window he bent quizzically and whimsically to tickle James's bare calf with a sprig of something, she twitted him for having dispatched "that poor young man", Charles Tansley. Tansley had had to go in and write his dissertation, he said.

"James will have to write *his* dissertation one of these days," he added ironically, flicking his sprig.

Hating his father, James brushed away the tickling spray with which in a manner peculiar to him, compound of severity and humour, he teased his youngest son's bare leg.

She was trying to get these tiresome stockings finished to send to Sorley's little boy to-morrow, said Mrs. Ramsay.

There wasn't the slightest possible chance that they could go to the Lighthouse to-morrow, Mr. Ramsay snapped out irascibly.

How did he know? she asked. The wind often changed.

The extraordinary irrationality of her remark, the folly of women's minds enraged him. He had ridden through the valley of death, been shattered and shivered; and now she flew in the face of facts, made his children hope what was utterly out of the question, in effect, told lies. He stamped his foot on the stone step. "Damn you," he said. But what had she said? Simply that it might be fine to-morrow. So it might.

Not with the barometer falling and the wind due west.

To pursue truth with such astonishing lack of consideration for other people's feelings, to rend the thin veils of civilisation so wantonly, so brutally, was to her so horrible an outrage of human decency that, without replying, dazed and blinded, she bent her head as if to let the pelt of jagged hail, the drench of dirty water, bespatter her unrebuked. There was nothing to be said.

He stood by her in silence. Very humbly, at length, he said that he would step over and ask the Coastguards if she liked.

There was nobody whom she reverenced as she reverenced him. (pp. 52–54)

Having recovered his equilibrium after having run into Lily Briscoe and William Bankes in the middle of the charge of the Light Brigade, Mr. Ramsay stops at the window, we see, to tickle James's calf with the sprig, stops, that is, to try in his own way to make up to his son for the disappointment he has caused him by his earlier announcement that it will not be possible to go to the lighthouse the next day. Following up the tickling with the remark about the dissertation, he tries once more to express his feeling for his son; but since the remark is "ironic" and the tickling "teasing," and neither succeeds in mollifying his son's hatred, what is revealed is not only the difficulty he has in expressing his love for his children but the degree to which he is out of touch with them. The lack of direct contact, the remoteness, that is figured by the tickling with a sprig is set against the reassuring love, the direct simplicities of touch, that Mrs. Ramsay's stroking of James's head exemplifies. Sitting on the floor between his father and mother, James is exposed not to a quantitative difference in the love his parents feel for him but to a temperamental disparity between male and female. That the opposition is one which as easily explodes in violence as reposes in balance is demonstrated by Mr. Ramsay's enraged outburst. It is what appears to him to be her "irrationality" that triggers the explosion, for he has a man's concern, uncompromising if abstract, for the truth, for the rational, in a word for "facts," while she in her woman's way cares only for the concrete situation, feels only the need for compassion for her son, and so with a fine disregard is ready to fly "in the face of facts." What is interesting is that Mr. Ramsay's insistence on facing the facts, the intellectual firmness which, when he stands on his spit of land at the edge of his lawn, is regarded as being of the stuff of which civilization is made, is here, for the woman sitting with her child, an outrage that wantonly rends "the thin veils of civilisation." Nothing, as the novel repeatedly insists, is simply one thing. And marriage, like everything else, subsists in balance, in the constantly delicate adjustment of the balance between man and woman: if Mr. Ramsay's outburst dazes Mrs. Ramsay into submission, as she bends her head and allows herself to be bespattered "unrebuked," her hurt elicits sudden humility on his part, and that, in turn, evokes her reverence—and so the previously disrupted balance is again (precariously) restored.

Sitting at the window, Mrs. Ramsay sustains not only her son but also her husband:

Mrs. Ramsay, who had been sitting loosely, folding her son in her arm, braced herself, and, half turning, seemed to raise herself with an effort, and at once to pour erect into the air a rain of energy, a column of spray, looking at the same time animated and alive as if all her energies were being fused into force, burning and illuminating (quietly though she sat, taking up her stocking again), and into this delicious fecundity, this fountain and spray of life, the fatal sterility of the male plunged itself, like a beak of brass, barren and bare. He wanted sympathy. He was a failure, he said. . . .

Filled with her words, like a child who drops off satisfied, he said, at last, looking at her with humble gratitude, restored, renewed, that he would take a turn; he would watch the children playing cricket. He went.

Immediately, Mrs. Ramsay seemed to fold herself together, one petal closed in another, and the whole fabric fell in exhaustion upon itself, so that she had only strength enough to move her finger, in exquisite abandonment to exhaustion, across the page of Grimm's fairy story, while there throbbed through her, like the pulse in a spring which has expanded to its full width and now gently ceases to beat, the rapture of successful creation. (pp. 61–62, 64)

Throbbing to the "rapture of creation," Mrs. Ramsay, who has redeemed her husband's "fatal sterility," filling him with life and so in a sense creating him afresh, may be said to experience in her marriage the sort of satisfaction that Lily Briscoe finds in her art—as is underlined by the fact that she, like Lily, creates from the fountain of life that wells up in her. But her experience is also presented as being depleting: feeding on her substance, "like a child who drops off satisfied," Mr. Ramsay appears to "exhaust" her rich store, so that "the whole fabric [falls] in upon itself." What is suggested, then, is that—for all the apparent equilibrating of man and woman—this, in essentials, is a marriage in which one partner lives on and off the other; and indeed the images of his being filled out and her falling in, together with the central image of the fountain, provide a striking parallel to the view of marriage presented in Henry James's *The Sacred Fount*. But as might be expected in a work that is permeated throughout with the same unifying vision, the Ramsay marriage is reciprocal in this respect too; and if balance, allowing for the permutations of the seesaw, implies mutual support, it is not Mr. Ramsay alone who is sustained. Mrs. Ramsay— like Virginia Woolf herself, we cannot help reflecting—is subject at times to a peculiar horror of flux: the sound of the waves then seems to her like the "ghostly roll of drums remorselessly [beating] the measure of life," and makes her think of "the destruction of the island and its engulfment in the sea," warning her that "it [is] all ephemeral as a rainbow." Succumbing to the impression, she has "an impulse of terror"; but it is the solid, substantial presence of her husband, "[beating] up and down the terrace" to another measure, that "soothes" her and assures her that "all [is] well" (pp. 30–31).

"Only connect . . ." would be as apt an epigraph to *A Passage to India* as it is to *Howards End*. Prominent symbols, indeed, in Whitman's "Passage to India," from which the title of the novel is taken,[1] are the Suez Canal and the Pacific railroad; and Forster's preoccupations in his last novel are not notably different from the concern with means of communication (whether between individuals, social classes or nations) that is manifested throughout his earlier work. Racial differences, the most formidable barrier between man and man, simply pose the most testing challenge in the oeuvre of a novelist pre-eminently concerned with the possibilities of personal relations.

What sharply distinguishes *A Passage to India* from Forster's earlier work, however, is his conception of it as a rhythmic unit. The rhythmic movement of the novel implies that human relations are subject to the same kind of ineluctable rhythms as the cosmos. This is the chastened conclusion that Forster would appear to have come to in *A Passage to India*, and it is this view that shapes the structure of the novel. "The three sections into which it is divided, Mosque, Caves, Temple," Forster tells us, "also represent the three seasons of the Cold Weather, the Hot Weather, and the Rains, which divide the Indian year."[2] What we are invited to witness, in other words, is a cyclic process, a rhythmic rise and fall, which we may describe (in terms of the action) as the establishment of relationship, the breakdown of relationship, and the reestablishment of relationship, with a further breakdown implied—as the end of the novel strikingly indicates. But "Mosque, Caves, Temple" are also the three main symbols of the novel, and they are linked together in a pattern of contrasted but interdependent meanings. The

rhythmic and symbolic patterns, moreover, are themselves closely related: the action that leads in turn to each of the stages in the rhythmic
process is initiated in or near the mosque, caves, and temple, which are
themselves symbolic of the tendencies exemplified in the action that
takes place in or near them. The symbolic pattern is the ground of the
rhythmic pattern, and I shall attempt to show the binding force of the
overall design.

2

THE CRUCIAL INCIDENT in part 1 is the encounter of Aziz and Mrs.
Moore at the mosque, for it is their movement beyond conventional
Anglo-Indian attitudes that precipitates the action of the novel. The
nature of some of these attitudes is revealed in parallel scenes that
frame the encounter. Before he goes to the mosque, Aziz dines with
Hamidullah and Mahmoud Ali. The Indians fall to discussing the Eng-
lish, and in a mood of "bitter fun" Mahmoud Ali maintains that Mrs.
Turton, the Collector's wife, "takes bribes":

"Bribes?"
"Did you not know that when they were lent to Central India over a Canal
Scheme, some Rajah or other gave her a sewing machine in solid gold so that
the water should run through his state."
"And does it?"
"No, that is where Mrs. Turton is so skilful. When we poor blacks take
bribes, we perform what we are bribed to perform, and the law discovers us in
consequence. The English take and do nothing. I admire them." (p. 13)[3]

Forster is adept at putting his social comedy to work. Peeping through
Mahmoud Ali's delightful anecdote is the deep-rooted Indian suspicion
of the English that throughout bedevils Anglo-Indian relations (even
those established between Aziz and Fielding)—a kind of suspicion that
(as here) is wholly irrational, for it persists despite the facts, and that is
more often than not quite unjustified, for the Turtons' honesty (whatever their faults) is beyond question.
    This suspiciousness is matched by English distrust of the Indians.
Mrs. Moore returns from the mosque to the club, and is introduced to
prevailing English attitudes toward the Indians:

[Adela] became the centre of an amused group of ladies. One said, "Wanting
to see Indians! How new that sounds!" Another, "Natives! why, fancy!" A
third, more serious, said, "Let me explain. Natives don't respect one any the
more after meeting one, you see."
"That occurs after so many meetings."

But the lady, entirely stupid and friendly, continued: "What I mean is, I was a nurse before my marriage and came across them a great deal, so I know. I really do know the truth about Indians. A most unsuitable position for any English-woman—I was a nurse in a Native State. One's only hope was to hold sternly aloof."

"Even from one's patients?"

"Why, the kindest thing one can do to a native is to let him die," said Mrs. Callendar.

"How if he went to heaven?" asked Mrs. Moore, with a gentle but crooked smile.

"He can go where he likes as long as he doesn't come near me. They give me the creeps." (pp. 27–28)

The racial arrogance of the English ladies, which is typical of the English response to the Indians, conceals qualities that only emerge fully at the time of Aziz's arrest and trial. The nurse's insistence on the need for English superiority to be rigorously asserted and maintained betrays an underlying insecurity, an insecurity that comes to the surface in the near-hysteria of the English colony when Adela makes her accusation against Aziz. We realize, moreover, that it is the physical aversion and repulsion, if not sexual fear, implicit in Mrs. Callendar's "creeps" that makes Adela's allegation of attempted rape so particularly horrifying to the English.

The meeting of Mrs. Moore and Aziz at the mosque should be viewed, then, in relation to this background of racial division and distrust. That the meeting takes place at the mosque is at once made significant:

[Aziz] had always liked this mosque. . . . The courtyard—entered through a ruined gate—contained an ablution tank of fresh clear water, which was always in motion, being indeed part of a conduit that supplied the city. . . . Where he sat, he looked into three arcades whose darkness was illuminated by a small hanging lamp and by the moon. The front—in full moonlight—had the appearance of marble, and the ninety-nine names of God on the frieze stood out black, as the frieze stood out white against the sky. The contest between this dualism and the contention of shadows within pleased Aziz, and he tried to symbolize the whole into some truth of religion or love. . . . Here was Islam, his own country, more than a Faith, more than a battle-cry, more, much more . . . Islam, an attitude towards life both exquisite and durable, where his body and his thoughts found their home.

. . . the mosque—that alone signified, and he returned to it from the complex appeal of the night, and decked it with meanings the builder had never intended. Some day he too would build a mosque, smaller than this but in perfect taste, so that all who passed by should experience the happiness he felt now. And near it, under a low dome, should be his tomb, with a Persian inscription:

> Alas, without me for thousands of years
> The Rose will blossom and the Spring will bloom,
> But those who have secretly understood my heart—
> They will approach and visit the grave where I lie.

He had seen the quatrain on the tomb of a Deccan king and regarded it as profound philosophy—he always held pathos to be profound. The secret under- standing of the heart! He repeated the phrase with tears in his eyes, and as he did so one of the pillars of the mosque seemed to quiver. (pp. 20–21)

This description suggests that the mosque conveys "meanings" on two levels: the impersonal "truth of religion or love" that Aziz tries to make it symbolize; and the personal "attitude towards life" that it rep- resents for him when he decks it with meanings the builder never intended. If Islam proclaims the oneness of God, the ninety-nine names or attributes of God, in testifying to His overall unity, seem to declare that the mosque itself be viewed as a symbol of unity. The nature of this unity is defined by the "dualism" of the black names standing out on the white frieze: it is a unity that is attained through a reconciliation of opposites, the "dualism" itself contesting (as a har- monious whole) with the shadows within the mosque. The same sort of reconciliation is imaged in the general play of light and darkness, for the dark mosque is illuminated by a lamp and by the moon; and in the evocation of simultaneous containment and flow in the description of the tank of water, for the water is always in motion. Aziz, moreover, finds a home for both his body and his thoughts in the mosque and in Islam. As he decks the mosque with his own meanings, he also seems to find in it and make it symbolize his guiding principle in personal relations—"the secret understanding of the heart." The two levels of symbolism are connected since it is through the secret understanding of the heart, we begin to see, that opposites may be reconciled and unity attained. This is precisely what is dramatized in the scene that follows between Mrs. Moore and Aziz.

The pillar that seems to quiver and that disturbs Aziz's reverie is of course Mrs. Moore. When he sees that it is an Englishwoman who has stepped out into the moonlight, he is "furiously angry" and shouts: "Madam! Madam! Madam!"

> "Oh! Oh!" the woman gasped.
> "Madam, this is a mosque, you have no right here at all; you should have taken off your shoes; this is a holy place for Moslems."
> "I have taken them off."

"You have?"

"I left them at the entrance."

"Then I ask your pardon."

Still startled, the woman moved out, keeping the ablution-tank between them. He called after her, "I am truly sorry for speaking."

"Yes, I was right, was I not? If I remove my shoes, I am allowed?"

"Of course, but so few ladies take the trouble, especially if thinking no one is there to see."

"That makes no difference. God is here." (p. 21)

The encounter initially follows the established mode of contact between Indian and Englishman in India. The fact of English intrusion at once provokes hostile Indian suspicion; the English reaction to the hostility is a fearful keeping of distance; and the upshot (as Mrs. Moore prudently places the ablution-tank between herself and Aziz) is, as it were, the creation of a gulf between the two. If the Collector's Bridge Party—"not the game, but a party to bridge the gulf between East and West," as he explains (p. 28)—is miserable evidence of the extent of the gulf, Aziz and Mrs. Moore are notable for being able to cross it. This is partly because in their meeting at the mosque they both seem eventually to be influenced by what D. H. Lawrence called "the spirit of place"; and partly because Mrs. Moore, when she says "God is here," herself demonstrates that quality of heart which the mosque symbolizes to Aziz, and he cannot help moving toward her in glad astonishment and recognition. Soon they sit down "side by side" at the entrance to the mosque (p. 22), and before he escorts her to the club, he expresses his joy at the establishment of this new relationship:

The flame that not even beauty can nourish was springing up, and though his words were querulous his heart began to glow secretly. Presently it burst into speech.

"You understand me, you know what others feel. Oh, if others resembled you!"

Rather surprised, she replied: "I don't think I understand people very well. I only know whether I like or dislike them."

"Then you are an Oriental." (p. 24)

The quality of their relationship is defined by the image of the flame and by the colloquy that follows. The flame that not even beauty can nourish is, I take it, a disinterested warmth of feeling for another, a warmth that contrasts sharply with the cold formality that is manifested on all sides at the Bridge Party; and this flame is fed by the secretly glowing heart. Aziz's excited assertion of kinship springs from the recognition that they both bring to their personal relations with others the same kind of direct, intuitive, emotional response. It is on this kind of response, of course, that their own relationship is based.

One of the important consequences of the encounter of Mrs. Moore and Aziz is the bringing together of Aziz and Fielding. They meet at the tea party Fielding gives for Mrs. Moore and Adela, and quickly take to each other. When Fielding later calls on Aziz, who is ill, he is disconcerted by his churlishness; but before he leaves, the relationship takes a sudden turn:

"Before you go, for you are evidently in a great hurry, will you please unlock that drawer? Do you see a piece of brown paper at the top?"
"Yes."
"Open it."
"Who is this?"
"She was my wife. You are the first Englishman she has ever come before. Now put her photograph away."
He was astonished, as a traveller who suddenly sees, between the stones of the desert, flowers. The flowers have been there all the time, but suddenly he sees them. He tried to look at the photograph, but in itself it was just a woman in a sari, facing the world. He muttered, "Really, I don't know why you pay me this great compliment, Aziz, but I do appreciate it."
"Oh, it's nothing, she was not a highly educated woman or even beautiful, but put it away. You would have seen her, so why should you not see her photograph?"
"You would have allowed me to see her?"
"Why not? I believe in the purdah, but I should have told her you were my brother, and she would have seen you. Hamidullah saw her, and several others."
"Did she think they were your brothers?"
"Of course not, but the word exists and is convenient. All men are my brothers, and as soon as one behaves as such he may see my wife."
"And when the whole world behaves as such, there will be no more purdah?"
"It is because you can say and feel such a remark as that, that I show you the photograph," said Aziz gravely. . . .
"Put her away, she is of no importance, she is dead," said Aziz gently. "I showed her to you because I have nothing else to show. You may look round the whole of my bungalow now, and empty everything. I have no other secrets, my three children live away with their grandmamma, and that is all."
Fielding sat down by the bed, flattered at the trust reposed in him, yet rather sad. He felt old. He wished that he too could be carried away on waves of emotion. . . . What had he done to deserve this outburst of confidence, and what hostage could he give in exchange? He looked back at his own life. What a poor crop of secrets it had produced! There were things in it that he had shown to no one, but they were so uninteresting, it wasn't worth while lifting a purdah on their account. (pp. 113–15)

This scene should be viewed in relation to the earlier scene at the mosque. Aziz, it is clear, approaches Fielding in much the same way that he approached Mrs. Moore. His impulsive showing of the photograph is analogous to his assertion of kinship with the Englishwoman: it is equivalent, that is, to taking Fielding behind the purdah, and so is a symbolic affirmation of brotherhood. The gesture is motivated, moreover, by his desire to make amends for his earlier rudeness and tacitly constitutes an appeal to the secret understanding of the heart. The simile of the traveler defines the nature of Fielding's response to the appeal, and is itself glossed by previous references to flowers. After her encounter with Aziz, Mrs. Moore's "sense of unity, of kinship with the heavenly bodies" is associated not only with the mosque but with flowers: "cocktails and cigars" (the symbols of English exclusiveness) are said to "[die] into invisible flowers" when she leaves the club and suddenly feels at one with the universe (p. 30). The luckless Dr. Panna Lal's smashing of the hollyhocks in the garden of the club, as he drives up in his tum-tum, further develops the flower image by providing an ironic comment on the pretensions of the Bridge Party (p. 41). Fielding's astonishment, as defined by the image, thus suggests his joyful recognition of the meaning of Aziz's gesture, which is intended to convey his desire for union—though this (like the flowers among the desert stones) has hitherto been obscured by the hard aridity of their meeting.

Fielding's question, "Did she think they were your brothers?" serves sharply to differentiate him from Mrs. Moore. Fielding is warm and sympathetic, but he is not prepared to rely on his intuitive understanding. Above all he is intellectual—his question is an attempt to make sense of Aziz's attitudes—and if he brings to his relationship with Aziz the good will of a liberal, enlightened man, it is a good will which is dependent on the understanding of the head rather than that of the heart. Fielding, indeed, is emotionally inhibited—as his failure to give Aziz a "hostage in exchange" reveals. He clearly rationalizes a temperamental incapacity to make a corresponding gesture of emotional intimacy when he attributes a lack of interest to his "secrets"; there is nothing intrinsically interesting about the photograph: "in itself" it is "just a woman in a sari."

If Aziz and Fielding thus represent radically different attitudes toward friendship, it seems clear that Forster endorses neither, for the emotionalism of the former and the reserve of the latter are in about equal measure responsible for the breakdown of the relationship. In this respect the book (like *Howards End* again) would appear to be a plea for yet another kind of connection, of head and heart, of prose and passion. The consistency of Forster's position would be admirable were it not for Mrs. Moore. About her he is ambiguous. *Her* understanding of the heart *is* endorsed—and yet it is not tested, for it is not exposed to the strains of a close personal relationship.

Neither is Aziz's at this point. When Fielding leaves him, he drops
off to sleep; and the sentence that describes his passing into a region of
dream (and that concludes part 1) effectively sums up the action of this
section of the novel: "He passed into a region where these joys had no
enemies but bloomed harmoniously in an eternal garden, or ran down
watershoots of ribbed marble, or rose into domes whereunder were in-
scribed, black against white, the ninety-nine attributes of God" (p. 119).
The "joys" referred to, significantly associated with flowers and with
the mosque, are clearly the joys of unity. If Aziz is primarily delighted
at the "compact" with Fielding that has been "subscribed by the photograph" (p. 119), the references to the mosque recall his relationship
with Mrs. Moore; and the passage as a whole can be taken to point to
the apparently successful bridging of the gulf between the races in
these two instances—which is the crux of part 1. But the fact that the
region where the joys have no enemies is a dream region suggests the
tenuous insubstantiality of even these two relationships, and looks
ahead to the reality where caves are as potent a factor as mosques.

3

THE DESCRIPTION of the Marabar Caves (with which part 2 begins) provides us with all that we need to know in order to interpret their symbolic meaning:[4]

[The hills] rise abruptly, insanely, without the proportion that is kept by the
wildest hills elsewhere, they bear no relation to anything dreamt or seen. To call
them "uncanny" suggests ghosts, and they are older than all spirit. . . .
    The caves are readily described. A tunnel eight feet long, five feet high, three
feet wide, leads to a circular chamber about twenty feet in diameter. This arrangement occurs again and again throughout the group of hills, and this is all,
this is a Marabar Cave. Having seen one such cave, having seen two, having seen
three, four, fourteen, twenty-four, the visitor returns to Chandrapore uncertain
whether he has had an interesting experience or a dull one or any experience at
all. He finds it difficult to discuss the caves, or to keep them apart in his mind, for
the pattern never varies, and no carving, not even a bees'-nest or a bat, distinguishes one from another. Nothing, nothing attaches to them, and their reputation—for they have one—does not depend upon human speech. . . .
    They are dark caves. Even when they open towards the sun, very little light
penetrates down the entrance tunnel into the circular chamber. There is little
to see, and no eye to see it, until the visitor arrives for his five minutes, and
strikes a match. Immediately another flame rises in the depths of the rock and
moves towards the surface like an imprisoned spirit: the walls of the circular
chamber have been most marvellously polished. The two flames approach and
strive to unite, but cannot, because one of them breathes air, the other stone. A
mirror inlaid with lovely colours divides the lovers, delicate stars of pink and
grey interpose, exquisite nebulae, shadings fainter than the tail of a comet or

the midday moon, all the evanescent life of the granite, only here visible. Fists and fingers thrust above the advancing soil—here at last is their skin, finer than any covering acquired by the animals, smoother than windless water, more voluptuous than love. The radiance increases, the flames touch one another, kiss, expire. The cave is dark again, like all the caves.

. . . But elsewhere, deeper in the granite, are there certain chambers that have no entrances? Chambers never unsealed since the arrival of the gods. Local report declares that these exceed in number those that can be visited, as the dead exceed the living . . . One of them is rumoured within the boulder that swings on the summit of the highest of the hills; a bubble-shaped cave that has neither ceiling nor floor, and mirrors its own darkness in every direction infinitely. If the boulder falls and smashes, the cave will smash too—empty as an Easter egg. The boulder because of its hollowness sways in the wind, and even moves when a crow perches upon it: hence its name and the name of its stupendous pedestal: the Kawa Dol. (pp. 123–25)

The place of the caves in the general symbolic pattern of the novel is suggested by the fact that the Marabar hills are "older than all spirit": the caves, that is, should be regarded as an epitome of nonhuman India, primal India, and as such they are set against the human endeavor that is represented by the mosque, the temple, and the club. Certainly the hills appear as a threatening denial of human aspiration: rising "abruptly, insanely, without . . . proportion," they negate all idea of harmonious relationship; and thrusting "fists" above the soil, they image an enmity that is antithetical to the human hope expressed in the outstretched hand of friendship. The sense of negation that the hills impress on the observer is strengthened by the caves they contain. The darkness of the caves is in strong contrast to the reconciliation of light and dark that characterizes the mosque; the darkness here suggests a negation of light, a turning away from the sun. But above all the caves defy and deny connection. Since it is impossible to distinguish one cave from another, it is impossible to make any meaningful connection with them. The attempt to do so that is represented by a visitor's striking of a match is productive only of the final negation, for the light shed on the prevailing darkness is sufficient only to define the futility of all that "strives to unite"—like the two flames, "the lovers." The caves are a divisive force, a solid barrier of stone to the "imprisoned spirit" that would break free into union. The only union that the caves allow is that of the dark, and the two flames can meet only in the kiss of death. The caves indeed typify "the spirit of the Indian earth" that (we are told elsewhere) "tries to keep men in compartments" (p. 127).

Then there are the caves that have no entrances. Their very inaccessibility is in keeping with the sense of impenetrable isolation that is suggested by the flame in the cave wall. It is suggested too by the "bub-

ble-shaped cave" that swings on the summit of one of the hills. The
Kawa Dol seems almost to stand as an emblem of the hollow, meaningless void that is Marabar—of the void into which Mrs. Moore peers.

Some confirmation for this interpretation of the symbolism is provided by the effect of the echo, which we may regard as the voice of the
caves:

> A Marabar cave had been horrid as far as Mrs. Moore was concerned, for she
> had nearly fainted in it, and had some difficulty in preventing herself from
> saying so as soon as she got into the air again. It was natural enough: she had
> always suffered from faintness, and the cave had become too full, because all
> their retinue followed them. Crammed with villagers and servants, the circular
> chamber began to smell. She lost Aziz in the dark, didn't know who touched
> her, couldn't breathe, and some vile naked thing struck her face and settled on
> her mouth like a pad. She tried to regain the entrance tunnel, but an influx of
> villagers swept her back. She hit her head. For an instant she went mad, hitting
> and gasping like a fanatic. For not only did the crush and stench alarm her;
> there was also a terrifying echo.
> . . . The echo in a Marabar cave . . . is entirely devoid of distinction. What-
> ever is said, the same monotonous noise replies, and quivers up and down the
> walls until it is absorbed into the roof. "Boum" is the sound as far as the
> human alphabet can express it, or "bou-oum", or "ou-boum",—utterly dull. (p.
> 145)

The echo, which reduces everything to a dull "boum," has the same
effect as the unvarying caves: it negates the making of meaningful distinctions. To Mrs. Moore, indeed, it murmurs, "Pathos, piety, courage—they exist, but are identical, and so is filth. Everything exists,
nothing has value"; and it consequently begins to "undermine her hold
on life" (p. 147). The extent to which Mrs. Moore in fact loses hold is
strikingly indicated by the scene in the cave. What she takes to be a
"vile naked thing" that strikes her face and settles on her mouth "like
a pad" turns out, when the visitors emerge from the cave, to have been
"a poor little baby, astride its mother's hip" (p. 146). Her mistake, made
in the darkness of the cave and under the influence of its echo, is a
distressing revelation of her loss of the capacity to make distinctions
and of the denial or distortion of true relationship that this entails. The
touch of the baby turns her into a "fanatic," hitting out with her fists,
raised—like those of the Marabar hills—in violent repudiation. Her
losing of Aziz "in the dark" becomes the prelude to further disruptions; shortly after her experience in the cave she realizes that she does
not want "to communicate with anyone, not even with God." Finally,
she loses "all interest, even in Aziz," and the "affectionate and sincere

words" that she has spoken to him seem "no longer hers but the air's" (p. 148).

The caves have an even more drastic effect, of course, on Adela. What happens to her at Marabar must be considered in relation to her reactions and behavior prior to her entry to the cave on the Kawa Dol, for Forster has given the incident a full and illuminating context. There is, first, the mistake she makes as the party moves toward the hills. The scene is such that everything seems "cut off at its root, and therefore infected with illusion":

For instance, there were some mounds by the edge of the track, low, serrated, and touched with whitewash. What were these mounds—graves, breasts of the goddess Parvati? The villagers beneath gave both replies. Again, there was a confusion about a snake which was never cleared up. Miss Quested saw a thin, dark object reared on end at the farther side of a watercourse, and said, "A snake!" The villagers agreed, and Aziz explained: yes, a black cobra, very venomous, who had reared himself up to watch the passing of the elephant. But when she looked through Ronny's field-glasses, she found it wasn't a snake, but the withered and twisted stump of a toddy-palm. So she said: "It isn't a snake." The villagers contradicted her. She had put the word into their minds, and they refused to abandon it. Aziz admitted that it looked like a tree through the glasses, but insisted that it was a black cobra really, and improvised some rubbish about protective mimicry. (p. 139)

This apparently trivial episode serves in fact as a concentrated preview of the later incident, parallels between the mistake Adela makes here and that she makes about Aziz being forcefully suggested. We notice, first, that her mistake about the snake is in part due to the scenery, which infects everything "with illusion," just as her later mistake is in part due to the atmosphere—or, as it were, the spirit—of the caves. But the mistake about the snake is also clearly in part a reflection of her own fears (Freudian symbolism being in this regard suggestive); the episode would accordingly seem to point to the role played by her fears in the cave. Second, it is only when she looks through Ronny's field-glasses, when she is able, that is, to clarify her vision through some external aid, that she sees the truth. Similarly, it is when she suddenly sees through Mrs. Moore's eyes at the trial, using Mrs. Moore as her field-glasses, so to speak, that she realizes her terrible error. Third, the refusal of Aziz and the villagers to abandon their belief in what Adela has put into their minds is a prefigurement of the reaction of the English colony when she withdraws her accusation against Aziz—as it is also testimony not to the power of "the word" but the credulity of man.

This episode is followed by an unpleasant brush between Adela and

Aziz. In her earnest way she tells Aziz she wants to consult him about "this Anglo-Indian difficulty," and asks him whether he can give her any advice:

> "You are absolutely unlike the others, I assure you. You will never be rude to my people."
> "I am told we all get rude after a year."
> "Then you are told a lie," he flashed, for she had spoken the truth and it touched him on the raw; it was itself an insult in these particular circumstances. He recovered himself at once and laughed, but her error broke up their conversation—their civilization it had almost been—which scattered like the petals of a desert flower, and left them in the middle of the hills. "Come along," he said, holding out a hand to each. They got up a little reluctantly, and addressed themselves to sightseeing. (p. 144)

Adela's "error" here is of a different kind from that made in regard to the stump of toddy-palm, but it is equally revealing. It shows a complete want of tact and delicacy on her part; and her crudity is viewed as a disruptive force, scattering the petals of the desert flower, the flower that Aziz has so carefully nurtured. If the desert flower particularly recalls the relationship of Fielding and Aziz, we realize that the ultimate consequence of Adela's later error is to smash the friendship of the two men, just as it widens the gulf between the two races. The accusation of assault, indeed, should be seen as an extreme form of the kind of crudity Adela manifests here, for it betrays a total lack of that sensitivity to people (that secret understanding of the heart) which would have made it impossible for her to accuse Aziz of such a crime—which enables Mrs. Moore, for instance, to "know" that he is innocent. The caves exert their dark influence, blotting out the mosque, but it is also crudity and insensitivity that are set against the understanding of the heart.

It is Adela's crudity that sets the scene for the culminating incident. Making her way up a track to the Kawa Dol with Aziz and the guide, she asks Aziz, in "her honest, decent, inquisitive way," whether he has "one wife or more than one." The question so appalls him that he plunges into a cave "to recover his balance"; she follows "at her leisure" and also goes into a cave (p. 151). It is her crudity which parts them and makes possible all that follows as a result of the separation. If her hallucination in the cave is partly attributable to the overpowering heat and to the echo that "appears to have frightened her" (p. 165), the form it takes is a reflection of her psychological state. Adela has been preoccupied with thoughts of her coming marriage, and just before she puts her question to Aziz, she has a sudden revelation that she and Ronny do "not love each other." She decides not to break off her engagement, however, since she is not convinced that "love is necessary to a successful union"; but she is wondering "about marriage" when she enters the cave (pp. 150–51). Her hallucination of an attempted criminal assault by Aziz is thus clearly referrable to her own shocked and confused state of mind—the discovery that she does not love Ronny comes so suddenly that she feels "like a mountaineer whose rope [has] broken" (p. 150); the imagined rape, it seems, symbolizes her fear of what a marriage without love will mean.[5] But rape is also one of the extreme forms that a denial of relationship can take, and this appropriately is the word that comes out of Marabar on the day of the expedition.

Intimations of the likely repercussions of Marabar are soon forthcoming. Fielding is with Aziz when he is arrested at the Chandrapore railway station, and showing a commendable loyalty he demonstratively walks "arm in arm" with him. But Fielding is "called off" by Turton, and Aziz goes on to prison alone (p. 159). Even *their* friendship is not proof in the end against the disruptive force generated in and by the Marabar; and (despite Fielding's continued and courageous support of Aziz throughout the period of the trial) their separation here is premonitory of what is to follow. It is again Adela, who later comes between them:

"So you and Madamsell Adela used to amuse one another in the evening, naughty boy," [said Aziz].

Those drab and high-minded talks had scarcely made for dalliance. Fielding was so startled at the story being taken seriously and so disliked being called a naughty boy, that he lost his head and cried: "You little rotter! Well, I'm damned. Amusement indeed. Is it likely at such a time?"

"Oh, I beg your pardon, I'm sure. The licentious Oriental imagination was at work," he replied, speaking gaily, but cut to the heart; for hours after his mistake he bled inwardly.

"You see, Aziz, the circumstances . . . also the girl was still engaged to Heaslop, also I never felt . . ."

"Yes, yes; but you didn't contradict what I said, so I thought it was true. Oh, dear, East and West. Most misleading. Will you please put your little rotter down at his hospital?"

"You're not offended?"

"Most certainly I am not."

"If you are, this must be cleared up later on."

"It has been," he answered, dignified. "I believe absolutely what you say, and of that there need be no further question." (p. 267)

If Aziz's heart fails him here as much as his head, if it is a failure in understanding that exposes the friendship to a strain it cannot withstand, it is his lack of candor that both marks its actual collapse and effectively prevents the matter from being "cleared up." Suspicion of Fielding remains in his mind, ramifying eventually into the belief that Fielding has committed the ultimate betrayal of marrying Adela, having first cunningly persuaded him to renounce the compensation money she owes him. That Aziz's suspicion should burgeon so monstrously from a casual piece of gossip, always fixing on Adela and Fielding as sexual partners, can perhaps be seen as an unconscious settling of accounts, an extreme reaction to Adela's unjust suspicion of himself. It would certainly seem to be attributable, at all events, to a hardening of his general distrust of the English as a result of the Marabar experience, a distrust from which not even Fielding is exempt. Nor is Fielding able to counter this distrust. Having withstood the tide of Marabar that flowed into the club, he is finally powerless against its surge in his friend. He is handicapped, too, by his own characteristic reserve and reticence; at the crucial moment he is quite incapable of responding to the gibe about Adela in a way that Aziz could understand. A touch of coarseness, we cannot help feeling, would have weighed more heavily with Aziz than his ponderous indignation. But then the infuriating way in which Aziz (to start with) taxes his naughty friend is a reminder that it is once again a lack of tact and delicacy that is shown to be a disruptive factor.

Though the relationship of Mrs. Moore and Aziz is not subjected to this kind of strain, it too is affected by Marabar. Mrs. Moore's response to the vision of the meaninglessness of existence that she has in the cave is to withdraw into herself and so to deny connection with those round her. Adela, for instance, is sure that her friendship with Mrs. Moore is "so deep and real" that it will "last," whatever happens; but she is disconcerted to find on her return from the McBrydes' bungalow that Mrs. Moore does not get up to greet her and withdraws her hand when she takes it (p. 194). The Mrs. Moore who ventured out alone to the mosque is now incapable, it is clear, of making a move toward anyone. Certainly she remains indifferent to the fate of Aziz, whom she believes to be innocent: "[Adela] has started the machinery," she says; "it will work to its end" (p. 201). This indifference, this negativism, amounts in practical terms to a desertion of Aziz, to a failure to act in some way on the understanding of the heart that tells her he is not guilty. This, it would seem, is her "way of evil":

"I am not good, no, bad." She spoke more calmly and resumed her cards, saying as she turned them up, "A bad old woman, bad, bad, detestable. I used to be good with the children growing up, also I meet this young man in his mosque, I wanted him to be happy. Good, happy, small people. They do not exist, they were a dream . . . But I will not help you to torture him for what he never did. There are different ways of evil and I prefer mine to yours." (p. 200)

The state of psychological withdrawal that Mrs. Moore now consistently manifests generates, in turn, a desire for a physical withdrawal from India. Arrangements are made for her departure, and she has all she wishes: "she [escapes] the trial, the marriage, and the hot weather" (p. 202). But this withdrawal is symptomatic of a desire, ultimately, to withdraw from life itself; and if her death on the voyage home is in part attributable to an overtaxing of her strength—"May is no month to allow an old lady to travel in," says Hamidullah (p. 240)—it would seem to be at least in part the result of her loss of the will to live.

Mrs. Moore also abandons Adela, leaving her to her echo. The echo "[spouts] after her" when she escapes from the cave, and thereafter "[rages] up and down like a nerve in the faculty of her hearing"; she believes that "only Mrs. Moore" can drive it away (p. 190). Adela's echo has both symbolic and psychological dimensions. If it symbolizes her continued failure to make distinctions, to distinguish, that is, between her hallucinatory image of Aziz and his true nature; it is also a manifestation of the unconscious working of her conscience. It disappears when she suddenly maintains that Aziz is innocent (p. 198), but it returns when she decides to go through with the trial. It is Mrs. Moore's name, if not Mrs. Moore, that finally drives the echo away. When her name is mentioned at the trial, it is taken up by the crowd in the street outside the court, being "Indianized" into "Esmiss Esmoor" (p. 219). As the crowd repeats "Esmiss Esmoor," the chant itself constitutes an echo, a human echo that is now set against the echo of the caves. It is under its influence that Adela is led to make her recantation and so win release from *her* echo.

As a result of the expedition to Marabar one new relationship is established: Fielding befriends Adela when she is basely deserted by Ronny (and the English colony) after her recantation. Their friendliness, we are told, is "as of dwarfs shaking hands" (p. 275); and the phrase, like the relationship itself, is a bridge between the preceding action and that which is to follow. The image points to the contrast between this relationship and the relationships that are established in part 1 of the novel; lacking the emotional force of those, this appears, by comparison, a diminished, dwarflike association. The image, furthermore, suggests that we view the establishment of this relationship against the background of the widespread disruptions of part 2—and so judge it of small significance. But in fact it is through his association with Adela that Fielding meets Mrs. Moore's children and marries her daughter,

and it is therefore ultimately through it that his reconciliation with
Aziz in part 3 is brought about. The tiny shaking of hands at the height
of the Hot Weather, in other words, leads us on to the Rains.

4

PART 3 opens with a description of the Krishna festival at the shrine in
the palace at Mau. The reconciliation between Aziz and Fielding takes
place against the background of the Hindu ceremony, the symbolism of
this description (like that of the mosque and the caves) pointing to
what is to come:

The assembly was in a tender, happy state unknown to an English crowd, it
seethed like a beneficent potion. When the villagers broke cordon for a glimpse
of the silver image, a most beautiful and radiant expression came into their
faces, a beauty in which there was nothing personal, for it caused them all to
resemble one another during the moment of its indwelling, and only when it
was withdrawn did they revert to individual clods. And so with the music.
Music there was, but from so many sources that the sum-total was untrammelled. The braying banging crooning melted into a single mass which trailed
round the palace before joining the thunder. Rain fell at intervals throughout
the night.
  It was the turn of Professor Godbole's choir. . . .

> "Tukaram, Tukaram,
> Thou art my father and mother and everybody.
> Tukaram, Tukaram,
> Thou art my father and mother and everybody.
> Tukaram, Tukaram. . ."

They sang not even to the God who confronted them, but to a saint; they did
not one thing which the non-Hindu would feel dramatically correct; this approaching triumph of India was a muddle (as we call it), a frustration of reason
and form. . . . Hundreds of electric lights had been lit in [the God's] honour
(worked by an engine whose thumps destroyed the rhythm of the hymn). Yet
His face could not be seen. . . . The inscriptions which the poets of the State
had composed were hung where they could not be read, or had twitched their
drawing-pins out of the stucco, and one of them (composed in English to indicate His universality) consisted, by an unfortunate slip of the draughtsman, of
the words, "God si Love."
  God si Love. Is this the final message of India? . . . Godbole consulted the
music-book, said a word to the drummer, who broke rhythm, made a thick
little blur of sound, and produced a new rhythm. This was more exciting, the
inner images it evoked more definite, and the singers' expressions became fatu-
ous and languid. They loved all men, the whole universe, and scraps of their
past, tiny splinters of detail, emerged for a moment to melt into the universal
warmth. Thus Godbole, though she was not important to him, remembered an

old woman he had met in Chandrapore days. Chance brought her into his mind while it was in this heated state, he did not select her, she happened to occur among the throng of soliciting images, a tiny splinter, and he impelled her by this spiritual force to that place where completeness can be found. Completeness, not reconstruction. His senses grew thinner, he remembered a wasp seen he forgot where, perhaps on a stone. He loved the wasp equally, he impelled it likewise, he was imitating God. (pp. 279–82)

The kind of force the temple represents is suggested by the effect on the villagers of their glimpse of the silver image. As they press toward the image, they are united in their adoration of it, but they lose their individuality: they cease to be "personal," they "resemble one another." The temple as a symbol of unity, that is to say, is sharply distinguished from the mosque, for it represents an attainment of unity not through a reconciliation of opposites that preserves separate identity but through a submergence of individual differences. The words of the song to Tukaram formally express this: the song seems to celebrate the elimination of individual differences in the greater identity of the saint; "everybody" is united, for all alike have ceased to be merely themselves and have become the saint. Finally, the music translates into sound what is imaged in the faces of the villagers and sung by the choir: the many separate sounds, "the braying banging crooning," lose their distinctive (discordant) quality and "melt" into a "single mass" in "untrammelled" harmony. The motif of merging, melting, submerging, which is insistent here, recurs (as we shall see) in the climactic scene of this section of the novel.

The temple clearly also represents the force of love. If opposites may be reconciled through the secret understanding of the heart, then (it is now suggested) individual differences may be submerged in an all-encompassing love, the love of "all men," of "the whole universe"; they may, indeed, "melt" into a "universal warmth." Godbole's love of Mrs. Moore is an instance of this kind of love; remote and impersonal, utterly different from Aziz's feeling for her, it is simply the expression of a universal benevolence that encompasses the wasp "equally" with her. If the love that is associated with the temple thus denies the making of distinctions, it is not, however, by way of negation (the way of the caves); the "hundreds of electric lights" blaze in implicit affirmation against the darkness of the caves. The muddle of "God si Love" might not be the final message of India, but it does well enough as the message of the temple. The "si" mutely asserts a connection between God and Love in much the same way that the temple asserts unity through love—through a love that transcends reason, that includes the wasp equally.

The meeting (after some two years) of Aziz and Fielding is cold, and Aziz keeps it impersonal. Even when he discovers that Fielding is in fact married to Mrs. Moore's daughter Stella—and not to Adela as he had supposed—he bursts out with: "What does it matter to me who you marry? Don't trouble me here at Mau is all I ask. I do not want you, I do not want one of you in my private life, with my dying breath I say it" (p. 298). Nevertheless, he personally takes to the Guest House the embrocation that he has promised to send over for Ralph's bee-stings, and his encounter with Mrs. Moore's son becomes the prelude to his reconciliation with Fielding. When he examines Ralph, he is startled to hear him say, "Your hands are unkind"; and to realize that "the extraordinary youth [is] right":

"You should not treat us like this," [Ralph] challenged, and this time Aziz was checked, for the voice, though frightened, was not weak.

"Like what?"

"Dr. Aziz, we have done you no harm."

"Aha, you know my name, I see. Yes, I am Aziz. No, of course your great friend Miss Quested did me no harm at the Marabar."

Drowning his last words, all the guns of the State went off. A rocket from the Jail garden gave the signal. The prisoner had been released, and was kissing the feet of the singers. Rose-leaves fall from the houses, sacred spices and coconut are brought forth . . . It was the half-way moment, the God had extended His temple, and paused exultantly. Mixed and confused in their passage, the rumours of salvation entered the Guest House. They were startled, and moved on to the porch, drawn by the sudden illumination. . . . The song became audible through much repetition; the choir was repeating and inverting the names of deities.

> "Radhakrishna Radhakrishna,
> Radhakrishna Radhakrishna,
> Krishnaradha Radhakrishna,
> Radhakrishna Radhakrishna,"

they sang, and woke the sleeping sentry in the Guest House; he leant upon his iron-tipped spear.

"I must go back now, good night," said Aziz, and held out his hand, completely forgetting that they were not friends, and focusing his heart on something more distant than the caves, something beautiful. His hand was taken, and then he remembered how detestable he had been, and said gently, "Don't you think me unkind any more?"

"No."

"How can you tell, you strange fellow?"

"Not difficult, the one thing I always know."

"Can you always tell whether a stranger is your friend?"

"Yes."

"Then you are an Oriental." He unclasped as he spoke, with a little shudder. Those words—he had said them to Mrs. Moore in the mosque in the beginning of the cycle, from which, after so much suffering, he had got free. Never be friends with the English! Mosque, caves, mosque, caves. And here he was starting again. He handed the magic ointment to him. "Take this, think of me when you use it. I shall never want it back. I must give you one little present, and it is all I have got; you are Mrs. Moore's son." (pp. 304–6)

If the transformation depicted in this scene cannot be attributed to the "magic" properties of Aziz's ointment, it is clearly connected with the ghostly presence of Mrs. Moore. Everything combines to evoke her. It is above all "the extraordinary youth," of course, that recalls her, the youth that has apparently inherited his mother's capacity for intuitive understanding, for the secret understanding of the heart. But it is also the Hindu song, the chanting of "Radhakrishna Radhakrishna," that recalls the chanting of Mrs. Moore's name ("Esmiss Esmoor") outside the courtroom; and indeed the "rumours of salvation" that sound here later become identified in Aziz's mind with the "syllables of salvation" that "sounded during his trial at Chandrapore" (p. 308). This evocation of Mrs. Moore suggests that she, as well as Godbole, presides over the coming reconciliation; suggests, that is to say, that the syllables of salvation associated with her and with the feeling engendered in the mosque merge and combine with the rumors of salvation associated with the temple to "save" Aziz from the spirit of the caves. They combine to produce a typically Forsterian view of "salvation," a saving from the denial of connection.

This is what is dramatized in the scene between Aziz and Ralph. It is the noise of the guns, which marks the freeing of the prisoner in honor of the Hindu God, that "drowns" Aziz's mention of the Marabar: the echo of the caves, we might say, is here submerged in the noise of the temple. But it is not the Hindu prisoner alone that is set free. If his release is testimony to the spirit of love and forgiveness that is at work, it also points to the possibility of a release from hatred in the case of Aziz. For Aziz too this is "the half-way moment." Then, with the chant sounding in his ears and "focusing his heart on something more distant than the caves, something beautiful," responding (it would seem) to the memory of Mrs. Moore—he holds out his hand. With Marabar drowned, something else that has been submerged can now rise to the surface: Mrs. Moore, Aziz reflects, "had not borne witness in his favour, nor visited him in the prison, yet she had stolen to the depths of his heart, and he always adored her" (p. 307).

Wishing to undertake some "act of homage to Mrs. Moore's son" (p. 307), Aziz invites Ralph to go out on the water with him. Fielding and his wife are out in another boat, and the Krishna festival is reaching its climax:

> [Aziz] tried to keep the boat out of the glare of the torches that began to star the other shore. . . . Suddenly, closer than he had calculated, the palanquin of Krishna appeared from behind a ruined wall, and descended the carven glistening watersteps. . . .
>
> The village of Gokul reappeared upon its tray. It was the substitute for the silver image, which never left its haze of flowers; on behalf of another symbol, it was to perish. A servitor took it in his hands, and tore off the blue and white streamers. He was naked, broad-shouldered, thin-waisted—the Indian body again triumphant—and it was his hereditary office to close the gates of salvation. He entered the dark waters, pushing the village before him, until the clay dolls slipped off their chairs and began to gutter in the rain, the King Kansa was confounded with the father and mother of the Lord. Dark and solid, the little waves sipped, then a great wave washed and then English voices cried: "Take care!"
>
> The boats had collided with each other.
>
> The four outsiders flung out their arms and grappled, and, with oars and poles sticking out, revolved like a mythical monster in the whirlwind. The worshippers howled with wrath or joy, as they drifted forward helplessly against the servitor, who awaited them, his beautiful dark face expressionless, and as the last morsels melted on his tray, it struck them.
>
> The shock was minute, but Stella, nearest to it, shrank into her husband's arms, then reached forward, then flung herself against Aziz, and her motions capsized them. They plunged into the warm, shallow water, and rose struggling into a tornado of noise. The oars, the sacred tray, the letters of Ronny and Adela, broke loose and floated confusedly. Artillery was fired, drums beaten, the elephants trumpeted and drowning all an immense peal of thunder, unaccompanied by lightning, cracked like a mallet on the dome. (pp. 309–10)

The confounding of the clay dolls at the height of the religious ceremony points the significance of the collision that follows. Gokul, we have earlier been told, is the equivalent of Bethlehem in the "nebulous" Hindu story of the birth of the God, and King Kansa, the enemy of the father and mother of the Lord, is Herod (pp. 282–83). Enmity, we realize, is thus symbolically dissipated as the clay figures melt in the rain and merge together. Similarly, the four outsiders are "confounded" as the result of the collision of the boats, and as they revolve, they and the boats seem to merge into a single "mythical monster." It is Stella's "motions" that thereafter capsize them, but she moves in response to the impact of the tray, "minute" though this is; she reacts to the Hindu mystery, and if she (the daughter of Mrs. Moore) is directly instrumental in bringing Fielding and Aziz together, it is suggested that they are brought together in the first instance by their contact—no matter how indirect—with the unifying force represented by the temple and its ritual. The outsiders' plunge into the water is the dramatic climax of the scene and the crux of the symbolism. The ducking represents both a submergence of differences and an immersion in the waters of renewal, for the water is associated with the rebirth of the Hindu God. Certainly it at once gives new life to the friendship of Fielding and Aziz: "After the funny shipwreck there had been no more nonsense or bitterness, and they went back laughingly to their old relationship as if nothing had happened" (p. 312).

The reestablishment of their relationship is thus brought about not by an act of understanding, whether of the heart or the head, but by the sense of an identity that is deeper than their differences—just as Godbole loves Mrs. Moore and the wasp equally. Alike outsiders to the crowd of Hindu worshippers, Fielding and Aziz find themselves in the same boat, as it were; and they are united by the good will of laughter that their common predicament releases in them. Their laughter is the spontaneous laughter of old friends, and it is this that reestablishes "their old relationship." It diffuses too a general good will (a "universal love" in face of the human predicament) on Aziz's part. He has an impulse to "wipe out the wretched business of the Marabar for ever," to submerge all differences, we might say, and he decides to make it up with Adela. "As I fell into our largest Mau tank under circumstances our other friends will relate," he writes to her, "I thought how brave Miss Quested was, and decided to tell her so, despite my imperfect English. Through you I am happy here with my children instead of in a prison, of that I make no doubt. My children shall be taught to speak of you with the greatest affection and respect" (p. 313).

"Friends again, yet aware that they [can] meet no more," Fielding and Aziz go for a "last ride" together in the Mau jungles (p. 312); and their horses and the earth conspire to confirm their coming separation: the horses "[swerve] apart," and the earth sends up rocks "through which riders must pass single file." Forster implies that it is politics more than anything else that is the divisive force at this point: the two will be able to be friends, it seems, only when "every blasted Englishman" (as Aziz puts it) has been driven into the sea (p. 317). But we cannot help feeling that there is something more than politics at issue, for we are not convinced that a relationship that is founded on a submergence of individuality can be proof against the assertion of difference. It has been strongly indicated, moreover, that the relationship is fundamentally vulnerable, for caves do appear to follow mosques in the human cycle. In making the final separation of Fielding and Aziz primarily a mark of political differences rather than of the human condition, it seems as if Forster shirks the conclusions of his own art; and this evasion is perhaps not unrelated to his long silence after *A Passage to India*.[6]

PART TWO

UNITY IN DISUNITY:
STRUCTURES OF SELF-DIVISION

D. H. LAWRENCE AND GEORGE ELIOT: THE GENESIS OF *THE WHITE PEACOCK*

One of the features of Lawrence's achievement as a novelist is the uncanny inwardness of his presentation of women and, particularly, of their sexuality—as in the notable instances of Ursula Brangwen (especially in *The Rainbow*) and Lady Chatterley. We may perhaps best place Lawrence in the tradition of the English novel in this respect if we compare his heroines with those of Jane Austen some hundred years earlier. Sex is a decided factor in Jane Austen—it is, indeed, *the* explosive and disruptive force in the otherwise stable world she depicts, breaking out calamitously in characters such as Lydia Bennet in *Pride and Prejudice* or Maria Bertram (Mrs. Rushworth) in *Mansfield Park*—but it is not for heroines. Or not so that we can notice it, for though a Fanny Price or an Emma Woodhouse may be presumed to have sexual needs and desires, the novelist does not allow these to rise to consciousness or overtly to influence behavior. This tacit differentiation of women into sheep and goats was subsequently extended and sharpened in the work of two other major novelists. Dickens stamped two opposed images of woman on the Victorian consciousness in his presentation, at the outset of his career, of the two contrasted young women of *Oliver Twist*, Rose Maylie, the heroine, and Nancy, the prostitute. In his portrayal of Rose, Dickens contrives both to evoke a burgeoning womanhood and to spiritualize it out of existence, epitomizing in her, nearly twenty years before Coventry Patmore put a name to it, an Angel in the House. Home, in Dickens, is no place for lust. That is for the likes of Nancy, a Fallen Woman of the Streets, who exists unmitigatedly in the flesh. And Thackeray was working in the same tradition that produced a Rose and a Nancy, though with a greater subtlety and complexity of characterization, in his representation in *Vanity Fair* of the seemingly angelic, sexless Amelia Sedley, as opposed to the demonic, sexy Becky Sharp.

When Lawrence speaks of literary images of woman, his account is broader—and racier—but he makes essentially the same kind of distinction:

> The real trouble about women is that they must always go on trying to adapt themselves to men's theories of women, as they always have done. When a woman is thoroughly herself, she is being what her type of man wants her to be. . . .
> . . . Dickens invented the child-wife, so child-wives have swarmed ever since. He also fished out his version of the chaste Beatrice, a chaste but marriageable Agnes. George Eliot imitated this pattern, and it became confirmed. . . .
> There is, also, the eternal secret ideal of men—the prostitute. Lots of women live up to this idea: just because men want them to. . . .
> Now the real tragedy is not that women ask and must ask for a pattern of womanhood. The tragedy is not, even, that men give them such abominable patterns, child-wives, little-boy-baby-face girls, perfect secretaries, noble spouses, self-sacrificing mothers, pure women who bring forth children in virgin coldness, prostitutes who just make themselves low, to please the men; all the atrocious patterns of womanhood that men have supplied to woman; patterns all perverted from any real natural fulness of a human being. . . . [T]he one thing [man] won't accept her as is a human being, a real human being of the feminine sex.[1]

Lawrence rightly maintains that the centrally opposed images of woman as Angel or Whore (and their derivatives) are a product, whether directly or indirectly, of the male imagination. And he correctly insists that what the varying images have in common is that they leave the woman out, a woman who has the "real natural fulness of a human being." But he does George Eliot an injustice. It was she, if anyone, who made a concerted effort to reassemble the polarized images and put woman together again. Following the lead given her by Emily Brontë in *Wuthering Heights* and Charlotte Brontë in *Jane Eyre*, it was she, tentatively in her portrayal of Hetty Sorrel in *Adam Bede*, and then magisterially in that of Maggie Tulliver in *The Mill on the Floss* and Dorothea Brooke in *Middlemarch*, who created lasting embodiments of "a real human being of the feminine sex." It would seem to be more than a coincidence of literary history that the challenge to the Dickensian conception of woman came most strongly from women novelists—though in making it they in turn proceeded to polarize the men to whom their heroines are attracted; and though Hardy's subsequent rendering of Tess Durbeyfield is as memorably full a portrayal as any they essayed. But the split remained, even though it was now internalized within unitary images of the heroine, and it is not until Lawrence's Ursula Brangwen that we are given a depiction of an achieved wholeness of being.

Lawrence should thus be regarded as having been engaged, among other things, in the same enterprise as George Eliot, and the quoted reference to her should accordingly be viewed as an instance of the kind of "misreading" of a precursor that Harold Bloom discusses in *The Anxiety of Influence*, a misreading that is liberating. For I believe that George Eliot was the major initial influence on Lawrence, and that he indeed found himself through her. The signs of her influence are stamped everywhere on his first novel, where we might expect to see them most innocently displayed—to a degree that *The White Peacock* may rewardingly be read as Lawrence's rewriting of *The Mill on the Floss*.

2

The White Peacock, Raney Stanford has remarked, is "generally regarded as the most Hardyesque of any of Lawrence's work, and generally dismissed as derivative therefore. This influence, most of Lawrence's critics agree, is in the description of and in some vague feeling for nature and rural setting that both writers share."[2] A similar view has been reiterated more recently by John Alcorn: "*The White Peacock*, then, reflects the spirit of Hardy on every level of theme and technique. Above all, Lawrence has invested his landscape with those elements of teeming fertility, wild abandon, and secret wisdom which were the hallmarks of Hardy's nature description."[3] It is true that it is Hardy-like descriptions of nature which most immediately compel attention in Lawrence's first novel—the descriptions are as sharply meticulous and passionately evocative as any comparable passages in Lawrence's later work—but Alcorn's relating of the novel to *Jude the Obscure* (the theme of entrapment in marriage as figured in George Saxton; the supposed modeling of Lettie Beardsall on Sue Bridehead) does not seem to me to illuminate its central concerns. Its provenance should be sought rather in the work of George Eliot. This is not of course to deny the influence of Hardy, but I should say it is more significant at a later stage of Lawrence's career and is indeed directly reflected then in his "Study of Thomas Hardy" (1914).

The opening pages of *The White Peacock* at once reveal small but suggestive links with *The Mill on the Floss*. Where George Eliot's main setting is Dorlcote Mill, Lawrence's is Strelley Mill; and his setting is the more notable in that it is a composite location, merging the real-life Haggs Farm (home of the Chambers family, the prototypes of the Saxtons in the novel) and the nearby Felley Mill Farm. Jessie Chambers has described how from the stackyard of the Haggs "the land dipped to the valley where we could see in the hollow the red roofs of Felley Mill";[4] but in the novel it is the Saxton farm that becomes "the Mill"—as if it were a mill that had a hold on Lawrence's imagination. Where the narrator of *The Mill on the Floss* begins her narrative by musing on the past, "dreaming" that she is "standing on the bridge in front of Dorlcote Mill, as it looked one February afternoon many years ago";[5] Cyril Beardsall, the narrator of *The White Peacock* (who proves to be a semiabsentee narrator, possessed of a striking talent for describing events at which he is not present), begins his narrative by telling his friend George he has been thinking how "the place" he has just described "[seems] old, brooding over its past."[6] And both narrators, the one in her reverie and the other in fact, start by staring into the mill-ponds, she "in love with moistness" and experiencing "a dreamy deafness, which seems to heighten the peacefulness of the scene" (*MF*, 8), he taken by how "intensely still" everything is, for "the whole place [is] gathered in the musing of old age" (*WP*, 13). For good measure, *The Mill on the Floss* even has its own peacock, a less portentous creature, no doubt, than that imaged by Lawrence, but there nonetheless (*MF*, 78, 84, 271).

In addition, there is external testimony that George Eliot and *The Mill on the Floss* were in Lawrence's mind when he began writing his first novel. Jessie Chambers has told us that "Lawrence adored *The Mill on the Floss*"; that "Maggie Tulliver was his favourite heroine. He used to say that the smooth branches of the beech trees (which he especially admired) reminded him of Maggie Tulliver's arms"; and that he consciously modeled *The White Peacock* on George Eliot's work:

Lawrence now began to talk definitely of writing. He said he thought he should try a novel, and wanted me to try to write one too, so that we could compare notes.

"The usual plan is to take two couples and develop their relationships," he said. "Most of George Eliot's are on that plan. Anyhow, I don't want a plot, I should be bored with it. I shall try two couples for a start."[7]

Emily Saxton and Cyril Beardsall are presumably one of the couples Lawrence intended writing about, but in the event their relationship is not "developed," as prescribed. In the published novel it is no more than vaguely adumbrated—these characters were to await their more vital reincarnation as Miriam Leivers and Paul Morel in *Sons and Lovers*—and the action is set in motion by the dynamics of a triangle, not of coupling, since Lettie Beardsall is attracted to George Saxton when she is already involved with Leslie Tempest. But Lawrence's actual structural pattern does in fact follow that of George Eliot in *The Mill on the Floss;* for once the long and loving delineation of the childhood of Maggie and her brother Tom is completed and the book moves belatedly to its main concern in the depiction of Maggie's adult relationships,[8] Stephen Guest and Lucy Deane prove to be no more substantial a "couple" than Cyril and Emily, and the motivating principle of the action is Maggie's triangular relationships with Stephen and Philip Wakem. It is notable that Lawrence also incorporates a relationship between a sister and brother to mediate between the relationships of the various couples and lovers, as does George Eliot, though the depiction of Lettie's relations with Cyril is nowhere near as vivid or as important as that of Maggie's with Tom.

What seems to have caught Lawrence's imagination, however, and what was to prove to be so decisive a factor in his own development as a novelist, was the underlying significance of the love-triangle in *The Mill on the Floss.* Philip and Stephen, the two men to whom Maggie is attracted, are not only presented as thoroughgoing opposites but (as remains to be discussed) embody opposed tendencies within Maggie herself. In her relationship with each of her lovers, she negates or suppresses one part of herself, which is activated in relation to the other man. The opposition within the self of the heroine is thus concretized in the opposition between the two lovers, just as her self-division is externalized in her attraction to both men—and in her ultimate incapacity to choose between them. What her story dramatizes, therefore, is her inability to reconcile the opposed forces within herself. And Lawrence follows the same pattern in his love-triangle in *The White Peacock.* Leslie and George are as strongly opposed as Philip and Stephen; and, I shall argue, figure an opposition which is embodied in Lettie, and which is also strikingly similar in nature to that presented in the earlier novel. Lettie is as much torn between Leslie and George as Maggie between her lovers. Though she, unlike Maggie, does finally choose one man, for ten years she is unable to give the other up, and her story is similarly one of self-division.[9]

Lawrence would seem to have been impelled to follow the pattern laid down by George Eliot in *The Mill on the Floss* for three main reasons. First, it exemplified a simple but effective method of organizing a novel. The love-triangle enabled him both to dramatize his heroine's self-division and to project the sort of opposition he was concerned with in his presentation of her lovers—and at the same time to contain the narrative within a unifying configuration. Second, it offered a tangible means of realizing the aim he wished to set for himself as a novelist, even though he once again "misread" George Eliot in formulating this aim—as Jessie Chambers's report of one of their conversations indicates:

> A fragment of conversation about writing and writers comes back to me. We were in the wood . . .
> "You see, it was really George Eliot who started it all," Lawrence was saying in the deliberate way he had of speaking when he was trying to work something out in his own mind. "And how wild they all were with her for doing it. It was she who started putting all the action inside. Before, you know, with Fielding and the others, it had been outside. Now I wonder which is right?"
> I always found myself most interested in what people thought and experienced within themselves, so I ventured the opinion that George Eliot had been right.
> "I wonder if she was," Lawrence replied thoughtfully. "You know I can't help thinking there ought to be a bit of both."[10]

The love-triangle in *The Mill on the Floss* clearly offers a model of how to put "a bit of both" in a novel, how to incorporate both the "inside" and the "outside," for it figures the externalization of inner conflict. It was a model that Lawrence made his own in the first stage of his career, adopting it not only in *The White Peacock* but more memorably in *Sons and Lovers*. In *Sons and Lovers* the protagonist is a man—it is perhaps a further indication of the hold Lawrence's "favourite heroine" had on him that in his first novel the character with whom he is most significantly identified should have been a woman—but Paul Morel's relations with Miriam Leivers and Clara Dawes follow the same pattern and have the same kind of import. It is notable, however, that whereas George Eliot throughout her career continued to combine inner and outer views, nowhere more strikingly perhaps than in *Middlemarch*, in the end it was Lawrence himself who, in *The Rainbow*, made one of the most sustained efforts in the English novel to put all the action inside. He called the method he employed in *The Rainbow* "exhaustive," and must have felt he had fully exploited its possibilities in this work, for in *Women in Love* and subsequent novels he returned to a more even balance between inner and outer worlds.

Third, we may assume Lawrence was especially struck by the love-triangle in *The Mill on the Floss* because it spoke to his own deepest experience as a young man. The broad opposition it projects is one that he grew up with, for it is not dissimilar to that represented by the dire clash between his parents, which he was later to chronicle in the description of the marriage of Mr. and Mrs. Morel in *Sons and Lovers*. And the self-division of the heroine of George Eliot's novel made vivid a condition that he himself was heir to, a condition that he first attempted to objectify and grapple with in his portrayal of Lettie. It proved to be an attempt that left him with an abiding sense of individual duality as an ontological principle and so as a rule of characterization, and it became his life's work to seek for a means of reconciling opposed forces within the self, however they were variously defined. It also left him not only with a heroine but a world divided in two, for in time he was roundly to declare that "everything that exists, even a stone, has two sides to its nature."[11]

3

IN HER CHILDHOOD Maggie Tulliver enjoys a notable wholeness of being though the opposed elements within her are sharply depicted. On the one hand, she is constantly pictured as a young animal, being compared to a Shetland pony and a Skye terrier and so on; on the other, she is shown to have a challengingly keen mind, and is so quick-witted that her father fears she is "too 'cute for a woman" (*MF*, 12). Animal-like vitality and intellectuality, however, coexist in her quite comfortably, neither in any way frustrating the free expression of the other. It is as an adult and in her relations with men that she falls into self-division. Lettie Beardsall is an adult when we meet her, and from the outset her self-division is apparent in her responses to the two men she is interested in. The opposing forces in Lettie are remarkably similar to those in Maggie, though the opposition in her case is perhaps best described, if we follow Lawrencean terminology, as one between mental consciousness and blood-consciousness. Lettie, like Maggie, is a woman with a mind. Though she is proud of her physical appearance, even a little vain, she seems to place the highest value on her mind (*WP*, 40); and as a mature hostess she is said to "overflow" with "clever speeches and rapid, brilliant observations" (*WP*, 322). At the same time, she abundantly possesses "blood-being," has a natural capacity, that is, for untrammeled existence in the flesh, and it is this (as well as "the subtle sympathies of her artist's soul") that is revealed in "her poise and harmonious movement" (*WP*, 117). It is also apparent in the way she is at one with nature, "[glinting] on like a flower" when she moves "brightly through the green hazels" (*WP*, 21).

When Maggie is drawn to Philip Wakem, it is clear that his appeal is to her intellect. He is in many ways a kindred spirit, is himself a Maggie, as it were, with all animality thoroughly tamed, if not quite left out. During the year that they meet secretly he gives her much-needed intellectual companionship and stimulation, but he himself unwittingly indicates what the inevitable result for her of a prolonged association with him would be when he laments the "benumbing and cramping" of her nature which, he says, is the consequence of her self-imposed "rule of renunciation" (*MF*, 284, 287). For Philip's humpback, his physical deficiency, ensures that "the thought of his being her lover never [enters] her mind" (*MF*, 289). When he finally confesses he loves her, she tacitly allows him to believe she is ready to return his love; and it is at this point that she begins the willed negation of one half of her being which thereafter characterizes her relationship with him.

Maggie registers that a love relationship with Philip will demand a "sacrifice" of her, but it is one that she initially believes she will be glad to make. It goes against the grain, however, as becomes evident when her brother Tom compels her to agree not to see Philip again. She becomes conscious then of "a certain dim background of relief in the forced separation"; and the narrator's suggestion that this is "surely . . . only because the sense of a deliverance from concealment [is] welcome at any cost" (*MF*, 305) as surely emphasizes the hidden nature of her relief. Some two years later, when Lucy Deane undertakes to arrange for her to marry Philip, Maggie is startled into an involuntary betrayal of her physical shrinking from him: she "[tries] to smile, but [shivers], as if she [feels] a sudden chill" (*MF*, 338). She persists, however, in declaring her wish to marry him, and maintains that this "would be the best and highest lot" for her (*MF*, 384), seeming to admit to herself that it is a lower, inferior self that has impelled her towards Stephen Guest.

With one part of him Lawrence would seem to affirm such a view: "The little cripple in *Mill on the Floss* was strong—but a woman despised his frailty. Pah—I hate women's heroes. At the bottom women love the brute in man best, like a great shire stallion makes one's heart beat."[12] It is notable, therefore, that Leslie Tempest, who is the equivalent figure to Philip in the love-triangle of *The White Peacock*, is given a firm physicality. He has a "fine, lithe physique, suggestive of much animal vigour"; his "person" is "exceedingly attractive"; and one is said to feel pleasure when one watches him "move about" (*WP*, 59–60). But his relationship with Lettie is nonetheless founded on the word. Banter is a feature of their relations; and when they make love, they characteristically make words, he even asking her on one occasion what she is "making so many words about" (*WP*, 105). Leslie says he thinks "there's more in the warm touch of a soft body than in a prayer" and declares he will "pray with kisses," but what more immediately seems to attract him to Lettie is her cleverness: "you are clever, you are rare," he announces with delight when she embroiders one of his allusions (*WP*, 103–4). If he is able to titillate her mind, however, he is unable in the irrational and mysterious ways of blood-being to warm her blood, and he is forced to recognize that to him she is "a cold little lover" (*WP*, 101). It is not Leslie but the flattering self-image he can command for her through his social position that kindles Lettie.

Lettie becomes engaged to Leslie, and during the period of the engagement they sleep together. When they meet the next day, she is "angry" with him and makes "a swift gesture of repulsion"; but it is her own hands that she says "disclaim" her and that she "can't bear the sight of," and her own hand that she "hides . . . swiftly against her skirt" when she catches sight of it (*WP*, 204–5). Lettie, that is, is filled with self-disgust, and we are to infer that, after all her hesitations in regard to Leslie, what she has now discovered—what her "blood" has now made incontrovertibly clear to her—is that she does not love him and cannot respond physically to him. Yet she is now doubly his. She does subsequently make an effort to break with him, telling him that they cannot be "flesh of one flesh," but by then he is recovering from serious injury as a result of a motor accident, and when he responds by betraying an utter dependence on her, his unmanning distress is too much for her. She puts her arms round him and finally commits herself to him. But what the price of her support of him—of such an abrogation of the blood—is likely to be is intimated by the end of the scene: "Oh—do you want to go away from me again?" Leslie suddenly asks; and she replies, "No—only my arm is dead," and she draws it "from beneath him, standing up, swinging it, smiling because it [hurts] her" (*WP*, 227–28). It is almost as if Lettie enacts the "benumbing and cramping" that is implicit in Maggie's relationship with Philip. And though Jessie Chambers reports that Lawrence declared George Eliot had "gone and spoilt [*The Mill on the Floss*] half way through" because he "could not forgive the marriage of the vital Maggie Tulliver to the cripple Philip," saying, "It was wrong, wrong. She should never have made her do it";[13] he makes his heroine do what Maggie of course did not do, for Lettie marries Leslie, whereas Maggie is drawn away from Philip to Stephen.

In contrast to Philip, Stephen (like Maggie) abundantly possesses bodily potency and a rich physical vitality. It is to his physical force—and attractiveness—that Maggie responds, as he to hers, each becoming "oppressively conscious of the other's presence, even to the finger-ends." It seems almost as if George Eliot is evoking a Lawrencean blood-consciousness here—and then again: "Maggie only felt that life was revealing something quite new to her; and she was absorbed in the direct, immediate experience, without any energy left for taking account of it and reasoning about it." She is also said to have "no distinct thought—only the sense of a presence like that of a closely-hovering broad-winged bird in the darkness" (*MF*, 352, 355). Yet when Stephen passionately declares his love for her, Maggie rejects him.

At one point during the exchange between Stephen and Maggie at her aunt Moss's, she is said to look at him "like a lovely wild animal timid and struggling under caresses" (*MF*, 393). The simile vividly suggests his power to call to life in her what she has repressed for so long; but their relationship and attraction to each other are entirely on a physical level. When she, therefore, insists that she remains tied to Philip while admitting she loves Stephen, it would seem this is not only a matter of principle: Maggie, we realize, needs and wants both men, wants Philip too for what Stephen cannot give her. Wanting both, she is finally unable to choose one. Pulled in two directions at once, she is incapable of resolving her conflict. The incapacity declares itself in the way she renounces Stephen in the same breath that she confesses she loves him (*MF*, 394).

What it means to Maggie to give Stephen up is powerfully suggested by her response to the letter (written some two months after she has left him at Mudport) in which he begs to be allowed to come to her:

When Maggie first read this letter she felt as if her real temptation had only just begun. At the entrance of the chill dark cavern, we turn with unworn courage from the warm light; but how, when we have trodden far in the damp darkness, and have begun to be faint and weary—how, if there is a sudden opening above us, and we are invited back again to the life-nourishing day? The leap of natural longing from under the pressure of pain is so strong, that all less immediate motives are likely to be forgotten—till the pain has been escaped from. (*MF*, 449–50)

The dark cavern evokes a tomb; and indeed Maggie has condemned herself to a kind of living death in choosing to be without either Philip or Stephen. Immediately prior to this she seems almost to have lost the will to carry on: "she must begin a new life, in which she would have to rouse herself to receive new impressions—and she was so unspeakably, sickeningly weary!" (*MF*, 449). The "sudden opening" above her that Stephen's letter makes in the cavern thus offers her a chance to rise from the tomb. The "leap of natural longing" to escape from pain which possesses her is also the leap of the lovely wild animal which Stephen again stirs into being and would make its own bid for life.

But, in a culminating instance of Maggie's self-division, the animal is negated by mind: "her mind [recoils]," we are told, and swings her back to her old position (*MF*, 450). Her decision to stand by her renunciation of Stephen may be viewed as a climactic exercise of restraint on her part, the sort of restraint that signifies a truly civilized response to life and an achieved maturity. That would seem to be the view the novelist expects us to take. But what we are also shown is that the decision places Maggie firmly back in the cavern. Facing a life without both Stephen and Philip, she may determine to cleave once again to Thomas à Kempis and bear her cross "till death," but she is in fact reduced to the kind of despair that knows and wants only death, to a despair that can issue only in what Philip once called a "long suicide." It is precisely at this point that the flood begins, but its advent, though carefully prepared for, comes across as sentimentally contrived. In the flood scenes Maggie is granted an access of strength, and with a re- newed wholeness of being evocative of her childhood, she rescues Tom and is reunited with him before they drown together—but not even this ending can offset the impression of her irreparable self-division, of the "cry of self-despair" with which she opts for the cavern and which leaves her wanting only to "[bury] her sorrow-stricken face" as her soul goes out to "the Unseen Pity" that will be with her "to the end" (*MF*, 451).

LETTIE is as powerfully drawn to George as Maggie to Stephen. In both cases it is the woman who stirs the man to life. Before Maggie appears on the scene, Stephen is presented as a lethargic fop, whose "diamond ring, attar of roses, and air of nonchalant leisure, at twelve o'clock in the day, are the graceful and odoriferous result of the largest oil-mill and the most extensive wharf in St. Ogg's" (*MF*, 316). Cyril, at the start of his narrative, tells George that his "life is nothing else but a doss," and declares he will "laugh when somebody jerks [him] awake" (*WP*, 13). The awakening follows speedily: when Lettie visits the Mill and plays "a love song" for him at the piano—it is notable that the rela- tionship of Maggie and Stephen likewise develops in scenes at the piano at Lucy's home—George is roused to look at her "with glowing brown eyes, as if in hesitating challenge," and she answers with "a blue blaze of her eyes" (*WP*, 27). If she is compelled by his physical presence, however, she is also made fearful by it, for it "[scatters] her words like startled birds" (*WP*, 26), seeming for a time to annul mental con- sciousness. On another occasion, when he looks at her with "wide and vivid" eyes, she first shrinks back, "as if flame [has] leaped towards her face," but then returns his gaze and they both "tremble with a fierce sensation that [fills] their veins with fluid, fiery electricity"; both then feel "the blood beating madly in their necks" (*WP*, 43–44). Lettie's rela- tionship with George, in contradistinction to that with Leslie which is based on the word, is anchored in the blood, but she is not willing to submit to its mad beat. In the end she seems to opt for the mind as a modus operandi: "she, who had always been so rippling in thoughtless life, sat down in the window-sill to think" (*WP*, 92). The result is that she chooses Leslie as a clearly better match.

But she still remains drawn to George, and even intimates her doubts about the choice she has made. "No, I won't come down [to tea]," she says to George, "—let me say farewell—*jamque Vale!* Do you remember how Eurydice sank back into Hell?" (*WP*, 146). On the same occasion—it is shortly before her marriage to Leslie—she suggests to George that they walk together into the wood. She repeatedly seeks physical contact with him, ruffling his hair, leaving her hand lying on his knee, leaning softly against him; roused, George passionately declares his love:

"No, Lettie," he pleaded, with terror and humility. "No, Lettie; don't go. What should I do with my life? Nobody would love you like I do—and what should I do with my love for you?—hate it and fear it, because it's too much for me?"
She turned and kissed him gratefully. He then took her in a long, passionate embrace, mouth to mouth. In the end it had so wearied her that she could only wait in his arms till he was too tired to hold her. He was trembling already.
"Poor Meg!" she murmured to herself dully, her sensations having become vague.
He winced, and the pressure of his arms slackened. She loosened his hands, and rose half dazed from her seat by him. She left him, while he sat dejected, raising no protest. (*WP*, 248–49)

This is the climactic moment of Lettie's relationship with George. She is now given a chance to climb out of the Hell into which she feels she is sinking—just as Maggie in relation to Stephen has the opportunity to leap out of the dark cavern in which she finds herself and return to "the life-nourishing day." But Lettie allows the chance to slip through her fingers because she wills herself into being deaf to what her blood-consciousness tells her, just as, analogously, Maggie allows her mind to recoil and swing her back into the cavern. Accordingly, Lettie does not heed George's appeal even though she is overcome by his embrace—and though she is as much overcome by the knowledge the passionate kiss conveys. "Poor Meg," she says, registering the unhappiness that George, loving her as he does with all his being, will doom Meg to by marrying her. And "poor Leslie," she might have murmured as well, for she has not been an unwilling partner in the embrace, has even provoked it, showing unequivocally how much she wants George even while insisting she is bound to Leslie. Though George characteristically "slackens" and accepts her departure, she must be assumed to submerge the truth of that kiss in her sense of the superior attainments, social position, and wealth of Leslie, for she proceeds to marry him in spite of it.

At this point Lawrence may be regarded, in Harold Bloom's terms, as executing a *clinamen* or "swerve" in relation to his precursor. The ending of *The Mill on the Floss* is unsatisfactory because, in effect, George Eliot evades a full confrontation of the issues her fiction has raised. The "long suicide" that is implicit in Maggie's condition when she rejects Stephen's appeal is transformed into an heroic death; and what her death means for both Philip and Stephen is not pursued, though we are told that they visit her grave and that "one of them" visits it again "with a sweet face beside him . . . years after" (*MF*, 457). What Lawrence does, devoting about one-third of his novel to this, is to explore the consequences for all three protagonists of Lettie's decision to marry Leslie.

An immediate indication of Lettie's lack of fulfillment in her marriage is that she can "never quite let [George] be," and that she is subject to "a driving force" that impels her "against her will to interfere in his life" (*WP*, 336). Though she desists from visiting him at his home after he is married because Meg proves to be "too antagonistic," she keeps up the friendship with him "in spite of all things," and he visits her at Highclose "perhaps once in a fortnight." Some ten years after the announcement of her engagement to Leslie, she seems to be no less engaged by George; and while she lets Leslie "forget her birthday" and so be away from home on the occasion, "for some unknown reason, she [lets] the intelligence slip to George," whom she invites to dinner. And ten years after the engagement, they still have much the same effect on each other (*WP*, 339–40).

George says that he looks "to marriage" to set him busy on his "house of life, something whole and complete, of which it will supply the design" (*WP*, 274); but the very foundation of his life is undermined when he marries Meg though still in love with Lettie. Years later he tacitly admits his responsibility for the failure of his marriage, unknowingly establishing a parallel between himself and Lettie in relation to her husband: "I can't give [Meg] any of the real part of me," he tells Cyril, "the vital part that she wants—I can't, any more than you could give kisses to a stranger" (*WP*, 342–43). The result is that Meg, who is "secure in her high maternity," humiliates him and is "hostile to his wishes" (*WP*, 314); and he feels "like a vacuum . . . all loose in the middle of a space of darkness, that's pressing on you" (*WP*, 328). Without marriage as a firm base from which to operate, moreover, George cannot really make a success of anything else. At first he sets out to make money, but, though he becomes quite well-to-do, his money-making is at bottom an escape from an inner nullity, from the vacuum of his being. Becoming disillusioned with mere prosperity, he begins to work for the socialist cause, but his political ardor soon peters out. In the end he lets everything go, and subsides into a gradual

drunken deterioration. Even the fire of his "evil-drunk" rages soon dies
out, and he sinks in the prime of his life into a feeble alcoholic passivity. When Cyril sees him for the last time, he is "lamentably de-
cayed," leaning against a gate "like a tree that is falling, going soft and
pale and rotten, clammy with small fungi" (WP, 366–67).

Leslie, like George, also goes in for public life after his marriage,
becoming a county councillor and speaking authoritatively as a mine
owner on economic questions of the day; but we are to understand that
he too does not excel as a public man. This would also seem to be
attributable to the nature of his marriage—Lettie encourages him in
his political ambitions because "it [relieves] her of him" (WP, 339)—
though we are not told much about his view of it. Cyril states that after
his marriage he seems to "[lose] his assertive self-confidence," and almost at once reports that "Lettie and he [have] separate rooms" when
they stay at Woodside (WP, 296). As Cyril sees it, the marriage for
Leslie, far from being vitalizing, is notable for the ease with which he
makes it nonexistent: "As Lettie was always a very good wife, Leslie
adored her when he had the time, and when he had not, forgot her
comfortably" (WP, 330).

The change in Lettie after her marriage is first apparent when she
makes no attempt to conceal a general sense of disillusionment, and
Cyril offers the following summing up of her condition:

Having reached that point in a woman's career when most, perhaps all of the
things in life seem worthless and insipid, she had determined to put up with it,
to ignore her own self, to empty her own potentialities into the vessel of another or others, and to live her life at second hand. This peculiar abnegation of
self is the resource of a woman for the escaping of the responsibilities of her
own development. Like a nun, she puts over her living face a veil, as a sign that
the woman no longer exists for herself: she is the servant of God, of some man,
of her children, or may be of some cause. As a servant, she is no longer responsible for herself, which would make her terrified and lonely. Service is light and
easy. . . . [Lettie] had . . . now determined to abandon the charge of herself to
serve her children. (WP, 323–24)

Cyril formulates his view of Lettie as a general proposition about the
life of women, but her disillusionment is clearly personal, and as clearly to be attributed to the vacuity of her marriage. Her condition, pulled
as she still is between the man she has married and the man she cannot
let be, is analogous to that of Maggie, torn irrevocably between Philip
and Stephen; and, like Maggie, she would seem to be poised for breakdown. Lettie does not overtly break down, but she falls apart at the
innermost core of her being—and in effect ceases to be, certainly as
Lawrence understands meaningful being. The central indication of this

is her determination "to empty her own potentialities into the vessel of another or others": Lettie allows herself to lapse into the life of her child, permitting the core of the self to dissolve, as it were, and pouring herself into her son. The result is her own vital inanition, and a negation of self that constitutes her "long suicide" as she lives her life at second hand and "abandons the charge of herself to serve her children." Such a sacrifice of self is a denial of "the responsibilities of her own development"—as she has previously denied her sexual being.

In the end Lettie tells Cyril that she has "nothing at all in her life," and declares it is "a barren futility": "I hope I shall have another child next spring," she writes; "there is only that to take away the misery of this torpor. I seem full of passion and energy, and it all fizzles out in day-to-day domestics" (*WP*, 330). When, after ten years of continued flirtation, George forces the issue, insisting "it must be one way or another," she "coldly" opts for a final parting (*WP*, 345)—but then she again defrauds herself, and her own blood is now virtually stilled: "Lettie's heart would quicken in answer to only one pulse, the easy, light ticking of the baby's blood" (*WP*, 357).

It is in his having gone beyond George Eliot in his first novel that Lawrence may be said to have found himself through her—to have discovered, that is, some of the basic thematic material that he was steadily to mine in his future career. The two bad marriages with which *The White Peacock* concludes come to serve as a springboard. First, the failure of both George and Leslie, but particularly George, to make anything significant of their lives concretizes what Lawrence was to declare in direct expository terms (and to dramatize again and again in his fiction) to be the dependence of man's "purposive activity," whether individual or collective, on sexual fulfillment:

Sex holds any *two* people together, but it tends to disintegrate society, unless it is subordinated to the great dominating male passion of collective *purpose*.

But when the sex passion submits to the great purposive passion, then you have fullness. And no great purposive passion can endure long unless it is established upon the fulfilment in the vast majority of individuals of the true sexual passion.[14]

Second, George (and not Annable the gamekeeper, as often asserted, though he clearly has his links with Mellors in *Lady Chatterley's Lover*) becomes an archetypal Lawrence character, leading in his vivid physical being and its squalid drunken extinction to Walter Morel in *Sons and Lovers*, and in his money-making as an escape from an inner vacuity to both Gerald Crich in *Women in Love* and Clifford Chatterley; just as Leslie, the mine-owner, in his childlike dependence on a woman leads in his own way to both Gerald and Clifford. Third, the women who remain unfulfilled in their marriages become archetypal too. Meg, who is denied "the real part" of George even though she proceeds to bear him five children, leads to Anna Brangwen in *The Rainbow* in the high maternity that is implacably hostile to her husband. And Lettie, who sacrifices herself in order to serve her children, leads not only to Mrs. Morel in *Sons and Lovers* but to Lawrence's insistence on the perniciousness of all such sacrifice of self, and to his exploration of the effects of such ministrations on the children who are its beneficiaries.

But above all *The White Peacock* initiates Lawrence's pursuit of an alternative outcome to the kind of self-division Lettie exemplifies. In the figure of Paul Morel in *Sons and Lovers*, Lawrence was to depict such a condition even more profoundly and vividly, and the crucial development occurs at the end of that novel. Unlike Lettie, Paul does not choose the "halfness" or "partness" which is offered him, for he rejects both Miriam Leivers and Clara Dawes, seeking a wholeness of being away from both of them. And unlike Maggie's rejection of Philip and Stephen, his is positive, for whereas she knowingly opts for the dark cavern, he turns his back on the darkness and walks toward "the faintly humming, glowing town, quickly." With *Sons and Lovers* behind him, Lawrence was ready for the attempt to determine how the two opposed modes of consciousness could be integrated in a unified self—was ready, that is, for his Ursula Brangwen.

VICTORY:
THE BATTLE FOR HEYST

I take it that virtually the sole interest of *Victory*, given the absence in it of the characteristic Conradian virtues, is the presentation of Heyst. The main action is melodramatic rather than epiphanic, the narrative method is arbitrarily inconsistent rather than intricately functional, the language is frequently flat or rhetorical, and the characterization of most of the figures surrounding Heyst hovers between the crudity of caricature and the bluntness of allegory—but Heyst himself has the distinctive complexity of being that graces more memorable characters in Conrad's earlier and better work. Heyst, indeed, is so complex that Conrad criticism is full of contradictory statements about him. On the one hand, the detachment of this "man of universal detachment," as the novelist himself describes him in his 1920 Author's Note,[1] is held by some critics to be no more than a "pose"[2] or an "adopted role";[3] it is also said to be "unnatural"[4] and, insofar as it reflects "his father's angry scepticism," to be "alien to his temperament."[5] On the other hand, it is asserted that Heyst's detachment is so deeply part of him as to be incapacitating; he is said to exhibit "an inability to act or to love,"[6] an "incapacity . . . for love,"[7] and an "incapacity to act";[8] where he does show pity, this is deemed to be "suspect."[9]

There is no need of a deconstructionist analysis in order to see how the text has given rise to such contradictory views, for they seem to thrust themselves at us. If it is intimated that Heyst is fundamentally a man of detachment since we are told that it is "the very essence of his life to be a solitary achievement, accomplished . . . by the detachment of an impermanent dweller amongst changing scenes" (p. 90) and, furthermore, that he is "temperamentally . . . a spectator" (p. 185), it is also categorically stated that he is "temperamentally sympathetic" (p. 70). It would seem to be clear, therefore, that Heyst is temperamentally prone both to a solitary detachment and a sympathetic involvement with others, and so it is misleading to conclude that only one of these opposed tendencies is genuine.[10] The personality that is presented to us is essentially dualistic in nature, and it is striking that the opening sentences of the novel should advert us to a notion of duality: "There is, as every schoolboy knows in this scientific age, a very close chemical relation between coal and diamonds. It is the reason, I believe, why some people allude to coal as 'black diamonds'" (p. 3). These statements recall D. H. Lawrence's use of a similar image to convey his sense of the duality of being and of the "allotropic states" that the individual "passes through": "Like as diamond and coal are the same pure single element of carbon. The ordinary novel would trace the history of the diamond—but I say, 'Diamond, what! This is carbon.' And my diamond might be coal or soot, and my theme is carbon." The Rainbow, which exemplifies Lawrence's apprehension of the carbon of character, appeared in the same year as Victory, but its central impetus is toward the integration of the dualistic self, and consequently it does not throw much light on Conrad's novel. Victory is illuminated, rather, by two nineteenth-century novels that are concerned, as I shall argue Conrad is in this work, with self-division. This is not to suggest that the novels I have in mind—Emily Brontë's Wuthering Heights and Thomas Hardy's Jude the Obscure—should be regarded as having directly influenced Conrad, but merely that the patterns of self-division they present are close enough to the configurations of Victory to help us clarify its difficulties.[11]

In these nineteenth-century novels the two main opposed forces within the protagonists are concretized in two characters with whom they are each brought into close relationship. Thus in Wuthering Heights the animal-like wildness of Heathcliff is set against the refined cultivation of Edgar Linton, and the two men may be regarded as embodying opposed tendencies within Catherine Earnshaw, who is drawn to both of them. In Jude the Obscure Arabella Donne is portrayed as "a complete and substantial female animal—no more, no less," while Sue Bridehead is said to be "so uncarnate" that "her spirit" may be seen "trembling through her limbs," and the opposition between them reflects the conflict between flesh and spirit within Jude Fawley, who moves back and forth between the two women. In Victory the central relationships are not patterned in a love-triangle as in the nineteenth-century novels, but they too are bound together in a triangle, and it seems to me that Heyst's self-division is projected in an analogous manner: the doctrine of detachment propounded by his father is set against an instinctive capacity for attachment in Lena, and the opposition within Heyst between urges to detachment and attachment is figured in his strong feeling for both his father and the young woman.

When he leaves school at the age of eighteen, Heyst lives with his father for three years, and since the father is an epitome of "disillusion and regret," we are told that "such companionship at that plastic and impressionable age" could not but "leave in the boy a profound mistrust of life" (p. 91). The father's influence, indeed, is deadly, as is first suggested when, during their last talk together before the elder Heyst dies, the very houses in the moonlit London street begin to look to the son "like the tombs of an unvisited, unhonoured cemetery of hopes." The father's final exhortation to his son on this occasion is: "Look on—make no sound"; but since he recognizes that the boy may not yet be capable of so perfect a detachment, he advises him "to cultivate that form of contempt which is called pity" as a preliminary to the attainment of "a full and equable contempt" which will do away with all belief in "flesh and blood" (pp. 174–75). It is one of the ironies of this injunction that pity is not only a form of contempt but also of compassion, and that if Heyst doggedly seeks to "sustain" himself on contempt (p. 177), it is his compassion that leads him to the more tangible sustenance of attachment. The immediate effect of the father's influence, however, is to turn him decisively against any such possibility:

Great achievements are accomplished in a blessed, warm mental fog, which the pitiless cold blasts of the father's analysis had blown away from the son.
  "I'll drift," Heyst had said to himself deliberately.
  He did not mean intellectually or sentimentally or morally. He meant to drift altogether and literally, body and soul, like a detached leaf drifting in the wind-currents under the immovable trees of a forest glade; to drift without ever catching on to anything.
  "This shall be my defence against life," he had said to himself with a sort of inward consciousness that for the son of his father there was no other worthy alternative. (p. 92)

The "pitiless cold blasts of the father's analysis" may have the salutary effect of dissipating all "mental fog" in his son, but it is evident that they also detach the leaf from the tree and leave it to drift in the wind. The fallen leaf is no doubt a vivid image of detachment, but it has a number of subversive undertones. To drift is to lack purposive direction, and in Conrad from as early as *The Nigger of the "Narcissus"* drift is associated with a general meaninglessness. A drifting leaf, moreover, is vulnerable as a defensive posture since it may be presumed to be at the mercy of every breeze. Most damagingly of all, the detached leaf is a dying leaf—cut off from that which might sustain it, removed, as it were, from the body of life—and in a related image Heyst is on another occasion said to be "like a feather floating lightly in the work-a-day atmosphere" (p. 60).

The father's influence on his son is thus clearly pernicious, but it is misleading to regard the view of life that Heyst holds to as having been imposed on him or adopted as an affectation. After his father's death he proceeds to drift for some fifteen years, and this would seem to indicate that something already deep in himself was merely reinforced by his father's directives. The point may perhaps be clarified by reference to what happens to the young Cathy Earnshaw when she first leaves Wuthering Heights and spends some time at Thrushcross Grange. The "wild . . . little savage" who left the Heights returns to it "a lady," and Nelly Dean is quick to conclude that her refinement is a pose, deliberately adopted for her own devious purposes. It is evident, however, that the Grange only fosters and develops what is from the outset potential in Cathy. Nelly believes Cathy simply conceals what she (Nelly) calls "her rough side," and that this is the real Cathy, but what we might call her smooth side is every bit as much part of her. Similarly, when Heyst says of himself that he is "a man of universal scorn and unbelief," and Lena accuses him of "putting it on," he replies: "No. I am like that, born or fashioned, or both" (p. 199); and we realize, with him, that his father has merely drawn out what is inherent in him. His drifting like a detached leaf for fifteen years suggests he is driven by an inner compulsion. Just what it is that drives him is intimated by his adoption of this mode of being as a "defence against life." That he feels the need to defend himself implies a general fear of life, and he certainly envisages life in threatening terms: "I often asked myself, with a momentary dread," he tells Lena, "in what way would life try to get hold of me?" (p. 202). It is for this reason that he insists so strenuously on emulating a detached leaf, abjuring all connection. "I only know," he says to her too, "that he who forms a tie is lost"; and though he explains this pronouncement by referring to "the germ of corruption" that then enters the soul (pp. 200–201), the language he uses suggests his specific fear is a fear of giving himself to another—of the loss of self such giving may be deemed to entail.

Where Heyst's father typifies the disengagement of a position of detachment, Lena figures the embrace of attachment. When Heyst shows a compassionate interest in her, it is she who flings herself into his arms (p. 83), as she readily admits: "You took me up from pity," she tells him. "I threw myself at you" (p. 354). For her the embrace of love is both a raison d'être—"She thought . . . that she would try to hold him as long as she could—till her fainting arms, her sinking soul, could cling to him no more" (p. 246)—and the emblem of her being:

he bent down and took her under the arms, raising her straight out of the chair into a sudden and close embrace. Her alacrity to respond, which made her seem as light as a feather, warmed his heart at that moment more than closer caresses had done before. He had not expected that ready impulse towards himself which had been dormant in her passive attitude. (p. 223)

It is notable that the feather image should recur in this passage, for in its evocation of a light alacrity of response it is set against the floating feather of Heyst's unaccommodating and unaccommodated detachment. Where the influence of Heyst's father is deathly in effect, moreover, Lena's responsiveness is heart-warming, a force for life. Where the father teaches the young man to reflect, which, we are assured, is "a destructive process" (p. 91), unleashing icy blasts, Lena instructs him in the hidden power of a sudden spontaneity, for her "ready impulse" has been "dormant in her passive attitude," and this, as it warms him, is restorative. Lena's very sense of self seems to inhere in a ready acceptance of connection: "Do you know," she says to Heyst, "it seems to me, somehow, that if you were to stop thinking of me I shouldn't be in the world at all!" (p. 187).

Attachment may thus be viewed as leading to the establishing of self, but this would appear to be dependent on a readiness to lose the self. Certainly Lena's willingness in this respect is repeatedly indicated: we are told, for instance, that whenever she speaks to him she seems "to abandon to him something of herself" (p. 188); and that she feels "in her innermost depths an irresistible desire to give herself up to him more completely, by some act of absolute sacrifice" (p. 201). A capacity for such abandon, moreover, is not only in contrast to the tight withholding of self that characterizes the posture of detachment; it is also, in its courageous audacity, set against the fear which underlies the withholding. The expression on Lena's face when Heyst first meets her is said to have in it "something indefinably audacious and infinitely miserable—because the temperament and the existence of that girl [are] reflected in it" (p. 74); and Lena at once demonstrates her audacity in insisting that Heyst accept the responsibility of his interest in her: "*You* do something," she says to him. "You are a gentleman. It wasn't I who spoke to you first, was it? I didn't begin, did I? It was you who came along and spoke to me when I was standing over there. What did you want to speak to me for? I don't care what it is, but you must do something" (p. 80). The courage to give the self is also, in its concomitant trustfulness, posed against that "profound mistrust of life" which both breeds and epitomizes detachment: "He could not believe that the creature he had coveted with so much force and with so little effect, was in reality tender, docile to her impulses, and had almost offered herself to [him] without a sense of guilt, in a desire of safety, and from a profound need of placing her trust where her woman's instinct guided her ignorance" (p. 95).

Heyst's own readiness for attachment, like his inclination to detachment, issues from his deepest being. "There must be a lot of the original Adam in me, after all," he reflects, and the nature of the old Adam in him is implicitly defined not as inherent evil but as a compulsion to bring himself into relation with his circumambient world: "There was in the son a lot of that first ancestor who, as soon as he could uplift his muddy frame from the celestial mould, started inspecting and naming the animals of that paradise which he was so soon to lose" (pp. 173–74). The old Adam repeatedly and incongruously declares itself in the proclaimed solitary, for if he wanders the world alone, he is also "a ready letter-writer," and during his wanderings writes "pages and pages" about his experiences to "his friends in Europe," so it is said (p. 6). Nor does he always withdraw from more direct contact. On the contrary, when business brings him to Sourabaya, he seems to be naturally gregarious, being rash enough, for instance, quite gratuitously to invite the notorious Mr. McNab to "come along and quench [his] thirst" with him (p. 8). But it is, of course, in relation to Morrison that he first conclusively gives way to an instinctive and spontaneous fellow-feeling—and invites the attachment that changes the course of his life.

The occasion of Heyst's involvement with Morrison, indeed, is the attachment of the latter's brig by Portuguese officials in Delli. What is notable about his encounter with Morrison is the way in which Heyst involves himself with him when there is no apparent need to do so. He is a "stranger" to Morrison (p. 15), and anyway Morrison does not even see him. When they meet, Morrison is "walking along the street, his eyeglass tossed over his shoulder, his head down, with the hopeless aspect of those hardened tramps one sees . . . trudging from workhouse to workhouse," and it is only when he is hailed from across the street by Heyst that he looks up "with a wild worried expression" (p. 12). Heyst's response is to invite Morrison to join him for a drink, and then, when he discovers the trouble he is in, to offer him a loan that will enable him to get his brig back. Heyst acts on his impulses, being directed by a strong feeling of compassion for Morrison, not contempt, and his action has far-reaching implications, for he is later said to have "plunged after the submerged Morrison" (p. 77). The image of the plunge, in its evocation of generous abandon, suggests that this man, who fears a loss of self, is also capable of risking the self, for it is after a "submerged" man that he plunges, pursuing a rescue by means of attachment.

2

IN *Wuthering Heights* and *Jude the Obscure*, the clash of conflicting qualities within the central protagonists is sharpened and pointed by the active rivalry of the two characters who in each case embody the opposed qualities. Thus Heathcliff and Edgar and Arabella and Sue are brought in one way or another into direct, hostile confrontation. In *Victory* Heyst's father is long dead before his son even meets Lena, but the opposition between them, the battle for Heyst that is implicitly waged, is nonetheless central to the main action. The death of the father if anything intensifies his influence:

> A few slow tears rolled down [Heyst's] face. The rooms, filling with shadows, seemed haunted by a melancholy, uneasy presence which could not express itself. The young man got up with a strange sense of making way for something impalpable that claimed possession, went out of the house, and locked the door. A fortnight later he started on his travels—to "look on and never make a sound." (p. 176)

It is not of the house alone that the spirit of Heyst's father "claims possession," nor only those rooms which from this point on are haunted by the "melancholy, uneasy presence." The "something impalpable" takes a more palpable form in the attitudes and pronouncements of the son who is possessed. It is in this respect that Conrad may be regarded as moving beyond the nineteenth-century novelists and sounding a characteristic modern note. There is little indication in their work of the source of the split in their protagonists; Conrad, with a Freudian-like awareness, makes us see Heyst as a man who carries his family ghosts with him.

The elder Heyst also inhabits the possessions that he leaves to his son. Heyst eventually brings these to his island retreat—"a lot of books, some chairs and tables, his father's portrait in oils . . . [and] a lot of small objects"; and we are told that it is "their presence there which [attaches] him to the island" when he wakes up to "the failure of his apostasy" (p. 177). When Lena comes to the island, she finds the main room of their house "lined with the backs of books halfway up on its three sides. . . . In the dusk and coolness nothing [gleams] except the gilt frame of the portrait of Heyst's father, signed by a famous painter, lonely in the middle of a wall" (p. 186). And the elder Heyst is an active ghost: when his son reads one of the books his father has written, "shrinking into himself, composing his face as if under the author's eye, with a vivid consciousness of the portrait on his right hand, a little above his head, a wonderful presence in its heavy frame on the flimsy wall of mats," he seems to hear his father's voice, and half believes that "something of his father [dwells] yet on earth—a ghostly voice, audible to the ear of his own flesh and blood" (pp. 218–19).

The elder Heyst, however, is not the only ghost with a claim on the son's attention. When Lena comes out to Heyst in the garden of the hotel, it is a "white, phantom-like apparition" that he sees and which proceeds to cling to him (p. 83); and a little later he again registers that, "white and spectral, she [is] putting out her arms to him out of the black shadows like an appealing ghost" (p. 86). It is thus that Lena confronts Heyst's father, and she is often placed in direct opposition to the portrait of the elder Heyst, in which his presence is most palpable: "[Heyst] glanced at the portrait of his father, exactly above the head of the girl, and as it were ignoring her in its painted austerity of feeling" (p. 359). At the climax of the novel, indeed, when Lena prepares to do battle with Ricardo for his all-too-phallic stage knife, our interest is focused on what proves to be her final struggle with a more dangerous opponent: "She had come out after Heyst's departure, and had sat down under the portrait to wait for the return of the man of violence and death" (p. 394).

In the nineteenth-century novels the disintegrating effect of the protagonist's self-division is held in abeyance by the temporary dominance of one of the opposed tendencies within the self and the repression of the other. The two characters with whom the protagonists are each in close relationship alternately call out one of the opposed qualities within them, and at the same time incline them to submerge the other. Thus Heathcliff elicits Cathy's tempestuousness, and she is not concerned to exhibit her refinement in relation to him; but Edgar fosters "the lady" in her, and with him she for the most part holds her wildness in check. Similarly, Jude tries to repress his sexuality in relation to Sue, and the connection with her is primarily intellectual or spiritual in nature; but in relation to Arabella this side of himself tends to be dormant and the sexual is predominant.

In *Victory* something like the same kind of alternation is apparent when Heyst meets Lena, though the change, if not as clear-cut as in the nineteenth-century novels, has perhaps greater psychological verisimilitude. The ghost of Heyst's father, in its long-accustomed presence, is not easily repressible. Prior to the meeting with Lena, the ghost remains in virtually unchallenged possession of Heyst, and there are no more than sporadic forays against his dominance—as in the letter writing and the conviviality with McNab previously referred to. Heyst's involvement with Morrison is a more serious manifestation of the suppressed part of himself, but though his compassion for Morrison is genuine enough, he never really commits himself to the relationship, and merely suffers stoically the consequences of the tie that he sees himself as having formed "in a moment of inadvertence" (p. 199). The dominance of the ghost, prior to the advent of Lena, is apparent, first in Heyst's fifteen long years of solitary wandering, and then in his lone existence on the island for two years before he brings Lena to it—though it is true he is tended by Wang, another ghostly presence.

When Heyst meets Lena, his life is transformed. An immediate indication of such transformation is the impetuous way he, the detached solitary for whom life is no more than a spectacle, forms an attachment, proceeds to act decisively on the basis of it, and then gives himself in love. If he is surprised, when he embraces Lena in the passage already quoted, by "that ready impulse towards himself which [has] been dormant in her passive attitude," it would seem that the force which impels him toward her is of a similar nature. He is certainly active enough then, and the plain facts of what follows should be sufficient to refute any suggestion that he is unable either to act or to love. It is with unaccustomed "audacity" (p. 77) that he snatches the girl from the Zangiacomo band and takes her back with him to his island; and the audacity is accompanied by a readiness to give of himself: "I am here," Lena tells him, "with no one to care if I make a hole in the water the next chance I get or not" (p. 78)—and, with his compassion aroused, Heyst shows that he is as ready to plunge after her as he was with Morrison. At this point his household ghost is held at bay, and we are told that "his sceptical mind" is now "dominated by the fulness of his heart" (p. 83).

The couple thereafter consummate their love, and once again the facts of the matter should scotch the view that Heyst is subject not only to an emotional incapacity for love but also to sexual impotence or deficiency. On the island he is said to be "under the fresh sortilege of their common life, the surprise of novelty, the flattered vanity of his possession of this woman; for a man must feel that, unless he has ceased to be masculine" (p. 201); and his feeling is matched by Lena's own sense of magical fulfillment, for she lives in "the appeased enchantment of the senses she [has] found with him, like a sort of bewitched state" (p. 303). At the same time Heyst feels that he "no longer [belongs] to himself" (p. 245), and his readiness to lose the self not unexpectedly proves (in this sexual context) to be the means of a finding of self: "The girl he had come across, of whom he had possessed himself, to whose presence he was not yet accustomed, with whom he did not yet know how to live; that human being so near and still so strange, gave him a greater sense of his own reality than he had ever known in all his life" (p. 200). Heyst's sense of an enhancement of self, however, does not enable him to establish an equable relationship with Lena since it is countermanded by old fears and reservations. It is on this very occasion, when he registers his gain, that he tells her that "he who forms a tie is lost." The remark is made apropos of his relationship with Morrison, but its crass insensitivity to her feeling—and to his own—in contradistinction to his habitual percipience, betrays its obsessive nature. This, we realize, is the voice of inculcated habit—is, indeed, the voice of his father who speaks through him. It is as if the old ghost rises up to challenge the old Adam that has been so bountifully released in him, and from this point on Heyst is divided between his two allegiances.

When the protagonists in the nineteenth-century novels are pulled with equal force in opposite directions by their divided allegiances and inclinations, one of two things happens: either the pull of one force neutralizes the other and produces a state of immobility, a kind of paralysis, as it were; or the opposed pulls are so overwhelming that they result in a tearing apart of the self, in breakdown. *Wuthering Heights* is illustrative of both processes. When things reach such a pass that Edgar tells Cathy she has no alternative but to choose between him and Heathcliff, the pulls exerted by her wish to remain Mrs. Linton of Thrushcross Grange and by her profound feeling for Heathcliff are so equal in strength that she is unable to choose. When the pressure becomes intolerable, she experiences a breakdown, succumbing to a brain fever. A disintegration of self is also projected in a loss of the will to live; and though Cathy recovers from her illness and it is in childbirth that she dies, she seems after the brain fever to want to die. In *Jude the Obscure* Jude's death figures a prior disintegration of self. Married once again to Arabella but still in love with Sue and longing for her, though she is married again to Phillotson, he is torn in two and deliberately courts death. He seeks, as he says, "to do for [himself]," and in effect commits suicide.

The two processes of paralysis and disintegration are also exemplified in the case of Heyst. His paralysis takes two forms. In relation to Lena, it manifests itself in his inability to say what he feels, issuing in his failure on three significant occasions to declare his love for her. On the first occasion she reproaches him, saying: "You should try to love me!":

He made a movement of astonishment.
"Try!" he muttered. "But it seems to me—" He broke off, saying to himself that if he loved her, he had never told her so in so many words. Simple words! They died on his lips. "What makes you say that?" he asked. . . .
. . . He did not know what to say, either from want of practice in dealing with women or simply from his innate honesty of thought. All his defences were broken now. Life had him fairly by the throat. (p. 221)

Heyst, we register, has not seemed to suffer from a "want of practice" in all the other ways in which he has "dealt" with Lena. Nor is it life that has him "by the throat," preventing speech; it is his skeptical mind, bound by the habits and beliefs of a lifetime—and bound also to a demanding ghost—that prevents him from declaring his love. We may assume he is inhibited in a similar way on the last night of Lena's life. First, as the danger posed by the predatory trio grows more palpable, Heyst ensures that Lena will not stay alone in the house when he goes to confront Jones, but when they part and she puts his hand to her lips, he can do no more than speak her name "under his breath": "He dared not trust himself—no, not even to the extent of a tender word" (p. 373). Then, even when she is dying, he cannot bring himself to tell her he loves her: "Heyst bent low over her, cursing his fastidious soul, which even at that moment kept the true cry of love from his lips in its infernal mistrust of all life" (p. 406).

In relation to Jones, Heyst's paralysis takes the form of an inability to act decisively against him. On the climactic night of confrontation he misses his opportunity when Jones, who has been covering him with a revolver, is disconcerted by the announcement that there is a woman on the island:

> Backed hard against the wall, [Jones] no longer watched Heyst. He had the air of a man who had seen an abyss yawning under his feet.
> "If I want to kill him, this is my time," thought Heyst; but he did not move. (p. 387)

Heyst's immobility here is expressive of the way in which his wish to protect Lena and safeguard their life together, which makes him perceive clearly enough that this is the moment to act against his flabbergasted opponent, is neutralized not only by a reluctance to kill but by an engrained belief in the futility of all such action. That it is not the morality of killing which is at issue is indicated when Jones marches Heyst at the point of a gun to the house in which Lena, unknown to Heyst, has received Ricardo:

> In [Heyst's] breast dwelt a deep silence, the complete silence of unused faculties. At this moment, by simply shouldering Mr. Jones, he could have thrown him down and put himself by a couple of leaps, beyond the certain aim of the revolver; but he did not even think of that. His very will seemed dead of weariness. He moved automatically, his head low, like a prisoner captured by the evil power of a masquerading skeleton out of a grave. (p. 390)

As in the case of Heyst's failure to declare his love for Lena, it is not "unused faculties" which are the problem, for he has shown that he can act decisively enough when he wants to. In this episode, moreover, in contradistinction to the scene in Jones's house, Heyst does "not even think" of taking action against his adversary, though the necessary action would mean no more than a shouldering. The paralysis of his will, which seems "dead of weariness," is attributable to the force that neutralizes his readiness to put up a fight, and indeed he is "like a prisoner captured by the evil power of a masquerading skeleton out of a grave." The simile refers directly, no doubt, to Mr. Jones, who literally has him prisoner, and who just previously is twice called a skeleton (pp. 383, 389), but it is the ghost of Heyst's father that effectively holds him back and so paralyzes him here.

The upshot of Heyst's failure to act is the death of Lena. When he first sees her with Ricardo and doubts her fidelity, he thinks that a man who has experienced "such a feeling" has "no business to live" (p. 392). We may infer that when he discovers that, far from being unfaithful, she has in effect died for him, his life is made even more intolerable. The prisoner of another ghost now, torn apart by the two spirits that contend for his soul, he takes his own life.

HOWARDS END:
GOBLINS AND RAINBOWS

About midway through *Howards End*—in a passage that is right at its center—the novelist describes a pervading condition of personal fragmentation:

> Margaret greeted her lord with peculiar tenderness on the morrow. Mature as he was, she might yet be able to help him to the building of the rainbow bridge that should connect the prose in us with the passion. Without it we are meaningless fragments, half monks, half beasts, unconnected arches that have never joined into a man. With it love is born . . .
>
> It did not seem so difficult [i.e., for Margaret to help Mr. Wilcox]. She need trouble him with no gift of her own. She would only point out the salvation that was latent in his own soul, and in the soul of every man. Only connect! That was the whole of her sermon. Only connect the prose and the passion, and both will be exalted, and human love will be seen at its highest. Live in fragments no longer. Only connect, and the beast and the monk, robbed of the isolation that is life to either, will die. (pp. 187–88)[1]

The "sermon" may be Margaret's, but Forster uses its text as the epigraph to the novel, and it is the "salvation" not only of Mr. Wilcox but of "every man" that is at issue. What men have to be saved from is the kind of self-division that is implicit in Mr. Wilcox's sexual attitudes, the split between spirit and flesh that makes him in turn a monk and a beast. The "rainbow bridge" Margaret hopes to help him build in order to connect the everyday casualness of prose with the special intensity of passion is itself—much as in D. H. Lawrence—a symbol of the harmonious reconciliation or integration of opposites. In a meeting of sun and rain, it joins earth and sky and signifies an achieved wholeness in contradistinction to the fragmentation of the "unconnected arches." It is love that resolves the specific opposition referred to, for it is born of the connection of monk and beast, but destroys its progenitors by depriving each of the isolation that is essential to its existence. It issues, indeed, as a tenderness that is the product of the union of flesh and spirit, a "tenderness that kills the monk and the beast at a single blow" (p. 219).

The drama of personal fragmentation is enacted against a background of social disintegration: "the city herself, emblematic of their lives, rose and fell in a continual flux, while her shallows washed more widely against the hills of Surrey and over the fields of Hertfordshire. This famous building had arisen, that was doomed. Today Whitehall had been transformed; it would be the turn of Regent Street tomorrow" (p. 115). It is the lack of stability, the "continual flux" of urban life, that particularly concerns the novelist. The flux is inherent in the city itself. It is the very city that rises and falls as old buildings are destroyed in order to make way for new in a continuous process that spills out over the countryside. The quintessential scene in Forster's London is of "an old house . . . being demolished to accommodate [two blocks of flats]": "It [is] the kind of scene that may be observed all over London, whatever the locality—bricks and mortar rising and falling with the restlessness of the water in a fountain, as the city receives more and more men upon her soil" (p. 59).

Fragmentary buildings, which are to be seen everywhere in London, provide an effective image of the lack of integration that is Forster's theme. Indeed it is in this regard, as well as in relation to the phenomenon of flux, that the city may be viewed as being "emblematic" of the lives of the Schlegels—and of the other characters who inhabit it— for the novelist posits a direct connection between the personal and the social predicament, presenting one as the consequence of the other. When the Schlegels are forced to vacate their home at Wickham Place so that it can be demolished, this is said to "[disintegrate] the girls more than they [know]" (p. 253). What the individual needs in the flux of modern city life is a locus of stability, and this, it is intimated, is best provided by a long-standing home. "Can what they call civilization be right," asks Mrs. Wilcox, "if people mayn't die in the room where they were born?" (p. 93). Margaret does not know "what to say" in reply to this, but the novelist insists that modern man is being reduced to "a nomadic horde" and reverting to a "civilization of luggage." The Schlegels, at all events, are denied what Mrs. Wilcox takes to be their natural right, and so are deprived of that which has hitherto "helped to balance their lives" (p. 154).

Given such a view of life in London, it is not surprising that the novel takes its title from the name of a house, a house in the country.

Given such a view, moreover, the plot, which turns on the Schlegels' loss of their home and their search for a new one, readily takes on a symbolic dimension: their loss is representative of a general predicament; and their search is for something more than a house. It is a search for that which can provide a secure anchorage for the self.

That the Schlegels eventually find a new home at Howards End is assertive, on the symbolic level, of more than is actually shown to be accomplished, for true personal stability is as much dependent on an inner cohesion and balance as on a stable environment—and I shall argue that none of the Schlegels achieve that. But the conclusion is indicative of the novel's strong contrapuntal structure: Howards End is set against Wickham Place, the country against the city, wholeness against disintegration. It has, indeed, the kind of musical structure so appreciatively described in the account of Helen's response to the third movement of Beethoven's Fifth Symphony:

the music started with a goblin walking quietly over the universe, from end to end. Others followed him. They were not aggressive creatures; it was that that made them so terrible to Helen. They merely observed in passing that there was no such thing as splendour or heroism in the world. After the interlude of elephants dancing, they returned and made the observation for the second time. Helen could not contradict them, for, once at all events, she had felt the same, and had seen the reliable walls of youth collapse. Panic and emptiness! Panic and emptiness! The goblins were right. . . .

[Then] as if things were going too far, Beethoven took hold of the goblins and made them do what he wanted. . . . he blew with his mouth and they were scattered! Gusts of splendour, gods and demigods contending with vast swords, colour and fragrance broadcast on the field of battle, magnificent victory, magnificent death! . . . [But] the goblins really had been there. They might return— and they did. It was as if the splendour of life might boil over and waste to steam and froth. In its dissolution one heard the terrible, ominous note, and a goblin, with increased malignity, walked quietly over the universe from end to end. Panic and emptiness! Panic and emptiness! Even the flaming ramparts of the world might fall. (pp. 46–47)

In a work evocative of heroic splendor, Beethoven, it is held, found it necessary to include an antiheroic statement. This counterstatement is comparable structurally to Forster's own assertion, in a world of unconnected arches, of the existence of rainbows. But the images in the quoted passage make the description of Beethoven's procedures in the Fifth Symphony more than an analogue of Forster's in the novel, for his goblins are heralds of disintegration. What they point to is the possibility of breakdown, a falling apart in which even "the reliable walls of youth" and "the flaming ramparts of the world" may disintegrate, a

collapse which is a "dissolution," a boiling over and a wasting to steam
and froth. The goblins, that is, lead straight to the landlord of Wickham
Place, who knocks it down and so spills "the precious distillation of
the years" which "no chemistry of his can give . . . back to society
again" (p. 155). The kind of collapse the goblins announce, moreover,
reveals—amid falling walls and ramparts—an inner hollowness, a
nothingness at the heart of things, the "panic and emptiness" that Hel-
en (who serves as the center of consciousness in the quoted passage)
has discerned behind the confident facade of Paul Wilcox. It is a hollowness that Conrad had some years earlier found at the core of Kurtz
in "Heart of Darkness"; it is the kind of void that Forster himself later
has Mrs. Moore memorably peer into in a Marabar cave in *A Passage to
India*. It is a "terrible, ominous note" that is sounded by the goblin that
quietly walks "with increased malignity . . . over the universe from
end to end" because what it prophetically foretells is dissolution on a
global scale—and the disintegration in 1914 of the society of those
who sit listening in the Queen's Hall to Beethoven. With such goblins
loose in the world, Forster may well essay the rainbow. When he
chooses "to make all right in the end" (p. 47), as Beethoven does despite
the goblins, the question is whether we can trust Forster—as he asserts
"one can trust Beethoven," who has bravely said "the goblins [are]
there" and "could return" (p. 47).

2

THOUGH it is the monk and the beast who are the focus of Margaret's
sermon, it is not with the opposition between spirit and flesh that Forster is directly concerned. His interest is in the contrasted qualities and
value systems of two families, the Schlegels and the Wilcoxes, who are
posed against each other in an elaborate balance, a point counterpoint,
that is the unifying principle of the novel. They figure an opposition
between the private and the public self.[2] What is involved in the opposition is neatly brought out in an apparently trivial incident. Margaret is traveling with a wedding party to celebrate Evie Wilcox's wedding at Oniton when the front car in which she is driving suddenly
stops. The second car pulls up, and Charles Wilcox is "heard saying:
'Get out the women at once.' " The women are "hustled out" into the
second car, which drives off, but at that point a girl comes out of a
cottage and "[screams] wildly at them." When the ladies want to know
what has happened, Charles says, "It's all right. Your car just touched a
dog"; and he adds, "It didn't hurt him" (pp. 211–12).

Charles, we note, at once takes command of the situation. When it
comes to acting, the Wilcoxes, as Helen remarks, seem "to have their

hands on all the ropes" (p. 41); and this capacity manifests itself in the "public qualities" Margaret believes have produced the material civilization on which they all depend (p. 177). The Wilcoxes, furthermore, seem to Helen to represent a "robust ideal" (p. 38): they are not only "competent" but have great "energy," "grit," and "character" (pp. 37, 41). They are also strongly male: Margaret is glad that in Mr. Wilcox she is marrying "a real man" (p. 176).

The capacity for acting in the world, however, not unexpectedly breeds a less admirable worldliness. Like the landlords who are busy demolishing old houses in London, the Wilcoxes' foremost concern is with making money; and they exemplify the nomadic civilization that is the result of these labors, restlessly moving from house to house and seeming to prize their motor cars above all. For the worldly, moreover, "love means marriage settlements; death, death duties," as Helen asserts (p. 41); and accordingly the way in which the Wilcoxes handle the accident is to dispense "compensation" for the loss of a pet, the chauffeurs being left to "[tackle] the girl" in this respect—and the insurance company to pay (p. 213). In the name of the efficient transaction of the business in hand, the Wilcoxes also naturally accommodate themselves to misleading distortion and suppression of the truth. Margaret, who is a woman and appears agitated, must be treated like a child and told the car "didn't hurt" the dog it ran over; as "a possible tenant," she is not told by Mr. Wilcox of the mews behind his Ducie Street house though as a prospective wife who has to be persuaded not to live there she is informed of its "huge drawbacks." She concludes that such behavior is not really devious and stems from "a flaw inherent in the business mind," the novelist commenting—with a show of objectivity that in its lameness is disquieting—that she "may do well to be tender to it, considering all that the business mind has done for England" (p. 184). But the business mind, it appears, is not prepared to do very much for the girl who has lost her pet. When it comes to her, it shows a total incomprehension that anything other than compensation and a hasty retreat are called for—an incomprehension that is extended to Margaret when, "horrified," she asks Charles to stop the car so that she can go back to the girl; he simply "[takes] no notice" (p. 212). We are told that all the Wilcoxes "[avoid] the personal note in life" (p. 101), but the sort of incomprehension Charles displays on this occasion amounts to a blankness that is expressive of a radical incapacity where the personal is concerned, an inner hollowness.

For the Schlegels such behavior is unthinkable. Margaret's most pronounced quality is said to be "a profound vivacity," which is defined as "a continual and sincere response to all that she [encounters] in her path through life" (p. 25). Such responsiveness makes her place a high value on "personal relations," which she and her sister think are "supreme" and "the real life" (p. 41). Where the Wilcoxes are "practical," they are "intellectual" (p. 151); and they pursue an inner life of cultivated sensibility that may rest, amid the prevailing flux, on the "island" of a private income (p. 72), but otherwise has few material preoccupations. Wickham Place may not have a precise location in *Howards End*, but it would appear to be not very far from Bloomsbury. The Schlegels certainly adhere to a distinctive ethos; and Margaret, who is "not a Christian in the accepted sense," is not without her own religion: "It is private life," she reflects, "that holds out the mirror to infinity; personal intercourse, and that alone, that ever hints at a personality beyond our daily vision" (p. 91).

The vistas of private life, however, are somewhat more restricted when it comes to mundane matters. Margaret admits that she and Helen "have never touched" the "great outer life" in which the Wilcoxes move so confidently, though she suspects it may be "the real one" (p. 41)—and indeed the Schlegels appear to be incapable of acting effectively outside a friendly drawing-room. This incapacity is strikingly shown in their inability to find a new house when they have to leave Wickham Place: "I want a new home in September," Margaret says, "and someone must find it. I can't" (p. 157). There is, in a word, something "bloodless" about the Miss Schlegels (p. 42)—and their effeminate brother Tibby. Nor, when the Schlegel blood is up, does it prove to be any more effective. Sitting in the car as Charles drives away from the scene of the accident, feeling the urgent need to take personal responsibility for what has happened, Margaret is faced by his steady refusal to heed her repeated requests that he stop. What she does is in keeping with the impulsiveness she shares with her sister—it is the only way they can act—and reckless of her own safety: she jumps out of the car. It is a courageous protest, but utterly ineffectual, the rage of impotence. In the end she "[yields], apologizing slightly," and is "led back to the car"—leaving the field to Charles. When it emerges it is a cat that has been killed and not a dog, he exclaims "triumphantly": "There! It's only a rotten cat" (pp. 212–13).

The Wilcox propensity for such distinctions is even more damagingly revealed in what they make of the note Mrs. Wilcox writes from her deathbed, which reads: "To my husband: I should like Miss Schlegel (Margaret) to have Howards End." It is written in pencil, and has no date and no signature (pp. 105–6). The "question" raised by the note—which the Wilcoxes meet to consider—is one that cuts right across the two worlds of the novel, squarely opposing a personal to a business ethic. The Wilcoxes dispose of the private world of "feminine" caprice that the note discloses to them by simply ignoring its existence. The pressing personal question that the note poses—are they not called upon to honor a dying wish, the last request of a wife and a mother?— is easily avoided because it is not even formulated. Nor is the question—which might have "driven them miserable or mad" (p. 107)—of what is implied by such a wish on Mrs. Wilcox's part. Instead they dodge the personal and the emotional; and, "assuming the manner of the committee-room" (p. 106), convert the question into the public and practical one of the note's legality. In the end, the question is reduced to what should be done with the piece of paper; and since it is "not legally binding" (p. 106), they proceed with characteristic decisiveness to "tear the note up and throw it onto their dining-room fire" (p. 108). The irony is that Margaret, had she been informed of Mrs. Wilcox's wish, would also have "rejected [it] as the fantasy of an invalid" (p. 110). But the fact remains that the destruction of the note, though perhaps not technically criminal, is certainly dishonest. Once again it is disquieting that the novelist should seek to minimize the weakness he has so devastatingly exposed. We are told that "the practical moralist" (who presumably believes the end justifies the means) "may acquit them absolutely"; while he "who strives to look deeper," even if conceding they should not be acquitted altogether, is merely palliative: "For one hard fact remains. They did neglect a personal appeal" (p. 108).

A personal appeal of another kind is productive of the central crisis in the novel when Helen decides to throw the Basts at the Wilcoxes on Evie's wedding day. Storming into the Wilcox domain to repudiate what they stand for, Helen emerges in this scene as the epitome of all that is opposed to their way of doing things. Defiantly dressed in "her oldest clothes" as a measure of her personal identification with the Basts in their difficult circumstances, betraying in her "tense, wounding excitement" the degree of her personal involvement with them (p. 222), she has generously accepted a personal responsibility for their plight. But she is as much given to converting reality to her own terms as the Wilcoxes, declaring the Basts to be starving and thus theatrically heightening their condition, in much the way that the Wilcoxes reduce the significance of the deathbed note. And the moment it comes to remedial action, Helen's admirable motives fade into utter inconsequentiality. What she does—much like Margaret in the car—is to abandon herself to her impulse, not considering at all whether it is wise to take the Basts with her to Oniton. Whereas Mr. Wilcox, when tactfully approached by Margaret, shows himself amenable to helping Bast (p. 228), his unfortunate meeting with Mrs. Bast, his former mistress, makes any further suggestion of such aid out of the question. The net result of Helen's attempt to save the Basts is that she helps to ruin them, for the expedition "[cripples them] permanently" since she forgets "to settle the hotel bill" and takes "their return tickets away with her"; without a job and evicted from his flat, Bast thereafter "[degrades] himself to a professional beggar" (p. 309).

In her haste to set the world to rights, Helen nearly brings about another unanticipated development. Even Margaret is moved to anger at her "bursting into Evie's wedding" in a manner that might seem calculated to cause everyone distress (p. 223), though nothing is further from her intention. In fact she comes close to destroying the relationship of Margaret and Mr. Wilcox: after the scene with Mrs. Bast, Mr. Wilcox, assuming the worst, releases Margaret from her engagement, and it is only Margaret's decision to regard the matter as Mrs. Wilcox's "tragedy," not hers, that saves the marriage (pp. 230–31). It is, of course, Bast's tragedy, too, and it is when Helen guesses that Mr. Wilcox has "ruined him in two ways," that she gives herself to him (p. 305). The ultimate consequences of the expedition to Shropshire are Helen's pregnancy—and Bast's death (though this last event does not have the painful effect that might be expected since the Basts are so utterly unconvincing in all they do and say, so clearly and in more than one sense beings of a different order of existence from that of the Schlegels and Wilcoxes, that they are never more than discordant creaks in the mechanism of the plot).

In episodes such as the killing of the cat, the destruction of Mrs. Wilcox's note, and the invasion of Evie's wedding party, what it means to be a Schlegel or a Wilcox is effectively revealed, and the attributes of the private and public self clearly established. What is notable is the degree to which, in each case, one aspect of the self is subdued to the other. In the Wilcoxes the private is suppressed by the public to an extent that there is only an emptiness where the personal should be. But in the Schlegels the ability to act is equally missing, and the personal reduces the public self to impotence. In both the Wilcox and the Schlegel personality, therefore, there is a radical deficiency, a blankness—like that into which an unconnected arch gapes.

The driving force of *Howards End* is the search for a means of supplying these deficiencies. But how does one connect a broken arch to a blankness? The novel, not unexpectedly, gives no very clear answer to this question, but does explore certain possibilities. An obvious resource is to attempt to develop the missing capacity. This, it would appear, can best be done in relation to a person who abundantly possesses it. Margaret, for instance, knows that the Wilcoxes are "not 'her sort,'" and that they are "deficient where she [excels]"; but nevertheless "collision with them [stimulates] her": "She desired to protect them, and often felt that they would protect her, excelling where she was deficient" (p. 111). The stimulus Margaret derives from contact with the Wilcoxes is clearly that generated by an opposite; the protection she both wishes to extend and to receive would seem to be not so much practical as a mutual fostering of qualities, an offering from a rich store in the area of the other's deficiency. If such casual provisioning might be expected to yield modest results, the best hope of continued supply might be supposed to lie in the maintenance of the closest possible relation with the opposite—in a word, in marriage.

It is a metaphorical union of opposites, at all events, that seems to posit the attainment of completeness—as it is the balance of opposites that integrates the narrative. Margaret experiences such "a feeling of completeness" when she is in the country: "In these English farms, if anywhere, one might see life steadily and see it whole, group in one vision its transitoriness and its eternal youth, connect—connect without bitterness until all men are brothers" (p. 264). And that is what the "peculiar glory" of the wych-elm, which Forster has stated was intended to be "symbolical" and "the genius of the house,"[3] seems to signify: "It was a comrade, bending over the house, strength and adventure in its roots, but in its utmost fingers tenderness, and the girth, that a dozen men could not have spanned, became in the end evanescent, till pale bud clusters seemed to float in the air" (p. 206). As Margaret stands in the house and looks at the tree, "truer relationships" are said to "gleam" (p. 206). Massively rooted in the earth, but "bending over the house," the wych-elm connects the house to the earth of its garden; and the tree itself is indicative of how opposites may be reconciled in indisputable wholeness. The "strength" of its roots counters the "tenderness" of its furthermost shoots; its enormous "girth" is balanced by its floating "evanescence."

What the tree at Howards End represents is given further embodiment in Mrs. Wilcox. Of her, Margaret, who is usually level-headed, says: "She knows everything. She is everything. She is the house, and the tree that leans over it" (p. 305). And on another occasion Mrs. Wilcox gives her "the idea of greatness" and makes her "conscious of a personality" that "transcends" and "dwarfs" the activities of her and her friends (p. 86). Clearly Mrs. Wilcox is one of those characters in Forster—Mrs. Moore in *A Passage to India* is another—who are more impressive to other characters than to the reader, for nothing that Mrs. Wilcox does or is would seem to accord with such estimates. But she would appear, if a little tenuously, to be the one character in the novel who is able to reconcile public and private worlds and achieve something like a state of wholeness.

Perhaps our most vivid impression of Mrs. Wilcox is in one of the early scenes in the novel, when we really see her moving into action. Charles Wilcox, seeking to go straight to the heart of the supposed affair between his brother Paul and Helen, at once asks his brother whether there is any truth in it; and, when Paul dithers, demands a plain answer to a plain question:

> "Charles dear," said a voice from the garden. "Charles, dear Charles, one doesn't ask plain questions. There aren't such things."
> They were all silent. It was Mrs. Wilcox.
> She approached just as Helen's letter had described her, trailing noiselessly over the lawn, and there was actually a wisp of hay in her hands. She seemed to belong not to the young people and their motor, but to the house, and to the tree that overshadowed it. One knew that she worshipped the past, and that the instinctive wisdom the past can alone bestow had descended upon her—that wisdom to which we give the clumsy name of aristocracy. High-born she might not be. But assuredly she cared about her ancestors, and let them help her. When she saw Charles angry, Paul frightened and Mrs. Munt in tears, she heard her ancestors say: "Separate those human beings who will hurt each other most. The rest can wait." So she did not ask questions. Still less did she pretend that nothing had happened, as a competent society hostess would have done. She said: "Miss Schlegel, would you take your aunt up to your room or to my room, whichever you think best. Paul, do find Evie, and tell her lunch for six, but I'm not sure whether we shall all be downstairs for it." And when they had obeyed her she turned to her elder son, who still stood in the throbbing, stinking car, and smiled at him with tenderness, and without saying a word turned away from him towards her flowers.
> "Mother," he called, "are you aware that Paul has been playing the fool again?"
> "It is all right dear. They have broken off the engagement."
> "Engagement—!"
> "They do not love any longer, if you prefer it put that way," said Mrs. Wilcox, stooping down to smell a rose. (pp. 36–37)

Once again Wilcoxes and Schlegels meet in a question; but this time the formulation, "plain question, plain answer," is one to which both in their different ways—no-nonsense and businesslike as against the personally direct and sincere—would subscribe. Mrs. Wilcox, however, is sharply differentiated from all of them, and not merely by her sense of a complexity that will not permit of plainness. They belong, not only the Wilcoxes but—whether they like it or not—the Schlegels also, to the restless present of modern city life, to the life that seems to be epitomized in "the throbbing, stinking car." She "worships the past," the sense of continuity and stability that is derived from being in touch with her "ancestors"—and from belonging "to the house, and to the tree that [overshadows] it." Unlike them, she is in touch with nature: she makes her entry with "a wisp of hay in her hands"—the rhythmic hay that ever since E. K. Brown has been pointed to again and again with admiration—and departs smelling a rose.[4] But she is even more strongly differentiated from them all by what she herself is, by the combination of qualities that in this scene she notably shows herself to possess. She is not clever like the Schlegels and their friends, not an intellectual, but she has an "instinctive wisdom" that expresses itself in a penetrating intuition where people are concerned. Though neither Paul nor Helen has spoken to her about their relationship, she has accurately sized it up, showing a sensitivity and delicacy of perception that are the obverse of the obtuseness the Wilcoxes habitually exhibit in the sphere of the personal. And unlike the Schlegels, who veer between paralysis and an impulsive courting of disaster, she knows how to act: she shows a real capacity for arriving at a swift decision as to the right action to take—and for carrying it out. In short, in contradistinction to the typical fragmentariness of both Schlegels and Wilcoxes, Mrs. Wilcox here exhibits a serene wholeness of being that may serve as a touchstone among the broken arches. And it is with "tenderness"—the tenderness that connects the monk and the beast—that she smiles at her irate son before turning to her flowers.

3

THE MARRIAGE of Margaret and Mr. Wilcox seems designed to test the possibility of the achievement of wholeness (of a kind epitomized by Mrs. Wilcox) through the union of opposites. The trouble is that it is difficult to accept the verisimilitude of the marriage on a literal level, it being hard to believe Margaret could marry a man who is so obviously lacking in all the qualities she values most; and since the marriage is a central event in the plot, the status of the fiction as a whole is undermined. Nor does the strenuousness of the novelist's asseverations help us suspend our disbelief: "Some day—in the millenium—there may be no need for [Mr. Wilcox's] type. At present, homage is due to it from those who think themselves superior, and who possibly are" (p. 165).

The superiority is all on Mr. Wilcox's side in the first difference between the couple that materializes after their marriage. When Helen, who is keeping her pregnancy from the family, refuses to see Margaret and Tibby though she is back in England, Margaret finds her behavior so strange as to lead her to believe she must be ill—and turns for help to Mr. Wilcox. He proposes that they trick Helen into going to Howards End, and that Margaret should meet her there. Margaret's immediate response is to reject the plan as "quite impossible" because "it's not the particular language" that she and Helen talk (pp. 277–78). Mr. Wilcox becomes impatient, demanding to know whether she wants his help or not, and (as the wheel comes full circle) requiring a "plain answer" to a "plain question":

By now Margaret wished she had never mentioned her trouble to her husband. Retreat was impossible. He was determined to push the matter to a satisfactory conclusion, and Helen faded as he talked. Her fair, flying hair and eager eyes counted for nothing, for she was ill, without rights, and any of her friends might hunt her. Sick at heart, Margaret joined in the chase. She wrote her sister a lying letter, at her husband's dictation; she said the furniture was all at Howards End, but could be seen on Monday next at 3.0 p.m., when a charwoman would be in attendance. It was a cold letter, and the more plausible for that. Helen would think she was offended. And on Monday next she and Henry were to lunch with Dolly, and then ambush themselves in the garden. (pp. 278–79)

What Mr. Wilcox does is to force Margaret to assume the manner of the committee-room, and so transform Helen, who "fades as he talks," from a person into a problem, to be dealt with as effectively as possible. But the ethic of action in the "great outer life" is exposed, as references to the hunt and the chase and ambushes multiply, as the way of the jungle, an ethic drawn, indeed, "from the wolf-pack" (p. 277). Mr. Wilcox's management of the matter is as efficient as ever; when Margaret, however, capitulates to the business mind that dictates the cold, lying letter, she does not so much learn how to supply the deficiency in her own makeup as forfeit all integrity. Her own earlier reflections on Helen's too easy dismissal of "the outer life" are instructive in this regard:

Perhaps Margaret grew too old for metaphysics, perhaps Henry was weaning her from them, but she felt that there was something a little unbalanced in the mind that so readily shreds the visible. The businessman who assumes that this life is everything, and the mystic who asserts that it is nothing, fail, on this side and on that, to hit the truth. "Yes, I see, dear; it's about halfway between," Aunt Juley had hazarded in earlier years. No; truth, being alive, was not halfway between anything. It was only to be found by continuous excursions into either realm, and though proportion is the final secret, to espouse it at the outset is to ensure sterility. (pp. 195–96)

It is one of the important passages in the book, an indication of how oppositions within the self which do not admit (like that of the monk and the beast) of resolution through the catalyst of sexual tenderness may be reconciled—a passage, like that on the rainbow bridge which immediately precedes it, that strikingly prefigures D. H. Lawrence's views. No easy balance between the opposed attributes of the self—

like that of equal weights on a seesaw—no simple "proportion," is possible. The balance required is that of relationship, the maintenance—
as the effort is made to give maximum expression to the opposed aspects of the self by "continuous excursions" into both "realms"—of a
connection with the opposite, a connection that is retained at all
times, even on an excursion into the furthermost regions of one of the
realms. It is such habitual connection, I take it, that leads to "the final
secret" of proportion. And it is this connection, as she ventures into
the "public" sphere of businesslike action, that Margaret lets drop, for
she altogether obliterates the "personal."

On the day of the ambush, however, Margaret suddenly decides that
she will have to be "on [Helen's] side" (p. 282); and when she sees her
and realizes the explanation of her behavior, her conflict is resolved.
She then persuades Mr. Wilcox to leave her alone with Helen, and they
are reconciled:

> And the triviality faded from their faces, though it left something behind—
> the knowledge that they never could be parted because their love was rooted in
> common things. Explanations and appeals had failed; they had tried for a com-
> mon meeting-ground, and had only made each other unhappy. And all the time
> their salvation was lying round them—the past sanctifying the present; the
> present, with wild heart-throb, declaring that there would after all be a future,
> with laughter and the voices of children. Helen, still smiling, came up to her
> sister. She said: "It is always Meg." They looked into each other's eyes. The
> inner life had paid. (pp. 291–92)

In this passage the novelist begins an astonishing reversal of direction
(which he maintains from this point to the end of the narrative), a reversal in which all that has previously been aimed at is quietly abandoned. When the triviality "[fades] from their faces," as Helen previously faded in the making of plans for the ambush, the novelist's
impelling desire to reconcile opposites seems to fade too. The "inner
life" has not only "paid" but done so in its own coin, routing the other.
Though it was previously in the connection of opposites that "salvation" was said to lie, it now appears to inhere in the irresistible pull of
like to like. It is now mutuality that is supreme, whose hold is un-
breakable and productive of an enduring oneness or wholeness, for it is
the fact that they and their love are "rooted in common things" that
ensures they "never [can] be parted."[5] As like pulls close to like in
negation of a great deal that has gone before, it appears, at least in part,
to be because of the pressure of unacknowledged matter which enters
the novel at this point—the pressure, we may infer, of Forster's own
unacknowledged homosexuality (though of course there are no sexual

overtones of any kind in the actual relationship of the sisters). That something like a disturbance of this nature is taking place is subsequently suggested when Helen, who has announced she intends to have her child in Germany and knows nothing of the rupture that has in the meanwhile developed between Margaret and Mr. Wilcox, seems equal to destroying their relationship once again—this time with malice aforethought—for she suddenly, and "seriously," asks Margaret to go to Germany with her (p. 306), to leave her husband, we must assume, for her. Furthermore, if "the past [sanctifies] the present" and begets the reunion of the sisters, the future that the present "declares" (with such a "wild heart-throb") will come "with laughter and the voices of children" proves to be more than niggardly, for Margaret seals it with a declaration of her own: "I do not love children," she tells Helen in the closing pages of the novel. "I am thankful to have none" (p. 327). The laughter, therefore, is confined to one child, the illegitimate child Helen bears after Bast's death, who grows up at Howards End in the ménage of the two sisters and a broken man.

The rupture between Margaret and Mr. Wilcox develops when she goes to ask his permission for Helen and herself to spend the night at Howards End. Mr. Wilcox, it appears, has in no way been prepared by marriage to Margaret for what is to be "the crisis of his life," nor taught how to respond to people. He weighs the request as if it were "a business proposition," and evasively turns it down, finally saying he cannot treat Helen "as if nothing [has] happened," and that he would be "false to [his] position in society" if he did (pp. 298–99). Margaret makes a last effort and asks him to forgive Helen, as he may "hope to be forgiven," and as he has "actually been forgiven":

Perhaps some hint of her meaning did dawn on him. If so, he blotted it out. Straight from his fortress he answered: "I seem rather unaccommodating, but I have some experience of life, and know one thing leads to another. I am afraid that your sister had better sleep at the hotel. I have my children and the memory of my dear wife to consider. I am sorry, but see that she leaves my house at once."

"You have mentioned Mrs. Wilcox."

"I beg your pardon?"

"A rare occurrence. In reply, may I mention Mrs. Bast?"

"You have not been yourself all day," said Henry, and rose from his seat with face unmoved. Margaret rushed at him and seized both his hands. She was transfigured.

"Not any more of this!" she cried. "You shall see the connection if it kills you, Henry!" (p. 300)

In his "fortress" Mr. Wilcox remains impenetrable, holding to the public duties of his "position in society" and his role as father and husband of the late Mrs. Wilcox—and also, as he declares to his son, defending "the rights of property" (p. 317). It is evident, moreover, that a sanctimonious and unredeemed monk still peeps from behind the ramparts. Helen, by contrast, is altogether vulnerable in her exposed situation, but asks for nothing more than the right to make her personal choices and lead her private life. When Margaret chooses between the two, she is "transfigured": it is a momentous development, for it marks her abandonment of the role of loyal wife and her recovery of an old self, which insists now on a "connection" that may break rather than make Mr. Wilcox—and is prepared to storm the fortress even "if it kills" him. This self is moved to repudiate him utterly, and she sees him as if for the first time in all his stupidity, hypocrisy, cruelty, and contemptibility (p. 300). The "crime," she will have him recognize at last, is not Helen's but his.

After Margaret has made her way back to Helen at Howards End, she determines to leave her husband and go with her sister to Germany (p. 318). She is prevented from doing so only by Bast's death and—when Charles is sentenced to three years' imprisonment—by Mr. Wilcox's collapse: "Then Henry's fortress gave way. He could bear no one but his wife, he shambled up to Margaret afterwards and asked her to do what she could with him. She did what seemed easiest—she took him down to recruit at Howards End" (p. 325). When the fortress finally gives way, Mr. Wilcox must be thought to disintegrate into nothingness since this is what we have consistently been led to expect. But the novelist seems rather to wish to leave us with the impression that the long-sought "connection" is somehow finally achieved in the marriage, despite the fact that the broken arch has been left to lean on nothing. Helen is made to say enviously to Margaret, "I see you loving Henry, and understanding him better daily, and I know that death wouldn't part you in the least"; and Margaret, with an unaccustomed smugness, is made to say in reply:

"All over the world men and women are worrying because they cannot develop as they are supposed to develop. Here and there they have the matter out, and it comforts them. . . . Don't you see that all this leads to comfort in the end? It is part of the battle against sameness. Differences—eternal differences, planted by God in a single family, so that there may always be colour; sorrow perhaps, but colour in the daily gray." (pp. 327–28)

As we consider the devastations of the goblins, we cannot help feeling that this late appearance of a rainbow in the daily gray is novelistic legerdemain.

PART THREE

GENERIC UNITY: THE
BILDUNGSROMAN TRAJECTORY

MANSFIELD PARK: THE PLACE OF SELF

The opening discussion between Sir Thomas Bertram and Mrs. Norris as to the desirability of taking the young Fanny Price off the hands of her hard-pressed parents and offering her a home at Mansfield Park poses questions on which the rest of the narrative turns. Sir Thomas perceives that, if Fanny is to be brought up at Mansfield, they will be morally obligated "to secure to her . . . the provision of a gentlewoman" (p. 7);[1] for otherwise she might ultimately be suspended between two spheres, having been lifted above Portsmouth but left without the means to maintain herself in the Mansfield style. From the outset, that is, Sir Thomas is concerned with the problem of Fanny's social place, and the question raised by the narrative is what that place will be. At the same time Sir Thomas is equally concerned that Fanny be given a due sense of her proper place in his own household. It must be quite clear that his two sons are beyond her, and that there be no possibility of "cousins in love" (p. 6). Equally a needed distinction must be made between her and his daughters, though it prove difficult "to preserve in the minds of [his] *daughters* the consciousness of what they are, without making them think too lowly of their cousin; and . . . , without depressing her spirits too far, to make her remember that she is not a *Miss Bertram*" (p. 10). The distinction between Fanny and Sir Thomas's daughters—and her indeterminate position at Mansfield—are both nicely pointed by the location of the room she is given:

"I suppose, sister," [Mrs. Norris says to Lady Bertram], "you will put the child in the little white attic, near the old nurseries. It will be much the best place for her, so near Miss Lee, and not far from the girls, and close by the housemaids, who could either of them help dress her you know, and take care of her clothes, for I suppose you would not think it fair to expect Ellis to wait on her as well as the others. Indeed, I do not see that you could possibly place her any where else." (pp. 9–10)[2]

For the ten-year-old child Mansfield is a far cry from Portsmouth, a world apart, but that is nothing like the distance she travels as she moves from the attic to the nearby parsonage, when she finally goes there as Edmund Bertram's wife.

Where Sir Thomas concentrates on the question of Fanny's place, Mrs. Norris, in seeking to answer his objections to the proposed move, insists on the degree to which Fanny may be shaped by Mansfield and so fitted for her due place in life. One need not worry about having to provide for her, she intimates, since she may be expected to win "a creditable establishment" for herself: "Give a girl an education, and introduce her properly into the world, and ten to one but she has the means of settling well, without farther expense to any body" (p. 6). Mrs. Norris, that is, affirms that a child whom one has "in a manner taken into one's own hands" (p. 6) may be appropriately molded; and so alerts us to the fact that Fanny, when she first comes to Mansfield, is like so much unworked clay. Much has been made in critical discussion of *Mansfield Park* of the difference between the unappealing personality of Fanny Price and that of Jane Austen's sparkling—and more typical— heroines, such as Elizabeth Bennet and Emma Woodhouse; but it may perhaps be as well to comment on an essential difference between them that the narrative of *Mansfield Park* forces on our attention. Elizabeth and Emma are fully formed at the outset, needing only to be tempered and chastened by experience, but Fanny is in more than one sense a nonentity at the start of her story. The other major question posed by the opening discussion of Sir Thomas and Mrs. Norris is the nature of the self Fanny will develop at Mansfield; and, starting ab ovo, as it were, Fanny may be regarded as a prototypical *Bildungsroman* heroine, a forerunner of such figures as Jane Eyre and Maggie Tulliver.[3]

In the same discussion Mrs. Norris also sets out to allay another of Sir Thomas's anxieties, but, in doing so, she adverts us to a problem which, I shall argue, is never satisfactorily resolved. Fanny, she maintains, may not only be made eligible for desirable suitors but also inaccessible to the Bertram boys. It is all a question, she suggests, of "bringing up" and "breeding," of another kind of molding. "You are thinking of your sons," she says to Sir Thomas, "but do not you know that of all things upon earth *that* is the least likely to happen; brought up, as they would be, always together like brothers and sisters? It is morally impossible. I never knew an instance of it. It is, in fact, the only sure way of providing against the connection." And she roundly adds: "breed her up with them from this time, and suppose her even to have the beauty of an angel, and she will never be more to either than a sister" (pp. 6–7). Fanny's movement along one line of the narrative from attic to parsonage runs parallel to—and is dependent on—her transformation on another line from sister to wife. Regrettably, it is only by sleight of hand that the novelist makes the lines converge; but they traverse the narrative and shape its main concerns. The attic is an insignificant part of Mansfield, but Fanny is at the center of *Mansfield Park*. The account of her growth to maturity is the focus—as it is the unifying principle— of the narrative; and the depiction of her development effectively subsumes the stories of greater personages whose lives meet in the house.

2

REMOVED from the place she has always known at Portsmouth, Fanny is transplanted to Mansfield, to take root there as she can. The opening description of this most problematic of Jane Austen's heroines is striking for its negations, as if Fanny exists more by what she is not than what she is:

> Fanny Price was at this time just ten years old, and though there might not be much in her first appearance to captivate, there was, at least, nothing to disgust her relations. She was small of her age, with no glow of complexion, nor any other striking beauty; exceedingly timid and shy, and shrinking from notice; but her air, though awkward, was not vulgar, her voice was sweet, and when she spoke, her countenance was pretty. (p. 12)

Not only, we register, is Fanny not captivating—and since this is a deficiency which is never remedied, she is at once opposed to that most captivating pair, Henry Crawford and his sister Mary, when they duly appear. Not only is she small physically, taking up very little room; she is so shrinking by nature that she hardly seems to be there at all. This apparent absence of even a minimum sense of self is further evident in the first scene in which she figures dramatically. After she has been at Mansfield a week, Edmund finds her "sitting crying on the attic stairs." Though he is compassionate—and his continued kindness to her from this point on ensures her devotion to him—he is at first unable to elicit what is the matter. Finally it emerges that her desolation is not merely due to her homesickness but that she has promised to write to her brother William and is crying because she does not have any paper on which to do so (pp. 15–16). What Fanny lacks, therefore, is not so much writing paper as even the modicum of self-confidence that would have enabled her to ask for it. Nor does continued residence at Mansfield give her that confidence. Though she begins to find things "less strange," Fanny's initial way of coping with her situation is to fit herself to her circumstances, striving "to catch the best manner of conforming" to the people round her (p. 17), seeking, that is, to take the shape of the place offered her in her new home. It is possible, indeed, to describe the major trajectory of the action of *Mansfield Park*, in so far as it follows the fortunes of its heroine, in terms of place and self, and of the changing relation between them. In the first phase of the action, which extends more or less to the end of volume 1 in the first edition, it is Fanny's sense of her place that determines the shape of her self. In the second phase, it is the size and shape of the self she has developed that determines the nature of the place she finally takes in the world. And it is the extent of the change in Fanny by the end of the novel that significantly differentiates her from Elizabeth Bennet and Emma Woodhouse—and that makes the opening presentation of her childhood so important, for her subsequent development is measured against it.

Not that there is evidence of much change in Fanny up to the time the Crawfords arrive for their visit at the parsonage when she is eighteen and the main action of the novel begins. As a child she suffers a great deal at the hands of the Bertram sisters, Maria and Julia, but though she is "often mortified" by their "treatment" of her, she thinks "too lowly of her own claims to feel injured by it" (p. 20). And though Edmund does his best "to conquer the diffidence" that prevents her "good qualities" from being "more apparent" (pp. 21–22), her diffidence is an outward manifestation of her own inner lack of belief in the very existence of such qualities. She is fifteen when she first allows herself an open expression of resentment. The occasion is the death of Mr. Norris and the departure of Mrs. Norris from the parsonage, it being assumed by the Bertrams that she will take Fanny to live with her in her new house. When Lady Bertram tells Fanny this, she finds the news "as disagreeable . . . as it [has] been unexpected," but she is completely submissive in her aunt's presence. To Edmund, however, she speaks out: "Cousin," she says, "something is going to happen which I do not like at all; and though you have often persuaded me into being reconciled to things that I disliked at first, you will not be able to do it now" (p. 25). Clearly Fanny's readiness to reveal herself is dependent on feelings of security or insecurity aroused in her by her interlocutor, the sense of her own worth being so uncertain because it comes, in the first instance, from outside. Her general sense of insecurity is radical, for she is said to have a mind that has "seldom known a pause in its alarms or embarrassments" (p. 35). And even with Edmund, though she allows

herself an uncharacteristic rebelliousness in the scene referred to, this
is mitigated by the weakness of the self-pity that she also permits herself, the self-pity fusing her sense of place and self:

> "I can never be important to any one."
> "What is to prevent you?"
> "Every thing—my situation—my foolishness and awkwardness." (p. 26)

Trying to console her, Edmund assures her that, while at Mansfield
there are "too many" whom she "can hide behind," with Mrs. Norris
she will be "forced to speak" for herself and "to do justice" to her "natural powers" (p. 27). It is not so much a matter, however, of her hiding
behind other people as behind herself, withdrawing into herself to a
degree that the powers which at this stage Edmund alone discerns are
habitually obscured. When the Crawfords appear on the scene, Mary is
at a loss to know whether Fanny is "out" or not (p. 48); and her query
inadvertently points in more than one direction.

The visit to Sotherton is the first major episode after the arrival of
the Crawfords, an episode that has justly and widely been singled out
for praise. When Mrs. Norris proposes arrangements for the visit, it is
evident that there is no place for Fanny among the privileged—"I dare
say Mr. Crawford would take my two nieces and me in his barouche,"
she says, "and Edmund can go on horseback, you know, sister, and Fanny will stay at home with you" (p. 62)—and it is only Edmund's inter-
vention that enables Fanny to join the visiting party. Their departure is
the occasion of a fine enactment in miniature of what is to become a
significant concern in the novel:

> Wednesday was fine, and soon after breakfast the barouche arrived, Mr.
> Crawford driving his sisters; and as every body was ready, there was nothing to
> be done but for Mrs. Grant to alight and the others to take their places. The
> place of all places, the envied seat, the post of honour, was unappropriated. To
> whose happy lot was it to fall? While each of the Miss Bertrams were meditat-
> ing how best, and with most appearance of obliging the others, to secure it, the
> matter was settled by Mrs. Grant's saying, . . . "As there are five of you, it will
> be better that one should sit with Henry, and as you were saying lately, that you
> wished you could drive, Julia, I think this will be a good opportunity for you to
> take a lesson."
> Happy Julia! Unhappy Maria! The former was on the barouche-box in a mo-
> ment, the latter took her seat within, in gloom and mortification; and the
> carriage drove off. (p. 80)

It is not only in the barouche that the way in which the young people
"take their places" will be registered, and the departure for Sotherton,

like the visit itself, is suggestively proleptic of much that is to follow. Mrs. Grant's allocation of "the place of all places" to Julia is dictated by her sense of what is fit and proper: since the "post of honour" must clearly be given to one of the Bertram sisters, and since Maria is engaged to Mr. Rushworth, it is Julia who obviously has the right to it. But Maria wants "the envied seat" as much as her sister, and so shows—and continues to show throughout the visit—that she is not prepared to abide by accepted notions of what her proper place is. In due course she will be ready to go much further in order to secure that coveted place. It is notable that Fanny is not considered by anyone as having a possible claim to the choice position—she is not even mentioned—but in the whirligig of time it will be Crawford himself who will offer her a position beside him.

At Sotherton the party visits the chapel, which is no longer used for prayers. "Every generation has its improvements," says Mary Crawford to Edmund, "with a smile," and she continues:

"Cannot you imagine with what unwilling feelings the former belles of the house of Rushworth did many a time repair to this chapel? The young Mrs. Eleanors and Mrs. Bridgets—starched up into seeming piety, but with heads full of something very different—especially if the poor chaplain were not worth looking at—and, in those days, I fancy parsons were very inferior even to what they are now."

For a few moments she was unanswered. Fanny coloured and looked at Edmund, but felt too angry for speech; and *he* needed a little recollection before he could say, "Your lively mind can hardly be serious even on serious subjects. You have given us an amusing sketch, and human nature cannot say it was not so. We must all feel *at times* the difficulty of fixing our thoughts as we could wish; but if you are supposing it a frequent thing, that is to say, a weakness grown into a habit from neglect, what could be expected from the *private* devotions of such persons? Do you think the minds which are suffered, which are indulged in wandcrings in a chapel, would be more collected in a closet?"

"Yes, very likely. They would have two chances at least in their favour. There would be less to distract the attention from without, and it would not be tried so long." . . .

While this was passing, the rest of the party being scattered about the chapel, Julia called Mr. Crawford's attention to her sister, by saying, "Do look at Mr. Rushworth and Maria, standing side by side, exactly as if the ceremony were going to be performed. Have not they completely the air of it?"

Mr. Crawford smiled his acquiescence, and stepping forward to Maria, said, in a voice which she only could hear, "I do not like to see Miss Bertram so near the altar." (pp. 86–88)

What is dramatized here in the first instance is the clash of styles of Mary and Edmund. Mary is above all bright and lively—Edmund tries to mitigate her offense by taking her "lively mind" into account—vivid in her evocation of the "starched up" young ladies, quick, witty, ironic, unconventional, even a little scandalous. And she strikes the distinctive Crawford note, for though Henry does not say much in the quoted passage, his remark is of the same caliber and his habitual tone is much like hers. Edmund, by contrast, though he certainly reveals that his heart is in the right place, comes across as prosy and sententious, forbiddingly dull. Fanny does no more than color and look at Edmund, but her style is much like his, for it is he who has "formed her mind" (p. 64), and she thinks and speaks (when she allows herself) as he does. If Edmund will want to marry Mary and Henry Fanny, the demarcation of true compatibility is insinuated here—though the idea of Edmund and Fanny as Mr. and Mrs. Bertram has alarmed some readers: "What imagination will not quail before the thought of a Saturday night at the Edmund Bertrams, after the prayer-books have been put away?" remarks Marvin Mudrick;[4] while Kingsley Amis reflects that "to invite Mr. and Mrs. Edmund Bertram round for the evening would not be lightly undertaken."[5]

Clearly, however, it is not merely a clash of styles that is at issue but oppugnant values and conceptions of the self. What lies behind the Crawfords' liveliness is the need for a constant provision of amusement, both for others and themselves, and to that end everything is grist to their mill, even the sort of "serious subject" which Edmund expects Mary to take seriously. On another occasion Fanny indignantly asks Edmund what right Mary has to suppose that he "would not write long letters" if he were away from home, and Edmund answers: "The right of a lively mind, Fanny, seizing whatever may contribute to its own amusement or that of others" (p. 64). There is something predatory about Mary's readiness to "seize" on amusement, a readiness that has its coordinate in a "natural" assertiveness on her part. Mary as instinctively thrusts herself forward as Fanny inclines to hide behind others or withdraw into herself, her self-abnegation being contrasted to Mary's self-assertion and that of her brother. His is the more dangerous because it is more decidedly predatory—and issues in action rather than in mere talk. When he makes his joke about the altar, he intimates to Maria that he is no more ready than she to accept conventional notions of a woman's place, particularly as regards marriage, and he initiates a course of action that leads ultimately to the breakup of her marriage to Rushworth. But the point is that he engages in this game, to start with, at any rate, as no more than an amusement, being pleased to flirt as provocatively with Julia as Maria.[6] "The sisters," we are told, "handsome, clever, and encouraging, [are] an amusement to his sated mind," and he is not accustomed to consider what the "indulgence of his idle vanity" may lead to (pp. 114–15). The narrator's comment is of profound importance, for it establishes the perspective in which the ensuing action is to be viewed. It is not merely a Lady Bertram, lolling on her sofa, who is to be seen as a monitory example of self-indulgence; Crawford, in his very liveliness, is as firmly viewed as self-indulgent. Crawford's kind of self-indulgence, indeed, is set against its ideal opposite (as that is also defined at Sotherton) and is presented as the pole to which the errant self swings.

From the chapel the party goes into the wilderness, "a planted wood of about two acres." When Maria and Crawford want to move into the park beyond, they find that the gate to it is locked. Rushworth volunteers to fetch the key, and the two remain together with Fanny, Edmund and Mary having gone off together. Crawford pursues the game he has started with Maria, remarking on her fair prospects: "You have a very smiling scene before you," he says:

"Do you mean literally or figuratively? Literally I conclude. Yes, certainly, the sun shines and the park looks very cheerful. But unluckily that iron gate, that ha-ha, give me a feeling of restraint and hardship. I cannot get out, as the starling said." As she spoke, and it was with expression, she walked to the gate; he followed her. "Mr. Rushworth is so long fetching this key!"

"And for the world you would not get out without the key and without Mr. Rushworth's authority and protection, or I think you might with little difficulty pass round the edge of the gate, here, with my assistance; I think it might be done, if you really wished to be more at large, and could allow yourself to think it not prohibited."

"Prohibited! nonsense! I certainly can get out that way, and I will. Mr. Rushworth will be here in a moment you know—we shall not be out of sight."

"Or if we are, Miss Price will be so good as to tell him, that he will find us near that knoll, the grove of oak on the knoll."

Fanny, feeling all this to be wrong, could not help making an effort to prevent it. "You will hurt yourself, Miss Bertram," she cried, "you will certainly hurt yourself against those spikes—you will tear your gown—you will be in danger of slipping into the ha-ha. You had better not go."

Her cousin was safe on the other side, while these words were spoken, and smiling with all the good-humour of success, she said, "Thank you, my dear Fanny, but I and my gown are alive and well, and so good bye. (pp. 99–100)

This scene has been much praised for the way in which Jane Austen's art effortlessly accommodates a realistic surface to symbolic depths, pointing in the most natural manner to the future development of the relationship between Crawford and Maria. The general drift of meaning is clear enough, but the question is what precisely is symbolized once Maria picks up the gauntlet Crawford throws down. Tony Tanner, in what seems to me to be the best critical account of the novel, offers the following reading of the scene: "The gate—perfect image for the rigid restrictions imposed by the conventions of civilized life—is locked. Mr. Rushworth goes to fetch the key. Being engaged to Maria, he is in many ways the lawful person to 'open the gates' (there is perhaps a reference to virginity here, just as the locked garden represents virginity in medieval paintings)."[7] This is suggestive but perhaps over-specific. The gate is not the only "image" we have to deal with, for the ha-ha is as important in the scene, and what both the gate and the ha-ha directly figure for Maria and Crawford are obstacles to going where they want. By natural extension, these obstacles may be seen as evocative not so much of "the conventions of civilized life" as of any imposed, external restraint to doing what one wants. Maria, indeed, says that the gate and the ha-ha give her "a feeling of restraint and hardship." It is no doubt Rushworth's place to open the gate for Maria in the sense suggested by Tanner; but, more directly, the key figures as a means to a legitimate way out, and it is Rushworth who holds the key, who alone can release Maria and sanction her exit from the "wilderness" in which she finds herself. Crawford, on the other hand, is eager to demonstrate to Maria that he can safely lead her round the obstacles to their continuing on their way together— despite Rushworth. What the scene beautifully dramatizes, therefore, as Maria and Crawford safely proceed to the other side of the gate and the fence, is the inefficacy of external restraints, for one can always get round or over them, and the lack of self-restraint on the part of Maria and Crawford. The wilderness at Sotherton may be as distant from the jungles of Africa or of a desert island as one would normally consider Jane Austen to be from both Joseph Conrad and William Golding; but in *Mansfield Park* her presentation of the need for self-command—when external restraints are removed or ineffective—is as insistent as that in "Heart of Darkness" and *Lord of the Flies*. It is when Sir Thomas has to go to Antigua that the Miss Bertrams are "relieved by [his absence] from all restraint" and feel themselves "to have every indulgence within their reach" (p. 32). What the scene at Sotherton also does is to define self-command as the value opposed to self-indulgence, these two possibilities being set up as the opposed poles between which the characters move. And at Sotherton self-command is viewed as subsuming a number of other qualities: Julia is said to lack "that higher species of self-command" that stems from a "just consideration of others," a "knowledge of [one's] own heart," and a "principle of right" (p. 91). The central opposition between self-command and self-indulgence thus also generates other polarities: a consideration of others is set against amusing one's self at their expense, self-knowledge against self-deception, and principle against desire.[8]

Fanny's response in the scene at the iron gate is interesting. Her sensitivity to the implications of what is going on between Maria and Crawford makes her "[feel] all this to be wrong," but at the same time her sense of her own place in relation to them makes it extremely difficult for her to say anything. Despite this, she does "make an effort" to prevent their going off into the park; and, in emphasizing the risks that Maria appears to be indifferent to, Fanny seems to me to do all that can reasonably be expected of her.[9] Certainly she shows more awareness than anyone else of what Henry is up to:

> Fanny was the only one of the party who found any thing to dislike; but since the day at Sotherton, she could never see Mr. Crawford with either sister without observation, and seldom without wonder or censure; and had her confidence in her own judgment been equal to her exercise of it in every other respect, had she been sure that she was seeing clearly, and judging candidly, she would probably have made some important communications to her usual confidant. As it was, however, she only hazarded a hint, and the hint was lost. "I am rather surprised," said she, "that Mr. Crawford should come back again so soon, after being here so long before, full seven weeks; for I had understood he was so very fond of change and moving about, that I thought something would certainly occur when he was once gone, to take him elsewhere. He is used to much gayer places than Mansfield."
> "It is to his credit," was Edmund's answer, "and I dare say it gives his sister pleasure. She does not like his unsettled habits."
> "What a favourite he is with my cousins!"
> "Yes, his manners to women are such as must please. Mrs. Grant, I believe, suspects him of a preference for Julia; I have never seen much symptom of it, but I wish it may be so. He has no faults but what a serious attachment would remove."
> "If Miss Bertram were not engaged," said Fanny cautiously, "I could sometimes almost think that he admired her more than Julia."
> "Which is, perhaps, more in favour of his liking Julia best, than you, Fanny, may be aware; for I believe it often happens, that a man, before he has quite made up his own mind, will distinguish the sister or intimate friend of the woman he is really thinking of, more than the woman herself. Crawford has too much sense to stay here if he found himself in any danger from Maria; and I am not at all afraid for her, after such proof as she has given, that her feelings are not strong."
> Fanny supposed she must have been mistaken, and meant to think differently in future. (pp. 115–16)

This passage marks an important stage in Fanny's development. What it highlights, first, is the growth of her perceptiveness. She alone, of all the people at Mansfield, sees through Crawford, for it is she alone—even though she may doubt herself—who "sees clearly." And her in-

sight is firmly set here against Edmund's blindness, his blatant failure
to understand either his sisters or Crawford, even though he is more
often than not presented as a model of right thinking. Fanny, moreover,
does not only see clearly but knows what to make of what she sees, as
her "censure" of Crawford indicates. Though her developing powers are
thus plainly registered, she still manifests an undermining lack of confidence, a lack which makes her conclude, in the end, that she is mistaken when she is right. This lack, however, is an indication of the
novelist's sureness of touch, for she presents Fanny as only slowly
growing into herself and not at all as the paragon she is often taken to
be. In this scene, indeed, she emerges as distinctively human: as she
moves from slight hint to broad insinuation in regard to Crawford, it is
evident that, at any rate in the security of her relationship with her
"confidant," she is not above sly innuendo, even (a cautious) meanness.

That Fanny is certainly fallible is further indicated in the other major
episode of volume 1, the theatricals. This episode has perhaps attracted
more critical attention than any other in the novel, and reasons for the
condemnation of those taking part in the theatricals have been re-
hearsed as assiduously as *Lovers' Vows* at Mansfield. Suffice it to note
that, when Sir Thomas is at home, he "keeps every body in their place,"
as Mrs. Grant says (p. 162); and that, in general terms, it is the failure of
his children to maintain a due sense of their place in his absence—and
in view too of what Edmund calls Maria's "very delicate" situation (p.
125)—that accounts for their condemnation. Furthermore, their choice
of play exacerbates the offense: Coleridge drew attention in *Biographia
Literaria* to what he called "pernicious barbarisms and Kotzebuisms in
morals and taste";[10] and Marilyn Butler has stated that *Lovers' Vows*
was "notorious" at the time the novel appeared, for "critics and sati-
rists from *The Anti-Jacobin* on had made it a byword for moral and
social subversion."[11] The question that is worth pursuing further is the
precise bearing of the episode on the developing drama of self.

Lionel Trilling, in his famous but overrated essay on the novel, has
stated that what makes the theatricals "decisively objectionable" is "a
traditional, almost primitive, feeling about dramatic impersonation":
"It is the [Platonic] fear that the impersonation of a bad or inferior
character will have a harmful effect upon the impersonator; that, indeed, the impersonation of any other self will diminish the integrity of
the real self."[12] Some support for this view is provided by the way in
which Crawford initially responds to the idea of the theatricals:

Henry Crawford, to whom, in all the riot of his gratifications, [acting] was yet
an untasted pleasure, was quite alive at the idea. "I really believe," said he, "I

could be fool enough at this moment to undertake any character that ever was written, from Shylock or Richard III down to the singing hero of a farce in his scarlet coat and cocked hat. I feel as if I could be any thing or every thing." (p. 123)

Crawford's eagerness for the theatricals is not merely an additional instance of his unrelenting search for amusement, acting being an as yet "untasted pleasure" for him; that acting should be related to "the riot of his gratifications" suggests the abandon with which he turns to it. His willingness to "be any thing or every thing" points to his readiness to cease to be himself—and to the equanimity with which he risks that diminution of integrity of which Trilling writes. But that this is not the decisive issue soon becomes apparent when the jockeying for coveted roles in *Lovers' Vows* begins. Maria, hoping to play Agatha and feeling "all the interest" of the part in the matter of who plays Frederick, clears the way for Crawford, thus making "certain of the proper Frederick," by inducing Yates to take the role of Baron Wildenhaim (pp. 132–33). Maria, that is, far from ceasing to be herself in the play, is determined to remain herself while acting the part of Agatha, and to exploit to the full the opportunities afforded by the text for close contact with Crawford. But first she has to secure the part against the claims of her sister. The question is decided by Crawford, who, not slow to seize his opportunity after he has glanced at the first act of the play "with seeming carelessness," eliminates Julia: "I must entreat Miss *Julia* Bertram," he says, "not to engage in the part of Agatha, or it will be the ruin of all my solemnity" (p. 133). Similarly, Mary Crawford, who is to play Amelia, is more concerned with her own "fate" than that of the character: "Who is to be Anhalt?" she asks. "What gentleman among you am I to have the pleasure of making love to?" (p. 143). Even Rushworth, who chooses to play Count Cassel, is solely "engaged with what his own appearance [will] be" (p. 138).[13] It is with quiet calculation, therefore, that the party at Mansfield embark on the theatricals, each reckoning how his own desires may best be satisfied. This is nowhere more strongly evident than in the case of Edmund, who at first steadfastly opposes putting on the play, but then succumbs to the temptation of playing opposite Mary Crawford, manifestly concocting a justification for doing so (pp. 153–54). Just as self-knowledge is said to be necessary for self-command, as we have seen, so self-deception is now shown to be a concomitant of self-indulgence; and it is left to Fanny to wonder whether Edmund is "not deceiving himself" (p. 156).

It is not long before Fanny is compelled to apply such a query to herself as attempts are made to draw her too into the theatricals—and she is confronted by the first major test of her independent selfhood:

"Fanny," cried Tom Bertram . . . , "we want your services."

Fanny was up in a moment, expecting some errand, for the habit of employing her in that way was not yet overcome, in spite of all that Edmund could do.

"Oh! we do not want to disturb you from your seat. We do not want your *present* services. We shall only want you in our play. You must be Cottager's wife."

"Me!" cried Fanny, sitting down again with a most frightened look. "Indeed you must excuse me. I could not act any thing if you were to give me the world. No, indeed, I cannot act." (p. 145)

Fanny's own sense of her place at the time of the theatricals is neatly figured by the way in which she jumps up in response to Tom's demand for her services: clearly not considering herself to be one of them, she can only conceive of service to the assembled group in menial terms. When she realizes what is wanted of her, her reaction is complex. With one part of her, as her "most frightened look" indicates, everything that is shrinking in her shies away from the public exposure of acting. At the same time her emphatic statment that she "cannot act" points not so much to her own disabilities, for she goes on to insist that "it is not that [she is] afraid of learning by heart" (p. 145), as to her morally based refusal to take part in the given circumstances in that play, for she has earlier judged it to be "totally improper for home representation" (p. 137).[14] The ambiguity of her response epitomizes the indeterminateness of her development at this stage. On the one hand, she is now spirited enough and sufficiently sure of who she is not to let herself be misrepresented when Rushworth assumes she is "afraid of [learning] half a dozen speeches" (p. 145); on the other hand, she is not sure enough either of herself or her place to articulate her objection to participating. The pressure on her is enormous, for Tom's repeated "requisition" is then "backed" by the Crawfords and Yates and Mrs. Norris. The test that Fanny is called on to face here is whether she can stick to her principles in opposition to the whole social group which surrounds her. At issue is a capacity for resistance that is a precondition of self-command, for this is opposed not only to a yielding to one's own desires but also the desires of others. Fanny's emergent self may appear to be shaped by negation, as she continues to insist that she "cannot act," that it is "absolutely impossible" for her, that they "must excuse" her (p. 146)—and it is perhaps because she is shown as typically refusing to do things rather than doing them that she is less appealing than other Jane Austen heroines—but it is in such refusals that she is slowly steeled.

Not that Fanny is immune to doubt:

Was she *right* in refusing what was so warmly asked, so strongly wished for? what might be so essential to a scheme on which some of those to whom she owed the greatest complaisance, had set their hearts? Was it not ill-nature—selfishness—and a fear of exposing herself? And would Edmund's judgment, would his persuasion of Sir Thomas's disapprobation of the whole, be enough to justify her in a determined denial in spite of all the rest? It would be so horrible to her to act, that she was inclined to suspect the truth and purity of her own scruples. (p. 153)

As Fanny seeks to determine whether she is not deceiving herself about the impulses in which her refusal is grounded, her self-distrust is turned to positive account, for it consists in an awareness of self that is the basis of true strength—and of unusual insight. It is not by chance in the narrative design that this passage is immediately followed by Edmund's self-deceiving announcement to her of his decision to take part in the play.

The self-command that Fanny demonstrates, however, is short-lived. She is led, first, to compromise the absoluteness of her opposition to the theatricals: believing herself "to derive as much innocent enjoyment from the play as any of them," it becomes "a pleasure to *her* to creep into the theatre, and attend the rehearsal of the first act—in spite of the feelings it [excites] in some speeches for Maria"; and she makes herself "useful" both as prompter and spectator (p. 165). Then, when Mrs. Grant is unable to attend "the first regular rehearsal of the three first acts," the whole group begs Fanny to take Mrs. Grant's place. Even Edmund says, "Do Fanny, if it is not *very* disagreeable to you"; but still she "[hangs] back":

"You have only to *read* the part," said Henry Crawford with renewed entreaty.
"And I do believe she can say every word of it," added Maria, "for she could put Mrs. Grant right the other day in twenty places. Fanny, I am sure you know the part."
Fanny could not say she did *not*—as they all persevered—as Edmund repeated his wish, and with a look of even fond dependence on her good nature, she must yield. She would do her best. Every body was satisfied—and she was left to the tremors of a most palpitating heart, while the others prepared to begin. (pp. 171–72)

It is a significant moment of choice. Once again it is Fanny's shyness and sense of what she knows to be wrong that make her "hang back"—as her being unable to "endure the idea of it" (p. 171) richly if ambiguously suggests—and her recoil is set against her "yielding" to the pressure of the group. When her self-command falters in response to Edmund's renewed appeal, which assumes her willingness to comply, she finally gives way. It is true that Julia announces the return of Sir Thomas at this juncture, and that Fanny is consequently saved by the gong from actually participating in the rehearsal, but it needs to be stressed that she does give way here, for some influential critics seem to ignore this conclusion to the episode of the theatricals—perhaps misled by the account Edmund gives to his father: "We have all been more or less to blame," he says, "every one of us, excepting Fanny. Fanny is the only one who has judged rightly throughout, who has been consistent. *Her* feelings have been steadily against it from first to last. She never ceased to think of what was due to you. You will find Fanny every thing you could wish" (p. 187).[15] The point of Fanny's capitulation here is to prepare us for a recognition of her strength when she subsequently stands firm against much greater pressures in the much weightier matter of Crawford's proposal.

3

WHEN MARIA finally marries Rushworth, feeling that Crawford in abandoning her has "destroyed her happiness" (p. 202), the young couple proceed to Brighton, and Julia accompanies them. The departure of the Bertram sisters brings about a change in Fanny's place at Mansfield, for her "consequence [increases]" as a result (p. 205). Fanny's own sense of her changed status is registered by her beginning to have thoughts of what may be her due: when Dr. Grant one day invites Edmund to dine with him and ignores Fanny, she does not even try to repress "an unpleasant feeling." The fact of the change is given external confirmation by Mrs. Grant on the same occasion: "Mrs. Grant, with sudden recollection, [then] turned to her and asked for the pleasure of her company too. This was so new an attention, so perfectly new a circumstance in the events of Fanny's life, that she was all surprize and embarrassment" (p. 215). Not that Mrs. Norris is slow to tell her that if Julia "had been at home, [she] would not have been asked at all"; and that she should remember she "must be the lowest and last": "though Miss Crawford is in a manner at home, at the Parsonage," Mrs. Norris furthermore instructs her, "you are not to be taking place of her" (pp. 220–21). Nor is Fanny's habitual tendency to shrink into herself much altered, for when she dines at the parsonage, she is glad to be "suffered to sit silent and unattended to." What is noteworthy is that her wish to do so is characterized as "her favourite indulgence" (p. 223). In *Mansfield Park*, we realize, self-indulgence is shown to take many forms, ranging from the self-assertion of a Henry Crawford at one extreme to the self-abnegation of a Fanny Price at the other—with the indolence of a Lady

Bertram (reclining on her sofa) epitomizing a simple position in the middle.

Crawford, having returned suddenly to the area, is also one of the party at the parsonage, and on the morning after the dinner he announces his intention to spend another fortnight at Mansfield:

> "And how do you think I mean to amuse myself, Mary, on the days that I do not hunt? I am grown too old to go out more than three times a week; but I have a plan for the intermediate days, and what do you think it is?"
>
> "To walk and ride with me, to be sure."
>
> "Not exactly, though I shall be happy to do both, but *that* would be exercise only to my body, and I must take care of my mind. Besides *that* would be all recreation and indulgence, without the wholesome alloy of labour, and I do not like to eat the bread of idleness. No, my plan is to make Fanny Price in love with me." (p. 229)

Recurrent chords sound out strongly in this passage. It is in order "to amuse" himself that Crawford sets out quite coldly to play with Fanny's feelings; and though he differentiates this from the amusements offered him by Mary, it is not distinguished by the "labour" involved from mere self-indulgence. Crawford, that is, sets out here to repeat with Fanny the game he has played so successfully with the Bertram sisters, particularly Maria. He thus pays Fanny the compliment of regarding her in the same light as her cousins, and the fact that she is singled out by a man such as Crawford is dramatic testimony to her new status. But it is also indicative of his own propensities: "I never was so long in company with a girl in my life—trying to entertain her—and succeed so ill!" he says to Mary on the same occasion. "Never met with a girl who looked so grave on me! I must try to get the better of this. Her looks say, 'I will not like you, I am determined not to like you,' and I say, she shall" (p. 230). Jane Austen here anticipates Thomas Hardy, having Crawford enunciate a law of love that is repeatedly enacted in the work of the later novelist—namely, that there may be no greater attraction to some lovers than the indifference of the prospective beloved. To a man like Crawford it is the challenge to his own powers posed by the need to "get the better" of an unresponsive woman that is irresistible. Indeed, he is finally undone when he gives way to such an impulse in relation to Maria at the end of the narrative:

> He saw Mrs. Rushworth, was received by her with a coldness which ought to have been repulsive, and have established apparent indifference between them for ever; but he was mortified, he could not bear to be thrown off by the woman whose smiles had been so wholly at his command; he must exert himself to subdue so proud a display of resentment; it was anger on Fanny's account; he

must get the better of it, and make Mrs. Rushworth Maria Bertram again in her treatment of himself. (pp. 467–68)

Crawford is shown to be a prey not to the seductive wiles of a woman but to her coldness—which is to say that he is a prey to himself, to a compulsion to indulge his own desire for supremacy.

Given the intensity of Crawford's pursuit of her, it might appear that Fanny would inevitably succumb to him. The narrator, indeed, insists that she could not have "escaped heart-whole from the courtship . . . of such a man as Crawford, in spite of there being some previous ill-opinion of him to be overcome, had not her affection been engaged elsewhere" (p. 231). It is Fanny's love for Edmund that provides her with a protective armor—just as Emma Woodhouse's unconscious love for Knightley safeguards her against Churchill, another Crawford—but the ironic effect of Fanny's continued resistance is to attract Crawford more and more until he falls genuinely in love with her. When he tells his sister he intends to marry Fanny, he attempts to define the qualities that have attracted him to her, to describe "what sort of woman it is that can attach" him:

"Had you seen her this morning, Mary," he continued, "attending with such ineffable sweetness and patience, to all the demands of her aunt's stupidity, working with her, and for her, her colour beautifully heightened as she leant over the work, then returning to her seat to finish a note which she was previously engaged in writing for that stupid woman's service, and all this with such unpretending gentleness, so much as if it were a matter of course that she was not to have a moment at her own command, her hair arranged as neatly as it always is, and one little curl falling forward as she wrote . . . Had you seen her so, Mary, you would not have implied the possibility of her power over my heart ever ceasing." . . .

. . . "And [Maria and Julia] will now see their cousin treated as she ought to be . . . Yes, Mary, my Fanny will feel a difference indeed, a daily, hourly difference, in the behaviour of every being who approaches her; and it will be the completion of my happiness to know that I am the doer of it, that I am the person to give the consequence so justly her due. Now she is dependent, helpless, friendless, neglected, forgotten."

"Nay, Henry, not by all, not forgotten by all, not friendless or forgotten. Her cousin Edmund never forgets her." (pp. 296–97)

As Crawford spells out his sense of Fanny's "dependent, helpless, friendless, neglected, forgotten" condition, we are reminded of the opening discussion between Sir Thomas and Mrs. Norris and register that the baronet's fears about having to make adequate material provision for Fanny have proved groundless. To Crawford it appears to be an

added attraction that Fanny has neither money nor status to recommend her; and if there is a subtle taint of patronage in his contemplation of the way "the behaviour of every being who approaches her" will
change when he elevates her to his position and she is "treated as she
ought to be," his assertion that his ability to bring about such a change
will be "the completion of [his] happiness" is also sincere. It is significant, however, that he views "the consequence" he will bestow on her
as being no more than "her due." The wheel, we see, has come full
circle: if Fanny started by trying to fit herself to the place allocated her
at Mansfield, the place that Crawford now wants to offer her is regarded as no more than fitting for the kind of person she has become.
What is striking is that Crawford's noting of the qualities in Fanny
which have won his heart should so signally miss her essence. He
stresses her "sweetness and patience," her "unpretending gentleness,"
her tolerance in the face of her "aunt's stupidity," and the selflessness
with which she accepts she is "not to have a moment at her own command." Though doubtless admirable in themselves, these qualities all
point to Crawford's sense of Fanny's pliant malleability; what he has
not realized is that the meek and mild Fanny has that in her which will
not simply submit to being molded to his desires—that she has iron in
her soul.

Sir Thomas, acting in loco parentis, is the one who conveys
Crawford's formal proposal to Fanny. Sir Thomas has previously indicated that he now indeed wishes to treat her like one of his own
daughters: he has specially given a ball "for" her and her brother at
Mansfield (p. 252), which was the occasion not only of her "coming
out" but appearing as "the Queen of the evening" (p. 267). Sir Thomas
also insisted that she "lead the way and open the ball," thus ensuring
that she be "placed above . . . many elegant young women" and treated
just "like her cousins" (p. 275). It is with much satisfaction, therefore,
that he asks Fanny to accompany him downstairs in order to accept the
offer of so eligible a young man as Crawford. He is startled by her response: "Oh! no, Sir, I cannot, indeed I cannot go down to him"; and
when Sir Thomas intimates that she has given Crawford "encourage-
ment," she flares up: " 'You are mistaken, Sir,'—cried Fanny, forced by
the anxiety of the moment even to tell her uncle that he was wrong—
'You are quite mistaken. How could Mr. Crawford say such a
thing? . . . I begged him never to talk to me in that manner again' " (pp.
314–15). The scene at once invites comparison with that in which Fanny is requested to participate in the theatricals. Once again her immediate and instinctive response is negative, a declaration that she "cannot" do what is asked of her; what is striking now is that there is no
shrinking on her part, that, on the contrary, she is ready to explain and

justify her position by criticizing others, not merely Crawford, but even her dreaded uncle himself. Nor does she subsequently falter:

> "Am I to understand," said Sir Thomas, after a few moments silence, "that you mean to *refuse* Mr. Crawford?"
> "Yes, Sir."
> "Refuse him?"
> "Yes, Sir."
> "Refuse Mr. Crawford! Upon what plea? For what reason?"
> "I—I cannot like him, Sir, well enough to marry him."
> "This is very strange!" said Sir Thomas, in a voice of calm displeasure. "There is something in this which my comprehension does not reach. Here is a young man wishing to pay his addresses to you, with every thing to recommend him; not merely situation in life, fortune, and character, but with more than common agreeableness, with address and conversation pleasing to every body. And he is not an acquaintance of to-day, you have now known him some time. His sister, moreover, is your intimate friend, and he has been doing *that* for your brother, which I should suppose would have been almost sufficient recommendation to you, had there been no other. It is very uncertain when my interest might have got William on. He has done it already."
> "Yes," said Fanny, in a faint voice, and looking down with fresh shame; and she did feel almost ashamed of herself, after such a picture as her uncle had drawn, for not liking Mr. Crawford.
> . . . "I am half inclined to think, Fanny, that you do not quite know your own feelings."
> "Oh! yes, Sir, indeed I do. His attentions were always—what I did not like."
> (pp. 315–16)

As Sir Thomas slowly builds up what seems to be an overwhelming case for the acceptance of Crawford, who appears to have "every thing to recommend him," Fanny is called on to face the most demanding test of her selfhood, to place her personal inclination before all the worldly advantages the match offers—and so to pit herself against the world, her little world, which speedily endorses Sir Thomas's incomprehension of her refusal. Her position is made the more difficult in that it is impossible for her to divulge to Sir Thomas the two main reasons for her refusal, though she hints at both in saying she cannot "like" Crawford. She cannot admit to Sir Thomas that she is not in love with Crawford because she is in love with his son (though he does not appear to return her feeling), but she does from the first try to take a stand on principle, to insist on the need for what Sir Thomas leaves out, trusting that in time he will come to feel "how wretched, and how unpardonable, how hopeless and how wicked it [is], to marry without affection" (p. 324). She also cannot admit to Maria's father that she has not been able to like Crawford, that is, respect him, ever since she grasped what he was up to with his daughter, and that she has long registered how "dishonourably and unfeelingly" he can behave, and "what a corrupted mind" he has (p. 225). Fanny may be unable to speak out in both these respects, but what is notable in this scene is the absolute firmness of her stand, both her refusal at the beginning of the quoted passage and her insistence at the end being strong, direct, un- qualified, and uncompromising. Her stand is the more remarkable in that she takes it, in the first instance, in opposition to the man who of all men is the most awesome to her—and to whom she owes the most. Yet throughout the scene her behavior is characterized, despite her sense of shame, by her unwavering self-command, by a self-possession which is the most telling indication that she has now truly found her- self. And her firmness is based, in contradistinction to what Sir Thom- as says, on the quiet certainty with which she does know her own feel- ings—because she has now learned to know herself. She later reflects that though "romantic delicacy" is "not to be expected" of Sir Thomas, who has "married a daughter to Mr. Rushworth," she must "do her duty" (p. 331); it is a duty, it is evident, that she conceives of as being owed only to herself, to her sense of her own integrity—to the self in its wholeness as well as its probity.

Sir Thomas's attempt to sway Fanny is but the first of a series of pressures that are brought to bear on her—by Crawford himself, by Edmund, and by Mary—but none can move her. In the end Sir Thomas determines to try to make her see reason by sending her on a visit to her family in Portsmouth, trusting that her experience of conditions there will shake her into a due appreciation of the importance of a proper place in the world, the kind of place that Crawford can com- mand for her. Ironically, the visit to Portsmouth, though disturbing, succeeds only in shaking her the more firmly into herself. A trivial incident there—when Fanny joins a circulating library in order to ob- tain books for her sister Susan—becomes the occasion for the setting of a symbolic stamp on her already achieved selfhood: "She became a subscriber—amazed at being any thing *in propria persona*, amazed at her own doings in every way" (p. 398).

There remains the bringing together of Fanny and Edmund in mar- riage. Though this is a consummation devoutly to be wished, the nov- elist makes it appear somewhat perverse on Edmund's part. His disillu- sionment in Mary is convincing enough, for when Maria abandons her husband and runs off with Crawford, Edmund is shocked to realize Mary views this "only as folly," and that it is "the detection, not the offence which she [reprobates]" (p. 455). Fanny, moreover, to the end nothing like the paragon she has so often been alleged to be, takes good care to inform him that, with Tom apparently dying, Mary's interest in the putative heir to a title was not exactly disinterested, for Fanny feels "more than justified in adding to [Edmund's] knowledge of [Mary's] real character, by some hint of what share his brother's state of health might be supposed to have in her wish for a complete reconciliation" (p. 459). But Edmund's affections are displaced too easily from Mary to Fanny:

Edmund had greatly the advantage of [Mary] in this respect. He had not to wait and wish with vacant affections for an object worthy to succeed her in them. Scarcely had he done regretting Mary Crawford, and observing to Fanny how impossible it was that he should ever meet with such another woman, before it began to strike him whether a very different kind of woman might not do just as well—or a great deal better; whether Fanny herself were not growing as dear, as important to him in all her smiles, and all her ways, as Mary Crawford had ever been; and whether it might not be a possible, an hopeful undertaking to persuade her that her warm and sisterly regard for him would be foundation enough for wedded love.

I purposely abstain from dates on this occasion, that every one may be at liberty to fix their own, aware that the cure of unconquerable passions, and the transfer of unchanging attachments, must vary much as to time in different people.—I only intreat every body to believe that exactly at the time when it was quite natural that it should be so, and not a week earlier, Edmund did cease to care about Miss Crawford, and became as anxious to marry Fanny, as Fanny herself could desire.

With such a regard for her, indeed, as his had long been, a regard founded on the most endearing claims of innocence and helplessness, and completed by every recommendation of growing worth, what could be more natural than the change? (p. 470)

The superlative poise with which Jane Austen has conducted her narrative to this point wobbles badly here. First, Edmund's belief that Fanny's "warm and sisterly regard for him would be foundation enough for wedded love" suggests at the least, if one wishes to be charitable to him, a kind of naïveté which would indicate he is by no means ready for the married state. Moreover, her regard for him is not at all warm and sisterly; she has for long loved him as a woman. It is *his* regard for her that, as Mrs. Norris predicted, has from the start been warm and brotherly: at Fanny's first dinner party at the parsonage, for instance, Edmund tells her, "with the kind smile of an affectionate brother," how nice she looks (p. 222); when Fanny says goodbye to Edmund before leaving for Portsmouth, she has sadly to register that he is "giving her the affectionate farewell of a brother" (p. 374). His feeling remains unchanged as late as their reunion at Mansfield after the calamities that have fallen on the Bertram household: he presses her to his heart and says, "My Fanny—my only sister—my only comfort now" (p. 444). When he wishes to marry her, therefore, being suddenly "struck" by the possibility, we must conclude either that he is attracted by the prospect of a quasi-incestuous relationship or that something happens to change his view of her as a sister. The text preserves a discreet silence in both respects, but the narrator is loud in her embarrassment. The unwonted authorial intrusion in the first person here is an overt indication of a general loss of poise, the novelist betraying a defensive uneasiness about what she is doing, and seeming to rely on her authority and the reiteration of the word "natural" to cover a multitude of sins. And indeed Edmund goes into marriage with "regard" rather than passionate love for his sister-wife.

Though the novelist focuses on Edmund and his change of feeling in the quoted passage, her uncertainties at this crucial moment have the unfortunate effect of undermining Fanny's position too. First, Fanny would seem to be condemned once again to being taken for what she is not, and so is not recognized for what she is—even by the man who marries her, for he persists in regarding her feeling for him as sisterly. But this is to take the least damaging view of her situation. If we are to understand that Fanny, given her demonstrated capacity for fine discriminations and her special sensitivity to Edmund, is aware of the nature of his feeling for her, but accepts him nevertheless, this would constitute a surrender to a proposal which we might expect to be no less unacceptable to her than that of Crawford. Her marriage, in that event, would seem to question the priorities she has adhered to, her sense of the place of self, for her acceptance posits a readiness to settle for less than her due. Alternatively, if we are to believe that the proposal *is* acceptable to her because Edmund's wish to marry her is as strong as she "[can] desire," the fact remains that his brotherly feeling is no more than temperate; and we may be led to wonder whether this is perhaps welcome to Fanny, whether she gets not so much what she desires but what she "can" desire—is capable of desiring. We would then have to conclude that the self-command she has exhibited so firmly in other circumstances has been attained at the cost of considerable sexual repression; and this would in turn suggest that self-command is not the unmitigated virtue that its opposition to a reprehensible self-indulgence has hitherto implied. The narrator's loss of control at this juncture, therefore, raises a number of disturbing issues, and their impact is the more subversive in that the text in its silence offers no way of resolving them. We are no doubt informed that "it remained for a later period" for Fanny to tell Edmund "the whole delightful and astonishing truth" about her love for him, and for him to assure her of his affection (p. 471); but this does not alter the nature either of the proposal or its acceptance. Since the presentation of Fanny to this point has been so immaculate, we cannot help feeling that she deserves a better ending.

A SECRET HEART:
THE HISTORY OF HENRY ESMOND

The History of Henry Esmond, Esq., "A Colonel in the Service of Her Majesty Q. Anne," as the imitation eighteenth-century title page informs us, is "Written by Himself," but the novelist's narrative method ensures that Esmond's tale is subject to a number of refractions. For a start, it does not even begin with itself but with a preface by Esmond's daughter, Rachel Esmond Warrington, written some sixty years after the point at which her father chooses to end his story. Her introductory description of her father is fulsome in the extreme, strenuously evoking his nobility in a blast of superlatives and a refusal of all qualification:

After a long stormy life in England, he passed the remainder of his many years in peace and honour in [Virginia]; how beloved and respected by all his fellow-citizens, how inexpressibly dear to his family, I need not say. His whole life was a benefit to all who were connected with him. He gave the best example, the best advice, the most bounteous hospitality to his friends; the tenderest care to his dependants; and bestowed on those of his immediate family such a blessing of fatherly love and protection, as can never be thought of, by us at least, without veneration and thankfulness; and my sons' children . . . may surely be proud to be descended from one who in all ways was so truly noble. (p. 37)[1]

This clearly is the suspect tone of hero-worship, if not of fixation; and Rachel Esmond Warrington's preface in effect invites us to register a discrepancy between her view of her father and that which will emerge in his own narrative, for we assume that the actual story of any man will not be amenable to such wholly uncritical adulation. Her preface, that is to say, at once establishes an ironic frame for what follows.

Nor is hers the only preface. Though not formally labeled as such, the narrator's introductory remarks (which precede chapter 1 of book 1 of his story) constitute a preface to the whole history which follows, and not inappropriately deal with the role of the historian:

> I have seen in his very old age and decrepitude the old French King Lewis the Fourteenth, the type and model of king-hood—who never moved but to measure, who lived and died according to the laws of his Court-marshal, persisting in enacting through life the part of Hero; and, divested of poetry, this was but a little wrinkled old man, pock-marked, and with a great periwig and red heels to make him look tall—a hero for a book if you like . . . but what more than a man for Madame Maintenon, or the barber who shaved him, or Monsieur Fagon, his surgeon? I wonder shall History ever pull off her periwig and cease to be court-ridden? . . . [Queen Anne] was neither better bred nor wiser than you and me, though we knelt to hand her a letter or a washhand-basin. Why shall History go on kneeling to the end of time? I am for having her rise up off her knees, and take a natural posture. (pp. 45–46)

The traditional historian, it appears, has much in common with Rachel Esmond Warrington, being "court-ridden" where she is father-struck, and kneeling obsequiously before a great personage in a manner that suggests her position in respect of her father. Esmond himself, however, wants the historian to get off his knees and "take a natural posture," to pull off the king's periwig and show the man beneath. And since Esmond, as his title insists, is himself writing a history, he is to be seen as dedicating himself to the attempt to show things as they are, having "taken truth for his motto" (p. 113). The juxtaposition of the two prefaces, with Esmond's coming after that of his daughter, collapses a possible distinction between a "history" of public personages and that of private lives; and in this historical novel we are invited to see *all* bald heads for what they are.

The prefatorial apparatus, therefore, is complex, suggesting that we will have to try to save Esmond's story not only from his daughter but also from himself, for an ironic frame is no respecter of persons and an intention is no guarantee of performance. Nor is it anyway clear who exactly "Esmond himself" is, as another narrative device indicates: Esmond tells his own story, but he habitually refers to himself in the third person; it is only in the titles of chapters and on comparatively few occasions in the text that he uses the first person. The use of the third person in this respect is in the tradition of eighteenth-century memoir writing;[2] and may be regarded simply as part and parcel of Thackeray's magisterial attempt to produce a historical novel that should itself be the thing it is intended to evoke. Not only did he copy the form of an eighteenth-century title page and dedication but, as John

Sutherland tells us, he had the first edition of the novel "set up in the obsolete type of Queen Anne's age, with carefully old-fashioned spelling"; and, furthermore, adapted his own style to make it throughout "uniform with the famous *Spectator* paper in the third volume, . . . what [could not] be done unobtrusively [being] made virtuosic."[3] But the use of both the first and third persons to refer to Esmond also points to an important feature of the narrative.

In the text, as distinct from the chapter titles, the first person is used in two sharply different ways. On some rare occasions it is used to suggest a special stress that Esmond is subject to, as when he visits his mother's grave: "I felt as one who had been walking below the sea, and treading amidst the bones of shipwrecks" (p. 322). For the rest, the first person is used to refer to the older narrator as distinct from his younger self—though, when used in this manner, it sometimes slides slipperily between the two selves. "At this time," we are told, "Harry Esmond was a lad of sixteen" and strongly drawn to Nancy Sievewright's "bonny face": " 'Tis surprising the magnetic attraction which draws people together from ever so far. I blush as I think of poor Nancy now . . . and that I . . . made speeches in my heart, which I seldom had courage to say . . . Poor Nancy! . . . I remember thy kind voice as if I had heard it yesterday" (p. 115). What the play of pronouns does, however, for all the slippage, is effectively to signal, in the difference between "he" and "I," one between Esmond's "experiencing self" and his "narrating self." Such a distinction is operative in all retrospective first-person narrative, but it is specially important in this novel because it is a further means of refracting Esmond's story. The experiencing self is presented to us in all the blindness and obtuseness of the moment; and sometimes the narrating self is at pains to point this out to us: " 'Tis not to be imagined that Harry Esmond had all this experience at this early stage of his life, whereof he is now writing the history—many things here noted were but known to him in later days. Almost everything Beatrix did or undid seemed good, or at least pardonable, to him then, and years afterwards" (p. 172). Even when the narrating self chooses (in an important instance) to keep silent, another piece of apparatus alerts us to what the experiencing self does not know. The history comes equipped too with sporadic footnotes, most of them supplied by the putative editor (the novelist), but some initialed by members of Esmond's family. Two such notes are initialed "R."—who can only be Rachel, Lady Castlewood—and they are inserted at that point in the narrative when Esmond is passionately declaring his love for Beatrix Esmond, her daughter (pp. 342, 343). The mere presence of these footnotes, quite apart from their insignificant content, is indicative of the fact that Rachel is in a position to provide them—and so implies the outcome of Esmond's strange entanglement with mother and daughter. By such means, therefore, we become accustomed to forming our own judgments of the life of the experiencing self even when—or precisely when—the narrating self remains silent. For a feature of this narrative, which is so elaborately framed for ironic undercutting, is the silence of the narrator about some of the most crucial matters of his history. It becomes clear that he would prefer to keep quiet about certain things.[4]

Esmond's silences are most marked in respect of his relations with Rachel and Beatrix, and his omissions or evasions in this regard leave a gap at the very center of his self-portrait, for the two women matter more than anything else to him. The very idea of the triangle that is constituted by his relations with them is so original, and its presentation so complex (encompassing one of the subtlest portrayals of a woman in English fiction), that perhaps we should not expect a smooth narrative surface. But the necessary critical response to the portrait the narrator gives us of himself, I believe, should not be an attempt to deconstruct it, but rather to fill in the gap.[5] Only when Esmond's emotional life has been carefully pieced together, can we try to get at the heart of its mystery. That, indeed, is what we are tacitly invited to do: "So much and suddenly had grief, anger, and misfortune appeared to change [Rachel]. But fortune, good or ill, as I take it, does not change men and women. It but develops their characters. As there are a thousand thoughts lying within a man that he does not know till he takes up the pen to write, so the heart is a secret even to him (or her) who has it in his own breast" (p. 208). The last comparison is instructive. In life, it is intimated, we know nothing of our inmost selves. It is only in the act of writing that the secret heart is revealed to the man who writes. But it does not follow that he will disclose its secrets to others—directly, at any rate—or fully accept them himself. *The History of Henry Esmond* is at once the record, in respect of what is central to his life, of the narrator's discoveries and camouflages. Where his relations with Rachel and Beatrix are concerned, we have to refuse both to take him at his word and to let him escape into his silences.[6]

2

A WAY of approaching Esmond's story is suggested by his insistence, in the passage in which he talks about the secret heart, that the characters of men and women do not so much change as develop. This view reflects that which he gives great prominence to in the Latin epigraph on his title page: "Servetur ad imum / Qualis ab incepto processerit, et sibi constet." The full quotation from Horace is: "[If you bring a new

concept to the stage and boldly form a new character], let his development be subordinated to his initial personality, and remain self-con-
sistent." It is as an English form of the *Bildungsroman* that *Henry Esmond* should first and foremost be read; and it is the nature of the
protagonist's "initial personality"—a crucial feature of the form—that
not only is the basis of his development but provides a clue to its mysteries. Esmond's attempt to chart his development, moreover, to establish its consistency, is the raison d'être of his narrative, and it effectively unifies his experiences as a lover in the domestic world of the
Castlewoods and his seemingly disjunctive activities in the domain of
public affairs.

The opening discriminated occasion in a *Bildungsroman* is always
important, for it sets the scene for what is to follow with more careful
particularity than in an ordinary novel. In *Great Expectations*, that
prototypical English *Bildungsroman*, for instance, the major lines of
Pip's developing life lead straight from the opening scene in the
churchyard. In *Henry Esmond* the beginning of the narrative is not
only significant in much the same way but is given special emphasis by
being displaced chronologically: it is the beginning of the *sjuzet* but
not of the *fabula*, and after chapter 1 there is a lengthy flashback of
some fifty pages (chapters 2–6) before the chronological order is resumed and then maintained throughout. Looking back on his life, the
narrator clearly chooses to start his history at the point which constitutes its effective beginning for him, though he is twelve years old
when the new Viscount and his family come to take possession of their
house at Castlewood in 1691:

> The new and fair lady of Castlewood found the sad lonely little occupant of
> this gallery busy over his great book, which he laid down when he was aware
> that a stranger was at hand. And, knowing who that person must be, the lad
> stood up and bowed before her, performing a shy obeisance to the mistress of
> his house.
> She stretched out her hand—indeed when was it that that hand would not
> stretch out to do an act of kindness, or to protect grief and ill-fortune? "And
> this is our kinsman," she said; "and what is your name, kinsman?"
> "My name is Henry Esmond," said the lad, looking up at her in a sort of
> delight and wonder, for she had come upon him as a *Dea certè*, and appeared
> the most charming object he had ever looked on. Her golden hair was shining
> in the gold of the sun; her complexion was of a dazzling bloom; her lips smil-
> ing, and her eyes beaming with a kindness which made Harry Esmond's heart
> to beat with surprise.
> "His name is Henry Esmond, sure enough, my lady," says Mrs. Worksop the
> housekeeper . . . and the old gentlewoman looked significantly towards the
> late lord's picture. (pp. 48–49)

All the needs that shape Esmond's life are encapsulated in this scene. Rachel's coming upon him "as a *Dea certè*" becomes for him a controlling image for many years, an image that springs from a complex combination of his own emotions and her appearance and attitude. To her the boy no doubt seems only sad and lonely, but he is in the grip of ravening anxiety: an orphan, he has just previously been feeling "quite alone in the world," and has awaited the arrival of the new occupants of the house with "terror and anxiety," wondering how they will "deal with him," and knowing that those to whom he has "formerly looked for protection" are "forgotten or dead" (p. 51). In his overwhelming insecurity, Esmond's most immediate need is for a protector; and when Rachel stretches out her hand to him, her eyes "beaming with . . . kindness," it is as such that she appears to him. But the uncertainty of his new hold on life is soon made apparent: when Mrs. Worksop looks at the late lord's picture and Rachel sees "the great and undeniable likeness between this portrait and the lad," the Viscountess blushes, "[drops] the hand quickly," and walks off (p. 49). And indeed we learn later that her husband's initial response to the boy is to want to send him away. Esmond's illegitimacy is also a continuing source of shame to him. From an early age he knows to the full "the disgrace" of his birth, and he thinks "with many a pang of shame and grief of his strange and solitary condition" (pp. 104–5). His shame and anxiety are motivating forces in his life. A "nameless" as well as a "houseless" orphan (p. 141), Esmond determines to make a name for himself, seeking palpable answers to the questions that agitate him: "Who was he and what?" (p. 105).

Rachel's appearance when Esmond first sees her is supportive of the image he projects of her. With "her golden hair . . . shining in the gold of the sun," her complexion "a dazzling bloom," her "lips smiling," and her "eyes beaming," she comes into Esmond's life as an effulgence of light, an illumination, and the effect on him is as of an epiphany, for he sees her as a goddess certainly. The image is long-lived, and it has a compulsive force. When Rachel comes back into the gallery, she finds him as if spellbound, standing "exactly in the same spot, and with his hand as it [fell] when he dropped it on his black coat." She takes his hand again, looking at him with "infinite pity and tenderness," and he falls at her feet, kissing "the fair protecting hand as he [kneels] on one knee" (pp. 49–50). Worship is no doubt an appropriate response to a protective goddess, and its posture is one that he either literally or figuratively continues to take in relation to Rachel for many years to come. But the posture is also that adopted by the historians Esmond reviles in his preface; and in life, no less than in history, a man needs to get off his knees and see people and things as they are. That Esmond—

to the end—is not doing so in respect of Rachel is suggested in this opening scene by his parenthetic comment on the way she stretches out her hand to the boy, for it is the narrating self that speaks retrospectively here: "indeed when was it that that hand would not stretch out to do an act of kindness, or to protect grief and ill-fortune?" Esmond seems to have forgotten what he will later record so vividly, how in *his* grief and ill-fortune (as he lies wounded and in prison after the duel in which Lord Castlewood is killed) she proceeds to wound him again, cruelly and unjustly, with a wound that, he says, leaves its mark forever. Or is it, we wonder, that he is repressing the knowledge he has of her, seeking by means of such adulatory comments—from the start of his narrative and throughout—to make up to her, in his history if not in life, for what he knows the woman who becomes his wife has never had of him?

Nor is this all that the marvelously packed opening scene conveys. For in the *Aeneid* "*Dea certè*" registers Aeneas's response not only to a goddess but to his mother, Venus; and Rachel comes into Esmond's life in the figure of a mother as well as a goddess, even though she is only twenty. He cannot even remember his own mother, and Rachel clearly supplies a lack that has not hitherto been provided for. But the lack is not so much, as we might expect, a lack of love, the cross of all orphans, as a lack of someone to love. Esmond's suffering stems not from a desiccated heart but a full soul, as we are made to realize at a strategic moment—at the end of the long flashback that brings his story up to the night preceding the arrival of the new family at Castlewood: "The soul of the boy was full of love, and he longed as he lay in the darkness there for some one upon whom he could bestow it. He remembers, and must to his dying day, the thoughts and tears of that long night, the hours tolling through it" (p. 105). It is at this point in the narrative that Esmond asks the questions "Who was he and what?"—and one of the answers immediately suggested is that he is a person who must love somebody. As well as a full soul, he is said to have "a fond and affectionate heart, tender to weakness, that would fain attach itself to somebody"; and his feeling for Rachel speedily becomes "a devoted affection and passion of gratitude which entirely [fills] his young heart" (p. 107). The gratitude of "the orphan lad whom she [protects]" issues in a vow that "no power should separate him from his mistress," and he longs for a chance to "show his fidelity to her." That this boyhood vow of fidelity provides an important clue to the nature of Esmond's whole relationship with Rachel is suggested by his mature view of it: "Now, at the close of his life, as he sits and recalls in tranquillity the happy and busy scenes of it, he can think, not ungratefully, that he has been faithful to that early vow" (p. 109).

When Esmond is sixteen, having suddenly "grown from a boy to be a man" (p. 128), Rachel is led unwittingly to betray a change in her feeling toward him. He has been with Nancy Sievewright, holding her little brother on his lap, and when it is announced that the boy has the small-pox, Esmond tries to prevent Beatrix from coming to him, saying in French to Rachel, "Madam, the child must not approach me; I must tell you that I was at the blacksmith's to-day, and had his little boy upon my lap" (p. 118). Rachel's uncontrollable outbursts are a feature of her characterization, and the one that follows this admission of Esmond's is subtly evocative of her situation:

> For once her mother took little heed of [Beatrix's] sobbing, and continued to speak eagerly—"My lord," she said, "this young man—your dependant—told me just now in French—he was ashamed to speak in his own language—that he had been at the alehouse all day, where he has had that little wretch who is now ill of the small-pox on his knee. And he comes home reeking from that place—yes, reeking from it—and takes my boy into his lap without shame, and sits down by me, yes, by *me*. He may have killed Frank for what I know—killed our child. Why was he brought in to disgrace our house? Why is he here? Let him go—let him go, I say, to-night, and pollute the place no more." (p. 120)

Rachel's staccato ejaculations indicate how her words are jerked out of her, as if against her will, and what they reveal to the reader—and to herself (though to no one who hears her) is the extent of her erotic feeling for Esmond. It is in a passion of sexual jealousy of Nancy Sievewright that she turns on Esmond, her willful misrepresentation of his speaking in French showing how she needs first of all to wound him for his association with the blacksmith's daughter. At the same time her scorn for the object of Esmond's attentions is deflected on to "that little wretch" her brother, the perfectly harmless child now ill with the small-pox. But the true source of her anger, the physical passion that is transformed by her sense of affront into sexual revulsion, is beautifully caught in her horror at the idea of the reeking, polluted Esmond's having sat down by *her*. Once the revulsion and recognition of what underlies it penetrate her consciousness, she becomes quite distracted, her conjunction of fear for her son's life with the assertion that Esmond has "disgraced" their house being strikingly disjunctive. The disgrace of his birth is now seen as a premonitory sexual tainting, and Esmond's protector expresses the wish to "let him go." The disowning, of course, is also a disowning of her illicit feeling, the protector now being concerned to protect herself. Her husband prevents the boy's expulsion, and Rachel is reconciled to him; but she insists that "at [his] age, and with [his] tastes, it is impossible that [he] can continue to stay upon the intimate footing" in which he has been in the family (p. 122). When she comes into a legacy, she arranges for Esmond "to go to college," so that he can "make a name to [himself]." That this is not her only concern, however, is indicated in a neat tableau: " 'By G——d, Rachel, you're a good woman!' says my lord, seizing my lady's hand, at which she blushed very much, and shrank back, putting her children before her" (p. 139). It is not from her husband's touch that she shrinks but from his praise, her blush revealing her own sense of how much she has compromised herself, if only in her own feelings and thoughts. But she is determined to put her marriage—as well as her children—before herself, and Esmond's being sent to the university is not only for his own good.

Though the narrator continues to hint at Rachel's hidden feeling for Esmond—we are told, for instance, that thereafter she "scarce ever [sees] him" without the company of her children (p. 150)—he (as experiencing self) remains quite unaware of it. It is not until he is twenty-two and becomes involved in Lord Mohun's pursuit of her that he seems to have a first glimmering of a possible complication of their relationship. The recognition is a concomitant of a newly demonstrated maturity on his part. When Frank Castlewood becomes suspicious of Mohun's attentions to his wife and it seems as if the outcome will be a duel between them, it is the young Esmond who, with as much aplomb as unwonted self-assertion, succeeds in stepping between them and smoothing over the quarrel. The change in Esmond is notable, and one measure of it is that, no longer in need of protection, he has himself become a protector—as Rachel, who has overheard the dispute, seems tacitly to grant: "Thank you, and God bless you, my dear brother Harry," she says (p. 177). When the situation continues to deteriorate, Esmond takes it on himself explicitly to warn Mohun off; and his new standing is attested by Mohun's readiness to treat him as an equal, for he demands to know whether Esmond is "prepared to answer" for his insinuations (p. 183). Mohun also says he believes Esmond himself "[has] an eye to the pretty Puritan," and asks whether he is in love with her; but Esmond's reply is patently sincere, and (in the light of what follows) delimits the period of his innocence: " 'My lord, my lord,' cried Harry, his face flushing and his eyes filling as he spoke, 'I never had a mother, but I love this lady as one. I worship her as a devotee worships a saint. To hear her name spoken lightly seems blasphemy to me' " (p. 184). Esmond says this to Mohun just before they jump for their lives from the runaway carriage in which they are driving. Mohun falls on his head, and it seems as if he is dead. When Castlewood tells Rachel that "poor Harry" has been killed, she "gives a great scream" and "drops down." For the suspicious husband this is final proof of his wife's involvement with Mohun—and it leads to the

duel between them and his own death; but he is not the only one who
wonders about her reaction: "Musing upon this curious history—for
my Lord Mohun's name was Henry too . . . and not a little disturbed
and anxious, Esmond rode home" (pp. 185–86). It is unlikely that Esmond's disturbed anxiety, despite his syntax, is occasioned by a sudden
doubt of Rachel's virtue, for he has just previously declared that it is
such that Mohun "might as well storm the Tower single-handed" (p.
184); the disturbance springs rather from a first realization of the depth
of her feeling for him. Subsequently, in trying to dissuade Castlewood
from pursuing his quarrel with Mohun, Esmond gets out of his own
depth:

"But, my lord, *my* name is Harry," cried out Esmond, burning red. "You told
my lady, 'Harry was killed!' "
"Damnation! shall I fight you too?" shouts my lord in a fury. (p. 195)

But Castlewood at once retracts, and indeed has just before paid his
own tribute to Esmond's newly won stature, to his transformation into
an accepted protector of the family: "I leave my wife and you as guard-
ians to the children," he says to Esmond (p. 193). And before the duel he
adds: "By George, Harry! you ought to be the head of the house . . . You
had been better Lord Castlewood than a lazy sot like me" (p. 194).
     Castlewood's remark is a prelude to his confession on his deathbed
that Esmond is not illegitimate and is the true heir to his father's title
and property. The revelation comes precisely at a time when Esmond,
at real risk, has bravely and loyally stood by Castlewood in the duel,
and so proved his worth to himself and to those round him. It is as if an
inner self-assurance, a firm sense of who and what he is, now offsets
the insecurity that was formerly a consequence of his status—and
makes redundant the kind of outer confirmation of standing that is
given by a title. At all events—and *pace* J. Hillis Miller—far from trying to take Castlewood's place (as a first step to getting into his bed), as
he now literally could, he thinks only of protecting the family from a
"double misfortune": refusing to dispossess "those he [loves] best," he
throws the written confession into the fire. When Castlewood is told
what he has done, he blesses him with his last breath, but then "the
blood [rushes] from his mouth, deluging the young man" (pp. 201–2). In
a number of ways it is established that Esmond is of one blood with the
Castlewoods.
     When Rachel visits Esmond in prison, however (pp. 205–6), she re-
coils from him: "Take back your hand—do not touch me with it!" she
cries out. "Look! there's blood on it!" This sets the tone for the outburst that follows, and her wild denunciation of him now recalls her

earlier fury over Nancy Sievewright. Once again she expresses physical revulsion from him, though this time because he reeks not of the ale-house but of the blood of her husband. Again she pours out unjust accusations on Esmond: we know that he has tried to forestall Cas-tlewood by taking the quarrel with Mohun on himself (p. 197), but she says, "Why did you stand by at midnight and see him murdered?" and she repeats this: "My husband lies in his blood—murdered for defend-ing me, my kind, kind, generous lord—and you were by, and you let him die, Henry!" In effect she accuses Esmond of betraying her hus-band, and furthermore declares that he has brought the family only "grief and sorrow," has merely "pretended to love" them, and would have done better to have died when he "had the small-pox." Rachel, however, betrays that it is her own corrosive guilt she is projecting onto Esmond when she extravagantly praises Castlewood, from whom she had long been estranged, says she has lost "the husband of [her] youth" through Esmond, that young as he was she "knew there was evil" in keeping him, and that all that has happened is "a just judgment" on her "wicked jealous heart."[7] Subsequently she appoints Thomas Tusher to the Castlewood living that had been reserved for Esmond and has Tusher inform him that she never wishes to see him again (pp. 209–10).

Rachel does offer to help Esmond financially, but he rejects "her offer of alms":

After the sending of this letter, the poor young fellow's mind was more at ease than it had been previously. The blow had been struck, and he had borne it. His cruel goddess had shaken her wings and fled: and left him alone and friendless, but *virtute suâ*. And he had to bear him up, at once the sense of his right and the feeling of his wrongs, his honour and his misfortune. As I have seen men waking and running to arms at a sudden trumpet, before emergency a manly heart leaps up resolute; meets the threatening danger with undaunted countenance; and, whether conquered or conquering, faces it always. Ah! no man knows his strength or his weakness, till occasion proves them. If there be some thoughts and actions of his life from the memory of which a man shrinks with shame, sure there are some which he may be proud to own and re-member; forgiven injuries, conquered temptations (now and then), and difficul-ties vanquished by endurance.

. . . It seemed to Esmond as if he lived years in that prison and was changed and aged when he came out of it. . . . You do not know how much you suffer in those critical maladies of the heart, until the disease is over and you look back on it afterwards. . . . 'Tis only in after days that we see what the danger has been—as a man out a-hunting or riding for his life looks at a leap, and wonders how he should have survived the taking of it. O, dark months of grief and rage! of wrong and cruel endurance! He is old now who recalls you. Long ago he has forgiven and blest the soft hand that wounded him; but the mark is there, and the wound is cicatrized only—no time, tears, caresses, or repentance, can obliterate the scar. We are indocile to put up with grief, however. *Reficimus rates quassas*: we tempt the ocean again and again, and try upon new ventures. Esmond thought of his early time as a noviciate, and of this past trial as an initiation before entering into life—as our young Indians undergo tortures silently before they pass to the rank of warriors in the tribe. (pp. 210–12)

Rachel's disowning of Esmond may be regarded as the crisis of his life—it is a "critical" malady that he suffers—and constitutes the most decisive test he ever has to face. "Ah! no man knows his strength or his weakness," says the narrator, in a statement that anticipates an essential concern of Joseph Conrad's, "till occasion proves them"; and in his response to the disowning Esmond really discovers what he is. It is a discovery that is more important than the earlier revelation of who he is in Castlewood's confession. The test (as in Conrad) first of all exposes his weakness, the "soft spot" that is in all of us. When he is "left . . . alone and friendless," it is as if all the intervening years are cancelled at a stroke and he is returned to the helpless dependence of his childhood. The "temptation" that he then faces is to give way to his despair, and what that would mean (again as in Conrad) would be to embrace the release of death, for it is death that is the danger—as the riding simile indicates. Esmond must also be presumed to face another temptation, the temptation of repaying Rachel in kind for her treatment of him, either by staking his claim to the title (for Atterbury too knows of the confession) or, at the least, by making her aware that it is by his bounty that she and hers continue to enjoy what is not theirs. He discovers, however, that if he has been left with nothing, he is endowed "*virtute suâ*," and he finds the inner strength to withstand both these temptations, and to vanquish his difficulties "by endurance."

Esmond comes through the test, but only by being made new. When "his cruel goddess" shakes her wings and flees, it is not only a desertion that is recorded but a liberation. From this point on, Rachel ceases to be a goddess for him, and though her blows lay him low, they also force him to get up off his knees and see her for what she is. At the same time, his previous sense of self has, as it were, been anchored in his worship of her; when he ceases to regard her as a goddess, there is apparently nothing left for him to hold to, and the self runs aground and shatters. But there is something left, his own strength and a readiness to start again: "*Reficimus rates quassas*"—we repair our shattered vessels, says the narrator, quoting Horace, and "try upon new ventures." For Esmond the experience both reveals what he is and serves as "an initiation": it is an initiation "into life" and into full manhood, as the comparison with the "young Indians" suggests. It is also a consummation of self, and we might well expect it to mark the conclusion of a *Bildungsroman*; but the experience described in fact takes place at the beginning of the second of three books, and it is clear that Esmond's new or reconstituted self is not complete. His self is now founded on its own independent strength—he is not only off his knees but standing on his own two feet—but he still needs someone to love. The rest of the narrative is primarily concerned with his quest for love, which ends nominally in his marriage at the close of his story. *Henry Esmond* is thus unique among *Bildungsromane* in charting the protagonist's development in two trajectories, from childhood to maturity, and then—as he "tries upon new ventures"—from young manhood to a purported further fulfillment in marriage. But, as we shall see, it is the way he copes with his experience in prison that remains the more significant "initiation . . . into life."

When Esmond leaves prison, he tells the truth about the title to his father's widow, and my Lady Dowager shows a readiness to take him up; but he has "made up his mind to continue at no woman's apron-strings longer," and casting about "how he should distinguish himself, and make himself a name," he decides to go into the army (p. 227). He takes part in the Vigo Bay expedition, and during the campaign "his energies [seem] to awaken and to expand" (p. 239). On his return the dowager "[pushes] his fortunes" to such effect that she gets the "promise of a company" for him, and has him "make his appearance at the Queen's drawing-room occasionally" and "frequent my Lord Marlborough's levees" (pp. 242–43). In the midst of his activities, however, Esmond's "heart [often] fondly [reverts]" to Rachel and her family (p. 243); and when he hears a rumor that she is likely to marry her chaplain, Tom Tusher, he hurries down to Walcote, where he is reconciled to her after "the year of grief and estrangement" (p. 250):

> She smiled an almost wild smile as she looked up at him. . . .
> "Do you know what day it is?" she continued. "It is the 29th of December—it is your birthday! But last year we did not drink it—no, no. My lord was cold, and my Harry was likely to die; and my brain was in a fever; and we had no wine. But now—now you are come again, bringing your sheaves with you, my dear." She burst into a wild flood of weeping as she spoke; she laughed and sobbed on the young man's heart, crying out wildly, "bringing your sheaves with you—your sheaves with you!"
> As he had sometimes felt, gazing up from the deck at midnight into the boundless starlit depths overhead, in a rapture of devout wonder at that endless brightness and beauty—in some such a way now, the depth of this pure devotion (which was, for the first time, revealed to him quite) smote upon him, and filled his heart with thanksgiving. Gracious God, who was he, weak and friendless creature, that such a love should be poured out upon him? Not in vain, not in vain has he lived . . . that has such a treasure given him. . . .

"If—if 'tis so, dear lady," Mr. Esmond said, "why should I ever leave you? If God hath given me this great boon . . . let me have that blessing near me, nor ever part with it till life separate us. Come away—leave this Europe, this place which has so many sad recollections for you. Begin a new life in a new world. . . ."

"And my children—and my duty—and my good father, Henry?" she broke out. . . .

"I would leave all to follow you," said Mr. Esmond; "and can you not be as generous for me, dear lady?"

"Hush, boy!" she said, and it was with a mother's sweet plaintive tone and look that she spoke. (pp. 253–55)

This is one of the subtlest scenes in the novel, and the novelist's handling of his protagonists—and of their silences—is masterly. Once again a major scene is initiated by an outburst on Rachel's part, but this time it is one of joy. Her wildness, referred to three times in the first ten lines, is the overt sign of the way she at last feels free to let herself go, to abandon herself to the passion for Esmond that she has sought for so long to repress. And her references to Psalm 126 (she has just previously repeated the lines sung that day in the church: "When the Lord turned the captivity of Zion, we were like them that dream") express both her own sense of liberation and—in her reiteration of his having brought his sheaves with him—her invitation to him to rejoice in his return and reap in joy. Esmond's response is curious in the extreme. The nature of her feeling is apparently clear to him, unqualified by any of the uncertainty that characterized his suspicion of it at the time of Mohun's supposed death, for the narrator parenthetically remarks that it is "for the first time, revealed to him quite"; but he at once proceeds to transform it into something other than it is, turning her obviously sexual passion into a "pure devotion" and losing himself "in a rapture of [carefully] devout wonder" at it. He transforms himself too, for the returning warrior, the captain with influential friends, is hardly a "weak and friendless creature," though his self-image certainly reflects, in its involuntary regression to his childhood, his own unreadiness for her love. The regression is evident too in his passivity before the love that is "poured out upon him": he clearly regards "such a love" as of great value—it is "a treasure" and a "great boon"—but he does not seem to feel called on to do much in order to secure it. It is notable that at no point does he actually say that he loves her, and the omission is so marked that it suggests he is silenced by a profound inhibition in relation to her. At the same time, Esmond still feels bound by his childhood vow of loyalty to Rachel; and though he cannot fake any enthusiasm for the project, he does rise to the occasion and propose that she come away with him to Virginia. Rachel, however, is swift to understand the significance of his response, and she then backs away, though she was not much concerned with her various duties to start with. She later says to him, "You never loved me, dear Henry— no, you do not now, and I thank Heaven for it" (p. 255). But by then she has reverted to their accustomed relationship, calling him "boy," and speaking with "a mother's sweet plaintive tone." Esmond is only too glad, it seems, to accept the reversion: " 'I think the angels are not all in heaven,' Mr. Esmond said. And as a brother folds a sister to his heart; and as a mother cleaves to her son's breast—so for a few moments Esmond's beloved mistress came to him and blessed him" (p. 256). If he no longer regards Rachel as a goddess, he now has no difficulty in spiritualizing her into an angel.[8]

Immediately following this encounter, Rachel and Esmond walk back to the house at Walcote. As they stand in the hall, Beatrix comes down the stairs, illuminated by the candle she carries:

> Esmond had left a child and found a woman, grown beyond the common height; and arrived at such a dazzling completeness of beauty, that his eyes might well show surprise and delight at beholding her. In hers there was a brightness so lustrous and melting, that I have seen a whole assembly follow her as if by an attraction irresistible: and that night the great Duke was at the playhouse after Ramillies, every soul turned and looked (she chanced to enter at the opposite side of the theatre at the same moment) at her, and not at him. She was a brown beauty: that is, her eyes, hair, and eyebrows and eyelashes, were dark: her hair curling with rich undulations, and waving over her shoulders; but her complexion was as dazzling white as snow in sunshine; except her cheeks, which were a bright red, and her lips, which were of a still deeper crimson. Her mouth and chin, they said, were too large and full, and so they might be for a goddess in marble, but not for a woman whose eyes were fire, whose look was love, whose voice was the sweetest low song, whose shape was perfect symmetry, health, decision, activity, whose foot as it planted itself on the ground, was firm but flexible, and whose motion, whether rapid or slow, was always perfect grace—agile as a nymph, lofty as a queen—now melting, now imperious, now sarcastic: there was no single movement of hers but was beautiful. As he thinks of her, he who writes feels young again, and remembers a paragon. (p. 257)

Esmond's visit to Walcote certainly faces him with some troubling transformations. He has no sooner contended with Rachel's sea changes from mother figure to passionate woman and back again than he has to confront the metamorphosis of the child he has left into the lustrous beauty that Beatrix has become. She is now sixteen—his age when Rachel first woke to him as a man at the time of the Nancy Sievewright affair—and he is eight years her senior, as Rachel in turn is eight years older than he. Some parallels are clearly intended, and none is more significant than the description of Rachel's coming into his life as a *Dea certè* in comparison with that of Beatrix's irruption into it. He does not see Beatrix, he insists, as a goddess, for he grants that her mouth and chin might be considered "too large and full . . . for a goddess in marble," whereas such flaws are apparently becoming in "a woman." For a mere woman, however, she is seen as enjoying a large measure of perfection—her shape is "perfect symmetry, health, decision, activity," and her motion "always perfect grace"—and if she is not a goddess, there is no doubt about her being "a paragon."

Beatrix's appearance on the stairs is furthermore contrasted with Esmond's first view of Rachel by a repeated detail which, though apparently equating the effect of the two women on him, subtly differentiates it. Both are "dazzling," but whereas Rachel's dazzle is a radiance that obscures any human blemish in its strong light, Beatrix's is the brightness of a sexual brilliance that casts all round her into shadow— as she does "the great Duke . . . at the playhouse after Ramillies." The "irresistible attraction" that she exerts is pure sexual magnetism; it also, like fire, "melts" those on whom the brightness shines. At the same time her dazzle is associated with the whiteness of snow, a comparison that catches her essential coldness, for all her apparent fire. Esmond seems to register the fact of such coldness, but he remains oblivious to its implications. He is wholly given over to the recording of her beauty, with a loving particularity of physical detail that contrasts sharply with the few generalized features accorded the *Dea certè*. The "brown beauty" as dark temptress is set squarely against the fair (erstwhile) goddess, and it is clear where Esmond's eyes are fixed. Indeed, Rachel is "still hanging on his arm" as he looks at Beatrix, and when the older woman speaks, he turns "with a start and a blush": "He had forgotten her, rapt in admiration of the *filia pulcrior*" (p. 258). The close juxtaposition of the scenes of Esmond's response to Rachel's outburst and of his contemplation of Beatrix, together with his "forgetting" of the mother in his preoccupation with the daughter, makes it seem that the intensity of his feeling for Beatrix is generated by the force of his inhibition in relation to Rachel; it is as if a previously inhibited sexuality is now compulsively released. At all events, "rapt in admiration," he now falls as surely under the spell of the daughter—he later refers to her as "this Circe" (p. 394)—as he was formerly spellbound by the mother. Even though he is made well aware of her faults—she is "imperious," "light-minded," "flighty," "false," and has "no reverence in her character"—and though he notes she is "in everything . . . the contrast of her mother," who is "the most devoted and the least selfish of women," he is nevertheless compelled to her: "Well, from the very first moment he saw her on the stairs at Walcote, Es-

mond knew he loved Beatrix. There might be better women—he wanted that one. He cared for none other" (p. 343). At Walcote, that is, Esmond's need to love someone centers itself in Beatrix, and his
"passionate fidelity of temper" (p. 394) ensures that his feeling is concentrated there for a long time.

Esmond tells Rachel all about his love for Beatrix, though he registers his behavior (when he looks back on it) as base: "what will a man
not do when frantic with love? To what baseness will he not demean
himself? What pangs will he not make others suffer, so that he may
ease his selfish heart of a part of its own pain?" (p. 291). The pain that
Esmond eases himself of here, however, would seem to go deeper than
his thwarted love for Beatrix since his indifference (at the time) to
Rachel's pangs, though he knows what she is suffering, suggests he is
not averse to hurting her. The pain he eases would seem to be not
unrelated to the wound she inflicted on him in prison, which he says
nothing ("no time, tears, caresses, or repentance") can "obliterate" and
that scars him still (p. 211). It is not one of the Colonel's more glorious
exploits. An even more decisive reversal in the fluctuating relationship
of Rachel and Esmond takes place when she finds out about his renunciation of the title—and he announces his intention to abide by it. In a
characteristic outburst of feeling, she flings herself "down on her knees
before him," and kisses his hands in "passionate love and gratitude":
" 'Don't raise me,' she said, in a wild way, to Esmond, who would have
lifted her. 'Let me kneel—let me kneel, and—and—worship you' " (pp.
375–76). The scene is not without its relevance to their eventual marriage, as Beatrix, who is the sharpest of the Castlewoods, makes us see
in another context: " 'I'm afraid of you, cousin—there," she says to
Esmond; "and I won't worship you, and you'll never be happy except
with a woman who will" (p. 408).

A wiser and a better man in all things else, a man who has distinguished himself in the world, Colonel Esmond persists in his unre-
quited love for the ambitious and flirtatious Beatrix. She puts him off
with all sorts of reasons, but it is clear why he fundamentally has no
hope of winning her, and she eventually articulates this: "I feel as a
sister to you," she says, "and can no more. Isn't that enough, sir?" (p.
403). In the relationships of Esmond and Rachel and of Beatrix and
Esmond, it is in each case the younger of the two who is inhibited by
the familial situation in which they grow up. Consequently Esmond's
grand plan to win the throne for the Pretender, which he undertakes
primarily as a last desperate effort to impress and so win Beatrix, is
ironically beside the point. The episode, however, though quite unhistorical,[9] neatly serves to link the tale of Esmond's life to its historical setting, for Esmond's story serves as a dramatic counterpart to that

of the Pretender. Each man is dispossessed of a title which is his by right; but where the Pretender intrigues to regain his title only to forfeit it through his own ineptitude, Esmond magnanimously renounces the title he is offered and determines rather to make his own name. And it is of course in the (historical) battles in which he participates prior to the attempt to gain the throne for the Pretender that Esmond makes that name. The historical setting is thus more integral to Esmond's story than might at first appear; and it merges with it completely when Beatrix's flirtation with the Pretender is made the occasion of Esmond's breaking with her. At the same time, when he tells Rachel about his plan, she thinks the "Restoration [is] to be attributed under Heaven to the Castlewood family and to its chief, and she [worships] and [loves] Esmond . . . more than ever she [has] done" (pp. 454–55).

The Pretender pursues Beatrix to Castlewood and so forfeits a crown; Beatrix, in enticing him and surrendering to him if only in "the treacherous heart within her," forfeits Esmond's love. Or so he says: "He sickened at [the] notion [of "the young Prince's lips . . . feeding on" her]. Her cheek was desecrated, her beauty tarnished; shame and honour stood between it and him. The love was dead within him" (p. 504). It is Beatrix's treachery—to their cause, to her family, and to him personally—that Esmond, whose whole life has been predicated on allegiance and fidelity, cannot stomach; and it is this that finally makes him give her up. But whether his love is as dead as he says is another matter. The very intensity of the physical revulsion from her bespeaks his desire (as analogously, on several occasions, does Rachel's in relation to him). And an earlier (retrospective) passage makes us view his break with Beatrix somewhat differently:

Who, in the course of his life, hath not been so bewitched, and worshipped some idol or another? Years after this passion hath been dead and buried, along with a thousand other worldly cares and ambitions, he who felt it can recall it out of its grave, and admire, almost as fondly as he did in his youth, that lovely queenly creature. I invoke that beautiful spirit from the shades and love her still; or rather I should say such a past is always present to a man; such a passion once felt forms a part of his whole being, and cannot be separated from it; it becomes a portion of the man to-day, just as any great faith or conviction, the discovery of poetry, the awakening of religion, ever afterward influence him; just as the wound I had at Blenheim, and of which I wear the scar, hath become part of my frame and influenced my whole body, nay, spirit subsequently, though 'twas got and healed forty years ago. (p. 429)

Is is a fine passage, and tells us more than Esmond would seem ready to grant. On the one hand, it records his liberation from Beatrix, his escape from bewitchment, from the Circean enchantment in which she has held him for so long. It also records how the image of Beatrix that is set up in his imagination at the foot of the stairs at Walcote, the image of her as a "lovely queenly creature," a "paragon," is tumbled down, and how he understands, seeing things as they are, that he has been worshipping an "idol." But at the same time, though he declares that his passion for her is "dead and buried," it is clear—by his own admission—that it will not stay in "its grave," and that he "loves her still." When the admission of his continuing love is made, the narrator quickly amends what he has said—"or rather I should say such a past is always present to a man"—but his elaboration of this idea in fact amounts to the same thing. If his passion "forms a part of his whole being," just like "the wound" he received at Blenheim, and so "becomes a portion of [him] to-day," then indeed he loves her still. Colonel Esmond has three major wounds in his life, wounds that permanently scar him: the wound he receives at Blenheim; the wound Rachel inflicts on him when he is in prison; and the wound he gets when he falls irretrievably in love with an unworthy Beatrix.

It is with such a love still alive in him that Esmond marries Rachel. This perhaps explains why he needs so strenuously and repeatedly to assert his happiness in his marriage, though he involuntarily betrays his feeling on a number of occasions. Looking back on the crisis of his relations with Beatrix, for instance, he cannot help regretting that he conceived his plan to restore the Pretender and so "undid" himself. The word slips out, and is hastily qualified, but a lot is revealed: "He was not the first that has regretted his own act, or brought about his own undoing. Undoing? Should he write that word in his late years? No, on his knees before Heaven,—[that suspect position]—rather be thankful for what then he deemed his misfortune, and which hath caused the whole subsequent happiness of his life" (p. 464).

It is when Rachel feels "severed from her children and alone in the world" that she is ready to marry Esmond. Her need, it must be assumed, outweighs any doubt she may have as to the nature of his feeling for her; and the "duties" that nominally prevented her from accepting his earlier proposal have now fallen away. He finds her "one day in tears" and begs her "to confide herself to the care and devotion of one who, by God's help, [will] never forsake her" (p. 513). It is not indicated, however, how he overcomes his former inhibitions. It is rather like the end of *Mansfield Park*, when Edmund Bertram, equally without explanation, is able to displace a long-held view of Fanny Price as a sister and happily to marry her. But in *Mansfield Park* that is the end of the story; whereas *Henry Esmond* is a retrospective narrative. What it tells us, consequently, is that Esmond never really overcomes his inhibition, and can never really give Rachel the love she is entitled to. But he is an honorable man, and he stands by her in her need, determined not to "forsake" her. It is a repeated motif: "Years ago, [as] a boy . . . , he had made a vow to be faithful and never desert her dear service. Had he kept that fond boyish promise? Yes, before Heaven; yes, praise be to God! His life had been hers; his blood, his fortune, his name, his whole heart ever since had been hers and her children's" (p. 439). But we know that his whole heart is not hers; and even in the final account he offers of the "happiness" which "crowns" his life—for he is a successful pretender—it is notable that he celebrates the joys of being loved rather than loving: Rachel is the "tenderest and purest wife ever man was blessed with"; the "depth and intensity" of her love "[blesses him]"; the love that is "bestowed" on him is "a boon," and a "gift"; and "to have such a love is the one blessing, in comparison of which all earthly joy is of no value" (pp. 511–12). Gentlemen too may protest too much, and, in celebrating one thing, forget another—as Esmond, in his retrospective narrative, seems to do when he describes his departure from Rachel after the scene at Walcote:

As for his mistress, 'twas difficult to say with what a feeling he regarded her. 'Twas happiness to have seen her: 'twas no great pang to part; a filial tenderness, a love that was at once respect and protection, filled his mind as he thought of her; and near her or far from her, and from that day until now, and from now till death is past, and beyond it, he prays that sacred flame may ever burn. (p. 273)

By the end of his story, Esmond has long been standing on his own feet, has made a name for himself, and has loyally served as a constant protector of the Castlewood family. He is also suitably disillusioned, having learned to see both men and women for what they are. His need to love is ostensibly met in his relationship with Rachel; but he is not satisfied in love, and though "filial tenderness" may be a "sacred flame," it is not what should burn in a marriage. But Esmond is not prepared to face all the implications of his own narrative, and its evasions and contradictions suggest that there is one head at least that remains in need of a stately periwig.

THE DOUBLE BIND OF
CONSCIOUSNESS: *A PORTRAIT OF*
THE ARTIST AS A YOUNG MAN

Joyce's *A Portrait of the Artist* is perhaps the tightest example in English of the unifying force of the *Bildungsroman* form. The trajectory of its narrative—or, to use Joyce's own phrase, "the curve of [the] emotion" that he wished his "portrait" to be[1]—is precisely bounded by the novel's one-line epigraph and its final single-sentence diary entry. The line from Ovid's *Metamorphoses*—Et ignotas animum dimittit in artes (8:188)—invokes "the cunning one" at a moment when he turns his mind to unknown arts, but "the point of the epigraph" is surely not, as Hugh Kenner has claimed, that Daedalus should be regarded as doing "violence to nature."[2] He is evoked rather in two distinct but related capacities: he is the artificer about to devise a means of flying, and so, as "a winged form flying above the waves"— in the terms in which Stephen Dedalus thinks of him at a decisive stage in his life—he is "a symbol of the artist forging anew in his workshop out of the sluggish matter of the earth a new soaring impalpable imperishable being" (pp. 153–54).[3] But he is also the prisoner of Minos, and "weary of exile, hating Crete, his prison,"[4] he essays the unknown art in order to escape from the island. The epigraph thus gives a dual thrust to the movement of the narrative, for Stephen is propelled by the double recognition that he slowly comes to—a recognition that it is his vocation to be an artist and that he has to escape (to "fly by") the restrictive "nets" which his home and country and religion constitute for him.[5] This double recognition is implicit in Stephen's turning to Daedalus in his diary at the end of the novel: "27 April: Old father, old artificer, stand me now and ever in good stead." Having decided to follow in Daedalus's footsteps, and invoking his blessing, Stephen stands poised to leave his own island as a necessary preliminary to the pursuit of his art. The question Nasty Roche puts to Stephen Dedalus when he tells him his name (on the first discriminated occasion in the novel after the opening prelude)—"What kind of a name is that?" (p. 8)—has received a tacit answer.

Within the general *Bildungsroman* trajectory of a development from childhood to maturity, Joyce's curve thus delimits a more specific course, the movement to the protagonist's discovery of his vocation, and (running down from this high point of the curve) his consequent disengagement from anything that may impede his progress. Joyce's greater specificity of design makes for a more closely woven effect than we find in such novels as *Mansfield Park* or *The History of Henry Esmond*; and this effect is further intensified by his single-minded pursuit of his design and by the elimination of all matter not directly relevant to it. The result is a novel that, in its trim compactness, may be regarded as epitomizing a polar opposite of the kind of "large loose baggy monster" Henry James excoriated. The compactness stems, moreover, not only from the removal of excess weight but also from an inner harmony of parts. In his "portrait," Joyce is intent on finding the "individuating rhythm" of his protagonist's life, such a rhythm being defined, in the essay-narrative, as a "formal relation" of part to part (p. 41); and, in Stephen's aesthetic theory, as "the rhythm of . . . structure" that allows for the apprehension of an image as "complex, multiple, divisible, separable, made up of its parts, the result of its parts and their sum, harmonious" (p. 192). The *Portrait*, in its intermeshing complexity, is harmoniously unified in this way, for at any given point, as we look back to what has gone before, Stephen is perceived as being what he has ineluctably become—and as making choices in accordance with what he has been. His explanation of what he means in declaring he was "someone else" when he was at school nicely catches the "complex, multiple, divisible" attributes of the narrative: "—I mean, said Stephen, that I was not myself as I am now, as I had to become" (pp. 216–17).

A further unifying feature of the *Bildungsroman* form is its exclusive concern with the development of a single protagonist. This means, in all *Bildungsromane*, that both the plot and the other characters are subordinated to the portrayal of the protagonist; and we have seen how in *Mansfield Park* the account of Fanny's development subsumes that of other enterprises at Mansfield, and how in *The History of Henry Esmond* the depiction of Esmond's life bridges and unifies seemingly discordant spheres of activity. In the *Portrait* this effect is intensified to an unusual degree, for Stephen may well be regarded as the only character. Serving throughout as the unchanged focus of the narrative, a consistent "centre of consciousness," everything and everyone is not only perceived by him but filtered through his consciousness. This ensures a striking singleness and wholeness of effect as far as Stephen is concerned, but—in contradistinction to *Henry Esmond*, which also has one fixed focus—it makes for a lamentable thinning of the existence of others.[6] Stephen, for instance, from his early childhood to the eve of his departure from Ireland, is obsessed by the girl and then the young woman who has so little real (fictional) existence outside him that she is not even dignified by a name except on one memorable occasion when the depersonalizing personal pronoun is dropped and Stephen thinks of her as Emma (p. 107)—and we have to go to *Stephen Hero* to learn that the "E——C——" who appears in the title of some verses he addresses to her as a young boy is Emma Clery. Stephen, we are told, "[retains] nothing of all he [reads] save that which [seems] to him an echo or a prophecy of his own state" (p. 141), and he does the same by the world around him. The result is a triumphantly unitary text, but the cost of some victories, we may feel, is too high.

2

PROBABLY NO SECTION of the *Portrait* has had more critical attention lavished on it than the opening page and a half. The focus of attention, however, has generally been the thematic prefigurements discernible in the section, which has rightly been regarded as a concentrated prelude to what follows. But it is also paradigmatic of a central feature of the narrative, of Joyce's attempt to delineate the consciousness of his protagonist; and the opening rendering of a child's consciousness, of a child's-eye view of the world, is possibly unrivalled in English fiction. We may better appreciate the extent of Joyce's achievement if we compare his work in this respect with that of Dickens, the more especially since George Orwell has declared that "no English writer has written better about childhood than Dickens" and "no novelist has shown the same power of entering into the child's point of view." Orwell adds that when he first read *David Copperfield* at about the age of nine, he "vaguely imagined" that the opening chapters "had been written *by a child.*"[7]

It is instructive to compare a short passage from chapter 2 of *David Copperfield* with one from the opening section of the *Portrait*:

> The first objects that assume a distinct presence before me, as I look far back, into the blank of my infancy, are my mother with her pretty hair and youthful shape, and Peggotty, with no shape at all, and eyes so dark that they seemed to darken their whole neighbourhood in her face, and cheeks and arms so hard and red that I wondered the birds didn't peck her in preference to apples.

I believe I can remember these two at a little distance apart, dwarfed to my sight by stooping down . . .

. . . [in the back yard there are fowls] walking about in a menacing and ferocious manner. There is one cock who gets upon a post to crow, and seems to take particular notice of me as I look at him through the kitchen window, who makes me shiver, he is so fierce. Of the geese outside the side-gate who come waddling after me with their long necks stretched out when I go that way, I dream at night; as a man environed by wild beasts might dream of lions.

Once upon a time and a very good time it was there was a moocow coming down along the road and this moocow that was coming down along the road met a nicens little boy named baby tuckoo. . . .

His father told him that story: his father looked at him through a glass: he had a hairy face. . . .

When you wet the bed, first it is warm then it gets cold. His mother put on the oilsheet. That had the queer smell.

His mother had a nicer smell than his father. . . .

The Vances lived in number seven. They had a different father and mother. They were Eileen's father and mother. When they were grown up he was going to marry Eileen. He hid under the table. His mother said:

—O, Stephen will apologize.

Dante said:

—O, if not, the eagles will come and pull out his eyes.

The passages are readily comparable in two respects: the child's consciousness of the world around him, particularly of adults; and the child's experience of fear. David may look back into the blank of his infancy, but he sees as often as not with adult eyes. The most striking example of this is the adults who are "dwarfed" to his sight, and this evocation of the child's sense of things in terms of adult conceptions is apparent too in the references to his mother's "pretty" hair and "youthful shape," and to Peggotty's having "no shape at all." But then, with a sudden change of focus that makes us understand what Orwell meant, Dickens flashes into a child's world with the description of Peggotty's arms and cheeks, which the birds might have wanted to peck "in preference to apples." Joyce has nothing as vivid as this, but he steadily confines himself to a child's point of view, not only limiting himself to direct sense impressions—Stephen's father has "a hairy face"; his mother has "a nicer smell than his father"—but using a child's literalness of notation to defamiliarize an adult world: "his father looked at him through a glass." The literalness also empties potentially charged experiences of adult connotation—"When you wet the bed, first it is warm then it gets cold"—and strikingly conveys the child's grappling with the referentiality of language: since the words "father" and "mother" evoke his father and mother, Stephen makes a major adaptation to the facts of life when he registers that the Vances have "a different" father and mother. Much the same may be said of the two writers' rendering of a child's sense of fear. Dickens both seizes hold of a child's consciousness with David's fear of the cock who "seems to take particular notice" of him and loses it when David dreams of the threatening geese "as a man environed by wild beasts might dream of lions." Joyce, avoiding weak specifications, leaves Dante's awful threat to speak for itself, forcing adult readers to imagine its impact on a child, and letting it thud home in the child's jingle that follows.

The opening section of the *Portrait* should not be regarded, however, merely as a tour de force. If Joyce makes such a concentrated effort to evoke Stephen's consciousness as a child, it is because he intends to show that what Stephen becomes will evolve directly out of that consciousness as it ramifies and proliferates. In *A Portrait of the Artist*, unlike *Mansfield Park* or *The History of Henry Esmond*, for instance, it is not so much the child's circumstances as his consciousness that determines the sort of adult he becomes and colors his whole personality. The child's consciousness is the "embryo" of character that Joyce starts with and then sets into dynamic relation with circumstance: "In Dublin when [Joyce] set to work on the first draft of the novel, the idea he had in mind was that a man's character, like his body, develops from an embryo with constant traits. The accentuation of these traits, their reactions to hereditary influences and environment, were the main psychological lines he intended to follow, and, in fact, the purpose of the novel as originally planned."[8]

In the opening pages of the narrative, Joyce is at pains to show how this embryo begins to grow. Two examples should suffice. On the football field at Clongowes, the young Stephen's mind is busier than his body, and he thinks how Wells shouldered him into the square ditch "because he would not swop his little snuffbox for Wells's seasoned hacking chestnut, the conqueror of forty. How cold and slimy the water had been! A fellow had once seen a big rat jump into the scum" (p. 10). It is notable that, though the memory is of the square ditch, when the cause of the shouldering is registered, Wells's chestnut enters Stephen's consciousness trailing its clouds of glory. Thereafter it is as if for Stephen the chestnut is inseparably wedded to its attributes, and a subsequent encounter with Wells brings back the whole memory—though with a notable accretion of detail as far as the rat is concerned, a detail that now puts Stephen's own stamp on the experience: "It was Wells who had shouldered him into the square ditch the day before because he would not swop his little snuffbox for Wells's seasoned hacking chestnut, the conqueror of forty. It was a mean thing to do; all the fellows said it was. And how cold and slimy the water had been! And a fellow had once seen a big rat jump plop into the scum" (pp. 13–14). Similarly, on the football field Stephen thinks of some lines from a spelling book:

> *Wolsey died in Leicester Abbey*
> *Where the abbots buried him.*
> *Canker is a disease of plants,*
> *Cancer one of animals.*

(p. 10)

When he later falls ill and Wells begs him to keep quiet about the square ditch, Stephen guesses that Wells is afraid he has "some disease"—and the mere thought of the word triggers a fairly elaborate memory: "Canker was a disease of plants and cancer one of animals: or another different. That was a long time ago then out on the playgrounds in the evening light, creeping from point to point on the fringe of his line, a heavy bird flying low through the grey light. Leicester Abbey lit up. Wolsey died there. The abbots buried him themselves" (p. 20). The associative process in the two examples is simple, but it is by an analogous play of association, going back to his childhood though more indirect in nature, that some of the most important decisions of Stephen's life are determined.

The first momentous event in Stephen's life is his decision not to join the Jesuit order, not to find his vocation, as the director urges him to, in the Catholic Church. It is here that Stephen first begins to define himself, even though this is by way of clarifying what he is not. The significance of the setting of the scene in which the director circuitously makes his proposal to Stephen has been memorably analyzed by Hugh Kenner, particularly in respect of the manner in which the director, as he dangles and loops the cord of the blind, "coolly [proffers] a noose" to Stephen.[9] Though we see the director's position and movements through Stephen's perceiving consciousness—as we do everything else in the novel—it seems to me, however, that it is we who register the significance of the noose and not he, for there is no indication whatsoever that he responds to it or that it plays any part in the making of his decision. The decision is determined rather by an involuntary process of association that goes back to his first experience of the church and of the Jesuits at Clongowes.

When the bell rings for night prayers, the boys move along the corridors to the chapel:

The corridors were darkly lit and the chapel was darkly lit. Soon all would be dark and sleeping. There was cold night air in the chapel and the marbles were the colour the sea was at night. The sea was cold day and night: but it was colder at night. It was cold and dark under the seawall beside his father's house. But the kettle would be on the hob to make punch. . . .

There was a cold night smell in the chapel. But it was a holy smell. It was not like the smell of the old peasants who knelt at the back of the chapel at Sunday mass. That was a smell of air and rain and turf and corduroy. But they were very holy peasants. They breathed behind him on his neck and sighed as they prayed. . . . It would be lovely to sleep for one night in [a] cottage before the fire of smoking turf, in the dark lit by the fire, in the warm dark, breathing the smell of the peasants, air and rain and turf and corduroy. But, O, the road there between the trees was dark! You would be lost in the dark. It made him afraid to think of how it was.

He heard the voice of the prefect of the chapel saying the last prayer. He prayed it too against the dark outside under the trees. (pp. 16–17)

The idea of darkness, as Stephen thinks of being "lost in the dark," concentrates his childhood fears of all that is unknown and frightening; and what he opposes to the darkness is a belief in prayer, for he prays "against the dark." Yet his trust in the efficacy of prayer in this regard is ironically undercut since the chapel is itself associated with the dark: its very light, like that of the "darkly lit" corridors that lead to it, evokes darkness. The chapel is associated, furthermore, with a reiterated sense of coldness: it is full of "cold night air," its "marbles" suggest the cold night sea, and its "holy smell" is "a cold night smell." Nor is the cold offset, as is that which Stephen connects with the scene outside his father's house, by a comforting feeling of inner warmth. Instead the cold and holy smell of the chapel is contrasted with that of the peasants; and they, in contradistinction to it, are linked with life-giving properties—with the "smell of air and rain and turf" as well as corduroy, and with the light and warmth of a fire.

The director asks Stephen to consider his offer carefully, and when they part he gives his hand "as if already to a companion in the spiritual life." That Stephen is naturally drawn to another sort of life, however, is suggested, as he moves outside, by his becoming "conscious of the caress of mild evening air." This leads, when he sees in the priest's face "a mirthless reflection of the sunken day," to a defensive motion of disengagement as he slowly "detaches" the hand which has "acquiesced faintly in that companionship":

As he descended the steps the impression which effaced his troubled self-communion was that of a mirthless mask reflecting a sunken day from the threshold of the college. The shadow, then, of the life of the college passed gravely over his consciousness. It was a grave and ordered and passionless life that awaited him, a life without material cares. He wondered how he would pass the first night in the novitiate and with what dismay he would wake the first morning in the dormitory. The troubling odour of the long corridors of Clongowes came back to him and he heard the discreet murmur of the burning gasflames. At once from every part of his being unrest began to irradiate. A feverish quickening of his pulses followed and a din of meaningless words drove his reasoned thoughts hither and thither confusedly. His lungs dilated and sank as if he were inhaling a warm moist unsustaining air and he smelt again the warm moist air which hung in the bath in Clongowes above the sluggish turf-coloured water. (pp. 145–46)

Clearly the key image in this passage is that of the director's "mirthless mask" which "reflects a sunken day"; but though it is Stephen who vividly registers it, he does not at first grasp its significance, for he continues to muse about the life he envisages as "awaiting" him in the order. These thoughts give way, however, to the sudden recall of Clongowes. Though the memory immediately follows his wondering about waking in the dormitory, it is triggered by the mirthless mask. The director's face is like a death-mask, and it suddenly activates Stephen's childhood association of the Jesuits and their church with all that is cold and dark and lifeless, with an air that is "unsustaining." The way the image of the mask works in his consciousness is interesting. Even before he understands its meaning for him, it "effaces" his "troubled selfcommunion" as to whether he should join the order or not, supplanting intellectual consideration of the problem. Then, with the way cleared, there follows the memory of Clongowes, and that brings with it an involuntary "unrest" that irradiates "from every part of his being." It is this unrest which decides the issue. With his "reasoned thoughts" driven "hither and thither confusedly," he is possessed by a deep revulsion from the life offered him. Thereupon he proceeds to rationalize the decision he has already made instinctively, concluding that it is "his destiny" to be "elusive of social or religious orders," and that for him to be celibate and "not to fall" would be "too hard, too hard" (pp. 147–48).

There is a parallel between the director's attempt to get Stephen to join his order and that by fellow students, particularly Davin, to have him participate in the Irish nationalist struggle. The parallel extends also to the way in which Stephen's refusal to make either commitment is arrived at. His sense of the nature of Irish political passions may be traced back to one of the most vividly rendered scenes of his childhood, the Christmas dinner. The scene is presented dramatically, but Stephen is the narrative focus, the perceiving consciousness, and the point of the episode is the impact it makes on him. The impact is overwhelming, for when both Mr. Casey and his father weep over "poor Parnell" at the end of the argument with Dante, Stephen's face is "ter-

rorstricken." There is much to frighten a child in the dispute, which is
marked by its increasing violence: Mr. Casey "[throws] his fist on the
table . . . , frowning angrily," and then raises "his clenched fist," which
he brings "down on the table with a crash," while he "[shouts]
hoarsely"; Dante's "cheeks [shake]," she screams and "almost [spits] in
[Mr. Casey's] face," she "[shoves] her chair violently aside" when she
leaves the table, "[turning] round violently and [shouting] down the
room" before "the door [slams] behind her." And the fiery passion-
ateness of Mr. Casey and Dante leaps to their faces: his face "[glows]
with anger" and he stares "out of . . . dark flaming eyes"; Dante's
"cheeks [flush] and [quiver] with rage" (pp. 35–37). The violence and the
passion are alien to Stephen's temperament—to the boy who cannot
even throw himself into a game of football, keeping "on the fringe of his
line . . . , out of reach of the rude feet" (p. 8); and to the contemplative
young intellectual who maintains that "the esthetic emotion" is "stat-
ic," with "the mind . . . arrested and raised above desire and loathing"
(p. 186). We may assume therefore that Irish politics are associated with
qualities from which the child recoils; and in the argument the history
of Irish nationalism is seen in terms (which leave their mark too on
Stephen) of recurrent betrayal: Mr. Casey accuses the Catholic Church,
in instance after instance, of treachery to the nationalist cause, while
Dante brands a patriot such as Parnell "a traitor to his country" (pp. 35–
36).

Stephen's refusal as an adult to support the nationalist cause is enun-
ciated in a conversation with Davin:

—Try to be one of us, repeated Davin. In your heart you are an Irishman but
your pride is too powerful.
—My ancestors threw off their language and took another, Stephen said.
They allowed a handful of foreigners to subject them. Do you fancy I am going
to pay in my own life and person debts they made? What for?
—For our freedom, said Davin.
—No honourable and sincere man, said Stephen, has given up to you his life
and his youth and his affections from the days of Tone to those of Parnell but
you sold him to the enemy or failed him in need or reviled him and left him for
another. And you invite me to be one of you. I'd see you damned first.
—They died for their ideals, Stevie, said Davin. Our day will come yet, believe me.
Stephen, following his own thought, was silent for an instant.
—The soul is born, he said vaguely, first in those moments I told you of. It
has a slow and dark birth, more mysterious than the birth of the body. When
the soul of a man is born in this country there are nets flung at it to hold it back
from flight. You talk to me of nationality, language, religion. I shall try to fly by
those nets.
Davin knocked the ashes from his pipe.

—Too deep for me, Stevie, he said. But a man's country comes first. Ireland first, Stevie. You can be a poet or mystic after.
—Do you know what Ireland is? asked Stephen with cold violence. Ireland is the old sow that eats her farrow. (pp. 184–85)

Stephen's view of Ireland as "the old sow that eats her farrow" not only savagely expresses his feelings about his country but also his reasons for refusing to serve it. The image has the same decisive force in this context as that of the director's mirthless mask in the scene previously referred to; but whereas the mask triggers an association with Stephen's childhood, propelling him back to it, this image is generated by impressions made in his childhood and springs from them. Encapsulating Stephen's recoil from both the violence and the betrayals of Irish politics, the image of the repulsive mother who consumes her own offspring, betraying the trust put in her, may be traced back to the general turbulence of the Christmas dinner and to one scene in particular:

—Really, Simon, said Mrs. Dedalus, you should not speak that way before Stephen. It's not right.
—O, he'll remember all this when he grows up, said Dante hotly—the language he heard against God and religion and priests in his own home.
—Let him remember too, cried Mr. Casey to her from across the table, the language with which the priests and the priests' pawns broke Parnell's heart and hounded him into his grave. Let him remember that too when he grows up.
—Sons of bitches! cried Mr. Dedalus. When he was down they turned on him to betray him and rend him like rats in a sewer. (pp. 31–32)

The image of the old sow is also related to Stephen's more recent experience. When Davin tells him the story of the pregnant woman who invites him to spend the night with her when he stops to ask for a glass of water, Stephen thinks of her too as an epitome of the Irish, as "a type of her race and his own, a batlike soul waking to the consciousness of itself in darkness and secrecy and loneliness and, through the eyes and voice and gesture of a woman without guile, calling the stranger to her bed" (p. 166). The woman, artlessly ready to betray her husband, as she issues her invitation to the stranger, becomes (like the sow) a type of Irish betrayal. She also suggests Ireland's willing submission to England, its readiness to be taken by the stranger; and Stephen, as he tells Davin, feels no obligation to pay for what his ancestors have done since they "allowed a handful of foreigners to subject them."
In the conversation with Davin, Stephen propounds the idea of man's double birth, first of the body and then of the soul. He talks in general terms of nets being flung to hold back the "soul of a man" when it is "born in this country," but it is evident he has his own expe-

rience in mind, and that he is thinking of his discovery of his vocation as the birth of his own soul. Just how nets are flung to restrict the artist in nationalist Catholic Ireland is suggested by the play of association in Stephen's mind on an occasion shortly before his departure from his homeland. Standing on the steps of the library, he watches some birds in flight, and this makes him think, among other things, of "the hawklike man whose name he [bears] soaring out of his captivity on osierwoven wings." He decides that the birds "must be swallows," and this brings some lines of verse to mind:

> Bend down your faces, Oona and Aleel,
> I gaze upon them as the swallow gazes
> Upon the nest under the eave before
> He wanders the loud waters.

A soft liquid joy like the noise of many waters flowed over his memory and he felt in his heart the soft peace of silent spaces of fading tenuous sky above the waters, of oceanic silence, of swallows flying through the seadusk over the flowing waters. (pp. 203–4)

The verses continue to "[croon] in the ear of his memory," but then they suddenly give way to the remembered sound of the "catcalls and hisses and mocking cries" that filled the hall "on the night of the opening of the national theatre" (p. 204). The chain of association here seems, deceptively, to be direct: the birds suggest the lines about the swallow in Yeats's play *The Countess Cathleen*, and the quotation from the play brings back to him how the Dublin students howled down what they considered a "libel on Ireland" (p. 204). But the process of association is more devious—and more significant—than that. Stephen is unable to decide what the birds he watches symbolize—"departure or . . . loneliness?"—but their flight would seem initially to have represented to him the free flight of the artist, as his (otherwise random) recall of Daedalus suggests. And in nationalistic Dublin this in turn evokes the existence of impediments to such flight, the nets cast to hold the artist back. It is not only because of "the swallow" that Stephen remembers Yeats's play and savors the liquid sound of the verse; nor is it only with the weight of idle thoughts that his consciousness is burdened. He decides to "fly by" the nets he sees stretching before him as an artist by flying away.

At the end of the narrative, Stephen makes a defiant declaration to Cranly: "I will not serve that in which I no longer believe," he says, "whether it call itself my home, my fatherland, or my church: and I will try to express myself in some mode of life or art as freely as I can" (p. 222). His alienation from his family seems to be less a necessity of his art than his breaking away from his country and his church, but it is intense. Even as a boy he feels that he is "hardly of the one blood" with his family, and that he stands to them rather "in the mystical kinship of fosterage, fosterchild and fosterbrother" (p. 90)—an interesting metaphorical equivalent of the typical *Bildungsroman* motif of the protagonist as orphan. As in the case of church and country, Stephen's sense of alienation from his family, particularly his father, is sustained by the complex interaction of outer circumstance and an associative consciousness. The combination is nicely caught in an early scene:

Mr. Dedalus screwed his glass into his eye and stared hard at both his sons. Stephen mumbled his bread without answering his father's gaze.

—By the bye, said Mr. Dedalus at length, the rector, or provincial, rather, was telling me that story about you and Father Dolan. You're an impudent thief, he said.

—O, he didn't, Simon.

—Not he! said Mr. Dedalus. But he gave me a great account of the whole affair. We were chatting, you know, and one word borrowed another. And, by the way, who do you think he told me will get that job in the corporation? But I'll tell you that after. Well, as I was saying, we were chatting away quite friendly and he asked me did our friend here wear glasses still and then he told me the whole story.

—And was he annoyed, Simon?

—Annoyed! Not he! *Manly little chap!* he said. . . .

Mr. Dedalus turned to his wife and interjected in his natural voice:

—Shows you the spirit in which they take the boys there. O, a jesuit for your life, for diplomacy!

He reassumed the provincial's voice and repeated:

—*I told them all at dinner about it and Father Dolan and I and all of us we had a hearty laugh together over it. Ha! Ha! Ha!* (pp. 66–67)

Though Stephen does not utter a word in this scene—indeed his silence is one measure of the alienation he feels—we know that the episode his father refers to is perhaps the most significant thing that has happened to him in his young life. His appeal to the rector with regard to Father Dolan's punishment of him was not merely a daring protest against injustice (and acclaimed as such by his schoolfellows) but also his first rebellious questioning of authority and assertion of self. For Mr. Dedalus, however, when he can keep his mind on it, the whole affair is simply a good joke, a story that is neatly illustrative both of the impudence of his son—his own view of the matter slips out—and the subtle diplomacy of the Jesuits. The discrepancy between the views offered in the narrative of Stephen's appeal to the rector figures (without the aid of a word of commentary) the gap between father and son.

The Mr. Dedalus who tells this story, moreover, screwing his glass into his eye and staring hard at his sons, is associated in Stephen's consciousness with the father who tells him the story about the nicens little boy, looking at him through a glass as he does so. Stephen's earliest consciousness of his father is associated with that glass as an impediment to direct contact; and as more and more things come between them, as in this scene, his own withdrawal—his refusal to "[answer] his father's gaze"—becomes complete.

3

THE BIRTH of Stephen's soul when he discovers his vocation generates a new consciousness, as it were, a new consciousness of himself as an artist and of art. Because this is a beginning, his encounters with the swimming boys and the wading girl—the discovery scenes—are parallel to the opening sections of the novel and, like them, lay the ground of consciousness in his new life.

Stephen's revelations come immediately after his rejection of the director's invitation to him to join the Jesuits, his realization that "his destiny" is not what he has "thought [it] to be" (p. 150) seemingly clearing the way for new developments. What is most valuable to him, at this stage of his life, is suggested, as he sets off for the Bull, by his drawing forth "from his treasure" a phrase, which he speaks "softly to himself: —A day of dappled seaborne clouds" (p. 151).[10] This is followed by the meeting with his swimming schoolfellows that prepares the way for his first revelation, for when they call out to him, they play with his name: "Stephanos Dedalos! Bous Stephanoumenos! Bous Stephaneforos!" (p. 153). The Greek and the evocation of "the fabulous artificer" suddenly make "his strange name [seem] to him a prophecy," a prophecy of "the end he [has] been born to serve," and he has the vision (previously referred to) of Daedalus flying above the sea, "a symbol of the artist" (pp. 153–54). Stephen seems to see into the heart of himself, as if in an epiphany, for the word "radiant" is used three times to describe his state—"the body he knew was purified in a breath and delivered of incertitude and made radiant and commingled with the element of the spirit. An ecstasy of flight made radiant his eyes and wild his breath and tremulous and wild and radiant his windswept limbs" (p. 154)—and in his aesthetic theory Stephen will translate Aquinas's "claritas" as "radiance"—the "quidditas" or "whatness" of a thing (pp. 192–93). The birth of his soul is celebrated as a delivery from a living death, and the discovery of his vocation becomes the central affirmation of his life: "His soul had arisen from the grave of boyhood, spurning her graveclothes. Yes! Yes! Yes! He would create proudly out of the freedom and power of his soul, as the great artificer whose name he bore, a living thing, new and soaring and beautiful, impalpable, imperishable" (p. 154).

Stephen takes off his shoes and socks, and then climbs down the breakwater:

> There was a long rivulet in the strand and, as he waded slowly up its course, he wondered at the endless drift of seaweed. Emerald and black and russet and olive, it moved beneath the current, swaying and turning. The water of the rivulet was dark with endless drift and mirrored the highdrifting clouds. The clouds were drifting above him silently and silently the seatangle was drifting below him; and the grey warm air was still: and a new wild life was singing in his veins. . . .
>
> A girl stood before him in midstream, alone and still, gazing out to sea. She seemed like one whom magic had changed into the likeness of a strange and beautiful seabird. Her long slender bare legs were delicate as a crane's and pure save where an emerald trail of seaweed had fashioned itself as a sign upon the flesh. Her thighs, fuller and softhued as ivory, were bared almost to the hips where the white fringes of her drawers were like featherings of soft white down. Her slateblue skirts were kilted boldly about her waist and dovetailed behind her. Her bosom was as a bird's soft and slight, slight and soft as the breast of some darkplumaged dove. But her long fair hair was girlish: and girlish, and touched with the wonder of mortal beauty, her face.
>
> She was alone and still, gazing out to sea; and when she felt his presence and the worship of his eyes her eyes turned to him in quiet sufferance of his gaze, without shame or wantonness. Long, long she suffered his gaze and then quietly withdrew her eyes from his and bent them towards the stream, gently stirring the water with her foot hither and thither. The first faint noise of gently moving water broke the silence, low and faint and whispering, faint as the bells of sleep; hither and thither: and a faint flame trembled on her cheek.
>
> —Heavenly God! cried Stephen's soul, in an outburst of profane joy. (pp. 155–56)

If the prose here seems at times to mirror Stephen's adolescent fervor at the sight of the girl, it is also used to set the scene with a precision that supports the symbolic significance of the encounter. As Stephen wades up the rivulet, giving himself to the life that is "singing in his veins," what he is opting for is defined by the "endless drift" around him: there is an "endless drift of seaweed" and the water mirrors "the highdrifting clouds"; the clouds are "drifting above him silently" and the seatangle is "silently . . . drifting below him." As opposed to the stability and fixity and stillness of a life in a religious order, Stephen (having emerged from the grave of his past) here elects for "a new wild life" that is viewed as endless flux, change, and motion. The girl that he then sees is marked by two striking attributes. First, she is absolutely still: she stands, "alone and still," as she gazes out to sea, and this is twice repeated; it is only after she has "long, long . . . suffered his gaze" that she breaks the stillness and begins to stir the water with her foot. Second, she is literally marked, for her legs are said to be "pure save where an emerald trail of seaweed [has] fashioned itself as a sign upon the flesh." The girl, it is thus intimated, is herself part of the flux of life, bearing its sign on her flesh; but in her stillness she is at the same time detached from the flux around her. It is not merely to "the wonder of [her] mortal beauty" that Stephen responds. The girl images what the artist sets out to do in his work, to capture flux in stillness, the "eternal passing and flowing," in a memorable phrase in *To the Lighthouse*, being "struck into stability." And the bird imagery in which she is so insistently depicted speaks to much the same tension of opposites: instinct with life and motion, like a bird poised for flight—and it is on free flight that Stephen is to posit his existence— she is caught at this moment in utter stillness. As they gaze long at each other without speaking, the meeting—in its stasis—becomes emblematic too of what Stephen will believe should be the aim of art, as his impersonal contemplation of the girl is of a desired response to it. His calling on God in "an outburst of profane joy" before he turns away from the girl not only marks the end of his contemplation but his conversion to a worship of mortal beauty. As he determines in his art "to recreate life out of life" (p. 156), he is ready to pursue a new religion as well as a new life, to become in time a "priest of the eternal imagination" (p. 200).

Stephen thinks of himself directly in these terms in the scene in which he is shown composing his villanelle. The eternal imagination, in this regard, is shown to work in unexpected ways, and the poem itself only tenuously reflects the consciousness from which it springs. Nor is this a function of the fact that it was not specially written for the *Portrait*,[11] since the novelist depicts the process of its composition with care, deliberately relating the finished product to his protagonist's state of mind. The villanelle shows considerable technical accomplishment but, though Robert Scholes has made an effort to fill it with mythic content,[12] it is not a good poem.

More to the point, perhaps, than the kind of critical judgment the poem invites is the relation set up in the narrative between the poem and the circumstances in which it is composed. Joyce is not only highly original in depicting the process of composition but, it seems to me, settles the question of how the poem should be regarded by the nature of the frame he carefully sets it in. After he wakes "towards dawn," Stephen is shown composing the villanelle stanza by stanza; and then, just before the completed poem is written out in full, we have this description:

He spoke the verses aloud from the first lines till the music and rhythm suffused his mind, turning it to quiet indulgence; then copied them painfully to feel them the better by seeing them; then lay back on his bolster.

The full morning light had come. No sound was to be heard: but he knew that all around him life was about to awaken in common noises, hoarse voices, sleepy prayers. Shrinking from that life he turned towards the wall, making a cowl of the blanket and staring at the great overblown scarlet flowers of the tattered wallpaper. He tried to warm his perishing joy in their scarlet glow, imagining a roseway from where he lay upwards to heaven all strewn with scarlet flowers. Weary! Weary! He too was weary of ardent ways.

A gradual warmth, a languorous weariness passed over him, descending along his spine from his closely cowled head. He felt it descend and, seeing himself as he lay, smiled. Soon he would sleep.

He had written verses for her again after ten years. . . .

A glow of desire kindled again his soul and fired and fulfilled all his body. Conscious of his desire she was waking from odorous sleep, the temptress of his villanelle. Her eyes, dark and with a look of languor, were opening to his eyes. Her nakedness yielded to him, radiant, warm, odorous and lavishlimbed, enfolded him like a shining cloud, enfolded him like water with a liquid life: and like a cloud of vapour or like waters circumfluent in space the liquid letters of speech, symbols of the element of mystery, flowed forth over his brain. (pp. 200–201)

If, in deciding to be an artist, Stephen dedicates himself to new wild life and the wonder of mortal beauty, it is notable how, in actually composing a poem, he "shrinks" from the commonness of life, "making a cowl" of his blanket: in his art, it appears, he is not so much a priest of the eternal imagination as a monk, keeping himself remote from everyday life and turning to art as a refuge from the world around him. Whereas he is able to draw on his own deepest feelings in deciding not to join the Jesuits or the Irish nationalists, and does so by maintaining a continuity with a childhood consciousness of things, it is as if there is a break in consciousness where his art is concerned. What the encounter with the wading girl reveals to him is that the artist's task is to capture the fullness of ordinary life in all its rich suggestiveness, to "recreate life out of life"; but the poem he writes is retrogressive, binding him in effect—despite his scintillating aesthetic theory—to an immature view of art that long precedes the seminal meeting with the girl. The villanelle, indeed, would appear to spring from impulses not notably different from those that characterized his first poem to the temptress, his writing of the verses to E—— C—— some ten years before when he was a young boy. The tie to childhood proves incapacitating in this instance rather than liberating:

During this process [of brooding] all those elements which he deemed common and insignificant fell out of the scene. There remained no trace of the tram itself nor of the trammen nor of the horses: nor did he and she appear vividly. The verses told only of the night and the balmy breeze and the maiden lustre of the moon. Some undefined sorrow was hidden in the hearts of the protagonists as they stood in silence beneath the leafless trees and when the moment of farewell had come the kiss, which had been withheld by one, was given by both. After this the letters L.D.S. were written at the foot of the page and, having hidden the book, he went into his mother's bedroom and gazed at his face for a long time in the mirror of her dressingtable. (p. 65)

The villanelle is subject to the same kind of flight from what might be "deemed common" as the boyish verses, for the sexual ardor that generates it tends to "fall out of the scene" of the poem much as the tram and trammen and horses; it too, allowing for the actual lack of contact between Stephen and Emma, suggests the kind of wish-fulfillment that is evident in the kiss being "given by both"; and the boy's self-absorption with his reflection in the mirror is itself reflected in the young poet's concern with himself as he composes the poem.

Stephen's strongly sexual imaginings during the writing of the poem have been the subject of some speculation. Hugh Kenner states flatly that "the one piece of literary composition Stephen actually achieves in the book comes out of a wet dream," and others have followed him.[13] But the section that details the composition of the poem starts with Stephen's waking, and everything that follows takes place while he is awake. Robert Scholes, on the other hand, says that "Stephen's spiritual copulation with [the temptress] is a symbolic equivalent for that moment of inspiration when 'in the virgin womb of the imagination the word was made flesh'."[14] If we undoubtedly witness the conception of the poem, it is not as immaculate as this suggests—just as Stephen's copulation with the temptress would appear to be both imaginary and imaginative, rather than "spiritual." It also serves far more prosaic purposes, for the conclusion seems inescapable that he is masturbating while he composes his poem: his mind, we note, "turns" to "quiet indulgence"; a "gradual warmth" and a "languorous weariness" pass over him, "descending along his spine"; "seeing himself" as he lies, he "[smiles]"; he thinks that "soon he [will] sleep"; and finally "a glow of desire [kindles] again his soul and [fires] and [fulfills] all his body," the orgasm being described in liquid terms as "her nakedness [yields] to him." As he turns away from the world and creeps under his blanket in order to compose his poem, Stephen's art, we see, is very much that of "a young man," a matter of self-indulgence and self-gratification. When he gets ready to leave Ireland and invokes Daedalus as the "old father" in the final diary entry, Stephen is as much identified with Icarus as the "old artificer"; and there is a clear implication that if he flies too high in the attempt to fly by the nets spread for him and withdraws too far from ordinary life, he is heading for disaster as an artist.

FREE FALL:
THE BURSTING OF THE DOOR

Free Fall resounds to Sammy Mountjoy's reiterated declarations of his unbridgeable separateness from the child he was. That his life should be apprehended as a seamless whole, however, is dramatically implied by the striking—and difficult—opening of the novel:

I have walked by stalls in the market-place where books, dog-eared and faded from their purple, have burst with a white hosanna. I have seen people crowned with a double crown, holding in either hand the crook and flail, the power and the glory. I have understood how the scar becomes a star, I have felt the flake of fire fall, miraculous and pentecostal. My yesterdays walk with me. They keep step, they are grey faces that peer over my shoulder. I live on Paradise Hill, ten minutes from the station, thirty seconds from the shops and the local. Yet I am a burning amateur, torn by the irrational and incoherent, violently searching and self-condemned.

When did I lose my freedom? For once, I was free. I had power to choose. The mechanics of cause and effect is statistical probability yet surely sometimes we operate below or beyond that threshold. Free-will cannot be debated but only experienced, like a colour or the taste of potatoes. I remember one such experience. I was very small and I was sitting on the stone surround of the pool and fountain in the centre of the park. . . . I had bathed and drunk and now I was sitting on the warm stone edge placidly considering what I should do next. The gravelled paths of the park radiated from me: and all at once I was overcome by a new knowledge. I could take whichever I would of these paths. There was nothing to draw me down one more than the other. I danced down one for joy in the taste of potatoes. I was free. I had chosen. (pp. 5–6)[1]

The opening paragraph of the narrative may be regarded as the ultimate point in its temporal range: having lived through the experiences that

189

constitute the narrative, Sammy is now looking back on his life as he prepares to record it, and he begins by registering his current sense of the world he lives in. When he then starts the narrative proper by moving to one of his earliest memories, there could be no better indication that his end is in his beginning.

The opening, furthermore, delineates a concern of Sammy's that is central to his life and runs literally from the first to the last page of his narrative. As a boy, Sammy hovers—at a crucial moment—between choosing one or other of "two pictures of the universe," between what he calls "the world of miracle," of "Moses and Jehovah" and the burning bush, and "the other world," the "rational universe"; he opts for the latter (pp. 211, 217). On the final page of his narrative, however, he concludes that "both worlds are real" though "there is no bridge" between them (p. 253). And this is the perception that he gives vivid if obscure expression to at the start of his story, his sense of the coexistence of the mundane world of markets and the pentecostal "flake of fire." He tries, that is, to do justice both to the materiality of things, such as dog-eared books, and the spirit that may burst from them; to the simple material existence of ordinary men—the reference to crowned people, we realize later, is to his fellow prisoners of war—and to the majesty of the spiritual life he sees in them, to that which transforms them into "sceptred kings," as he subsequently calls them. He tries to do justice to both worlds, but he recognizes now that it is impossible to account for one in terms of the other, to reduce the flake of fire to "the mechanics of cause and effect," and vice versa.[2] And though he has himself experienced the miraculous fire—it is the climax of the prisoner of war episode, as we shall see, the "star" to his "scar"—he lives habitually in the material world of "the shops and the local," and so is no more than "a burning amateur," not committed to a full acceptance of the spiritual life and still "torn by the irrational," which he is forced incoherently to set side by side with "statistical probability." His search for unity, for a system which will bridge the two worlds, may be unsuccessful, but it unifies his own life, for he is still "violently searching" for the connection even though he believes there is none. He lives, after all, "on Paradise Hill."

Living where he does, Sammy is also a haunted man. He lives "almost next door" to a house, known to him in his days in Rotten Row, that has now become a mental hospital in which Beatrice is permanently resident, and he cannot free himself of her presence. His "yesterdays walk with [him]," he says, peering over his shoulder with "grey faces," faces, he adds, which "nothing can expunge or exorcise" (p. 7). Unable to break away from Beatrice's grey face, the question that preoccupies him as he begins his story is when he lost his freedom.

It is a question that determines the structure of the narrative. It seems at first, as Sammy depicts his childhood and his years at primary school (chapters 1–3), that the narrative will be chronological; but then he jumps to his life as an art student at the age of nineteen, and chapters 4–6 portray his relationship with Beatrice. The displaced section of the narrative—the account of his high school days and first meeting with Beatrice—comes much later (chapters 11–12); and we understand that the order of events is shaped by Sammy's attempt to pinpoint the loss of his freedom. Periodically the narrative is punctuated by the question "Here?" and the answer "Not here." After such a question and answer at the end of chapter 3, however, chapter 4 begins with the categorical assertion that by the age of nineteen he "was no longer free" (p. 79). The loss of freedom must have occurred, therefore, at a point between these two narrative blocks, at a time between his childhood and young manhood—and indeed the loss is eventually ascribed to a decision he makes at the end of his high school days—but Sammy first elects in chapters 7–10 to deal with his experience as a prisoner of war (with a flashback to his childhood in chapter 8). The narrative order thus suggests that he has to come to terms with his war experience before he is able to answer the question on which the narrative turns.[3] Encompassing this question is a concern with the nature of freedom and with the consequences of its loss; and since all the major episodes would appear to be selected with a view to their bearing on these central concerns, *Free Fall*—like *A Portrait of the Artist*—has a notably unified tightness of effect: it too, within the general *Bildungsroman* portrayal of the protagonist's development from childhood to manhood, follows a single, specific line of interest. Samuel Mountjoy, who "[hangs] in the Tate" (p. 7), is more of an artist than Stephen Dedalus, and *Free Fall* may in some ways be regarded as Golding's covert rejoinder to the earlier novel, which is certainly suffused with more traditional notions of the fall.

Golding's own idea of the fall is neatly caught in the title of his novel, and he is himself on record as to what he intended that to convey:

Everybody has translated ["free fall"] in terms of theology; well, okay, you can do it that way, which is why it's not a bad title, but it is in fact a scientific term. It is where your gravity has *gone*; it is a man in a space ship who has no gravity; things don't fall or lift, they float about; he is completely divorced from the other idea of a thing up *there* and centered on *there* in which he lives.

Do you see what I mean? Where for hundreds of thousands of years men have known where they were, now they don't know where they are any longer. This is the point of *Free Fall*. Perhaps I didn't mention this aspect at all in those days, possibly because I felt a little tiny bit ashamed of the kind of science-fiction overtones of *Free Fall*, but it is really and truly the idea. There is also the Miltonic idea; there is also the Genesis idea; there is also the ordinary daily life idea of something which is "for free," something which is also "fall." "Free" and "fall" are both caught up in it.[4]

We may be inclined to believe that men not knowing where they are is not quite "the point of *Free Fall*," since Sammy's narrative is dedicated to establishing just where he is and how he got there, but Golding's remarks are nevertheless suggestive. They indicate how the two "worlds" that contest for Sammy's exclusive allegiance coexist in the very title of the novel, which draws together in its primary meaning the Miltonic (or biblical) and scientific overtones of the phrase. Sammy, that is, is to be seen as free to choose what he wants to make of his life, having been endowed with free will and made "sufficient to have stood, though free to fall"; but at the same time he is to be viewed as subject to a force outside himself and so having no control over what he does, for his "gravity has gone." The apparent contradiction is resolved in the notion of a free choice that thereafter determines the irrevocable course of a life. Since this course is irreversible—an endless and perpetual floating in space, as it were—it is impossible for the fall to be followed by a redemption. It is in this sense that Sammy sets out to pinpoint "the decision made freely that cost [him his] freedom" (p. 7). But he begins his narrative by dwelling on what has been lost—the "taste of potatoes"—as he recalls his first overwhelming experience of the freedom of choice. Still "very small" but waking to sudden awareness, he is "overcome by a new knowledge" as he confronts the radiating paths of the park and realizes that he is free to take whichever path he likes. His joyous dance down the path he chooses—and his freedom then to move from path to path—is set against his inability now to put the straight and narrow way he has chosen behind him, to break out of its confinement.

2

SAMMY's illegitimacy and his being brought up by one parent are in line with the obscure origins of many *Bildungsroman* protagonists and/or their orphan or quasi-orphan status. Unlike Fanny Price or Henry Esmond or Stephen Dedalus (who confers the status on himself), however, Sammy does not appear to be overtly affected by the kind of start he is given in life. He remembers his mother as "enormous" and as filling "the backward tunnel": "These last few months I have been trying to catch her in two handfuls of clay—not, I mean, her appearance; but more accurately, my sense of her hugeness and reality, her matter-of-fact blocking of the view. Beyond her there is nothing, nothing. She is the warm darkness between me and the cold light. She is the end of the tunnel, she" (p. 15). Sammy's sense of his enormous mother, of the reality of her hugeness, nicely catches the security she gives him. It is as though she completely fills the space around him, flowing over into the missing father's place. As he tries to push back into the tunnel of memory, he cannot go further than the solid, matter-of-fact presence of his mother; his memories—and his life—start with her. At the same time, in a reversal of the image, she is at the opening of the tunnel too, "blocking the view" and interposing her warmth between him and "the cold light" of the outside world. Sammy, we note, both loves and is loved; and so he is not subject to the emotional insecurity that characterizes so many *Bildungsroman* protagonists. Nor does "Ma" smother him with the kind of overpowering maternal love a Paul Morel is exposed to in *Sons and Lovers*. Indeed, the only mark his illegitimacy seems to leave on Sammy is the symbolic one of his wanting intensely to know how he has been made into what he is. Despite the toughness of the material conditions of life in the Rotten Row slum, moreover, his description of his childhood suggests he is given everything needful for his development—sufficient for him to have stood.

Sammy's search for the point at which he lost his freedom begins as soon as he has sketched in the background of his life in Rotten Row; and accordingly he concentrates in the chapters devoted to his childhood on recapitulating one misdemeanor after another as he seeks to establish the occasion of his "fall." This, as has been indicated, comes at a later stage, but the account of these childhood episodes serves to clarify the necessary conditions of a fall in Sammy's terms. The first incidents of note in this respect are all literally instances of trespass— Sammy's encroachment on what is said to be (in regard to the first foray) "sacred and forbidden ground" (p. 39), as if the idea of wrongdoing in his childhood is concretized as an act of illegal entry: Sammy and Johnny Spragg climb through the wire fence surrounding the airfield and make their way to the patch where the planes land; they steal aboard a barge in the canal and hide under its tarpaulin; and they go through a break in the wall into the grounds of the general's house (which later becomes the mental hospital). A plane crashes on the airfield, and as they "bolt for the road" a man shouts at them, "You kids shove off! If I catch you here again I'll put the police on you" (p. 41); the bargee chases them out of the barge, but they manage to run away from him; and though they see a policeman in the gap in the wall of the general's house, he is gone when they return and they leave the grounds safely. Since to fall, in Sammy's view, means to lose one's freedom, we realize why none of these acts constitutes the turning point: though the boys do trespass, what the episodes dramatize is that they are not caught: "I see now what I am looking for and why these pictures are not altogether random. I describe them because they seem to be important. They contributed very little to the straight line of my story. If we had been caught—as later I was indeed caught—and taken by the ear to the general, he might have set in motion some act that changed my whole life or Johnny's. But they are not important in that way" (p. 46). Because Sammy and Johnny are not caught, because, for instance, they are able freely to roam around the grounds of the general's house, the very experience of trespass is presented as prelapsarian: they are said on that occasion to "[wander] in paradise" (p. 45). The notion extends beyond trespass to what Sammy calls "a technical crime" when he steals tuppence from their lodger: he gets "clean away with it," and so can think of that time as "days of terrible and irresponsible innocence" (p. 25). A primary attribute of the fall in Sammy's terms, then, is that it is a condition in which one is caught, trapped in some way. The point is driven home at the beginning of chapter 4, as the nineteen-year-old Sammy begins his pursuit of Beatrice and proclaims his loss of freedom: "I was lost. I was caught. I could not push my bike back again over the bridge . . . I was trapped again. I had trapped myself" (p. 81).

Two other episodes in Sammy's childhood, in both of which he *is* caught, throw further light on the central concept of the fall. In the first of these, Sammy is inveigled by Philip Arnold into taking fagcards by force from smaller boys and is finally discovered. The head teacher deals lightly with him:

"It's really because you like pictures, eh, Sammy? Only you mustn't get them that way. Draw them. You'd better give back as many as you can. And— here. You can have these."

He gave me three kings of Egypt. I believe he had gone to great trouble over those fagcards. He was a kindly, careful and conscientious man who never came within a mile of understanding his children. He let the cane stay in the corner and my guilt stay on my back.

Is this the point I am looking for?
No.
Not here. (p. 52)

It is notable that the final refrain is first explicitly used at this point in the narrative, being evoked apparently because this is the first time

Sammy is actually caught in a misdemeanor. But this is nonetheless not the occasion of his fall because though he is caught, he is not trapped. The headmaster, who is a much wiser man than Sammy (even as an adult) credits him with being, carefully provides him with a way out: in the future he can amass kings of Egypt by drawing them; and he can now make up for having taken the cards by giving back as many as he can. The episode implies two further attributes of the fall: it blocks all alternative paths; and it leaves open no possibility of reparation.

In the second episode, Philip dares Sammy "to defile the high altar," and Sammy is caught twice—first by Philip, as he follows him "in the net," and then by the verger, who holds him firmly: "It was a fair cop" (pp. 59, 62). The verger takes him to the parson, who proceeds to "interrogate" him in a scene that prefigures his experience in the prisoner of war camp. The parson offers, like Dr. Halde, the Gestapo officer, to "let [him] go" if he tells him what he wants to know—who put him up to it (as Halde wants to know who is planning to escape); and, looking back on his childhood, Sammy registers how already then he was "faced by the brute thing" that threatened "the breakdown of [his] integrated simplicity" though in the event his infected ear served to bring him release and saved him from "any suspicion of [his] own inadequacy" (pp. 65–66). Yet it is not his reprieve from the parson, who is forced to let him go, that differentiates this—the worst of the misdemeanors— from the act that costs him his freedom but the way in which he engages in the attempted defilement. The scene in the church dramatizes how Sammy, though dared to undertake the sacrilege by Philip and accepting the challenge, is unable to give himself to the act: he cannot urinate on the altar as planned because in his nervousness he has already "been three times"; and though he makes the motions, he cannot really spit (as an alternative) because his "mouth [is] dry, too" (p. 61). The fourth attribute of the fall that emerges in this episode is that the loss of freedom is predicated on a full commitment of the self to the path chosen.

The early sections of the novel also reveal how Sammy in childhood—in contradistinction to his later fallen condition—lives effortlessly in two worlds. The first reference to this capacity is deceptively innocuous: he has a vivid memory of "the antique shop" Evie and he pass on the way to school, and he accepts both the materiality of the objects they gaze at and the presence of Evie's uncle inside the suit of armor at the back of the shop. He accepts what Evie says, though this is "demonstrably ridiculous" since he can see "through the suit" where the pieces do "not quite join," for his "faith" is "perfect" (p. 31). Then, in the garden of the general's house when he and Johnny trespass, Sammy experiences an epiphany as he looks at a cedar tree, the very material specificity of his observation of it being the basis of other intimations:

> There was one tree between me and the lawns, the stillest tree that ever grew, a tree that grew when no one was looking. The trunk was huge and each branch splayed up to a given level; and there, the black leaves floated out like a level of oil on water. Level after horizontal level these leaves cut across the splaying branches and there was a crumpled, silver-paper depth, an ivory quiet beyond them. Later, I should have called the tree a cedar and passed on, but then, it was an apocalypse. (pp. 45–46)

And this matter of fact acceptance of the material and the spiritual and of their coexistence characterizes Sammy's later attitude at high school to the "two worlds" represented by Rowena Pringle and Nick Shales, the "world of miracle" and the "rational universe": "We crossed from one universe into another when we came out of her door and went into his. We held both universes in our heads effortlessly because by the nature of the human being, neither of them was real" (p. 211).

3

SAMMY'S relationship with Beatrice Ifor may be said to begin (though the account of this is delayed to the end of his narrative) when he sketches her in an art class at high school. Beatrice is acting that day as the model, and though Sammy concludes she is not worth his attention, he makes a quick sketch of her for Philip, who "[cannot] draw at all," "[scrawling] her in with about two lines and a couple of patches of offhand shading" (pp. 219–20). Miss Curtis praises the sketch highly, and when Sammy examines his "orphaned portrait," he is "astonished": "In carelessness and luck I had put the girl on paper in a way that my laborious portraitures could never come at. The line leapt, it was joyous, free, authoritative" (p. 221). The line is "free," we realize, because he is still free; it is "careless" in the sense that it comes from a "not caring" which fosters an "inspired ease" (p. 223), and the ease is the mark of an absence of self-consciousness on his part—or of any manifestation of self that might come between him and his subject. He then looks again at the model, and sees in her face what he can "neither describe or draw": her face is "lit from a high window," and he sees "a metaphorical light" that seems to him to be "an objective phenomenon" (pp. 221–22). That light, the "light of heaven," which he takes to be "a real thing," should no doubt have become the guiding light of his life; and it certainly should have served as "a counterpoise to Nick's rationalism." But "besides that unearthly expression, that holy light," Beatrice has "knees sometimes silk and young buds that [lift] her blouse when she [breathes]" (p. 222)—and it is these that interest Sammy. That he is not paying sufficient attention to something essential is indicated by his ability, as he develops as an artist, to draw any face except Beatrice's "in one swift line" so that "the likeness [leaps] from the paper"; but her face he "[can]not remember" at all (p. 225).[5]

Sammy's forgetting of Beatrice's face gives advance notice of the choice he will make between the worlds of Miss Pringle and Nick Shales. The grounds of his choice are more personal than anything else, for Nick is "good and . . . attractive" where Miss Pringle is thoroughly objectionable (p. 219); but when he opts for Nick's "rational universe" and concludes that "there is no spirit, no absolute," and that he is free to decide what is good or not, he in fact traps himself: "I transformed Nick's innocent, paper world. Mine was an amoral, a savage place in which man was trapped without hope, to enjoy what he could while it was going" (p. 226). If Sammy, as we have seen, feels "trapped again" as he rides over the bridge toward Beatrice, this is where he first lets himself get caught.

The sort of "place" Sammy now chooses to live in is concretized in the description of his walk in the forest on the day he leaves school:

all the forest, the bracken, the flies and uncatalogued small moths, the thumping rabbits, the butterflies, brown, blue and white, they murmured sexily for musk was the greatest good of the greatest number. As for the heavy sky, the blue to purple, it filled every shape between the trees with inch-thick fragments of stained glass, only at arm's length out of reach. The high fronds touched my throat or caught me round the thighs. There was a powder spilled out of all living things, a spice which now made the air where I waded thick. In basements of the forest among drifts of dried leaves and cracking boughs, by boles cathedral thick, I said in the hot air what was important to me; namely the white, unseen body of Beatrice Ifor, her obedience, and for all time my protection of her; and for the pain she had caused me, her utter abjection this side death. (pp. 235–36)

It is the natural and prolific animal world, a world in which "thumping rabbits" are prominent, that "murmurs sexily" in the forest, making sex—or the musky smell of sex—"the greatest good of the greatest number." But it is Sammy who responds to that murmur, hearing in it a validation of his own propensities, for he too has opted for musk— "Musk, shameful and heady, be thou my good" (p. 232). When Sammy makes sex the supreme good, he makes it an end in itself; he thus moves to a position which is at the opposite pole from that he adopts after his experience in the cell, the "vital morality" which posits living relationship as a good and so implicitly makes sex only a means to an end. When he deliberately parodies Milton's Satan, moreover—"Evil, be thou my good"—he shows how ready he is, intellectually, emotionally, psychologically, to embrace his fall. He is ripe now to make sex his religion, to become a priest of musk (as Stephen Dedalus is a priest of the imagination); and the forest accordingly becomes his church, with its "fragments of stained glass" between the tops of the trees, and the trees themselves like cathedral pillars. But turning the forest into a church is to convert it from an open to a closed space, confined within its own structure—is to make it, that is, an apt setting for a fall.

But first Sammy is given a last chance to preserve his freedom. He walks out of the forest, and "coming out below the weir," strips and plunges into the water before moving on:

Dressed and cooled, contained as an untouched girl I moved away from the providential waters and up the hill-side. Already there were stars, large glossy stars that had been put in one at a time with the thumb. I sat there between the earth and the sky, between cloister and street. The waters had healed me and there was the taste of potatoes in my mouth.

What is important to you?

"Beatrice Ifor."

She thinks you depraved already. She dislikes you.

"If I want something enough I can always get it provided I am willing to make the appropriate sacrifice."

What will you sacrifice?

"Everything."

Here? (p. 236)

Sammy's swim in "the providential waters"—which are also recuperative, for they "heal" him—is the last free movement he experiences, his bathing here being set against his bathing in the park pool as a child and his running down the path "for joy in the taste of potatoes." The waters below the weir wash away the musk, as it were, but then he "moves away" from them; and when he decides to sacrifice "everything" for Beatrice, he chooses a path that costs him his freedom, as the unanswered question "Here?" emphasizes. The nature of his fall exemplifies all except one of the attributes of the condition that are established in the childhood sections of the narrative (the exception being brought to bear later). We are adverted to the central characteristic of his fall by an unexpected simile: after Sammy comes out of the water he is said to be not only "dressed and cooled" but "contained as an untouched girl." The image suggests his self-sufficiency; and so links up with what Dr. Halde says to him in the interrogation: "There is no point at which something has knocked on your door and taken possession of you. You possess yourself" (p. 144). But "the Herr Doctor," as we are told by the commandant in the final gnomic pronouncement of the novel (which is given altogether disproportionate weight by its position), "does not know about peoples" (p. 253), and demonstrates this conclusively in his view of Sammy. For when Sammy chooses to sacrifice everything in order to possess Beatrice, he himself becomes possessed; ceasing to possess himself, he gives himself to an obsession. Once he does that, committing himself totally to his aim, he loses his freedom, for the monomania rules out any other alternative and (as he sees later) leaves him caught, bound hand and foot, "tied by this must" (p. 116). If he makes the possession of Beatrice an end in itself, moreover, it is not his only end. Something vicious enters into his pursuit of her, for he dedicates himself as well to ensuring "her utter abjection this side death" in order to pay her back for "the pain she has caused" him, for the sexual frustration she has subjected him to, presumably. Hence it is with a "pursuer's hate" that he stalks her as a young man, never really moving beyond it though he thinks it has been "swallowed up in gratitude" (p. 110), and never being able to "[cry] quits for the distraught bed of [his] school days" (p. 127). In his pursuit of Beatrice, that is, Sammy is the prisoner not only of a sexual obsession but also of a need for retaliation.

Locked in the self, Sammy longs to escape, and paradoxically he tries to do so in relation to Beatrice. He believes, as a general principle, that love is "a passionate attempt to confirm that the wall which [parts]" a couple "is down" (p. 14); but his wish for fusion with Beatrice seems to express not so much his love for her as a desperate need to break out of his own confinement: "I want to be with you," he says to her, "and in you and on you and round you—I want fusion and identity—I want to understand and be understood—oh God, Beatrice, Beatrice, I love you—I want to be you!" (p. 105). But to be her he must either cease to be himself—and he cannot do that without giving up his life at the same time—or obliterate her by taking her into himself, a desire (however impossible of attainment) which, in its narcissistic self-aggrandizement, further traps him in the self. Wanting to be one with her, he is quite unable to accept her otherness, and so condemns their sexual relationship to inevitable failure.

Beatrice, however, plays her own part in this failure since, in addition to her premarital "religious taboos" (p. 118), she is temperamentally unsuited to sexual relationship. She is said to be "contained in herself" (p. 87), like the "untouched girl" Sammy is compared to just before his fall. Her "emotions and physical reactions" are "enclosed as a nun";

and when he knocks and then hammers "at the door she [remains] shut
up within" (p. 110). Beatrice, that is, is incapable of giving herself—like
Philip Arnold (*mutatis mutandis*), who, "skimped in every line of his
body by a cosmic meanness," keeps himself "intact," and is "defended
against giving" (p. 100); and also like a number of heroines in Thomas
Hardy's fiction, Bathsheba Everdene, Grace Melbury, and Sue Bridehead. When she finally consents to be taken, she lies back "obe-
diently": "[she] closed her eyes and placed one clenched fist bravely on
her forehead as though she were about to be injected for T.A.B." (p. 117).
Sammy later reflects that they both seemed unconsciously to have
been "setting [themselves] to music": "The gesture with which she
opened her knees was, so to speak, operatic, heroic, dramatic and
daunting. I could not accompany her. My instrument was flat" (p. 118).
Sammy's impotence on this occasion is an expression of what is left of
a better self, and like his inability to urinate or spit on the altar, it
represents a refusal to lend himself to a violation. But he is now a fallen
man, and "of course there [are] other occasions" (p. 118). Beatrice, in
Lawrence's memorable phrase, is duly "crucified into sex"; and Sammy, accepting the role of torturer, keeps his "victim on the rack" (p.
118). What he continues to leave out as he pursues this course with her
is indicated in his paintings of her in the nude. He cannot "paint her
face"—the face, we remember, that had the light playing about it—but
he paints her body: "I painted her as a body and they are good and
terrible paintings, dreadful in their story of fury and submission" (p.
123).

Sammy and Beatrice go on in this fashion "for nearly two years until
the ripples and then waves of war" wash round them. But it is not the
war that separates them. Their separation is implicit in the image that
evokes the form their relationship takes after it becomes sexual: "She
had found her tower and was clinging to it. She had become my ivy" (p.
122). It is inevitable that he should want in the end to break free of the
smothering ivy—just as it is that she should collapse when the tower is
removed—and his meeting with Taffy provides the occasion for his
desertion of Beatrice. On their first meeting, Sammy and Taffy recognize "without a moment's doubt" that they will "never let each other
go," and the same night they make love, "wildly and mutually" (p. 126).
Within a short time Sammy brutally abandons Beatrice, simply disap-
pearing from her life without word, and then marries Taffy.

In retrospect, Sammy states he had no alternative to behaving as he
did:

What else could I have done but run away from Beatrice? I do not mean what
ought I to have done or what someone else could have done. I simply mean that
as I have described myself, as I see myself in my backward eye, I could do

nothing but run away. . . . I had lost my power to choose. I had given away my freedom. I cannot be blamed for the mechanical and helpless reaction of my nature. What I was, I had become. (pp. 130–31)

At first sight this may seem merely like hairsplitting on Sammy's part as he makes an unconvincing attempt to justify himself. His fall may ensure his loss of a freedom of choice, and so may even determine his eventual abandonment of Beatrice, who is no more to him than a body; but it certainly does not deprive him of the "power to choose," and his desertion of Beatrice and marriage of Taffy are clearly choices. The hairsplitting, however, is symptomatic of the difficulty the novelist— rather than the narrator—gets into at this point, and his resolution of it very nearly undoes the novel. The ready means of bringing about a separation between Sammy and Beatrice, which is essential to the fur- ther development of the plot and the revelation of the ultimate im- plication of Sammy's fall, is to have him drawn away by another wom- an, and this is done with the introduction of Taffy. The trouble is that, on a primary level of verisimilitude, Taffy is simply nonexistent as a character; and, more damagingly, that Sammy's relationship with her is, in his own terms, quite impossible. Locked in self as he is, the "stag- nant pool" (p. 9) of the opening pages of the retrospective narrative, Sammy is not free for a relationship with her, is not free—without something happening to effect his prior release—for the immediate wild mutuality of the love that they celebrate on first meeting. Nor is he free to change the course of his life. He does win a measure of re- lease eventually, but it is brought about in the prisoner-of-war camp, not in relation to Taffy—and subsequent to his marriage to her.

4

THAT MEANINGFUL CHANGE does entail "a necessary preliminary" is at once asserted at the beginning of the prisoner-of-war section of the nar- rative: "I can tell when I acquired or was given the capacity to see. Dr. Halde attended to that. In freedom I should never have acquired any capacity. Then was loss of freedom the price exacted, a necessary pre- liminary to a new mode of knowing? . . . The Gestapo whipped the coverings off yesterday and unveiled the grey faces" (p. 133). Since Dr. Halde locks Sammy up in utter darkness, the "capacity to see" that he forces him to attain is a seeing which is understanding, insight. What he specifically enables him to see are the "grey faces," which presum- ably have been haunting him since the abandonment of Beatrice. When they are "unveiled," Sammy can at last see the past for what it is and begin to come to terms with it. This is one significance of the prisoner-of-war experience, and it is after he relives it that Sammy is able to pinpoint the exact moment of his fall. A further significance is that Sammy's being a prisoner of war concretizes the most important event of his past life, the loss of his freedom, for the "loss of freedom" referred to in the quoted passage clearly subsumes the physical as well as the metaphysical dimensions of his captivity. Both kinds of captivity are the "necessary preliminary" to "a new mode of knowing," and it is this which is the recompense of his suffering, the only recompense available indeed—notwithstanding Taffy—to one who (in the designated terms) has irrevocably lost his freedom.

After the fruitless interrogation, Halde blindfolds Sammy and locks him up in the dark cell, in solitary confinement. Left in the cell, Sammy conjures up one horror after another as the torture he assumes is intended for him, culminating in the monitory visions of the severed penis left in the center of the cell, the "fragment of human flesh, collapsed in its own cold blood" (p. 182), and of the subsiding ceiling that comes down "slowly with all the weight of the world" (p. 183):

Reason and common sense told me there was no body hanging crushed from which other pieces might fall and yet I believed in the body because Halde wanted me to.
I started to cry out.
"Help me! Help me!"

Let me be accurate now if ever. These pages I have written have taught me much; not least that no man can tell the whole truth, language is clumsier in my hands than paint. And yet my life has remained centred round the fact of the next few minutes I spent alone and panic-stricken in the dark. My cry for help was the cry of the rat when the terrier shakes it, a hopeless sound, the raw signature of one savage act. My cry meant no more, was instinctive, said here is flesh of which the nature is to suffer and do thus. I cried out not with hope of an ear but as accepting a shut door, darkness and a shut sky.
But the very act of crying out changed the thing that cried. Does the rat expect help? . . .
"Help me!"
But there was no help in the concrete of the cell . . . Here the thing that cried came up against an absolute of helplessness. . . . The future was the flight of steps from terror to terror, a mounting experiment that ignorance of what might be a bribe, made inevitable. The thing that cried fled forward over those steps because there was no other way to go, was shot forward screaming as into a furnace, as over unimaginable steps that were all that might be borne, were more, were too searing for the refuge of madness, were destructive of the centre. The thing that screamed left all living behind and came to the entry where death is close as darkness against eyeballs.
And burst that door. (pp. 183–85)

Sammy's experience in the cell brings him to the verge of breakdown, and it is then that he cries out for help. The cry—like "the cry of the rat when the terrier shakes it"—is wrung from him in spite of himself, in an instinctive need to alleviate his terror. The cry is "a hopeless sound" because it is uttered in the knowledge that there is no one to cry to and in the face of his acceptance of "a shut door, darkness and a shut sky." Yet his life "[remains] centred round" what follows because "the very act of crying" changes him and leads to the "new mode of knowing" previously referred to. It is not to the Germans that he cries out, for no help can be expected of them, and it is "not with hope of an ear" that he cries; there would seem to be no basis, therefore, for believing that he is now ready to betray his comrades, nor is the cry itself indicative of a willingness to talk. Despite his conviction of "a shut sky," it is to God he cries, forced in extremity to turn for help to some force outside himself. But that he should do so is itself a tacit admission of the existence of something beyond the "rational universe."[6]

No help, however, is forthcoming, and it is when he comes up against "an absolute of helplessness" that Sammy breaks. The only alternative seemingly open to him is the death he is sure Halde has prepared for him; and in an agonized desire to get it over with, he runs on his death, leaving "all living behind" as he comes to "the entry where death is close as darkness against eyeballs": "And burst that door." Those four monosyllables make up a sentence that is perhaps as difficult (and important) to interpret as any in the novel. In the immediate context, the door referred to seems to be that which leads from life to death, but the fact that Sammy is still there to tell the story effectively disposes of such a reading. It then appears that it must be the door of the cell that he bursts, and this view seems to be supported by the sentence that follows this statement: "Therefore when the commandant let me out of the darkness he came late and as a second string, giving me the liberty of the camp when perhaps I no longer needed it" (p. 186). We assume that he comes late because Sammy has already freed himself from the cell, and that he no longer needs "the liberty of the camp" because he has liberated himself. But Golding has a surprise in store for us, one that he keeps—as in earlier novels such as *Lord of the Flies* and *Pincher Martin*—for the last page of the narrative:

The bright line became a triangle sweeping in over a suddenly visible concrete floor.

"Heraus!"

Rising from my knees, holding my trousers huddled I walked uncertainly out towards the judge. But the judge had gone.

The commandant was back.

"Captain Mountjoy. This should not be happening. I am sorry."

The noise turned me round. I could see down the passage now over the stain shaped like a brain, could see into the cell where I had received what I had received. They were putting the buckets back, piles of them, were throwing back the damp floorcloths. I could see that they had forgotten one, or perhaps left it deliberately, when they emptied the cupboard for me. It still lay damply in the centre of the floor. Then a soldier shut the buckets and the floorcloths away with an ordinary cupboard door.

"Captain Mountjoy. You have heard?"

"I heard."

The commandant indicated the door back to the camp dismissively. He spoke the inscrutable words that I should puzzle over as though they were the Sphinx's riddle.

"The Herr Doctor does not know about peoples." (p. 253)

This passage seems to me to make it quite clear that it is not the door of the "cell" that Sammy bursts: the concrete floor that is made "suddenly visible" to him is the floor of the cell that is revealed to him when the door is opened, as he is revealed on his knees on the floor. And when he is ordered to go out, it is out of the cell that he "walks uncertainly."[7]

We are adverted to a third possible dimension of the door—and this reading is not subsequently challenged—later in the narrative, though the event referred to takes place well before the war. At high school, we remember, Sammy eventually opts for Nick Shales's "world": "In that moment a door closed behind me. I slammed it shut on Moses and Jehovah. I was not to knock on that door again, until in a Nazi prison camp I lay huddled against it half crazed with terror and despair" (p. 217). The reference to the door here serves to confirm our view of the import of Sammy's cry for help, suggesting that it is into "the world of miracle" that Sammy bursts in the Nazi camp, driven in his extremity to rediscover the spirit. But this reference, then, is no more than confirmatory of a reading we can arrive at independently; and it is in no way related to the elaborate last-page surprise—which suggests that the door has yet another significance.

Sammy's taking the commandant's pronouncement about "the Herr Doctor" so seriously serves to distract us from truly important revelations that are made at this juncture. When Sammy turns round in the passage and takes in that the object lying "damply in the centre of the floor" of the "cell" is not a severed penis but a floorcloth, he becomes aware—as we do—of the degree to which he has tortured himself during his incarceration. And when he registers that his cell is a cupboard and that it is "an ordinary cupboard door" that has been locked on him, what is revealed is how he has effectively imprisoned himself, for a

determined shove at that door would have been enough to bring him at
least a temporary release from his agony. The cupboard door therefore
becomes the ground of the most important metaphor in the novel. If
Sammy's being a prisoner of war concretizes a general loss of freedom,
his self-imprisonment in the Nazi camp projects a specific condition
he has long been subject to. We recall his own recognition, as he moves
over the bridge to begin his obsessive seduction of Beatrice, that he has
"trapped [himself]" (p. 81); and we recall too that what precedes this
moment and prepares for it follows the same pattern: when Sammy
opts for Nick's "world," he transforms it into "a savage place in which
man [is] trapped without hope" (p. 226)—in which Sammy, that is,
since he freely chooses this, traps himself. Furthermore, since the very
notion of self-imprisonment posits an inability to be free of self, we
realize that Sammy is confined too in the self-enclosure of his attitudes, in his self-aggrandizement and desire for retaliation in regard
to Beatrice, as we have seen. The point is underlined for us by Sammy's
conviction that Nick must surely be "familiar" with the taste of potatoes because he is "a selfless man" (p. 212).[8]

A further significance of the bursting of the door, therefore, is that as
a result of his experience in the cell Sammy bursts out of himself, as it
were. He takes the first step beyond his self-enclosure, beyond making
self the measure of all things as he has habitually done, when he cries
out for help, for he is forced in his despair to appeal to something outside the self. When the cry goes unanswered and he is reduced to "an
absolute of helplessness," he is compelled to confront his own absolute
inadequacy, the inability of the self to sustain itself amid such hope-
lessness. What follows is a collapse of self, a moral disintegration
rather than a mental breakdown, for he is not psychologically harmed
by his stay in the cell; but the experience undermines the basis of his
previous self-establishment: it is "destructive of the centre." With the
self in its disintegration no longer a barrier, Sammy also bursts the door
that has divided the self from everything outside it.

Support for this reading is offered by what follows. When the commandant sends Sammy back into the camp, he goes as "a man resurrected but not by him":

I saw the huts as one who had little to do with them, was indifferent to them
and the temporal succession of days that they implied. So they shone with the
innocent light of their own created nature. I understood them perfectly, boxes
of thin wood as they were, and now transparent, letting be seen inside their
quotas of sceptred kings. I lifted my arms, saw them too, and was overwhelmed
by their unendurable richness as possessions, either arm ten thousand fortunes
poured out for me. Huge tears were dropping from my face into dust; and this
dust was a universe of brilliant and fantastic crystals, that miracles instantly

supported in their being. I looked up beyond the huts and the wire, I raised my dead eyes, desiring nothing, accepting all things and giving all created things away. The paper wrappings of use and language dropped from me. Those crowded shapes extending up into the air and down into the rich earth, those deeds of far space and deep earth were aflame at the surface and daunting by right of their own natures though a day before I should have disguised them as trees. Beyond them the mountains were not only clear all through like purple glass, but living. They sang and were conjubilant. (p. 186)

The measure of Sammy's transcendence of self is that he comes out of the cell "desiring nothing, accepting all things" in their own right. But the loss of self is the means of finding it, for Sammy, the resurrected man, is "overwhelmed" by his own possession of himself, glorying in the "unendurable richness" of his own arms as "possessions": having broken out of the obsessed self, Sammy is now free to repossess himself. At the same time he ceases to interpose the self between the world around him and his perception of it. It is because he is now "indifferent" to the huts in the camp that they shine "with the innocent light of their own created nature"; and in the same way his fellow prisoners inside the huts are seen as "sceptred kings"—for Sammy is seeing again as he saw Beatrice when he sketched her for Philip. But, having burst the door, Sammy now also has access to the "world of miracle": "Standing between the understood huts, among jewels and music, I was visited by a flake of fire, miraculous and pentecostal; and fire transmuted me, once and for ever" (p. 188). His own transmutation, his willingness now to allow for the informing spirit that he denied in his subsequent view of Beatrice, works other transformations, for it is not only the huts that "shine." In an experience that recalls his vision of the apocalyptic cedar in the general's garden, he sees the trees around him—those "deeds of far space and deep earth"—as being "aflame at the surface"; and even the mountains are apprehended as "living." His new intuition of being also carries over into his work: "those secret, smuggled sketches of the haggard, unshaven kings of Egypt in their glory are the glory of my right hand and likely to remain so" (p. 188).

Sammy's sense of "a new mode of knowing" is immediate, but it is only in the days following his release from the cell that he begins to draw things together. Then "at last" he looks "where Halde [has] directed," turning his eyes in on himself and finding that "the human nature . . . inhabiting the centre of [his] own awareness" is "loathsome" (p. 190). Seeing himself in this way frees him to see Beatrice differently (though the basis of his new view of her is not clear). He is struck by "the beauty of her simplicity": "That negative personality, that clear absence of being, that vacuum which I had finally deduced from her silences, I now saw to have been full. . . . She was simple and loving and generous and humble" (p. 191). And from the new mode of knowing he fashions a new philosophy, what he calls "a kind of vital morality," that is based not on "the relationship of a man to remote posterity nor even to a social system" but on "the relationship of individual man to individual man— once an irrelevance but now seen to be the forge in which all change, all value, all life is beaten out into a good or a bad shape" (p. 189). It is man, not God, whom Sammy makes the source of "all value," and that is why, despite the "flake of fire, miraculous and pentecostal," he remains a "burning amateur." But his vital morality is in direct contradistinction to the amorality of his previous position, to the view that the world is a place where man must "enjoy what he [can] while it [is] going," for that effectively did away with true relationship—as Sammy proceeded to demonstrate in the case of Beatrice. The new recognition, however, comes too late to save her. She is insane, and though the doctor will say no more than that Sammy's desertion of her may have "tipped her over," the fact remains that her incarceration in the hospital (which was previously the general's house) dates from the time of her abandonment (p. 247). When Sammy goes to visit her after the war—she has then been in the hospital for seven years—he is unable to communicate with her, but she manages to repudiate him by turning her back on him. Living "only a hundred yards" from the hospital (p. 238), he has to go on living with the grey faces, and he reflects that he is "up to the neck in the ice on paradise hill" (p. 241). Despite the transmutation and the liberation he has experienced—and despite his (illegitimate) Taffy too—Sammy, held in that icy enclosure, remains a haunted and fallen man, for there is no reparation he can make.

PART FOUR

BEYOND THE SINGLE TEXT:
UNIFYING PREOCCUPATIONS

APHRODITE OF THE FOAM AND *THE LADYBIRD* TALES

The central issue of the three tales published in 1923 in the volume called *The Ladybird* is glossed by a pronouncement of Rawdon Lilly in *Aaron's Rod* (1922): "But the mode of our being is such that we can only live and have our being whilst we are implicit in one of the great dynamic modes. We *must* either love, or rule. And once the love-mode changes, as change it must, for we are worn out and becoming evil in its persistence, then the other mode will take place in us. And there will be profound, profound obedience in place of this love-crying, obedience to the incalculable power-urge. And men must submit to the greater soul in a man, for their guidance: and women must submit to the positive power-soul in man, for their being." Despite their difference of milieu and mode, the three tales are unified by a concern with the same theme, with the necessity for the abandonment of romantic love as a basis for relationship between the sexes and with its replacement by the woman's submission to the "power-soul in man." *The Ladybird* tales, indeed, are best read in relation to the novels of this period, particularly *The Plumed Serpent* (1926); for in this novel the conception of the new relationship that is first adumbrated in *Aaron's Rod* is fully developed, and Lawrence is explicit about the nature of the submission demanded of the woman in the sex act, whereas he is reserved on this matter in the tales. The sexual submission of the woman in *The Plumed Serpent* is total, involving, as it does, her voluntary forgoing of orgasm. This is a concealed preoccupation in the three tales, but it is revealed (in the light of *The Plumed Serpent*) by a recurrent symbolism.

Lawrence was led to advocate such an extreme form of sexual submission in reaction against the kind of assault on a man that is figured in Ursula Brangwen's ferocious "annihilation" of Skrebensky in *The Rainbow*—an assault that the novelist had come to envisage as a concomitant of romantic love. It is a position, however, that he abandoned, for in *Lady Chatterley's Lover* (1928) relationship between a man and a woman is based not on power and submission but on a reciprocal tenderness, and Connie Chatterley achieves a less questionable form of sexual fulfillment with Mellors. *The Ladybird* tales, in other words, should be regarded as exploratory ventures in a large undertaking that was to lead, eventually, to *Lady Chatterley's Lover*. But Lawrence's assertion in these tales of a male dominance unwittingly suggests that the concomitants of the doctrine of power are as unfortunate as those of romantic love. *The Ladybird* is a most impressive volume, a testimony to Lawrence's remarkable power and range in the long story; but it seems to me that both "The Ladybird" and "The Fox" are seriously marred.

2

LADY DAPHNE in "The Ladybird" is introduced as having "her whole will" fixed in "her adoption of her mother's creed," fixed, that is, in a belief in loving humanity and in a "determination that life should be gentle and good and benevolent." But it is at once intimated that her adherence to such a creed is a perverse denial of her essential self, for she has "a strong, reckless nature"—she is "Artemis or Atalanta rather than Daphne"—and her eyes tell of "a wild energy dammed up inside her" (pp. 13–14).[1] Such a fixing of the will in frustration of natural being is inevitably inimical to life, and Daphne moves, as it were, in death: her two brothers have been killed in the war, her baby has been born dead, and her appearance fills "the heart with ashes" (p. 13). She is, indeed, Proserpine—though in a sense different from that in which her husband, Major Basil Apsley, uses the name when he refers to her "wonderful Proserpine fingers" and says that "the spring comes" if she lifts her hands (p. 51). Daphne, though given to life, is wedded to death, embodying in herself the deathliness of the creed of Love.

This deathliness is further projected in the marriage of Daphne and Basil. When he comes back from the war, he is "like death; like risen death" (p. 47), and "a new icy note" in his voice goes "through her veins like death" (p. 44). We are meant to register, I think, that the death Basil carries in himself is not only the mark of his experiences in the war. A "white-faced, spiritually intense" man, Basil maintains that, having been through the ordeal of the war, he has arrived at "a higher state of consciousness, and therefore of life. And so, of course, at a higher plane of love" (pp. 54–55). It is the constant burden of Lawrence that, where life is viewed in terms of the achievement of a state of heightened mental consciousness, it is life as well as "blood-consciousness" that is denied; and it follows that the love which is a correlative of such a state of consciousness is as sterile as the life with which it is equated. This, at all events, is what Basil's love for Daphne is shown to be. After his lovemaking she has "to bear herself in torment," she feels "weak and fretful," she "[aches] with nerves," and cannot eat; he in turn becomes "ashy and somewhat acrid" (pp. 51–52). In Basil, we are to understand, the consciousness of loving has usurped the body of love, leaving him ineffectually prostrate before Daphne:

> He suddenly knelt at her feet, and kissed the toe of her slipper, and kissed the instep, and kissed the ankle in the thin black stocking.
> "I knew," he said in a muffled voice. "I knew you would make good. I knew if I had to kneel, it was before you. I knew you were divine, you were the one— Cybele—Isis. I knew I was your slave. I knew. It has all been just a long initiation. I had to learn how to worship you."
> He kissed her feet again and again, without the slightest self-consciousness, or the slightest misgiving. Then he went back to the sofa, and sat there looking at her, saying:
> "It isn't love, it is worship. Love between me and you will be a sacrament, Daphne. That's what I had to learn. You are beyond me. A mystery to me. My God, how great it all is. How marvellous!" (pp. 48–49)

The act of kneeling and the kissing of feet are charged with significance in Lawrence's work of this period. In this instance, we may feel, they are even somewhat overcharged, but their purport is unmistakable. Abnegating his independent manhood, Basil becomes a slavish idolater; and his worship of Daphne turns her into a goddess, turns her, indeed, into Cybele, whose name Birkin invokes when (in the scene at the millpond in *Women in Love*) he attempts to smash the reflection of the moon, thus demonstrating his opposition to the possessive *magna mater* figure that is destructive of a man's virility. When Basil says that his feeling for Daphne "isn't love" but "worship," what he means is that he has attained "a higher plane of love." It is too ethereal a plane to support life, however, and not unexpectedly his worship of her postulates the kind of sacrifice of self that conceals a desire for death: "I am no more than a sacrifice to you," he tells her, "an offering. I *wish* I could die in giving myself to you, give you all my blood on your altar, for ever" (p. 51).

Basil is distracted from his worship of Daphne when, returning to the sofa, he slides his hand down between the back and the seat and finds a thimble. The thimble belongs to Daphne, a present given her as a girl by a Bohemian count, Johann Dionys Psanek, with whom, wounded and a prisoner of war in England, she has renewed acquaintance. This interruption of Basil's adoration of his wife is premonitory of the Count's irruption into their relationship. The Count, whose own marriage has failed, regards himself (like the Indians in "The Woman Who Rode Away") as "a subject of the sun" rather than of a woman; and a "dark flame of life" seems to glow through his clothes "from his body." "I belong to the fire-worshippers," he tells Daphne; and what he slowly, even unwillingly, proceeds to do is to fire her into life, to release the wild energy that is dammed up in her. At the same time, contact with her also helps to heal him—"Let me wrap your hair round my hands, like a bandage," he says (p. 24)—for he does not at first wish to live.

Daphne's sewing of some shirts for both the Count and her husband is made to reveal the different demands that the two men make of a woman. Basil is enraptured at the thought of having a shirt she has sewn next to his skin: "I shall feel you all round me, all over me," he says to her (p. 50). What he wants in his relationship with her, we see, is to be encompassed, as in a womb. The Count, on the other hand, having told Daphne that the hospital shirt he is wearing is too long and too big, insists that she herself, and not her maid, should sew a shirt for him: "Only you," he maintains, "might give me what I want, something that buttons round my throat and on my wrists" (p. 28). What he wants of a shirt is that it be a good fit—just as what he wants of a woman is that she be a "mate." "Everything finds its mate," he is fond of remarking; and he makes it clear to Daphne that what interests him is not the gentle mating of doves but the fiercer mating of wild creatures. The tale, that is to say, seems to be moving to a mating of Artemis and Dionysus, for Daphne becomes aware of a "secret thrilling communion" (p. 34) with the Count, of a dark flow between them; and, though she resists him with her mind and will, she is nevertheless drawn by his account of a "true love" that is "a throbbing together in darkness, like the wild-cat in the night, when the green screen [with which her eyes are closed] opens and her eyes are on the darkness" (p. 35). She comes to recognize too that, in contradistinction to the "superconscious" finish of Basil and herself, the Count, like her father, has some of "the unconscious blood-warmth of the lower classes"; and she is prepared to grant that his "dark flame of life . . . might warm the cold white fire of her own blood" (p. 70). We are led to expect, in other words, that the union of these two will be the contrary of the deathly "white love" of Daphne and her husband; in fact the new relationship proves to be merely the obverse of the old.

The new form that Daphne's life appears about to take is symbolized by the thimble the Count has given her, which she puts on when she sews his shirt. The thimble has "a gold snake at the bottom, and a Mary-beetle of green stone at the top, to push the needle with" (p. 27). The Mary-beetle or ladybird, placed opposite the snake at the top of the thimble, may be thought of as instinct with flight; and the thimble, I suggest, figures the kind of union that is represented by Quetzalcoatl in *The Plumed Serpent*, a union of bird and serpent, of spirit and flesh. Certainly, as Daphne moves closer and closer to a vital relationship with the Count, it appears to be the hope of a release into unified being that is held out to her. It is the ladybird alone, however, that is the Count's crest, and as such, as "a descendant of the Egyptian scarabaeus," it is emblematic of a rather different urge on his part. Lord Beveridge declares that the ball-rolling scarab is "a symbol of the creative principle," but the Count suggests (though he smiles "as if it were a joke") that, on the contrary, it symbolizes "the principle of decomposition" (pp. 67–68). He is not joking, however, for, confronted with a world that "has gone raving," he has chosen "the madness of the ladybird" and found his God in "the blessed god of destruction." His God is a "god of anger, who throws down the steeples and the factory chimneys," and he proposes to serve him by helping to beat down "the world of man" (pp. 42–43). The Count, it emerges, is bent on disrupting the established order, an order founded on democracy and love, and substituting for it an order based on "the sacredness of power." Basil maintains that "there is really only one supreme contact, the contact of love," but the Count insists that he "must use another word than love" and suggests several: "Obedience, submission, faith, belief, responsibility, power" (pp. 57–59). The Count talks here like Lilly in *Aaron's Rod*, and it is in the novels, particularly in *The Plumed Serpent*, that the political implications of this doctrine of power are pursued to a logical conclusion. In "The Ladybird" the superiority of the doctrine of power over that of love is asserted domestically, as it were, in the Count's conquest of Basil's wife.

The Count's power as a man is evidenced by the "spell" he casts on Daphne when, prior to his departure from England, Basil invites him to spend a fortnight at Thoresway, the "beautiful Elizabethan mansion" of Lord Beveridge. At night, when he is alone in his room, the Count croons to himself "the old songs of his childhood." Daphne, who is "a bad sleeper," and whose nights are "a torture to her," hears the singing, which, "like a witchcraft," makes her forget everything. Thereafter it becomes "almost an obsession to her to listen for him." She is sure he is calling her "out of herself, out of her world," and in the day she is "bewitched" (pp. 71–72). One night she cannot resist going into his room, and they sit for some time apart, in the dark:

> Then suddenly, without knowing, he went across in the dark, feeling for the end of the couch. And he sat beside her on the couch. But he did not touch her. Neither did she move. The darkness flowed about them thick like blood, and time seemed dissolved in it. They sat with the small, invisible distance between them, motionless, speechless, thoughtless.
> Then suddenly he felt her finger-tips touch his arm, and a flame went over him that left him no more a man. He was something seated in flame, in flame unconscious, seated erect, like an Egyptian King-god in the statues. Her finger-tips slid down him, and she herself slid down in a strange, silent rush, and he felt her face against his closed feet and ankles, her hands pressing his ankles. He felt her brow and hair against his ankles, her face against his feet, and there she clung in the dark, as if in space below him. He still sat erect and motionless. Then he bent forward and put his hand on her hair.
> "Do you come to me?" he murmured. "Do you come to me?" (pp. 74–75)

Great stress is laid here on the lack of consciousness of the lovers: they sit "speechless, thoughtless," and the Count, having moved to Daphne "without knowing," sits "in flame unconscious." In contradistinction to the superconsciousness of Basil and Daphne, they are immersed in a flow that is thick and dark, "like blood"; and where Basil is prostrate before her, the Count sits "erect, like an Egyptian King-god in the statues," sits, that is (like Birkin in *Women in Love*) in "immemorial potency." The Count's sense of his own potency certainly communicates itself to Daphne, for it brings her sliding down to his feet. But the relationship that Daphne now embraces is not, after all, so different from that which obtains between her husband and herself. There is a significant reversal of roles, it is true, but the relationship is still founded on the worship of one partner by the other, even though it is now "the sacredness of power" that elicits the devotion. What is disturbing here is that Lawrence, intent on asserting the Count's power and on emphasizing the difference between his attitude to Daphne and that of Basil, seems to be unaware that Daphne, clinging to the Count's feet and with "her brow and hair against his ankles," is (for all the heightened prose of the description) in no less objectionable a position than Basil at her feet.

It is a position, we cannot help feeling, that figures more than a woman's necessary sexual submission to a man. The "small" man has brought the "tall" woman—their difference of stature is repeatedly stressed—to her knees; and her clinging to his feet is the overt sign of a kind of submission to him that has far-reaching implications for their sexual relations. This is how Daphne is described on the following morning: "She felt she could sleep, sleep, sleep—for ever. Her face, too, was very still, with a delicate look of virginity that she had never had before. She had always been Aphrodite, the self-conscious one. And her eyes, the green-blue, had been like slow, living jewels, resistant. Now they had unfolded from the hard flower-bud, and had the wonder, and the stillness of a quiet night" (p. 76). The reiterated allusions to Daphne's stillness at first sight seem to betoken no more than her achievement of the peace of fulfillment after the strain of her sexual relations with Basil, but taken in conjunction with the references to her "delicate look of virginity" and to her always having been "Aphrodite"—we remember that Basil, "in poetry," has called her "Aphrodite of the foam" (p. 46)—the emphasis on her stillness has a concealed significance. A passage in *The Plumed Serpent* makes clear, I think, what is only hinted at in the story:

> [Kate] realized, almost with wonder, the death in her of the Aphrodite of the foam: the seething, frictional, ecstatic Aphrodite. By a swift dark instinct, Cipriano drew away from this in her. When, in their love, it came back on her, the seething electric female ecstasy, which knows such spasms of delirium, he recoiled from her. It was what she used to call her "satisfaction". She had loved Joachim for this, that again, and again, and again he could give her this orgiastic "satisfaction", in spasms that made her cry aloud.

With Basil, we are told, Daphne has known "the fierce power of the woman in excelsis," the power of "incandescent, transcendent, moon-fierce womanhood," but her inability to "stay intensified" in her "female mystery" has left her "fretful and ill and never to be soothed" (p. 52). What the Count has done, it seems, presumably by refusing her "satisfaction," is to bring her not a release of, but from, her own wild energies. Hence the "quiet, intact quality of virginity in her" and her "strange new quiescence" (pp. 77–78) that Basil finds so puzzling; and hence her own sense of having "suddenly collapsed away from her old self into this darkness, this peace, this quiescence that [is] like a full dark river flowing eternally in her soul" (p. 79).

Daphne's achievement of a new self should be distinguished, therefore, from that of Connie Chatterley, of whom she is evidently a prefigurement, for it is said that at Thoresway "there was a gamekeeper she could have loved—an impudent, ruddy-faced, laughing, ingratiating fellow; she could have loved him, if she had not been isolated beyond the breach of his birth, her culture, her consciousness" (p. 70). Connie, responding to the tenderness of Mellors, also dies to the Aphrodite in her, but she is reborn as a woman who finds a different kind of "satisfaction," a consummation that I think we are to understand is denied Daphne, as it is denied Kate in *The Plumed Serpent:*

Oh, and far down inside [Connie] . . . , at the quick of her, the depths parted and rolled asunder, from the centre of soft plunging . . . , and closer and closer plunged the palpable unknown, and further and further rolled the waves of herself away from herself, leaving her, till suddenly, in a soft, shuddering convulsion, the quick of all her plasm was touched, she knew herself touched, the consummation was upon her, and she was gone. She was gone, she was not, and she was born: a woman.

Daphne's accession into new being, moreover, does not resolve the problem of her relations with the two men. She has to be satisfied, though her relationship with Basil has been demolished, with being "the wife of the ladybird," for the Count, a prisoner of war, has no alternative but to depart. It is significant, however, that he anyway feels he has "no future in this life" and that he cannot offer her "life in the world" because he has "no power in the day, and no place" (pp. 75–76). The Count, that is to say, having pledged his power to his god of anger and destruction, appears to have his being in death; and what he finally offers Daphne is a life in the underworld. "In the night, in the dark, and in death, you are mine" (pp. 75–76), he tells her; and when he parts from her, he says: "I shall be king in Hades when I am dead. And you will be at my side" (pp. 79–80). Proserpine, we see, is Proserpine yet, and the spring seems far behind.

3

"THE FOX," until the killing of Banford, has a fine and powerful inevitability of development that makes it, up to that point, one of the most translucent of Lawrence's tales. The established relationship, in this further instance of "the wicked triangle" (p. 62), is of two girls ("usually known by their surnames"), who have set up home and a farm together. March acts "the man about the place," but despite their feeling for each other, she and Banford are "apt to become a little irritable" and seem "to live too much off themselves." It is evidently a sterile relationship, March, indeed, being generally "absent in herself," as if she were not really held by Banford; and this sterility is mirrored in the unproductiveness of the farm, particularly in the "obstinate refusal" of their hens to lay eggs. Matters are made worse by the depredations of a fox, which carries off hens "under [their] very noses" (pp. 85–88).

One evening March, out with her gun, is standing with her consciousness "held back" when she suddenly sees the fox "looking up at her." His eyes meet her eyes, and "he [knows] her." She is "spellbound," does not shoot, and the fox makes off. Thereafter she wanders about "in strange mindlessness," but she is "possessed" by the fox and feels that he has "invisibly [mastered] her spirit" (pp. 88–89). What is enacted here with admirable economy is parallel to what takes place in repeated meetings between Daphne and the Count. Into the vacancy of March's being there suddenly irrupts, with the force of an epiphany, a manifestation of wild life. Immediately prior to the encounter March has been unaware of the vibrant life around her, of the "limbs of the pine-trees" shining in the air and the stalks of grass "all agleam," for she "[sees] it all, and [does] not see it" (p. 88). Now, at a level deeper than consciousness, she comes under the spell of newly apprehended energies and is possessed by them. What is perhaps specially significant is that she submits to the mastery of the fox—this and the strong sexual overtones of the description preparing the way for her response to the young soldier who suddenly arrives at the farm.

From the moment he appears Henry "[is] the fox" to March (p. 93). She tries "to keep her will uppermost" as she watches him, but soon ceases "to reserve herself" from his presence. Instead she gives herself up "to a warm, relaxed peace," and, "accepting the spell" that is on her, she allows herself to "lapse into the odour of the fox," remaining "still and soft in her corner like a passive creature in its cave" (p. 98). In the light of Daphne's experience in "The Ladybird," March's still, relaxed passivity under the spell is worthy of notice. That it is to a sexual potency in Henry that she is responding is indicated by the dream she has on the night of his arrival. Hearing a strange singing—a call (like the Count's crooning) to a new mode of life—she goes outside and suddenly realizes that it is the fox who is singing. She approaches the fox, but when she puts out her hand to touch him, he suddenly bites her wrist. At the same time, in bounding away, his brush (which seems to be on fire) "[sears] and [burns] her mouth with a great pain" (pp. 99–100). If March in her dream experiences the fire of passion that she desires (for when Henry later kisses her it is "with a quick brushing kiss" that seems "to burn through her every fibre" [p. 115]), she is also warned, as it were, not to play with fire, for the fox is no doll, as his bite testifies.

What playing with fire means, in the first instance, is resisting Henry's determination to master her. He is "a huntsman in spirit," and deciding that he wants to marry her (initially with the shrewd idea of gaining the farm for himself but soon with a genuine and disinterested passion), he sets out to hunt his quarry, knowing "he [is] master of her" (pp. 104–5). He also hunts the fox and kills it. It is a remarkable stroke. The killing of the marauder functions, first, as a ritual supplanting of the fox by which March is possessed. At the same time Henry is para-doxically aligned with the fox he kills, and his hunting of it is made the occasion of an extension of his significance:

As he stood under the oaks of the wood-edge he heard the dogs from the neighbouring cottage up the hill yelling suddenly and startlingly, and the wakened dogs from the farms around barking answer. And suddenly it seemed to him England was little and tight, he felt the landscape was constricted even in the dark, and that there were too many dogs in the night, making a noise like a fence of sound, like the network of English hedges netting the view. He felt the fox didn't have a chance. For it must be the fox that had started all this hullabaloo.
    . . . He knew the fox would be coming. It seemed to him it would be the last of the foxes in this loudly-barking, thick-voiced England, tight with innumera-ble little houses. (p. 121)

Henry, we see, should not be regarded merely as a rather nondescript young man who has been fired into the pursuit of a woman. He sud-denly emerges here as the representative of a wild, passionate spirit for which there seems to be no room in a tight England. It is a spirit, we are to understand, that has been assailed in England during the war, for the passage should be related to Lord Beveridge's bitter thoughts in "The Ladybird" of "the so-called patriots who [have] been howling their mongrel indecency in the public face" and of an "England fallen under the paws of smelly mongrels." Henry, like James Joyce's Stephen Deda-lus, is determined to fly by the nets that threaten to drag him down; and he wants a freer, more expansive life than seems possible in a land fenced in by the conventional pieties of such as Banford. It is a measure of Lawrence's despair of England at this time that Henry and March are made to leave for Canada at the end of the tale.

But before they can finally come together, Banford's hold on March has to be broken. The way in which Banford is disposed of arouses our gravest doubts; and it is at this point that the crystal-clear depths of the story become suddenly muddied with obsessive matter. Banford is dis-posed of when Henry, refusing to accept March's withdrawal from her promise to marry him, comes back to the farm to claim her and chops down a tree that falls on and kills his rival. It is true that this climactic event is carefully prepared for. Prior to it March dreams that Banford is dead and that the coffin in which she has to put her is "the rough wood-box in which the bits of chopped wood" are kept. Not wanting to lay her "dead darling" in an unlined box, March wraps her up in a fox-skin, which is all she can find (p. 123). The dream points clearly enough to March's desire for Banford's death, and, in its association of the dead woman with the fox that Henry has killed, seems to express a wish

that he will be the one to bring about her death. It is March's unconscious complicity in Banford's death that in part explains her immediate capitulation to Henry the moment the deed is consummated. It is
true, too, that the killing is technically an accident, and that Henry
warns Banford to move (though in a manner that ensures her refusal)
before he strikes the blows that fell the tree. "In his heart," however, he
has "decided her death" (p. 151)—and the fact remains that he murders
her.

It is furthermore true that the symbolism of the story insidiously
suggests that Henry kills Banford as naturally, almost as innocently, as
a fox kills chickens, and out of a similar need to live, March being
essential to his life. It may also be granted that the killing frees March
for life. That does not mean to say, however, that we should celebrate
the murder as "an inspired and creative deed," as Julian Moynahan has
suggested.[2] Henry, after all, is not a fox, and calling murder by another
name does not make it smell any sweeter. We can only conclude, I
think, that when Lawrence, who has such a reverence for life, can be
taken to justify murder, it is because the murder is incidental to a compulsive justification of something else.

What strikes us about the murder of Banford is that it is strictly
unnecessary. The moment Henry returns to the farm and faces March,
her upper lip lifts from her teeth in a "helpless, fascinated rabbit-look,"
and as soon as she sees "his glowing, red face," it is "all over with her";
she is as "helpless" as if she were "bound" (p. 148). She is as powerless,
that is, as a rabbit before a fox; and her helplessness surely implies that
Henry has only to insist on her leaving the farm with him for her to
yield, irrespective of the opposition they might be expected to encounter from Banford. That Henry is nevertheless made to kill Banford is a
means, I suggest, not of freeing March but of ensuring her submission
to him as a woman. In *The Plumed Serpent*, when Cipriano executes
the men who have tried to kill Don Ramón, he repeatedly intones
"The Lords of Life are Masters of Death"; it seems to be the covert
intention behind Henry's murder of Banford that his mastery of death
establishes him as a lord of life. For March not only has to be freed from
Banford; she has to be released into a new mode of being.

She has to be won, first, to a new conception of relationship between a
man and a woman. When she writes to Henry and goes back on her
promise to marry him, she says that she has "been over it all again" in
her "mind," and that she does not see "on what grounds" she can marry
him since he is "an absolute stranger" to her, they do not "seem to have a
thing in common," and she does not "really love" him (pp. 142–43).
What she has to be made to respond to, though not with her mind, is the
existence of an affinity between them that goes deeper than conven-

tional ideas of love and compatibility; what she has to be made to accept, in a word, is the compulsion of a life-force—and of a lord of life. It is this acknowledgment that is wrung from her when Banford is killed, it being an indication of the lengths to which Lawrence is driven in asserting the doctrine of power that murder should be made the means of ensuring the acknowledgment. March faces Henry, gazing at him "with the last look of resistance," and then "in a last agonized failure" she begins to cry. "He [has] won," we are told; and looking at him with "a senseless look of helplessness and submission," she realizes that she will "never leave him again" (p. 153).

Henry's demonstration of his mastery in the killing of Banford is intended to effect a further submission on March's part once they are married:

If he spoke to her, she would turn to him with a faint new smile, the strange, quivering little smile of a woman who has died in the old way of love, and can't quite rise to the new way. She still felt she ought to *do* something, to strain herself in some direction. . . . And she could not quite accept the submergence which his new love put upon her. If she was in love, she ought to *exert* herself, in some way, loving. She felt the weary need of our day to *exert* herself in love. But she knew that in fact she must no more exert herself in love. He would not have the love which exerted itself towards him. It made his brow go black. No, he wouldn't let her exert her love towards him. No, she had to be passive, to acquiesce, and to be submerged under the surface of love. (p. 154)

Lawrence is not as explicit here as he is in *The Plumed Serpent*, but in view of the previously quoted comments in that novel on Aphrodite of the foam, I think there can be little doubt what a woman's exertion in love should be taken to mean. March, having "died in the old way of love," is required (like Daphne) to be reborn into a new passive acquiescence and foamless submergence in the sex act. It is a saving grace that March is left not quite accepting her submergence.

4

F. R. Leavis has discussed "The Captain's Doll" at length, leaving little to be added to his account.[3] I should merely like to draw attention to the presence in the tale of what might be called the Aphrodite motif. It is perhaps only our recognition of the importance of this motif in "The Ladybird" and "The Fox" that makes us aware of it in the third tale in the volume, for in "The Captain's Doll" it is presented even more obliquely.

Captain Hepburn, like Count Dionys and Henry, possesses the kind of mastery that casts a spell over a woman. He speaks to Countess Hannele with a "strange, mindless, soft, suggestive tone" that leaves her "powerless to disobey" (p. 170); and when he makes love to her, she is "heavy and spellbound" (p. 172). Hannele, in a word, cannot "help being in love" with him. Nevertheless, Hannele, who makes dolls and cushions and "suchlike objects of feminine art," has made a doll of the Captain, a "mannikin" that is "a perfect portrait" of him as a Scottish officer (p. 162), and the making of the doll clearly indicates that his mastery over her is far from absolute. At the same time the doll projects an image of the Captain that is not altogether unfair, for we discover that his wife has made a living doll of him: "Why, on our wedding night," Mrs. Hepburn tells Hannele, "he kneeled down in front of me and promised, with God's help, to make my life happy. . . . It has been his one aim in life, to make my life happy" (p. 188). The mannikin, that is, suggests the diminishment of self, of true being, that is implicit in such a limitation of a man's purposive activity. Hepburn is thus both a masterful man and a doll, and it is this complexity that makes the conflict between old and new modes of love a more subtle affair in this story than it is in "The Ladybird," of which we may be reminded by the recurrence of a man on his knees before a woman. In "The Captain's Doll" the conflict is first internalized, as it were, for Hepburn himself comes to repudiate "the business of adoration" (p. 208). When his wife dies, he realizes that he no longer wants to love in that way; and he insists to Hannele that *any* woman . . . could start any minute and make a doll" of the man she loves: "And the doll would be her hero; and her hero would be no more than her doll" (p. 249). Hannele, however, is inwardly determined that "he must go down on his knees if he [wants] her love" (p. 235). The ostensible drama that is played out between them consists in his attempt to make her abandon this position.

But since a man's being no more than a woman's doll also implies that she may use him as a toy in the sex act—implies, indeed, the kind of relationship that Bertha Coutts is said to have forced on Mellors in *Lady Chatterley's Lover*—the drama here not unexpectedly turns out to have a further dimension. We are adverted to this dimension at the beginning of the long, superb description of the excursion that Hannele and Hepburn make to the glacier. Sitting silently in the car that is taking them to the mountains, they watch the glacier river. The river is "roaring and raging, a glacier river of pale, seething ice-water"; it is a "foaming river," a "stony, furious, lion-like river, tawny-coloured" (pp. 221–22). When the car can go no further, they begin to climb the mountain; and then there follows this passage:

This valley was just a mountain cleft, cleft sheer in the hard, living rock, with black trees like hair flourishing in this secret, naked place of the earth. At the bottom of the open wedge for ever roared the rampant, insatiable water. The sky from above was like a sharp wedge forcing its way into the earth's cleavage, and that eternal ferocious water was like the steel edge of the wedge, the terrible tip biting into the rocks' intensity. Who could have thought that the soft sky of light, and the soft foam of water could thrust and penetrate into the dark, strong earth? (p. 224)

What we have here, it seems clear, is another rendering of "the intercourse between heaven and earth" that is described at the beginning of *The Rainbow*; and what the "rampant, insatiable" water, the "ferocious" water, symbolizes, I suggest, is "the seething, frictional, ecstatic" Aphrodite of the foam. Such a reading helps us to understand the reactions of Hepburn and Hannele to the scene. He "hates" and "loathes" it, finding it "almost obscene" (p. 224); she is "thrilled and excited" by it "to another sort of savageness" (p. 225). They proceed on their way to the glacier, and Hepburn suddenly decides he wants to climb on to it: it is "his one desire—to stand upon it" (p. 238). The ascent of the glacier is for Hepburn an "ordeal or mystic battle" and, as he prepares for it, "the curious vibration of his excitement" makes the scene "strange, rather horrible to her"; she shudders, but the glacier still seems to her "to hold the key to all glamour and ecstasy" (p. 237). He has earlier declared that the mountains "are less" than he, and been filled with "a curious, dark, masterful force" (pp. 233–34). What he demonstrates, I take it, as he climbs "the naked ice-slope," the ice that looks "so pure, like flesh" (p. 238), is his determination to pit himself against the source of the seething water and so really to get on top of it.

On the way down Hepburn makes it clear to Hannele that he will not marry her "on a basis of love." What he demands of her in marriage, he tells her, is "honour and obedience: and the proper physical feelings" (p. 248). The word "proper," we may feel, is highly ambiguous, but he leaves it at that. Lawrence leaves it at that too, and "The Captain's Doll" is consequently not marred, as the other two tales are, by an attempt to enforce a total surrender on the woman. After a fierce argument Hannele finally makes her submission, movingly and convincingly, when she tells Hepburn she wants to burn the picture of the doll that he carries with him. The ascent of the glacier has shown beyond question that he is no doll.

HARDY'S
RELUCTANT HEROINES

Thomas Hardy's novels are notable for the most sustained attempt in English—prior to D. H. Lawrence—to portray the varied nature of sexual relations between men and women. Within his overall oeuvre, three of the novels—*Far from the Madding Crowd* (1874), his first mature work; *The Woodlanders* (1887), written at about the middle of his career; and *Jude the Obscure* (1896), the last and one of the greatest of his novels—are specifically linked by Hardy's recurrent preoccupation with a sexual incapacity on the part of his heroines. This incapacity has not attracted any critical attention, so far as I am aware, but its recurrence in the three novels not only suggests its significance to Hardy but provides a frame that enables us to read one work in relation to another. In *Far from the Madding Crowd* the problem created by the heroine's sexual attitudes is clearly revealed despite some attempt to camouflage it; and the characterization of Bathsheba Everdene in this respect provides us with a basis for interpreting the more obscure presentation of both Grace Melbury in *The Woodlanders* and Sue Bridehead in *Jude the Obscure*.

The view of the relationship of Bathsheba and Sergeant Troy which the novelist appears to endorse in *Far from the Madding Crowd* is that she is dazzled by his sexual brilliance (as in the famous scene of the sword exercise), becomes foolishly infatuated with him, and so marries a thoroughly irresponsible and dissolute man, who eventually deserts her as he has earlier abandoned Fanny Robin. Troy's sexual glamor and vitality are strongly conveyed, but otherwise he is consistently condemned. He is condemned not only by Boldwood, his jealous rival, who calls him "a rake" who has burst in on Bathsheba "without right or ceremony" (p. 262);[1] but out of his own mouth: "He had been known to observe casually that in dealing with womankind the only alternative to flattery was cursing and swearing. There was no third method. 'Treat them fairly, and you are a lost man,' he would say" (p. 221). He is condemned too by his own actions, as on the night of the great storm when, instead of taking steps to protect the ricks on Bathsheba's farm (which is now his responsibility), he leads the farmworkers in a "debauch" that makes for a "painful and demoralizing termination to the evening's entertainment" he has arranged (p. 303). And he is condemned furthermore by the consistently hostile commentary of the narrator, of which a few examples must suffice: his "deformities" are said to lie "deep down from a woman's vision," while his "embellishments" are "upon the very surface" (p. 244); when he plants the flowers on Fanny's grave with what I take to be genuine emotion—I shall discuss his attitude toward Fanny later—he is said "in his prostration at this time" to have "no perception that in the futility of these romantic doings, dictated by a remorseful reaction from previous indifference, there [is] any element of absurdity" (pp. 372–73); and we are told that what Troy has "in the way of emotion" is "an occasional fitful sentiment which sometimes [causes] him as much inconvenience as emotion of a strong and healthy kind" (p. 400).

Troy, clearly, is not an admirable character, but the failure of his marriage to Bathsheba is not solely to be attributed to him. Although he is again viewed critically when he and Bathsheba are seen alone together for the first time after the marriage, it is also suggested that something more is at issue between the couple than emerges (rather like the scene in Henry James's *The Portrait of a Lady*—published a few years later—in which we first see Mr. and Mrs. Osmond after their marriage and register the change in their relationship):

"And you mean, Frank," said Bathsheba sadly—her voice was painfully lowered from the fulness and vivacity of the previous summer—"that you have lost more than a hundred pounds in a month by this dreadful horse-racing? O, Frank, it is cruel; it is foolish of you to take away my money so. We shall have to leave the farm; that will be the end of it!"

"Humbug about cruel. Now, there 'tis again—turn on the water-works; that's just like you."

"But you'll promise me not to go to Budmouth second meeting, won't you?" she implored. Bathsheba was at the full depth for tears, but she maintained a dry eye.

"I don't see why I should; in fact, if it turns out to be a fine day, I was thinking of taking you." . . .

"But you don't mean to say that you have risked anything on [the race next Monday] too!" she exclaimed, with an agonized look.

"There now, don't you be a little fool. Wait till you are told. Why, Bathsheba, you have lost all the pluck and sauciness you formerly had, and upon my life if I had known what a chicken-hearted creature you were under all your boldness, I'd never have—I know what." (pp. 318–19)

The carping tones of the couple as they engage in mutual recrimination indicate how soon the marriage has lost its gleam, the point being made additionally and emblematically by some "early-withered leaves" that spin across the path of their gig (p. 319). But if Bathsheba is justifiably angered by his prodigal behavior, it is not clear why she—as distinct from her money—should be so diminished, for her voice is "painfully lowered" from its habitual "fulness and vivacity." And if Troy, in turn, is led to assert his mastery in the marriage, there is nothing in the scene itself to account for the kind of disenchantment he expresses, neither her nagging nor her chicken-heartedness being presented as so obnoxious as to warrant his implied regret that he has married her.

Shortly thereafter, when Troy is reduced to asking Bathsheba for money (which he wants to give to Fanny), we are told that he deems it "necessary to be civil" though he does "not now love her enough to allow himself to be carried too far by her ways" (p. 330). It seems that the decline of his love for Bathsheba may be linked to his chance encounter with Fanny, with whom he has lost touch but not deliberately abandoned; and this impression is strengthened when Bathsheba discovers he keeps another woman's "coil of hair" in the case at the back of his watch (p. 331). The discovery greatly upsets Bathsheba and forces her to review her situation. The account we are then given of her attitude to marriage suggests the cause of Troy's disenchantment with her—though the narrator carefully stops short of stating this himself:

Directly he had gone, Bathsheba burst into great sobs—dry-eyed sobs, which cut as they came, without any softening by tears. But she determined to repress all evidences of feeling. She was conquered; but she would never own it as long as she lived. Her pride was indeed brought low by despairing discoveries of her spoliation by marriage with a less pure nature than her own. She chafed to and fro in rebelliousness, like a caged leopard; her whole soul was in arms, and the blood fired her face. Until she had met Troy, Bathsheba had been proud of her position as a woman; it had been a glory to her to know that her lips had been touched by no man's on earth—that her waist had never been encircled by a lover's arm. She hated herself now. In those earlier days she had always nourished a secret contempt for girls who were slaves of the first good-looking young fellow who should choose to salute them. She had never taken kindly to the idea of marriage in the abstract as did the majority of women she saw about her. In the turmoil of her anxiety for her lover she had agreed to marry him; but the perception that had accompanied her happiest hours on this account was

rather that of self-sacrifice than of promotion and honour. Although she scarcely knew the divinity's name, Diana was the goddess whom Bathsheba instinctively adored. That she had never, by look, word, or sign, encouraged a man to
approach her—that she had felt herself sufficient to herself, and had in the
independence of her girlish heart fancied there was a certain degradation in
renouncing the simplicity of a maiden existence to become the humbler half of
an indifferent matrimonial whole—were facts now bitterly remembered. (pp.
333–34)

The narrator states that the sense of "spoliation" Bathsheba so bitterly
registers here is due to her "marriage with a less pure nature than her
own," but the rest of the passage suggests it stems from the brute fact
of marriage itself. It is not merely that she has "never taken kindly to
the idea of marriage." If it was a positive "glory" to her, prior to her own
marriage, to know she had remained sexually untouched by any man,
this feeling would seem to extend beyond a girlish pride in virginity
since she is said to "[hate] herself now"—to be disgusted, apparently,
by sexual experience per se. Certainly the feeling of self-hatred is
evoked in direct response to the recall of those untouched lips and
waist. This suggests that her resentment at being "conquered" may
also be related to the fact of her sexual submission, and that it is not
merely disillusionment in Troy that has brought "her pride" low. Similarly, her renunciation of "the simplicity of a maiden existence" for life
as "the humbler half of an indifferent matrimonial whole" is felt as a
"degradation," and the strength of the revulsion suggests a more profound kind of humbling. Indeed, she was only led into marriage in the
first place "in the turmoil of anxiety for her lover"—by her jealousy
and fear of losing him, that is, as she has previously confessed (p. 311).
It was this specific fear that allayed her more general fear of sexual
contact and impelled her to go against her own nature, for Bathsheba is
of the tribe of Diana—is temperamentally a virgin, "sufficient to herself." Marriage, even in its "happiest hours," is accordingly a "self-sacrifice" to her, for her martyrdom to sex entails the violation of her self-
sufficiency.

   In the quoted passage, therefore, the narrator both implies that
Bathsheba is temperamentally unsuited to marriage and contrives to
camouflage this by suggesting at the same time that it is her marriage
to Troy that is the trouble. What he leaves quite unsaid—though this is
of the essence—is what the effect of her attitude is on Troy. Troy is no
doubt a wastrel and a philanderer, but there is more to his side of things
than the novelist appears willing to admit. Troy's accusation of chicken-heartedness on Bathsheba's part now takes on another meaning, and
it is not her nagging over money that is the main cause of his rapid

disenchantment with her: we may assume that she has proved incapable of really giving herself to him, and it is because he does not feel they are truly married that he abandons her.

Support for this view is provided by one of the most striking scenes in the novel (and in Hardy)—the confrontation of Troy and Bathsheba over the open coffin that contains the bodies of Fanny and her child, whom he has fathered:

He had originally stood perfectly erect. And now, in the well-nigh congealed immobility of his frame could be discerned an incipient movement, as in the darkest night may be discerned light after a while. He was gradually sinking forwards. The lines of his features softened, and dismay modulated to illimitable sadness. Bathsheba was regarding him from the other side, still with parted lips and distracted eyes. Capacity for intense feeling is proportionate to the general intensity of the nature, and perhaps in all Fanny's sufferings, much greater relatively to her strength, there never was a time when she suffered in an absolute sense what Bathsheba suffered now.

What Troy did was to sink upon his knees with an indefinable union of remorse and reverence upon his face, and, bending over Fanny Robin, gently kissed her, as one would kiss an infant asleep to avoid awakening it.

At the sight and sound of that, to her, unendurable act, Bathsheba sprang towards him. All the strong feelings which had been scattered over her existence since she knew what feeling was, seemed gathered together into one pulsation now. The revulsion from her indignant mood a little earlier, when she had meditated upon compromised honour, forestalment, eclipse in maternity by another, was violent and entire. All that was forgotten in the simple and still strong attachment of wife to husband. She had sighed for her self-completeness then, and now she cried aloud against the severance of the union she had deplored. She flung her arms round Troy's neck, exclaiming wildly from the deepest deep of her heart—

"Don't—don't kiss them! O, Frank, I can't bear it—I can't! I love you better than she did: kiss me too, Frank—kiss me! *You will, Frank, kiss me too!*" . . .

"I will not kiss you!" he said, pushing her away. (pp. 359–60)

Hardy's characterization here is superb. Troy acts with complete sincerity and spontaneity, and so is unassailable. The commentary, otherwise so hostile, grants him this: as he begins to melt into motion, the unfreezing of his "congealed immobility" is given an affirmative connotation by the parallel established between it and the discerning of "light" in "the darkest night," just as the softening of his features bespeaks the tenderness with which he approaches the dead Fanny. (His feeling now, we may remark in passing, is not different in kind from that which he later exhibits at Fanny's grave, though the narrator is not as charitable to him then.) But the suffering that Troy inflicts on Bathsheba is also sharply rendered. His gentle kissing of Fanny is an

"unendurable act" for Bathsheba not alone for the quality of the feeling
it reveals toward the dead woman but in its utter negation of his wife,
as if he were unaware of her very presence there. The fear of losing him
that has led her into the marriage now operates to make her try to save
it, though paradoxically it has all along been a threat to "her self-completeness"—and this propels her into her grotesque competition with
Fanny. But Troy is remorseless. Putting an effective end to their marriage, he proceeds to spell out what has undermined it: "This woman,"
he says to Bathsheba, "is more to me, dead as she is, than ever you
were, or are, or can be," and he then calls Fanny his "very, very wife."
He also adds, "heartlessly": "You are nothing to me—nothing. A ceremony before a priest doesn't make a marriage. I am not morally yours"
(p. 361). Bathsheba, in the end, remarries; but when she gives herself to
Gabriel Oak, it is in a union that is based on *"camaraderie,"* not passion (p. 458).

2

ANALOGIES at once suggest themselves when we compare the marriage
of Grace Melbury and Edred Fitzpiers in *The Woodlanders* with that of
Bathsheba and Troy.[2] Fitzpiers, like Troy, has a strong sexual magnetism: Grace is conscious, when she first meets him, of his exercising "a
certain fascination over her—or even more, an almost psychic influence, as it is called" (p. 188).[3] Like Troy, Fitzpiers lets himself be swept
by his own sexual feeling and is led into marriage to Grace when he is
"at the spring-tide of a sentiment" that she is "a necessity of his existence," and allows himself "to be carried forward on the wave of his
desire" (p. 184). And like Troy too, he is a philanderer. Lying in wait for
Grace at the end of the Midsummer eve ceremony, he "captures" her
and, while she "[rests] on him like one utterly mastered," he says: "You
are in my arms, dearest; and I am going to claim you, and keep you
there all our two lives!" (p. 178). But no sooner does Grace leave him on
this occasion than he runs off after Suke Damson, "a hoydenish maid-
en of the hamlet," and we are told that "it [is] daybreak" before the
couple reenter Little Hintock (pp. 179–80). Within two and a half
months of his marriage to Grace, moreover, he becomes enamored of
Mrs. Charmond and begins his obsessive pursuit of her. At the same
time he is not merely a rake, for—like Troy again—he is capable of
inspiring a genuine passion in women other than his wife: when the
rumor spreads through the village that he is dying, both Suke and Mrs.
Charmond hurry to the Fitzpierses' house to obtain firsthand information about him, though they thus risk exposing themselves (p. 287).
    As in the case of *Far from the Madding Crowd,* the immediate ques-

tion posed by the narrative in *The Woodlanders* is what leads so quick-ly to the husband's disenchantment with his wife and his abandon-ment of her. The short answer provided is that Fitzpiers is "that kind of man," a man who is ready to play with a woman "as a toy" (p. 154). Probing more deeply, the narrator subsequently declares that Fitzpiers is a man who is capable of "spreading the same conjoint emotion" over a number of women at the same time, and that "the love of men like [him] is unquestionably of such quality as to bear division and trans-ference": "He had indeed once declared, though not to [Grace], that on one occasion he had noticed himself to be possessed by five distinct infatuations at the same time" (p. 239). And this is the view of Fitzpiers that we are left with at the end of the novel, for when Grace is finally reconciled to him, her father, for one, is not hopeful that a chastened Fitzpiers will be ready to give up joint stock enterprises:

> "Well—he's her husband," Melbury said to himself, "and let her take him back to her bed if she will! . . . But let her bear in mind that the woman walks and laughs somewhere at this very moment whose neck he'll be coling next year as he does hers to-night; and as he did Felice Charmond's last year; and Suke Damson's the year afore! . . . It's a forlorn hope for her; and God knows how it will end!" (pp. 389–90)

The marriage of Grace and Fitzpiers, then, would seem quite simply to founder because of his temperament, but the novelist will not allow us a simple explanation, and this proves to be only one of a number of contributory factors. There is, first, the metaphysical dimension of the failure. When the couple meet for the first time, he observes her reflec-tion in a mirror before seeing her in the flesh, as it were, and he is quick to relate the experience to "the work of a transcendental philosopher" he has been reading: "I did not see you directly," he says to Grace, "but reflected in the glass. I thought, what a lovely creature! The design is for once carried out. Nature has at last recovered her lost union with the Idea!" (p. 161). It is of some significance that Fitzpiers first sees a reflection of the woman he marries—not the reality that marriage alone discloses. And "the design" formed by the union of Nature and the Idea is that of "the Unfulfilled Intention" which rules the Hardy universe in *The Woodlanders*: "Here [in the wood], as everywhere, the Unfulfilled Intention, which makes life what it is, was as obvious as it could be among the depraved crowds of a city slum. The leaf was de-formed, the curve was crippled, the taper was interrupted; the lichen ate the vigour of the stalk, and the ivy slowly strangled to death the promising sapling" (p. 83). This sounds the bitter note of the mature Hardy but it is not gratuitous, being intended to reverberate in the main action of the narrative. With such a controlling force in the universe, nothing—neither in nature with its predatory struggles nor among men in their depravity—is enabled to realize its potentiality; and this applies equally to the human endeavor of marriage. Before they marry, Grace and Fitzpiers see "two large birds" tumble "one over the other into the hot ashes at their feet, apparently engrossed in a desperate quarrel that [prevents] the use of their wings." They quickly part, and fly up "with a singed smell," to be seen no more; but Marty South is there to say, "That's the end of what is called love" (p. 173). The birds preside over an Idea of marriage as a getting burnt prior to a separation. After their marriage, both Grace and Fitzpiers emphasize the point for us: "Sorrow and sickness of heart at last," he says, are "the end of all love" (p. 223); and Grace wonders if there is "one world in the universe where the fruit [has] no worm, and marriage no sorrow" (p. 234).

Given such a man as Fitzpiers, therefore, and such a world as that of *The Woodlanders*, Grace's marriage would not seem to stand much chance of lasting. But she, we come to realize, proves to be as much of a disappointment to him as he to her, though Hardy does not indicate this directly, and we need to see Grace through Bathsheba, so to speak, in order to take the measure of *his* predicament. That it is not merely a question of Fitzpiers's "conjoint emotion" that is at issue is implicitly conceded by Grace in her confrontation with Mrs. Charmond: "He'll get tired of you soon," she says, "as tired as can be—you don't know him so well as I!—and then you may wish you had never seen him" (p. 268).

What may lie behind Fitzpiers's having become tired of Grace so quickly is first intimated in his falling into "the scrupulous civility of mere acquaintanceship" in relation to her (p. 231), for this points to his feeling that they have failed to establish a real intimacy. But Grace is inclined to attribute her sense of distance from him to a different cause, and her view appears to be endorsed by the narrator:

Grace was amazed at the mildness of the anger which the suspicion [of her husband's involvement with Mrs. Charmond] engendered in her. She was but little excited, and her jealousy was languid even to death. It told tales of the nature of her affection for him. In truth, her ante-nuptial regard for Fitzpiers had been rather of the quality of awe towards a superior being than of tender solicitude for a lover. It had been based upon mystery and strangeness—the mystery of his past, of his knowledge, of his professional skill, of his beliefs. When this structure of ideals was demolished by the intimacy of common life, and she found him as merely human as the Hintock people themselves, a new foundation was in demand for an enduring and staunch affection—a sympathetic interdependence, wherein mutual weaknesses are made the grounds of a defensive alliance. Fitzpiers had furnished nothing of that single-minded confidence and truth out of which alone such a second union could spring; hence it was with a controllable emotion that she now watched the mare brought round [i.e., for his journey to Mrs. Charmond]. (p. 233)

What Grace discovers here—to her amazement—is that, though it was his passion for her that mastered her, her sexual feeling for him is not very strong, as the mildness of her anger and the languidness of her jealousy now indicate to her. But if the absence of strong feeling on her part tells (a surprising) tale of "the nature of her affection for him," it also bears witness to what she has brought to him in the marriage—though neither she nor the narrator seems to take account of this. The reflections that follow are characterized by the same kind of half-truth: they may have their own validity, but more needs to be said. If it was "awe towards a superior being" that drew her to Fitzpiers, it is not only "tender solicitude for a lover" that this displaced, nor is solicitude the only alternative to such awe. If "a new foundation" is needed for "an enduring and staunch affection" in their relationship, this is not merely because the awe has disappeared in "the intimacy of common life" but because the relationship has never had a firm sexual basis. The desired "second union" that should be founded on "a sympathetic interdependence" seems to be a new version of the *camaraderie* of *Far from the Madding Crowd*, which in that novel is said to be "the only love which is strong as death," in contradistinction to "passion," which is "evanescent as steam" (p. 459). But passion, we may feel, has never been brought to the boil in the marriage of Grace and Fitzpiers.

That Grace suffers from the same kind of inhibition as Bathsheba is suggested by the fact that for her too marriage is regarded as a "degradation to herself" (p. 239), the strong word hinting at her own disabilities as well as those of her husband. And indeed, when Fitzpiers returns home after having abandoned her for a time for Mrs. Charmond, her response implies more than moral revulsion on her part. Her father urges her to take him back, but the idea of his "reinstatement" strikes her as "intolerable," and she becomes "almost hysterical" (p. 324). When her husband actually appears on the scene, she flees from him:

A spasm passed through Grace. A Daphnean instinct, exceptionally strong in her as a girl, had been revived by her widowed seclusion; and it was not lessened by her affronted sentiments towards the comer, and her regard for another man. She opened some little ivory tablets that lay on the dressing-table, scribbled in pencil on one of them, "I am gone to visit one of my school-friends," gathered a few toilet necessaries into a hand-bag, and, not three minutes after that voice had been heard, her slim form, hastily wrapped up from observation, might have been seen passing out of the back door of Melbury's house. (p. 325)

It is interesting that—as in analogous circumstances in *Far from the Madding Crowd*—Hardy should again have recourse to mythology in order to account for the behavior of his heroine, the mythological reference, in the comparative openness of its connotation, serving perhaps to conceal as well as reveal, and so ensure that the question of female sexuality should remain decently veiled. Certainly he was concerned, as we shall see, by the response of a prudish public to his subject matter. Grace's "Daphnean instinct," at all events, suggests that she is the kind of woman for whom the preservation of her virginity means more than life itself (in ordinary terms), for it is at her own entreaty that Daphne is changed into a tree when pursued by Apollo. The instinct, which is said to have been "exceptionally strong" in Grace "as a girl," would not seem to have diminished in force in her maturity, for it now impels her to precipitate flight from her husband. We may assume, indeed, since instincts do not easily die, that it not only "revived" in her "widowed seclusion" but, prior to that, survived her marriage—and that she, like Bathsheba, was unable psychologically, if not physically, to give herself to her husband. There is no doubt that, in Hardy's imagination, Grace is another Bathsheba, for she is later said to have "more of Artemis than of Aphrodite in her constitution" (p. 341), more, that is, of Diana, who was widely identified with Artemis. We must suppose, therefore, that Fitzpiers, like Troy, has had to suffer an unresponsive wife; and that it is not in sheer promiscuity that he turns from Grace to pastures new. When he finally tries to win Grace back, it is to "a different kind of love altogether": "Less passionate," he says to her, "more profound. It has nothing to do with the material conditions of the object at all; much to do with her character and goodness, as revealed by closer observation" (pp. 366–67). We are not intended to believe, however, that Fitzpiers's conduct will change, as is indicated both by the previously quoted prophecy of Grace's father and in the following (extratextual) statement by the novelist himself—though no mention is made, either in the novel or outside it, of what Fitzpiers will continue to encounter in his renewed marriage to Grace:

You have probably observed that the *ending* of *[The Woodlanders]*, as hinted rather than stated, is that the heroine is doomed to an unhappy life with an inconstant husband.
I could not accent this strongly in the book; by reason of the conventions of the libraries etc. Since the story was written however truth to life is not consid-

ered quite such a crime in literature as it was formerly: and it is therefore a question for you [if you adapt the novel for the theatre] whether you will accent this ending; or prefer to obscure it.[4]

3

THE RELATIONSHIP of Sue Bridehead and Jude Fawley in *Jude the Obscure* seems, at first sight, to bear scant resemblance to that of either Bathsheba and Troy or Grace and Fitzpiers. Jude is no rake, and his fidelity to Sue is not an issue. And Sue, the emancipated, urban intellectual, has apparently little in common with the country girls Bathsheba and Grace. Their relationship, moreover, in its tortured complexity, is radically different in kind from the simple, more straightforward unions depicted in the earlier works; but when we restrict ourselves to their sexual relations, we find that Sue—"Sue the Obscure," as she has been called[5]—is less enigmatic when placed side by side with Bathsheba and Grace.

As Jude contemplates Sue on one notable occasion, it appears that, where sex is concerned, her problems are likely to be not so much psychological as physical:

Looking at his loved one as she appeared to him now, in his tender thought the sweetest and most disinterested comrade that he had ever had, living largely in vivid imaginings, so ethereal a creature that her spirit could be seen trembling through her limbs, he felt heartily ashamed of his earthliness in spending the hours he had spent in Arabella's company. There was something rude and immoral in thrusting these recent facts of his life upon the mind of one who, to him, was so uncarnate as to seem at times impossible as a human wife to an average man. (p. 245)[6]

If Sue seems to be "so ethereal a creature" that her spirit can "be seen trembling through her limbs," this is less because her spirituality is palpable—though she is indeed intended to be the opposite of Arabella, who is said to be "a complete and substantial female animal—no more, no less" (p. 81)—than because her physicality gives the impression of being so attenuated she hardly appears to be there in the flesh at all. As the vivid coinage "uncarnate" emphasizes, Sue's spirit seems to be disembodied, and she, the woman she is, no more than "a phantasmal, bodiless creature," as Jude says to her subsequently (p. 324). Yet paradoxically she is sexually attractive, rousing Jude to an enduring passion for her; and she herself declares, seeking to justify her marriage to Phillotson, that she feels she would not have been "provided with attractiveness unless it were meant to be exercised" (p. 265). The exercising, however, reveals to her that she is a woman "with aberrant passions, and unaccountable antipathies" (p. 266).

The antipathy seems, at first, to be due to the nature of the man she has married. Sue's aunt grants that Phillotson is "a very civil, honourable liver," but she adds: "—I don't want to wownd your feelings, but—there be certain men here and there that no woman of any niceness can stomach. I should have said he was one" (p. 249). Sue herself later admits to Jude that it is "a torture" to her to "live with him as a husband" (p. 273), but is hard put to it to explain what is the matter. On the one hand, she blames herself for having "a personal feeling" against married life, "a physical objection—a fastidiousness, or whatever it may be called" (p. 271), and then goes on to call it her "own wickedness," a "repugnance" on her part (p. 273). But at the same time she suggests that what she is experiencing is common to all women and to the nature of marriage:

> "I have only been married a month or two!" she went on, still remaining bent upon the table, and sobbing into her hands. "And it is said that what a woman shrinks from—in the early days of her marriage—she shakes down to with comfortable indifference in half-a-dozen years. But that is much like saying that the amputation of a limb is no affliction, since a person gets comfortably accustomed to the use of a wooden leg or arm in the course of time!" (p. 273)

Sue's comparison is instructive. If getting used to sexual relations is like getting used to an amputation, this reveals how unnatural such relations seem to her rather than what all women may be supposed to shrink from. And indeed the narrator, in offering an authoritative summing up of her condition, clearly indicates it is a personal disability Sue suffers from: "the ethereal, fine-nerved, sensitive girl" is said to be "quite unfitted by temperament and instinct to fulfil the conditions of the matrimonial relation with Phillotson, possibly with scarce any man" (p. 281).

Exactly what kind of "temperament" Sue has, however, and what particular "instinct" she is subject to are not specified; but in the light of *Far from the Madding Crowd* and *The Woodlanders*, we may make reasonable assumptions. The instinct would seem to be the "Daphnean instinct" that is so strong in Grace, as Sue proceeds to demonstrate in the ever-increasing desperation of her marriage to Phillotson. Sexual relations become so repugnant to her that she wants to leave him and go to Jude. Her husband refuses to allow this, but he nevertheless consents to "her living apart in the house" (p. 288). When the poor man goes absentmindedly into Sue's room one night—it is the room they originally occupied together—she jumps out of the window and falls to the earth below, though she does not "[break] her neck" (p. 289) (or turn into a tree). And that Sue's temperament, like that of Bathsheba, makes her adore the goddess Diana is implied by her own account of the "friendly intimacy" she forms with a Christminster undergraduate when she is eighteen and lives with him though separately, as later with Phillotson: "We shared a sitting-room for fifteen months," she tells Jude, and adds: "He said I was breaking his heart by holding out against him so long at such close quarters; he could never have believed it of woman. . . . His death caused a terrible remorse in me for my cruelty—though I hope he died of consumption and not of me entirely" (p. 202).

On the same occasion Sue engages in some self-analysis that allows us to clinch the comparison between her and Bathsheba. Jude, having listened to the story of the Christminster student, says he believes she is "as innocent as [she is] unconventional":

"I am not particularly innocent, as you see, now that I have

> twitched the robe
> From that blank lay-figure your fancy draped,

said she, with an ostensible sneer, though he could hear that she was brimming with tears. "But I have never yielded myself to any lover, if that's what you mean! I have remained as I began."

"I quite believe you. But some women would not have remained as they began."

"Perhaps not. Better women would not. People say I must be cold-natured,—sexless—on account of it. But I won't have it! Some of the most passionately erotic poets have been the most self-contained in their daily lives." (p. 203)

When Sue says, with an undercurrent of pride, that she has "never yielded" herself to any lover, we recall Bathsheba's boast—sounding over the more than twenty years that separate the two novels—that (prior to her marriage) "her lips had been touched by no man's on earth" as "her waist had never been encircled by a lover's arm." And this is not because Sue or Bathsheba is "sexless," as Sue rightly insists about herself, but because virginity is for each the prime value in its signification of their autonomy. What matters to Bathsheba is that she is "sufficient to herself"—and to Sue that she is "self-contained." This is first and foremost an instinctive physical feeling, but when held to so intensely the wish for it may survive sexual surrender and leave its stamp on it, as we have seen in the case of Bathsheba (and Grace). This becomes apparent too in regard to Sue, as Jude ruefully registers after the frightful death of their children: "Yes, Sue," he says, "—that's what I am. I seduced you. . . . You were a distinct type—a refined creature, intended by Nature to be left intact. But I couldn't leave you alone!" (p. 418).

The kind of tenderness Sue is capable of is nicely caught in an early exchange between her and Jude:

". . . we are going to be *very* nice with each other, aren't we, and never, never, vex each other any more?" She looked up trustfully, and her voice seemed trying to nestle in his breast.

"I shall always care for you!" said Jude.

"And I for you. Because you are single-hearted, and forgiving to your faulty and tiresome little Sue!"

He looked away, for that epicene tenderness of hers was too harrowing. (p. 208)

That nestling voice epitomizes Sue. With her voice she gives herself to him completely—but incorporeally, as it were. And that precisely, as the repeated image emphasizes, is what she would like in return from Jude: " 'Jude, I want you to kiss me, as a lover, incorporeally,' she said, tremulously nestling up to him, with damp lashes" (p. 350). Indeed, the novelist finds the exact word to describe Sue's tenderness: it is "epicene" in the sense that it takes no account of any difference of sex between Jude and herself, remains asexual, that is, in the very assertion of intimacy—and that is why for him it is so "harrowing."

Sue leaves Phillotson in the end and goes to Jude, but she insists on their living separately, in much the same way as she did with her husband and the Christminster student, even when their divorces come through and they are free to marry. The fact that they never actually marry, despite repeated resolutions on their part to do so, provides a symbolic underlining of her failure ever really to give herself to him. When she does eventually submit sexually, it is in a manner that again recalls the story of Bathsheba. One night Arabella suddenly erupts again into their lives, begging Jude to meet her at the inn where she is staying overnight, but Sue opposes his going:

"Well—Arabella has appealed to me for help. I must go out and speak to her, Sue, at least!"

"I can't say any more!—O, if you must, you must!" she said, bursting out into sobs that seemed to tear her heart. "I have nobody but you, Jude, and you are deserting me! I didn't know you were like this—I can't bear it, I can't! If she were yours it would be different!"

"Or if you were."

"Very well then—if I must I must. Since you will have it so, I agree! I will be. Only I didn't mean to! And I didn't want to marry again, either! . . . But, yes—I agree, I agree! I do love you. I ought to have known that you would conquer in the long run, living like this!"

She ran across and flung her arms round his neck. "I am not a cold-natured, sexless creature, am I, for keeping you at such a distance? I am sure you don't think so! Wait and see! I do belong to you, don't I? I give in!" (p. 332)

What finally brings Bathsheba to give in to Troy, we recall, is her fear of losing him to another woman, as Sue here fears Arabella will infallibly claim Jude if given a chance. And Sue, like Bathsheba, regards her giving in to her lover as a "conquest" on his part not because she is won sexually but because she is defeated in her desire to remain intact unto herself. Beaten by life, she is forced to surrender—and can only lament that she "didn't mean to." We are to understand that their relationship is consummated sexually that night; but though Sue proceeds to bear two children and is pregnant with a third when the tragedy strikes, there is no indication that their lives are much changed by the new development—though Hardy is more explicit about this outside the novel than in it:

> there is nothing perverted or depraved in Sue's nature. The abnormalism consists in disproportion: not in inversion, her sexual instinct being healthy so far as it goes, but unusually weak and fastidious; her sensibilities remain painfully alert notwithstanding, (as they do in nature with such women). One point illustrating this I could not dwell upon: that, though she has children, her intimacies with Jude have never been more than occasional, even while they were living together (I mention that they occupy separate rooms, except towards the end), and one of her reasons for fearing the marriage ceremony is that she fears it would be breaking faith with Jude to withhold herself at pleasure, or altogether, after it; though while uncontracted she feels at liberty to yield herself as seldom as she chooses. This has tended to keep his passion as hot at the end as at the beginning, and helps to break his heart. He has never really possessed her as freely as he desired.[7]

Jude has never really possessed Sue, we might add, because she—like Bathsheba and Grace—has never really been able to give herself. But where Troy and Fitzpiers quickly become disillusioned and disgruntled, Jude, with greater generosity, endures to the bitter end of her leaving him. He does so in part because his love for her is more profound than theirs for their wives, but also because in his own rending conflict between the flesh and the spirit he cannot help admiring Sue's capacity for being uncarnate. The novelist, however, in a fine symbolic scene, suggests how Jude, if only he were more at one with himself, might have saved Sue from herself. The occasion is their visit (together with Little Time) to the flower pavilion at the Agricultural Exhibition:

> Sue's usually pale cheeks [reflected] the pink of the tinted roses at which she gazed; for the gay sights, the air, the music, and the excitement of a day's out-

ing with Jude, had quickened her blood and made her eyes sparkle with vivacity. She adored roses, and what Arabella had witnessed was Sue detaining Jude almost against his will while she learnt the names of this variety and that, and put her face within an inch of their blooms to smell them.

"I should like to push my face quite into them—the dears!" she had said. "But I suppose it is against the rules to touch them—isn't it, Jude?"

"Yes, you baby," said he: and then playfully gave her a little push, so that her nose went among the petals.

"The policeman will be down on us, and I shall say it was my husband's fault!"

Then she looked up at him, and smiled in a way that told so much to Arabella.

"Happy?" he murmured.

She nodded. (pp. 365–66)

Sue's response to the roses is suggestive of more general attitudes she clings to. Even when she is aroused, when her "blood" is "quickened," she hangs back from doing what she wants, from pushing her face "quite into" the roses. It is when Jude, however, does not leave her to hang back but gently pushes her past her reluctance, that she—this being the only time in the novel that she does so in direct relation to him—spontaneously acknowledges him as her "husband."

ALAN SILLITOE:
THE NOVELIST AS MAP-MAKER

An inspired scene in *The Widower's Son,* one of Alan Sillitoe's most recent and finest novels, is set in a cemetery. The visitors to the cemetery are the widower, now a postman after twenty-four years in the army, and his son, who has lost his mother at the age of seven. They go to her grave every fortnight, but the widower never talks of her during these visits. On this occasion he takes out a prismatic compass, and tells his son that they are "going to do a survey of the cemetery," and that they will "feature her grave in red" when they "come to draw the map." He hands his son the compass, says, "What's the bearing of that big elm over there?" and gets down to the measuring of distances (1:1).[1] The scene vividly pinpoints the way in which the widower has set about bringing up his son: always teaching him to do what is right, never neglecting a chance to further his "training," he also systematically contrives to avoid what really matters, for if the map is a graphic means of forcing his son to register the fact of his mother's death, it also enables the old soldier to sidestep any emotional confrontation of it. The son, we are told, is not only taught "how to judge distance," but what goes with it, "to *keep* his distance as well" (1:1). Indeed, the widower's obsessive concern with the taking of his bearings betrays his fundamental insecurity, an uncertainty as to where he stands, especially in relation to his son.

The scene is also exemplary in another sense, for in novel after novel Sillitoe's characters are repeatedly shown taking their bearings, making maps, or consulting them. In *The General,* for instance, the symphony orchestra falls into Gorshek hands when the train driver loses his bearings (1); and the General, when he decides to free his captives, gives them precise directions: "Here are rifles, ammunition and food," he says. "Look at this map . . . Cross the railway-line and walk north. Pinpoint yourselves on 504, then trek at right-angles to the Northern Star" (12). In *Key to the Door* Brian Seaton as a young boy "passionately" studies a manual of map-reading and attains a sound knowledge of "conventional signs, grid references, scales and representative fractions and [of] how to allow for magnetic variation in true and compass north" (3:18); later, when he goes on the jungle expedition while serving with the RAF in Malaya, it is his job to "[sight] bearings on visible hillpoints and [plot] them" (4:23). In *A Tree on Fire* the guerrillas "[follow] a pocket compass" when they move at night through the Algerian desert (2:14); Frank Dawley, left on his own, takes his bearings from Ursa Minor and the North Star (2:20). In the anti-Utopian *Travels in Nihilon*, the geographers of Nihilon exemplify its nihilism by seeking to outdo one another in the inaccuracy of their maps; and Edgar Salt, on board the steamship *Nihilon*, taking his own sightings with a sextant and plotting the ship's position, is amazed to find how much the ship's chart is "out of true" (6).

That map-making is a personal interest of Sillitoe's is suggested by the elaborate map of Nihilonia that he provides for *Travels in Nihilon*, going one better in his invention of an imaginary territory than Thomas Hardy, who in his map of Wessex merely invented the names of his towns and villages. The interest is plain in an essay called "Maps," which appears in the collection *Mountains and Caverns*. Sillitoe remarks that when he served in Malaya as a ground radio operator in the RAF, one of his jobs was to use "Marconi direction-finding equipment to send bearings to aircraft which used radio-telegraphy to find their positions." He contracted tuberculosis in Malaya, and when he returned to England was hospitalized for eighteen months. In the hospital his childhood passion for maps revived, and he took a correspondence course in surveying: "The old obsession came back in my long and wearisome idleness. I studied for many months, and at last really got to grips with the proper science of surveying. In all seriousness, it seemed the only thing I was cut out for, to qualify so that I could bury myself in the mundane occupation of making maps." Simultaneously, however, he began "the task . . . of getting into the map of [his] own consciousness," and discovered that he wanted to be a writer. Sillitoe is clearly fascinated by the parallelism between maps and novels: "Why did I, as a child, teach myself to read a map at the same time as learning to read a novel? And why did I, as a young man in hospital, make my first conscientious attempt at constructing maps while beginning my first serious efforts to write a novel?" A connection between maps and novels is implicit in Sillitoe's description of map-reading as "the art of visualising reality from the symbols on a sheet of paper," which may readily serve as an account of novel-reading—or, inversely, of map-making and novel-writing. It is then but a short step to calling maps "poems of landscape" (as is done in *The General*), or to defining the novelist's task as the attempt "to map the spiritual turmoil of [himself] and other people."

The immediately distinctive feature of Sillitoe's work as a fictional map-maker is its accuracy. In his best novels the lives of working people—he detests the phrase "the working class"—are rendered with an authenticity and immediacy and matter-of-factness that are new in English literature, for not even D. H. Lawrence, who is his immediate forerunner on the Nottingham scene, succeeds in so uncompromisingly refusing to palliate either word or deed or circumstance. In a 1977 preface to *Key to the Door* (1961), Sillitoe (rebelling against his precursor) rather unkindly fixes on one difference between his work and that of Lawrence: "My book showed a comparatively sensitive young man from what was called 'the working classes' who instead of walking in the fields clutching an anthology of romantic poetry (misunderstood by an uncouth father and seared by an overloving mother, much as if he were still kicking and screaming to get out of *Sons and Lovers*) puts the experience of his life into political terms because they were the only ones he could dimly perceive at that time." The "uncouth father" in *Key to the Door*, a man who is forced to spend his time sitting at home, on the dole in the thirties, is memorably caught in the opening pages of the novel, presented with a concentrated quietness that does as much as the long tearing rows of *Sons and Lovers*:

He did not know he had a father, only that a man (what was a man?) sat always humped before a firegrate and was liable to throw out a fist like lightning if he went too close; until he came in one day and found his wailing mother bending over a bucket so that blood could drip into it from her forehead. "Your dad," she shouted. "That's what your dad's gone and done with a shoe." And so amid the weeping and blood-bucket he came to know what a dad was.

Key to the Door is a definitive map of the depression of the thirties—in my view it is Sillitoe's best novel to date, a major work of our time—but it is balanced by *Saturday Night and Sunday Morning* (his first novel), which strikes the same note of rigorous authenticity in its presentation of working-class life in England after the Second World War. With these novels behind him, Sillitoe's evocation of the Nottingham milieu in his later work, such as *The Widower's Son*, has become effortless, enabling him to capture an ethos in a sentence—"Charlie's son William was born in a street where, if the curtains of a house weren't open by half past six in the morning, it was thought that somebody had died during the night" (1:1)—or a whole way of life in a paragraph:

> The bed creaked at his unavoidable thrusts, but she slowed him again, a hand around his neck.
>   Jane was wide awake: "What are you doing?"
>   She must bloody know, he thought.
>   "What's he in our bed for?"
>   "Go to sleep," Helen said, breathlessly, and he felt her tense beneath him. "He's only staying for a minute."
>   "I know what's going on," she said in a resigned voice, and her head went down on the pillow, though she didn't turn to the wall as before.
>   It didn't put him off that she was in the same bed. He felt he knew her as much as Helen, having been with them both all day. (1:3)

2

The need to know where he is would seem to be one of the motivating forces of Sillitoe's fictional map-making. One may register where one is by taking bearings on where one has come from, and this he deliberately sets out to do in *Raw Material*, which he calls "part novel, part autobiography" (1:2). Where he has specifically come from as a writer is suggested by his reference to the two objects that preside over his writing table: "I sit and write at a somewhat unstable table with one of Burton's horseshoes in front of me, and Edgar's open-faced Gommecourt watch to keep the time" (3:67). A combination analogous to that of the horseshoe and the watch is implied by two of the large maps that line the walls of his study:

> Apart from bookshelves, the wallspace shows maps like beds of flowers, a street plan of Nottingham, a large-scale trench-map of the Gommecourt salient in 1916, marked by the advancing death-lines of the Sherwood Foresters, a relief chart of Deception Island, and a topographical map of Israel flanked by the Mediterranean and the Jordan River, topped by Mount Hermon and bottomed by the southern arrowhead of Sinai—different regions I cannot shut my eyes to. (3:67)

The maps of Deception Island and of Israel would seem to reflect what Sillitoe has characteristically added to his somewhat somber heritage—a belief that sudden, violent disappearance (for Deception Island is "all that remains of a volcanic cone suddenly pulled under by some insufferable whim of the earth" [3:69]) may be countered by a capacity for reestablishment.

Burton, the blacksmith and Sillitoe's maternal grandfather, is clearly the hero of *Raw Material* and the single figure of greatest importance in Sillitoe's early life. (He also figures memorably as Merton in *Key to the Door*.) If Sillitoe may be regarded as coming from Burton, Burton should be seen first and foremost as a working man and a man of Nottingham and its environs, and Sillitoe's twin allegiances are to working people and to Nottingham. In "Maps" he remarks that "we are all born navigators, and a born navigator has nothing if not a sense of place, and an anchor-like attachment to the locality he was born in." But Burton not only epitomizes Nottingham and an unremitting life of labor; he was a craftsman, proud and strong in his art, and in *Raw Material* the horseshoe that "presses down the pile of written sheets" on the novelist's table is said to be a "perfect specimen" (3:69). There is a fine symbolism in that use of the horseshoe, for it is Sillitoe's sense of Burton and people like him and of the weight of their lives that makes his work so down-to-earth, that prevents it from flying off into sentimentality or idealization.

Sillitoe himself is aware of an analogy between the crafts of the smith and the novelist: Stanley S. Atherton reports him as saying that the writer "works with words as a 'blacksmith uses the tools of his strong and often subtle art.'"[2] What the blacksmith does with his tools is to shape the hot iron into a shoe, and a mark of Sillitoe's own subtle art is the care he takes to shape his material, one immediate indication of this concern being the repeated division of his novels into parts or sections. Sometimes the logic of these divisions is not at once apparent. When *Key to the Door* first appeared, for instance, it was assailed by John Coleman in a review as being "incredibly episodic, jerking along from paddling-pool to school-room to love with a dancing girl in Kota Libis as if the nominal thread of Brian is enough to hold so much disparate experience together."[3] In fact the four parts of the novel are as tight as a horseshoe. Part 1 ("Prologue") presents Brian Seaton's antecedents, dealing not only with his early childhood but with the marriage and relationship of his parents and with the home from which his mother comes. Part 2 ("Nimrod") deals with various episodes in Brian's childhood at the ages of about eight to ten and culminates in the end of an era with the destruction of his grandparents' home, the Nook, and with the outbreak of World War II. In parts 3 and 4 ("The Ropewalk" and "The Jungle") the structure is daring. Whereas parts 1 and 2 form solid blocks of narrative, parts 3 and 4 alternate regularly from chapter to chapter between Brian's adolescent experiences in Nottingham and his life in the RAF in Malaya. The changed method of organization effectively sets off Brian's childhood from his adolescence and young

manhood, the first section (parts 1 and 2) being the basis and support of
the second (parts 3 and 4). The alternative chapters in the second section, moreover, dramatically emphasize that what Brian is and does in
Malaya is a direct consequence of what he was and did in Nottingham.
Which is what the book is about.

Uncle Edgar's watch provides us with another bearing on where Sillitoe comes from as a novelist. In *Raw Material* Sillitoe recounts how,
when he saw his uncle for the last time, he gave him a copy of his first
book of poems and Edgar insisted on giving him "an old fob-timepiece"
in exchange: "It's only gold-plated zinc," he said. "It was with me at
Gommecourt, and in Germany. Went all the time I was under fire.
Would you believe it? Hasn't gone for years now." Sillitoe had the
watch repaired a year later and reports that he still wears it (2:56). The
watch is as symbolic as the horseshoe, and Sillitoe's wearing it is expressive of the way he continuously carries with him the memory of
the Great War. Born some ten years after the armistice, he seems to be
haunted by the War, particularly by the battles of the Somme and the
specific slaughter of Nottingham men. In an apparent attempt to lay
the ghosts, he visited the battlefields—"From the low stone wall of
Gommecourt Wood Cemetery I looked through binoculars at the space
of that pathetic little battlefield Edgar had walked across in such terror," he relates in *Raw Material*. "It was not holed and pitted now, of
course, but was a rather wide, dipping meadow of rich green grass that
fifty years ago had fed on blood" (2:49)—but this attempt resulted only
in his uncharacteristically losing his bearings: "Walking through the
cemetery of Gommecourt and the vast collection of graveyards around
Ypres, where tens of thousands rest under crosses or the occasional
Star of David, the feeling is one of bewilderment and pity that brings
tears like a wall of salt up to the eyes. . . . I was lost, and began to
wonder if I would ever get out" (2:49). Though he finds his way back to
his car, he never, in a sense, "gets out," and in *Raw Material* he dwells
at length and in anguish on those battles that were fought before he
was born.

It is the terribleness of the toll of death that seems particularly to
have seized his imagination. For him July 1, 1916, when "Haig com-
menced his attack on the Somme"—and when "in the diversionary
attack at Gommecourt the 5th and 7th battalions of the Sherwood Foresters came out of their trenches . . . and went towards the German
lines"—is a "dark day in the history of the British nation": "Within ten
minutes or so of the attack starting 60,000 men had fallen to the fire of
a hundred German machine-gunners, and to their artillery" (2:38). The
Sherwood Foresters alone lost over 1,200 men at Gommecourt, and
"blinds were drawn in every Nottingham street" (2:38). Sillitoe's views

of both the effects and the significance of that day in July 1916 are
radical. He states that it "finished Britain as a world power, and as a
country fit for any hero to live in" (2:40); and he maintains that the
Somme slaughter was fundamentally a class slaughter:

> For every officer killed or wounded on the first day of the Battle of the
> Somme, twenty-two other ranks fell with him. During the whole of the Boer
> War, in which the total British casualties were under 17,000, the proportion
> was one officer to eleven other-ranks.
> If Waterloo was won on the playing fields of Eton, the British class war was
> fought out on the Western Front with real shells and bullets. The old men of
> the upper classes won by throwing the best possible material into the slaugh-
> ter, including their own high-spirited and idealistic young. . . .
> [The masses] were thrown away with prodigal distaste because they were
> coming to the point of stepping into their own birthright. Their potential was
> about to become manifest, and they would have demanded what had been de-
> nied them for so long. War seemed the only alternative to revolution. (2:43)

For Sillitoe, it appears, the Great War is an emotional and ideological
tinderbox, and it is his many-sided concern with it that would seem to
have led to the pronounced preoccupation—if not obsession—with
war that is unmistakable in his work as a novelist. Though he himself
has no direct experience of battle, for he was too young to serve in the
army in World War II, the novels are full of intensely imagined accounts of war. This is most notably the case with the brilliant reconstruction of the fortunes of an artillery unit as it retreats to Dunkirk in
The Widower's Son, but there are also striking battle scenes in other
works, even when these relate to wholly imaginary conflicts as in *The
General* and *Travels in Nihilon*. There is also a vivid depiction of guer-
rilla war in the Algerian desert in the Frank Dawley trilogy, particularly *A Tree on Fire*. But it is still the Great War that will not let Sillitoe
go: in his latest novel, *The Storyteller* (1979), a powerful account of
hand-to-hand combat at Passchendaele is provided by an eighty-year-
old Nottingham survivor of the battle.

More significantly, from a purely literary point of view, war provides
the ground for the most marked line of imagery in the novels. For Sillitoe, life—the kind of life he was born into in the England of the depression and the dole, a life which he seems to regard as having been a
continuation of the War by other means—is, quite simply, war. The
equation emerges explicitly in the analytical *Raw Material*: "Perhaps I
came here simply to write *Raw Material*—a tale of two Nottingham
families shattered by the Empedoclean progress of the Great War,
which may be the same as saying that they were broken by life itself"
(1:3); but it is implicit from the outset of his career in early works such

as *Saturday Night and Sunday Morning* and *Key to the Door*. One of its most bizarre manifestations is a scene in the latter novel which, in its combined strangeness and representativeness, is comparable to the scene in the cemetery in *The Widower's Son*. *Key to the Door* opens with an account of how the Seaton family flits from one condemned— or about-to-be condemned—house to another. A block in which they have previously lived is up for demolition, though this is said to take "a novel" form: "the Albion Yard area, deserted and cordoned off, was to be the target of bombs from buzzing two-winged aeroplanes, the side-show of a military tattoo whose full glory lay on the city's outskirts." Brian is told that if he is "a good lad" he will be taken to see the bomb-ing: "The bombing was to be on a Sunday afternoon, and Seaton hoisted Brian on to his stocky shoulders so that he felt one with the trams that swayed like pleasure-ships before the council house, ferry-ing crowds to the bombing." As the spectators wait, "three biplanes [dip] their wings from the Trent direction":

Each plane purred loudly along the rooftops, like a cat at first, then growling like a dog when you try to take its bone away, finally as if a roadmender's drill were going straight to the heart, so that he felt pinned to the ground. Two black specks, then two more, slid from the rounded belly of each. The gloved wheels beneath seemed to have been put down specially to catch them, but the dots fell through and disappeared into the group of ruined houses.
"Now for it," somebody announced, and an enormous cracking sound, a mil-lion twig-power went six times into the sky—followed by the muffled noise of collapsing walls somewhere in the broken and derelict maze. (1:1)

If the weird bombing literally turns the block of slum houses into a battlefield, this scene serves to concretize a war of existence that is steadily evoked in metaphorical terms in the early Nottingham novels. It is a war of existence that subsumes a notion of class war—in *Satur-day Night and Sunday Morning* Arthur Seaton registers a sense of kinship with Winnie's husband in the following terms: "If he worn't a sowjer he'd be on my side, grabbin' 'is guts out at a machine like mine, thinking about making dynamite to blow up the Council House" (2:15)—but usually it is more generalized than that, being regarded as both a limiting and governing condition of life itself, an on-going battle in which the enemy may just as well be a wife or a mother as an arm of government:

And trouble for me it'll be, fighting every day until I die [Arthur reflects at the end of the novel]. Why do they make soldiers out of us when we're fighting up to the hilt as it is? Fighting with mothers and wives, landlords and gaffers, coppers, army, government. If it's not one thing it's another, apart from the work we have to do and the way we spend our wages. There's bound to be trouble in store for me every day of my life, because trouble it's always been and always will be.

Consequently the metaphorical evocation of the battle of life—Mrs. Bull, for instance, whom Arthur prods into open enmity when he unintentionally nudges her in passing, is said to keep "a chock-a-block arsenal of blackmailing scandal ready to level with foresight and backsight at those that crossed her path in the wrong direction, sniping with tracer and dumdum from sandbags of ancient gossip" (1:7)—is of the same order as that referring more specifically to class war, as in the following passage in which Arthur is depicted drawing his wages at the bicycle factory at which he works:

[Robboe, the gaffer,] walked away, and Arthur slipped the wage-packet into his overall pocket. Truce time was over. The enemy's scout was no longer near. For such was Robboe's label in Arthur's mind, a policy passed on by his father. Though no strong cause for open belligerence existed as in the bad days talked about, it persisted for more subtle reasons that could hardly be understood but were nevertheless felt, and Friday afternoon was a time when different species met beneath white flags, with wage-packets as mediators, when those who worked in the factory were handed proof of their worth, which had increased considerably in market value since the above-mentioned cat-and-dog ideas had with reason taken root. (1:4)

The "bad days talked about" are, of course, the thirties, the period recorded so vividly in *Key to the Door*, and in that novel too there is a similar collocation of metaphors. On a "moonlight-flit" in which the Seaton family periodically engages, a helpful neighbor remarks, "You'd think the Jerries was after us," and Seaton replies, "The rent man is, and that's worse" (1:1); when eight-wheeled lorries are dumping the remains of demolished slum houses at the tips, "a piece of wall" is said to make "a splash like a bomb" (2:5), effectively recalling the novel demolition at Albion Yard. But the personal violence that is easily detonated among the people Sillitoe writes about is adverted to in analogous terms, as in the following scene (which incidentally epitomizes Grandfather Merton):

He let out a terrific "Ha!" like a bullet: "You'd take [the cutlery] off the table just because it's lightning?" he shouted [at his wife]. Brian drew back: what's he getting on to me for as well? Merton jumped up, so that Brian almost lost his fear of the storm in wondering what he was up to. "I'll show you there's no bloody need to be frightened at a bit o' lightning." He scooped a bundle of knives and forks, flung open the window and held them outside, waiting for a flash of lightning while Brian and his grandmother froze by the table. (2:4)

At school Brian is beaten by the teacher for "actually [*drawing*] a picture" when the class is told "to draw a pen-picture of the Old Sea Dog, when he comes to the Admiral Benbow Inn":

> With hands bent over his head he wondered: Why is he hitting me like this? It's bad enough hitting me, but why is he telling the class I've made such a daft mistake? It was hard not to weep at such thoughts, and he was saved from tears only by a surge of hate; he let forth in his mind a stream of awful words he had heard his father use under his breath to his mother. Mr. Jones still hovered, ready to crack him again, while vivid barbed-wire images flashed through Brian's mind. (2:8)

Even young love falls (though not without some sense of strain) into the same pattern—"[Brian] stood with Pauline by the back door of the Mullinders, and the end of their quiet evening blazed between them in a battlefire of kisses" (4:24)—as does the most ordinary everyday activity: "Water, gravel, cement and sand were shovelled and poured into the circling cannon-like mouth of the concrete mixer" (2:15). So insistent is the encompassing imagery that at times it deteriorates into mere mannerism: "At the beginning of September time threw in its reserves of frost and fog to break down the year's resistance, and he wore a coat . . . Rain came, cold and persistent, drainpipes and gutters working overtime to wash away the dead from a battlefield of leaves and matchsticks" (2:11).

In *Saturday Night* war imagery is interestingly combined with a complex drawn from another ground of battle—the jungle:

> [Arthur] did not ask whether he was in such a knocked-out state because he had lost the rights of love over two women, or because the two swaddies represented the raw edge of fang-and-claw on which all laws were based, law and order against which he had been fighting all his life in such a thoughtless and unorganised way that he could not but lose. Such questions came later. The plain fact was that the two swaddies had got him at last—as he had known they would—and had bested him on the common battleground of the jungle. (2:13)

If all laws are based on fang-and-claw, the particular "jungle commandments" Arthur seems implicitly to follow are not notably more altruistic than those held by Moggerhanger in *A Start in Life* which say "that you must get anything you want no matter at what cost to others" (4). And on the battleground of the jungle, the truce between Robboe the gaffer and Arthur is depicted in alternate terms: "Arthur and Robboe tolerated and trusted each other. The enemy in them stayed dormant, a black animal stifling the noise of its growls as if commanded by a greater master to lie low, an animal that had perhaps been

passed on for some generations from father to son on either side" (1:2).
In Sillitoe's work imagery drawn from the jungle is persistent, if less
pervasive than that from war—though it may be assumed to derive its
force from the novelist's own personal experience of the jungle in Malaya. But then the direct experience—or, at least, a fictional version of
it—is powerfully recorded in *Key to the Door*, the account of the first
expedition into the jungle being one of Sillitoe's most sustained and
impressive pieces of description.

3

AS NEW GROUND is covered in Sillitoe's work, positions—once ascer-
tained—are fixed and plotted in such a way as to reveal a clear line of
progress. What might be called his first phase is characterized by his
growing awareness of the implications of the war of existence his characters are heir to. It is self-evident, for a start, that war has its own
rules, and that playing the game is not one of them. The protagonists of
the novels of the first phase move steadily to more and more radical
manifestations of a refusal to play the game. Arthur Seaton, in *Saturday Night and Sunday Morning*, maintains that "that's what all these
looney laws are for, yer know: to be broken by blokes like me" (1:2);
and he proceeds with a debonair and anarchic nonchalance to break all
the rules he can get away with, particularly as regards sexual behavior.
Which is not to say he does not have his own rules, though they may
differ from those pertaining on the playing fields of Eton: "one of the
rules of his game," for instance, is that if a husband discovers that you
have been "knocking-on with his wife" and takes you up on it, you
must give her back (1:2). And he accepts that, on the battleground of
the jungle, he will have to pay for Saturday night with Sunday morning.
   The works that follow make a refusal to play the game a matter of
more meaningful protest, moving to stronger and stronger defiance of
the powers that be. "The Loneliness of the Long-Distance Runner" is a
short story, but it makes a major statement and marks a decisive change
in this respect. The protagonist-narrator distinguishes between "In-law
blokes," like the governor of the Borstal he is at and the law-abiding
citizens he represents, and "Out-law blokes" like himself; and he knows
"that it's war between [him] and them." He is the governor's hope for
"the Borstal Blue Ribbon Prize Cup for Long-Distance Cross-Country
Running (all England)." He could easily win, but he deliberately throws
the race in order to get "a bit of [his] own back on the In-laws and
Potbellies." He accepts that he will subsequently be victimized by the
governor, but he is determined to be "honest in the only way" he knows,

and since "this is war," to strike where he can—and where it hurts most. In *The General* metaphorical battlegrounds give way to imaginary ones, but a similar issue is explored. For the Gorsheks, standing orders rule that all prisoners should be shot at once, but the General arranges for the captured symphony orchestra to give a concert. Thereafter he not only refuses to obey the Marshal in Chief's specific instructions to kill the members of the orchestra but helps them to escape—even though this means he is sentenced to "exile until death." *Key to the Door* offers the most dramatic—and daring—enactment of a refusal to abide by the rules. When the revolt against the British breaks out in Malaya, Brian Seaton, though he is attacked by a communist rebel who is out to kill him, lets the man go free when he has him at his mercy. At the crucial moment he knows whose side he is on, and lets him go because he is "a comrade," just as he does not kill him because he is "a man." A little later Brian and his party are attacked by a whole group of rebels, but he deliberately fires wide: he is not prepared "to fire at [his] pals"—even though the fellow-soldier lying next to him has his face shot away (4:27). And in the first two volumes of the Frank Dawley trilogy the protagonist goes beyond Brian Seaton's refusal to kill rebels by actively joining them. Frank initially becomes involved in running guns from Morocco to the FLN for their war of independence against the French in Algeria; but, after a clash with a French patrol near the border, he insists— "ignoring the rules" of gun-running, as his friend tells him—on crossing the border, and then throws in his lot with the rebels, fighting with them against the French.

The Frank Dawley trilogy (*The Death of William Posters, A Tree on Fire,* and *The Flame of Life*) may thus be regarded, in one respect, as marking the end of a phase; but it is also transitional and (if one discounts the somewhat unreal *The General*) represents the beginning of a new stage that is characterized by the novelist's apparent decision to break away from the comparatively limited working-class world he had earlier depicted and map new areas of experience. Frank Dawley's story is itself emblematic in this regard: a mechanic in a factory, one day he "explodes" out of the life he has hitherto led, "leaving wife, home, job, kids and Nottingham's fair city where he [has] been born, bred and spiritually nullified" (*William Posters,* 1:1). In the end he leaves England too, traveling in Europe before going to Morocco and then Algeria, but prior to that he makes his way to London, where he is brought into contact with the world of the middle class. The new thrust in Sillitoe is manifest when Frank thinks about the owner of an art gallery he has become acquainted with: "He didn't dislike him, for Teddy was generous, outspoken, intellectual and rich, and who could ask for pleasanter company in which to learn about this sort of world?" (2:17). The presentation of this world is a prelude to the sparkling evocation of a London underworld in *A Start in Life*, a light-hearted romp in which the protagonist again leaves the North for a life in London. In Michael Cullen the novelist creates a genuine modern picaro, and in the portrayal of his adventures finds full scope for the display of the humor and zest and high spirits that are an integral component of his narrative energy but tend, in other works, to be subordinated to weightier matter. These qualities flag a little in *Travels in Nihilon*, a satirical fantasy, that offers an admonitory exposure of "the perfect system of regimented chaos" developed in that country.

The Widower's Son is a first-rate achievement, and it may well turn out to be a transitional work marking a move to another phase whose outlines are not yet clear, for it too seems to be both a summation of the old and an advance into new territory. It offers, as has already been pointed out in other contexts, a superb rendering both of the working-class Nottingham milieu and of the grim actuality of war in its account of William Scorton's part in the retreat to Dunkirk. It also shows how William succeeds both in maintaining his links with his working-class background and in transcending it, as he moves beyond it spiritually rather than physically; and it is as assured in its presentation of its middle-class characters as its working people. What is new in this novel is the psychological profundity of its treatment of personal relations, particularly the relationship of the widower and his son (which is so memorably caught in the scene in the cemetery) and that between William and his wife Georgina. There is nothing like the anatomy of their marriage in the work that goes before—if anything, in the presentation of their dark conflict it again calls D. H. Lawrence to mind—though its complexity is based on a familiar apprehension: "As soon as I saw you and fell in love," William tells Georgina, "I knew it was war to the death" (3:19). On a new "domestic battlefield," the novel details with bold particularity the "endless campaign of attrition" which "[grinds] them into invisibility for each other" (3:20), leading him to attempt suicide and forcing their separation.

Finally, in *The Storyteller*, a return to a lighter mode, Sillitoe maps a progress that is in a way parallel to his own as a novelist, for he recounts the adventures of a man who tells stories for gain, at first in pubs to working people but then to more select audiences. One of the interests of the novel is the exploration of what it is that impels Ernest Cotgrave to tell his tales, and some of his insights are revealing: "He stood condemned for having followed a private and obsessional drive to tell stories which, after all, was a prolonged attempt to break through a ceiling of ice that had always held down his spirit" (1:9); "he was still the voracious blood-sucking storyteller fuelled by an insatiable backbone hunger since birth. Even when not actually drawing the marrow from people by getting at their stories, he had only to walk the street and spot faces. One flash, and they were in" (1:13); "the longer he lived the more he knew that if he hadn't become a storyteller he would have been dead already" (1:14). It is almost as if *The Storyteller* is written in the margins of *Raw Material,* for it too—though in a different way—suggests where the novelist has come from. Where he is, at the mid-point of his career, is perhaps best indicated by registering that he—like his grandfather—is a master of his craft.

This essay was written in 1981 for a collection of essays entitled *The Contemporary British and Irish Novel,* ed. Hedwig Bock and Albert Wertheim. Accordingly, no reference is made to any of Sillitoe's work published after 1981, most particularly to *Her Victory,* a major novel (1982).

POSTSCRIPT: THE UNIVOCAL
AND THE EQUIVOCAL

To be univocal or not to be univocal—that is the critical question today. Whether the literary text, however, is intrinsically equivocal, as Deconstructionists maintain it is, is another matter. "Is it not," Paul de Man has asked, apropos of the New Critical belief in textual unity, "that this unity . . . resides not in the poetic text as such, but in the act of interpreting this text?"[1] We may well ask a similar question of the Deconstructionists in respect of their demonstration of the "unreadability" of texts. It is a question that was directly posed for me by J. Hillis Miller's recent, full-scale, deconstructionist analysis of *The History of Henry Esmond*.[2] With all respect to Miller, I do not see in *Henry Esmond* what he says is to be seen; and my essay on the novel (written after I had read Miller on it) may serve to suggest some other possibilities. I am under no illusions, however, that Miller, if he were to read me on *Henry Esmond*, would see what I see. Though we all like to believe that what we point to in a text is objectively there in it, the conclusion seems inescapable that it is the presuppositions—and, even more, the procedures—of critics that determine what they say about the nature of texts, and not vice versa. It is the procedures that are all-important, for, as Miller has said, "the test of the efficacity, if not of the 'validity,' of a given theory is the persuasiveness of the readings it enables."[3] In this regard I should like briefly to indicate how Miller's procedures—and he is surely a representative Deconstructionist—seem to me to be open to objection.

A basic tenet of Deconstruction is what might be called the free-floating quality of language. "Deconstruction," says Geoffrey Hartman, "refuses to identify the force of literature with any concept of embodied meaning," and he holds that one way of describing "the force of literature" is "the priority of language to meaning" in it.[4] Paul de Man says that "sign and meaning can never coincide" in literary language; and he refers both to "the necessarily figural nature of literary language" and to its "necessarily ambivalent nature."[5] The detachment of language from intention makes for its free play within a given text, and this in turn is taken to justify what Miller, in his well-known essay "The Critic as Host," calls "the deconstructive procedure" of "playing on the play within language."[6] But any game, if it is to be played by others as well as oneself, must have rules; and a rule which we might expect to pertain to the play of language, if we wish to ascribe meaning to a word, is that this be determined by its immediate context. Miller's procedure, however, allows the free play itself to determine a context, as becomes apparent in the game he plays with the words "parasite" and "host" in this essay.[7]

Miller begins the essay by referring to the joint view of Wayne Booth and M. H. Abrams—he cites a phrase of each—that "the 'deconstructionist' reading of a given work 'is plainly and simply parasitical' on 'the obvious or univocal reading' " (p. 217). It is this statement which should be the determining context in this instance, but Miller speedily establishes an alternative context when he declares that "one of the most frightening versions of the parasite as invading host is the virus" (p. 221). We may readily grant that " 'parasite' is one of those words which calls up its apparent opposite," that "it has no meaning without that counterpart," and that "there is no parasite without its host" (pp. 218–19). But we should also be clear that, in the quoted sentence about the virus, it is Miller who coins the metaphor of the parasite as host in the (archaic) sense of armed multitude; and that, in doing so, he offers a counterfeit meaning of the word "host" which the word "parasite" always "calls up," one that is entirely distinct from it etymologically and thus arbitrarily yoked to it here.[8] This questionable procedure, however, is used to suggest that any parasite is also necessarily a host in a "perpetual reversal" (p. 225), and so to deconstruct Booth, for it follows that it is Deconstruction that may well play the host to a parasitic univocality. Perhaps the best comment on this procedure is that provided by Miller himself when, in a different context, he implicitly proposes a normative rule for the linking of meanings. The meanings of all the key words in Stevens's "The Rock," Miller declares, are "incomparable, irreconcilable": "They . . . remain stubbornly heterogeneous. They may not be followed, etymologically, to a single root which will unify or explain them, explicating them by implicating them in a single source. They may not be folded together in a unified structure, as of leaves, blossom, and fruit from one stem."[9]

In his free play with language, therefore, Miller revels in a rejection of the restraints of context. But this rejection of context leads, in the end, to a larger refusal of meaning. One does not have to pretend to the definitive in order to offer a univocal reading of a literary work, but Miller seems to confound the two in his denial of the availability of clear meaning: "The poem ['The Triumph of Life'], like all texts," he says in "The Critic as Host," "is 'unreadable,' if by 'readable' one means a single, definitive interpretation" (p. 226). Nor is his final account, in the same essay, of the nature of unreadability less problematic. The critic, he maintains, will always be forced in interpreting a work to oscillate between opposed meanings: "In this oscillation two genuine insights . . . into a given text . . . inhibit, subvert, and undercut one another. This inhibition makes it impossible for either insight to function as a firm resting place, the end point of analysis" (p. 252). But this, one's own contrary experience of reading and interpreting suggests, is the mark not of all texts but only of strictly "ambiguous" works, in the sense in which these have been conclusively defined by Shlomith Rimmon—works, that is, in which "two hypotheses are mutually exclusive, and yet each is equally coherent, equally consistent, equally plenary and convincing, so that we cannot choose between them";[10] works like Henry James's *The Turn of the Screw*, for example.

The desiderated oscillation between meanings, moreover, seems to have a tendency in practice to come to a halt either in a reading which it is difficult to distinguish from univocality—or in an acceptance, in effect, of nonmeaning. In his analysis of Dickens's *Sketches by Boz*, for instance, Miller states that what has "seemed 'realistic' comes to be seen as figurative," and says: "Back and forth between these two interpretations the reader oscillates. Neither takes precedence over the other, but the meaning of the text is generated by the mirage of alternation between them."[11] A mirage, we must assume, can generate only another mirage; and, in fact, once Miller has himself subtly demonstrated that "the stories which rise from the door-knockers, the old clothes, the objects in the pawnshop are Boz's inventions, not objective facts" (p. 119), we are no longer free to countenance a "realistic" interpretation and have no alternative but to settle for the figurative. It seems at first as if Miller is involuntarily led to a similar position of rest in his discussion of *Henry Esmond*. He maintains that in this novel we are offered two portraits of the protagonist-narrator, one "the grand portrait of himself" that Esmond paints, and another unheroic, ironic portrait drawn behind Esmond's back, as it were, by the novelist.[12] I must confess that I do not at all see the second portrait that Miller affirms is there, and so took issue with his reading in my discussion of the novel. What I wish to consider now, however, is his contention that the second portrait serves "to obliterate the kinglike portrait"

(p. 97). If this were indeed the case, we would be left with it alone—and a univocal reading. Miller saves the day by undertaking to engage in further deconstruction (p. 104). Maintaining that irony "always masters the one who tries to master it or to take power with it" (p. 106), he grants that it also serves to undermine his own deconstructive reading:

> If the deconstruction of the first portrait depends on putting in question, by means of irony, the metaphorical connections Henry has made in order to draw a picture of himself, and if it unties all those connections, there is no reason why the same procedures should not be applied to the second metaphorical construction as have been applied to the first. What applies to the first must apply to the second. The undoing of the first by the second undoes also the second. (p. 107)

In such a scene of general devastation, however, of total undoing, we are left neither with the first portrait nor the second, nor with an oscillation between them since both are no longer there, but only with nothing—with a refusal of (univocal) meaning which is nonmeaning.

HAVING STATED these objections to Miller's procedures, I hasten to add that I would not seek to deny that Deconstruction has been most salutary in heightening our awareness of the slipperiness of language and the clash of meanings most texts present—and that Miller's own work serves as a constantly challenging example of this. But the thrust of Deconstruction, as the word insists, is disintegrative, toward the breaking down of unitary meaning. The idea of disintegration, however, "calls up" its opposite as surely as the word "parasite"; so too does the doctrine of "unreadability," and one cannot think of "oscillation" without the notion of rest. Alternative critical possibilities are sharply delimited. In the essays in this collection, trying to respond fully to contrary pulls, I have opted to forego perpetual oscillation and take a stand, to present *a* reading of the work under analysis. The artist, confronted with the flux of life, nevertheless aspires to contain it in his art, and he has to order his materials even when he wishes to represent disorder. In analogous terms, the critic is faced by the play of language in the work he is discussing, and he too must aspire to contain it, to order it in a reading.

In a vivid phrase in respect of a specific instance, Jacques Derrida has declared it is the "want of a saturating context" that permits the critic to assign more than one meaning to a given passage;[13] and it is no doubt true, with regard to any work of literature, that no critic can ever provide the kind of saturating context that will allow a final and definitive interpretation of it. This is not to say, however, that a literary work must by definition be "unreadable." The inability of any critic to provide such a context only ensures that there will always be something left out in any interpretation, enough to provide the basis for another (nonsaturating) context and a different kind of reading in the unending dialogue of critical commentary. But it is the individual critic's job, I believe, to make the best sense he can of the work he is studying, and—striving not to overlook anything of significance—to integrate as much as he can of its welter of detail in a coherent interpretation. The critical act, that is, should be a piecing together, not a taking apart, the patient and methodical establishment of the meaning the critic has discerned in the work. The essays in this book affirm such meanings, and I have tried to demonstrate various ways in which one may seek unitary meaning in a wide variety of texts. If I have committed the latter-day heresy of univocality in following such a critical procedure, I hope that the readings have not appeared to be necessarily "impoverishing" or "reductive," as Derrida and de Man, respectively, would seem to imply must be the consequence of such errant methodology.[14] More than anything else, comprehensiveness of insight, we may agree, determines the quality of an interpretation, but no theory per se ensures it. And if I have indeed opposed the univocal to the equivocal, it has been by way of trying to do as much justice to the rich ambiguity and complexity of literary texts as any exercise in oscillation. It is the readings, in the end, that count. As Miller rightly says, "A theory is all too easy to refute or deny, but a reading can be controverted only by going through the difficult task of rereading the work in question and proposing an alternative reading."[15]

NOTES

Preface

1. D. H. Lawrence to Helen Corke, 1 February 1912, *The Collected Letters of D. H. Lawrence*, ed. Harry T. Moore (London, 1962), 1: 98.

2. Gordon N. Ray, *Thackeray: The Age of Wisdom, 1847–1863* (New York, 1958), p. 110.

Strategies in *Vanity Fair*

1. The quotations are from "Before the Curtain." Page references are to the Penguin English Library edition of *Vanity Fair*, ed. J. I. M. Stewart (Harmondsworth, 1968). This edition reproduces the text of the 1853 edition, the last to be corrected by Thackeray. The novel was first published in book form in 1848.

2. In addition, see *Vanity Fair*, pp. 53, 286, 523, 587, 708, 753, and 790.

3. Geoffrey and Kathleen Tillotson, eds., Introduction to the Riverside edition of *Vanity Fair* (Boston, 1963), p. viii.

4. The narrator, however, is sometimes taken at face value—compare Robin Ann Sheets, who says: "[The narrator's] habitual willingness to confess his sins seems to indicate humility and self-knowledge, but it also serves to cast doubts on his own values. It is one thing for him to say that he, like George and Dobbin, is attracted by the follies of love; it is quite another for him to admit that he would be as hypocritical as the Crawley family if he had a wealthy old aunt and that he would go to Lord Steyne's party if he had an invitation" ("Art and Artistry in *Vanity Fair*," *ELH* 42 [Fall 1975]: 427–28).

5. See also *Vanity Fair*, pp. 43–44, 147, 197–98, 212, 272, 427, 440, 444, 559, 583–84, and 662.

6. Dorothy Van Ghent, *The English Novel: Form and Function* (New York, 1953), pp. 139–40.

7. Wolfgang Iser, *The Implied Reader: Patterns of Communication in Prose Fiction from Bunyan to Beckett* (Baltimore and London, 1974), pp. 105–6, 118.

8. J. Y. T. Greig, *Thackeray: A Reconsideration* (New York, 1967; first published 1950), p. 106.

9. Harriet Blodgett regards the narrator as "the principle of unification for the book," but she is concerned to show how "his attitudes unify its plot and modulate its tone" ("Necessary Presence: The Rhetoric of the Narrator in *Vanity Fair*," *Nineteenth-Century Fiction* 22 [December 1967]: 211).

10. Geoffrey and Kathleen Tillotson, Introduction, *Vanity Fair*, Riverside ed., p. xv.

11. See E. D. H. Johnson, who says: "For all its setting in Regency times, *Vanity Fair* is a novel about Victorian England." And in a footnote he adds: "A comparison between *Vanity Fair* and any one of Jane Austen's novels in terms of setting and action will immediately demonstrate the truth of this statement" ("*Vanity Fair* and *Amelia*: Thackeray in the Perspective of the Eighteenth Century," *Modern Philology* 59 [November 1961]: 107).

12. In the text the Emperor is said to perform such a part when Dobbin's regiment is ordered abroad, and his sisters are glad that he is "at any rate" spared the danger of Amelia's attentions since she is no longer engaged at that point to George.

Edgar F. Harden takes a similar view of the importance of the war imagery. In a short but excellent article, he says: "the Napoleonic struggles furnish a metaphor that is at the heart of Thackeray's novel, furnishing it with a major structural principle and an important moral standard. One of the novel's major ironies depends upon our awareness that the many-sided but microcosmic world of peace is constantly being described in terms of warfare and reflects that arena of human strife. At the same time, the Napoleonic conflicts in which the characters variously participate are presented to us in the language of their peacetime concerns" ("The Fields of Mars in *Vanity Fair*," *Tennessee Studies in Literature* 10 [1965]: 123–24). I have argued, however, that the metaphor is at the heart of the novel not merely in the sense that it provides a "series of major analogies" which are "complementary" to the "controlling idea" of *Vanity Fair* (p. 123), but that it is this metaphor which truly animates the whole work. And since it is "a major structural principle," it must also necessarily shape the stories of the two protagonists—as I will try to show. As a demonstrably unifying feature, furthermore, it provides the "single, stable perspective or standard" which Peter K. Garrett maintains the novel "never [allows] the reader" (*The Victorian Multiplot Novel: Studies in Dialogical Form* [New Haven and London, 1980], p. 127).

13. The war imagery recurs rhythmically—but not in any way monotonously or expectedly—throughout the text. See, in addition to the various examples noted in this essay, pp. 49, 52, 80, 82, 153, 196, 212, 217, 232, 235, 236, 254, 257, 262, 267, 306, 376, 385, 387–88, 390, 430, 433, 712, 714, 769, and 777.

14. Harden, "The Fields of Mars in *Vanity Fair*," p. 125.

15. This is not the view generally taken of her surrender. Compare, for instance, Gordon N. Ray, who says: "[Becky and Amelia] were established in

conscious contrast, like George Osborne and Dobbin, one accepting the usages of Vanity Fair, the other rejecting them" (*Thackeray: The Uses of Adversity, 1811–1846* [New York, 1955], p. 422); Barbara Hardy: "despite the need to sacrifice and sell George to his grandfather, who certainly buys him with real money, [Amelia] stands apart from the mercantile values. She does not sell her child because she wants the money but because she wants a decent life for him" (*The Exposure of Luxury: Radical Themes in Thackeray* [London, 1972], p. 101); and Laurence Lerner: "Amelia is subjected to a test (shall she give Georgy up to his grandfather?) and takes the decision that hurts her but will benefit the child" ("Thackeray and Marriage," *Essays in Criticism* 25 [July 1975]: 287).

Owning and Disowning:
The Unity of *Daniel Deronda*

1. Joan Bennett, *George Eliot: Her Mind and Her Art* (Cambridge, 1962), p. 183.

2. Ian Milner, *The Structure of Values in George Eliot* (Prague, 1968), p. 118.

3. Barbara Hardy, *The Novels of George Eliot: A Study in Form* (London, 1963), p. 111.

4. Page references to *Daniel Deronda* are to the Penguin English Library edition, ed. Barbara Hardy (Harmondsworth, 1967; first published 1876). The Penguin text is based on the Cabinet edition of 1878, the last George Eliot corrected.

5. Cynthia Chase, in a forceful deconstructive analysis, emphasizes the artificiality of that part of the plot which relates to the revelation of Deronda's Jewish origin; but his coming into his birthright has greater resonance in the narrative as a whole and is more meaningful than she seems ready to allow. See her essay, "The Decomposition of the Elephants: Double-Reading *Daniel Deronda*," *PMLA* 93 (March 1978): 215–27. Mary Wilson Carpenter maintains that Chase's "illuminating deconstruction" of *Daniel Deronda* "actually leads to discovery of the reader's blind spot, not the writer's," and that far from "[going] aground" (Chase's phrase) on the question of Deronda's circumcision, the novel is unified by it: "Ultimately, however, the reader must deconstruct his or her own reading of *Daniel Deronda*, for the interpretation of everything present in the text depends on the discovery of the crucial element missing from the *reader's* construction of the text—the Circumcision, in its full hermeneutical significance. Only if the reader inscribes the text with the contextual system of nineteenth-century Protestant interpretation of the circumcision rite will Eliot's statement that she meant everything in the novel to be related to everything else seem even remotely comprehensible" ("The Apocalypse of the Old Testament: *Daniel Deronda* and the Interpretation of Interpretation," *PMLA* 99 [January 1984]: 67).

Journeys to a Lighthouse

1. Page references to *To the Lighthouse* are to the Hogarth Press Special Edition (London, 1943; reprinted 1946; first published 1927).

2. Virginia Woolf, "Modern Fiction," *The Common Reader*, first series (London, 1948; first published 1925), p. 188.

3. Virginia Woolf, *A Writer's Diary*, ed. Leonard Woolf (London, 1953), p. 80.

4. Ibid., pp. 76−77, 138.

5. Ibid., pp. 80−81.

6. See the following extract from Arnold Bennett's review in the *Evening Standard* of 23 June 1927: "The middle part does not succeed. It is a short cut, but a short cut that does not get you anywhere. . . . I doubt the very difficult business of conveying the idea of the passage of a very considerable amount of time can be completed by means of a device . . . [it] has to be conveyed gradually without any direct insistence—in the manner of life itself." Quoted by Jean Guiguet in his chapter on *"To the Lighthouse"* in *Virginia Woolf and Her Works* (1962), which is reprinted in a collection of essays edited by Morris Beja, *Virginia Woolf: To the Lighthouse* (London, 1970), p. 245.

7. This view of the novel is similar to that advanced in what seems to me to be the best critical account of it, Norman Friedman's "The Waters of Annihilation: Double Vision in *To the Lighthouse*," *ELH* 22 (March 1955): 61−79. I shall argue, however, that the central opposition is other than that between involvement and detachment, as Friedman maintains.

8. Similarly, Lily and Mr. Bankes wonder at Mr. Ramsay's being so "strangely . . . venerable and laughable at one and the same time" (p. 74); and, to Mrs. Ramsay, James and Cam are "demons of wickedness, angels of delight" (p. 93).

9. See chapters 4 and 5 in Mitchell Leaska, *Virginia Woolf's Lighthouse: A Study in Critical Method* (London, 1970).

10. In his introduction to the casebook on *To the Lighthouse* that he has edited, Morris Beja says "just about all the critics in this volume recognize this danger [i.e., of finding the lighthouse "simply one thing"] and refrain from limiting too severely their view of this clearly central symbol. In an unguarded moment, Joseph Blotner is an exception" (pp. 21−22).

11. Amid the welter of meanings attributed to the lighthouse, some support for this reading is to be found in that advanced by Sharon Kaehele and Howard German: "A discussion of the androgynous nature of the Lighthouse symbol does not reveal its full meaning, for it is also associated with ideas about time, flux, death and egoism. Just as an actual Lighthouse functions to mark a fixed spot in moving waters, so the Lighthouse in this novel symbolizes fixed points or ways of creating fixed points in the flux of human life" (*"To the Lighthouse*: Symbol and Vision," first published in *Bucknell Review* 10 [May 1962], and reprinted in Beja, *Virginia Woolf: To the Lighthouse*, p. 194). Kaehele and German believe, however, that the lighthouse symbolizes many things: it "in part symbolizes both Mr. and Mrs. Ramsay" (p. 192); it also "symbolizes not only the individual traits of the Ramsays, but the harmonious union of their complementary qualities—courage with sympathy, intellect with intuition, endurance with fertility" (p. 193); and it further suggests "death" (p. 194).

William York Tindall, who maintains that the lighthouse, among other things, is "an image of man's remoteness and solitude," of "any absolute," and (specifically for James) of "a hunted father and a father found"; nevertheless also says: "Stable amid the waves, a light in darkness, bringing order to night and confusion, the tower suggests the ideal of Mr. Ramsay, a philosopher seeking the absolute, and that of Mrs. Ramsay, composing dinner parties; for the Lighthouse seems all that is hostile to flux, whether of wave or time: 'In the midst of chaos there was shape'" (*The Literary Symbol* [Bloomington, 1955], pp. 160–62).

12. William Troy, "Virginia Woolf and the Novel of Sensibility," *Selected Essays*, ed. Stanley Edgar Hyman (New Brunswick, N.J., 1967), p. 68.

13. Josephine O'Brien Schaefer, though from a different point of view, has also drawn attention to the effect of this description: "That dining room becomes a lighthouse as the group grows conscious of being a party. . . . The real lighthouse of the novel, therefore, is the one which Mrs. Ramsay carefully sets glowing and which illuminates a space of life even after her death" (*The Three-Fold Nature of Reality in the Novels of Virginia Woolf* [The Hague, 1965], p. 124).

14. Virginia Woolf, *A Room of One's Own* (London, 1946; first published 1929), p. 148. In a different connection, Kaehele and German also point to the link between this passage in *A Room of One's Own* and that which describes Lily painting. See Beja, *Virginia Woolf: To the Lighthouse*, p. 206.

15. Kaehele and German have also pointed out that the description of the stake "[suggests] the image of the Lighthouse." See Beja, *Virginia Woolf: To the Lighthouse*, p. 192.

Rhythmic and Symbolic Patterns
in *A Passage to India*

1. E. M. Forster confirms this in his notes to the Everyman edition of *A Passage to India* (London, 1942), p. xxxi.

2. Ibid.

3. Page references to *A Passage to India* are to the Penguin edition (Harmondsworth, 1959; first published 1924).

4. It seems to me that it is prudent to stick to the text in interpreting the symbolism. The dangers of not doing so are illustrated in the procedure followed by Glen O. Allen. He says, "The Marabar Hills . . . derive their essential meaning from sources outside the novel itself," namely Hindu philosophy, and proceeds to analyze the symbolism in terms of the Hindu distinction between Atman and Brahman and of the relation between the echo "Boum" and "the mystic syllable, *Om*." He quotes his Hindu sources and blandly concludes: "These few passages from Hindu scriptures will suggest what Forster has in mind in the symbols of cave, echo, and snake." There seems little warrant for this conclusion; less still for the tacit belief that Forster assumes such esoteric knowledge in his readers; and less still for foisting a Hindu system on the whole novel (as Allen does) when this is clearly irrelevant to the mosque sec-

tion and of doubtful aid for the rest. For the passages quoted, see "Structure, Symbol, and Theme in E. M. Forster's *A Passage to India*," *PMLA* 70 (1955): 941, 942, 943.

5. I am indebted to Gertrude M. White here. She says the echo speaks to Adela of "the last horror of union by force and fear, without love . . . the Marabar reveals to her what such union is: Rape" ("*A Passage to India*: Analysis and Revaluation," *PMLA* 68 [1953]: 648).

6. *A Passage to India* was published in 1924 when Forster was forty-five and at the height of his powers. He did not write another novel, though he lived until 1970.

D. H. Lawrence and George Eliot: The Genesis of *The White Peacock*

1. D. H. Lawrence, "Give Her a Pattern," *Phoenix II*, ed. Warren Roberts and Harry T. Moore (London, 1968), pp. 535–36.

2. Raney Stanford, "Thomas Hardy and Lawrence's 'The White Peacock,'" *Modern Fiction Studies* 5 (Spring 1959): 19.

3. John Alcorn, *The Nature Novel from Hardy to Lawrence* (London, 1977), p. 81. See also Ross C. Murfin, who states that both George Saxton and Lettie Beardsall are composite portraits, virtually compilations, derived from a number of Hardy characters in each case (*Swinburne, Hardy, Lawrence and the Burden of Belief* [Chicago and London, 1978], pp. 188–89).

4. E. T. [Jessie Chambers], *D. H. Lawrence: A Personal Record* (London, 1965; first published 1935), p. 21.

5. *The Mill on the Floss*, ed. Gordon S. Haight (Boston, 1961; first published 1860), p. 8. All further references are to this edition, designated *MF*.

6. *The White Peacock* (Penguin, 1976; first published 1911), p. 13. All further references are to this edition, designated *WP*.

7. Chambers, *A Personal Record*, pp. 97, 98, 103.

8. See George Eliot's own admission in this respect: "My love of the childhood scenes made me linger over them; so that I could not develop as fully as I wished the concluding book in which the tragedy occurs, and which I had looked forward to with attentive premeditation from the beginning." Letter to François D'Albert-Durade, 29 January 1861, *The George Eliot Letters*, ed. Gordon S. Haight (New Haven, 1954–55), 3:374.

9. It is true that a similar pattern may be discerned in Hardy's *Tess of the d'Urbervilles*; but—to go by Jessie Chambers—Lawrence's numerous comments on George Eliot and *The Mill on the Floss* and his apparent lack of interest in Hardy when he was writing his first novel suggest it was the earlier writer who held his attention then. It is striking that Chambers's "account of Lawrence's reading" in the chapter entitled "Literary Formation" in *A Personal Record*, while full of detailed references to a large number of writers and their books, contains only one bare mention of Hardy and makes no reference to a specific work: "Hardy's name had been familiar in our house since childhood days" (p. 110).

10. Chambers, *A Personal Record*, pp. 104–5.

11. D. H. Lawrence, ". . . Love Was Once a Little Boy," *Reflections on the Death of a Porcupine* (Philadelphia, 1925), p. 183.

12. D. H. Lawrence to Blanche Jennings, 4 November 1908, *The Letters of D. H. Lawrence*, ed. James T. Boulton, vol. 1 (Cambridge, 1979), p. 88.

13. Chambers, *A Personal Record*, pp. 97–98.

14. D. H. Lawrence, *Fantasia of the Unconscious* (London, 1931; first published 1923), p. 99.

Victory: The Battle for Heyst

1. Author's Note, *Victory*, Dent Collected Edition (London, 1948; first published 1915), p. x. All subsequent references are to this edition.

2. Douglas B. Park, "Conrad's *Victory*: The Anatomy of a Pose," *Nineteenth-Century Fiction* 31 (Summer 1976): 153, 157.

3. Sharon Kaehele and Howard German, "Conrad's *Victory*: A Reassessment," *Modern Fiction Studies* 10 (Spring 1964): 61.

4. Douglas Hewitt, *Conrad: A Reassessment* (London, 1969; first published 1952), p. 104.

5. C. B. Cox, *Joseph Conrad: The Modern Imagination* (London, 1974), p. 129.

6. Adam Gillon, "Conrad's *Victory* and Nabokov's *Lolita*: Imitations of Imitations," *Conradiana* 12 (1980): 58.

7. Donald A. Dike, "The Tempest of Axel Heyst," *Nineteenth-Century Fiction* 17 (September 1962): 103.

8. Frederick R. Karl, *A Reader's Guide to Joseph Conrad* (New York, 1960), p. 260.

9. Albert J. Guerard, *Conrad the Novelist* (Cambridge, Mass., 1958), p. 273.

10. Suresh Raval seems at first to take a similar view: "The very crux of the narrative turns upon the conflict generated by Heyst's divided loyalties. He is a man torn between, on the one hand, allegiance to the self of universal detachment implanted in him by his father, and on the other hand, his spontaneous adherence to the call of the human community as it is embodied in Lena and Morrison." But that he in fact often sees one of these tendencies as more genuine than the other is suggested by subsequent statements: "Heyst's rescues of Morrison and Lena occur in [a] context of skeptical detachment contaminated only by a pity that does not engage a deeper commitment to life"; "For Heyst, love, being grounded in reciprocal relationship, is impossible because his skeptical conception of life cannot liberate a response antithetical to itself"; "Lena seems to recognize . . . that Heyst . . . cannot possibly feel or experience love" ("Conrad's *Victory*: Skepticism and Experience," *Nineteenth-Century Fiction* 34 [March 1980]: 420, 421, 424, 427.

11. The patterns of self-division in *Wuthering Heights* and *Jude the Obscure* are much the same as those evident in *The Mill on the Floss* and *The White Peacock*, as outlined in the previous essay on D. H. Lawrence and George Eliot.

Howards End: Goblins and Rainbows

1. Page references to *Howards End* are to the Penguin Modern Classics edition, ed. Oliver Stallybrass (Harmondsworth, 1975; first published 1910). This text follows that of the Abinger Edition, 1973.

2. The opposition has been variously described. Formulations in some of the best discussions of the novel are: "Bloomsbury liberalism" as against "the great world" (Wilfred Stone, *The Cave and the Mountain: A Study of E. M. Forster* [Stanford, 1966], p. 235); "liberalism" as against "a kind of blunt and humorless materialism" (Frederick C. Crews, *E. M. Forster: The Perils of Humanism* [Princeton, N.J., 1962], p. 105); and "the inner life of intellect and spirit" as against "the outer life of the physical and the sensory" (Cyrus Hoy, "Forster's Metaphysical Novel," *PMLA* 75 [March 1960]: 126).

3. E. M. Forster, interview by P. N. Furbank and F. J. H. Haskell, *The Paris Review* 1 (Spring 1953): 34.

4. See E. K. Brown, *Rhythm in the Novel* (Toronto, 1950), pp. 46–50.

5. James Hall has suggestively drawn attention to this aspect: "For all the talk about personal relations, the novel is not optimistic about the possibility of personal relations with people outside the limited group who have been reared to have similar values" ("Forster's Family Reunions," *ELH* 25 [March 1958]: 75).

Mansfield Park: The Place of Self

1. Page references to *Mansfield Park* are to R. W. Chapman's edition (Oxford, 1923; reprinted 1978; first published 1814).

2. Alistair M. Duckworth makes a similar point: "[Fanny's] spatial position [i.e., in the attic] was clearly a definition of her intermediate social status, and Sir Thomas's intention was to make it clear to her that she was 'not a *Miss Bertram*'" (*The Improvement of the Estate: A Study of Jane Austen's Novels* [Baltimore and London, 1971], p. 79).

3. Gordon N. Ray, as I remarked in the Preface, has stated that Thackeray's *Henry Esmond* is "the first true *Bildungsroman* in English fiction," but *Mansfield Park* would seem to have a clear prior claim to that distinction. See *Thackeray: The Age of Wisdom, 1847–1863* (New York, 1958), p. 110.

4. Marvin Mudrick, *Jane Austen: Irony as Defense and Discovery* (Princeton, N.J., 1952), p. 179.

5. Kingsley Amis, "'What Became of Jane Austen?': *Mansfield Park*," *Spectator* (4 October 1957); reprinted in *Jane Austen: "Sense and Sensibility," "Pride and Prejudice" and "Mansfield Park,"* ed. B. C. Southam (London, 1976), p. 244.

6. Henry, in this respect, may be seen as a forerunner of Frank Churchill in Jane Austen's next novel, *Emma*, just as Mary, in her bright assertiveness, points ahead to Emma herself.

7. Tony Tanner, Introduction to *Mansfield Park*, Penguin English Library edition (Harmondsworth, 1966; reprinted 1971), p. 25.

8. This view of the main concern of *Mansfield Park* has something in common with that of Howard S. Babb, though I shall argue that "self-denial" is itself shown to be a form of "self-indulgence": "the novel's theme," writes Babb, ". . . contrasts the selfishness that results from indulging in one's own wishes with the principled behavior achieved through self-denial" (*Jane Austen's Novels: The Fabric of Dialogue* [Columbus, Ohio, 1962], p. 154).

9. This is not the view that is always taken of her behavior. Mark Kinkead-Weekes, for instance, says that "in fussing about the risk to Maria's dress, instead of speaking decisively about the implications of what she is doing, Fanny is silly—and is meant to sound so" ("This Old Maid: Jane Austen Replies to Charlotte Brontë and D. H. Lawrence," *Nineteenth-Century Fiction* 30 [Dec. 1975]: 407); and Marilyn Butler maintains that in the first half of the book (which includes the visit to Sotherton) Fanny's "consciousness is deliberately left slightly childish and unformed. Instinctively she tries to tell right from wrong, but as yet she lacks the ability" (*Jane Austen and the War of Ideas* [Oxford, 1975], p. 227).

10. Samuel Taylor Coleridge, quoted by Edward M. White, "A Critical Theory of *Mansfield Park*," *Studies in English Literature* 7 (Autumn 1967): 663.

11. Butler, *Jane Austen*, p. 93.

12. Lionel Trilling, "*Mansfield Park*," *The Opposing Self* (1954); reprinted in *Jane Austen*, ed. B. C. Southam, pp. 225–26.

13. Stuart M. Tave takes a similar view of the theatricals: "one of the objections to ladies and gentlemen acting at Mansfield Park is not a Platonic fear of assuming a role but, rather, their amateur inability to keep their private lives from taking over their assumed roles; they don't really act" (*Some Words of Jane Austen* [Chicago and London, 1973], pp. 191–92). See also Butler, *Jane Austen*, p. 232.

14. See Gary Kelly: "There is of course a wealth of ambiguity in her protest, because Fanny's statement [i.e., "I cannot act"] may be taken literally in reference to dramatic acting, or as a confession of physical incapacity resulting from moral disapproval (a consistency of principle and action), or yet again as a reference to Fanny's peculiar passivity and retiredness throughout the novel" ("Reading Aloud in *Mansfield Park*," *Nineteenth-Century Fiction* 37 [June 1982]: 41).

15. Compare, for instance, Tony Tanner: "Even Edmund exerts his pressure on her to participate in the play. And indeed, it seems finally that she too must succumb to the actors. . . . What we are to feel is that if Sir Thomas had not come back, then Fanny would have been forced to 'act' . . . [but] because Fanny does hold out, she will be the one who truly saves Mansfield Park . . . at the end of the book" (Introduction to *Mansfield Park*, Penguin ed., p. 29). See also Butler, *Jane Austen*, pp. 240–41.

A Secret Heart: *The History of Henry Esmond*

1. Page references to *Henry Esmond* are to the Penguin English Library edition, ed. John Sutherland and Michael Greenfield (Harmondsworth, 1970; first

published 1852). The text of the Penguin edition is based on the one-volume 1858 edition, the last that Thackeray supervised.

2. See John Loofbourow, who says "Esmond, in the tradition of memoirs of the period, habitually refers to himself in the third person" (*Thackeray and the Form of Fiction* [New York, 1976; first published 1964], p. 119).

3. John Sutherland, Introduction to *Henry Esmond*, p. 14.

4. Juliet McMaster suggests that the whole narrative should be read in terms of dramatic irony. She says that "if we take Esmond's memoirs at face value," we are given a picture of a man who "grows to wisdom and maturity, not only in knowledge of the world, but emotionally and morally as well"; and she maintains "there is something godlike about so much virtue and self-abnegation." If, however, we regard the novel "as a sustained piece of dramatic irony," we see that Esmond's "humility is inverted pride, and his self-abnegation an elaborate glorification of self"; moreover, "far from growing to maturity, he finally fulfils the infantile impulse to marry his mother." McMaster says her interpretation "has suggested the second reading because critical emphasis has usually been the other way," but that she does "not mean to exclude the first: there is again that double focus which is part of the complexity of Thackeray's moral vision." But this seems more like having it both ways than a double focus; and, if anything, her reading would appear in fact to exclude the second view. She finally grants that Esmond's "actions *are* noble even if he has himself a rather exaggerated sense of their nobility" (my emphasis), a qualification, no doubt, but one that does not invert their nobility. *Thackeray: The Major Novels* (Toronto, 1971), p. 124.

5. Pursuing deconstruction, J. Hillis Miller proposes an Oedipal reading of the text that produces a portrait of Esmond which "erases" and "obliterates" the narrator's "picture of himself"; but this reading seems to me to be open to serious objection. "Like the Oedipus of the legend," Miller says, "Henry has been responsible for the death of the man who stands in place of a father to him. He ultimately takes that father's place in the bed of the woman who has been a mother to him." But Esmond is *not* "like the Oedipus of the legend," for Oedipus is not "responsible" for the death referred to—he kills; and he kills his father, not "the man who stands in place of a father to him." Nor is Esmond in fact responsible for the death of Frank Castlewood: his death is the result of a quarrel about his wife with Lord Mohun, who tries to seduce her, and Esmond is responsible neither for the quarrel nor the death, having done everything possible to avert both. His responsibility is scarcely established by the assertion that "Mohun is Henry's malign double," and that Esmond acts "as it were" through him. Far from hurrying, moreover, to take his "father's" place in bed, Esmond backs away when "the woman who has been [like] a mother to him" offers it to him some time after her husband's death. *Fiction and Repetition: Seven English Novels* (Cambridge, Mass., 1982), pp. 97, 102, 103.

6. My view of the kind of response the narrative invites is akin to that of John Hagan, though I think Esmond is more self-aware than Hagan grants: "*Henry Esmond* is . . . a masterpiece of irony . . . in the sense that it requires us to penetrate the disguises, the understatements, and the indirections of the narrator, Esmond himself, and to discover the truth of his feelings which his

own narrative so effectively in part conceals both from his readers and very probably even from himself" (" 'Bankruptcy of His Heart': The Unfulfilled Life of Henry Esmond," *Nineteenth-Century Fiction* 27 [Dec. 1972]: 295).

7. See J. Y. T. Greig, who says that "the motives and feelings behind Rachel's hesitant severity are clear: her cruelty to Esmond is cruelty to herself; it is herself she is punishing for having been unfaithful in will, though not in deed, to her murdered husband" (*Thackeray: A Reconsideration* [New York, 1967; first published 1950], p. 162). John E. Tilford states "it is altogether clear now that, undone by a tragedy for which she feels responsible, she is overwhelmed by a profound feeling of guilt, though she distorts the reasons for that feeling. . . . Her feeling of guilt, we now know, is not due to jealousy; it is due to loving Henry beyond maternal bounds" ("The Love Theme of *Henry Esmond*," *PMLA* 67 [September 1952]: 690).

8. It is strange that John Hagan, who is extremely perceptive about Esmond's role in this scene, should fail to see how his attitude affects Rachel's: "the real reason for [Rachel's] refusal of Esmond's proposal [is that she is "still dominated by her old guilty feeling about having loved Esmond during her husband's lifetime"]. Why, otherwise, would she speak to him with the look and tone of a 'mother'? . . . she . . . tries to cope with [her guilty conscience] by transforming her erotic passion into an exalted, morally acceptable maternal love" (" 'Bankruptcy of His Heart,' " p. 309). See also John E. Tilford, who says "[Rachel] thanks heaven, perhaps [that "his proposal [is] inspired . . . by . . . his duty as a gentleman"], because she knows that if his love were erotic, she would likely yield" ("The Love Theme," p. 693).

9. See Sylvia Manning, who says that "the episode of James and Beatrix and Anne . . . is egregiously unhistorical: the Pretender was not even in England at the time of Queen Anne's death" ("Incest and the Structure of *Henry Esmond*," *Nineteenth-Century Fiction* 34 [September 1979]: 210).

The Double Bind of Consciousness:
A Portrait of the Artist as a Young Man

1. James Joyce, "A Portrait of the Artist," in *James Joyce: Dubliners and A Portrait of the Artist as a Young Man*, ed. Morris Beja (London, 1973), p. 41. "A Portrait" is an essay-narrative of about 2,000 words, written in January 1904, and it may be regarded as a first version of the novel, which Joyce dates "Dublin 1904 Trieste 1914."

2. Hugh Kenner, *Dublin's Joyce* (London, 1955), p. 120.

3. Page references to *A Portrait of the Artist as a Young Man* are to the Granada Triad Panther edition, ed. Richard Ellmann (Frogmore, St. Albans, 1979; first published 1916). The text of this edition is based on the Dublin Holograph, as amended by Chester G. Anderson and Richard Ellmann.

4. The quotation is from Horace Gregory's verse translation of Ovid's *The Metamorphoses* (New York, 1958).

5. A number of critics have drawn attention to the significance of the Daedalus motif in the novel. See Marvin Magalaner and Richard M. Kain,

Joyce: The Man, the Work, the Reputation (New York, 1956), pp. 119–20; A. Walton Litz, *James Joyce* (New York, 1966), pp. 70–71; and Velma F. Grant, "Stephen Dedalus and Classical Daedalus: A Symbolic Analogy," *CLAJ* 21 (March 1978): 411.

6. S. L. Goldberg says that even "the [aesthetic] theory in the *Portrait* serves to reveal not so much the nature of art as the nature of Stephen Dedalus" (*The Classical Temper: A Study of James Joyce's* Ulysses [London, 1961], p. 43). Both J. I. M. Stewart and William York Tindall draw attention to the shadowiness of the characters other than Stephen. See Stewart, *James Joyce* (London, 1957), p. 18; and Tindall, *A Reader's Guide to James Joyce* (New York, 1959), p. 63.

7. George Orwell, "Charles Dickens," *Critical Essays* (London, 1946), p. 17.

8. Stanislaus Joyce, *My Brother's Keeper: James Joyce's Early Years*, ed. Richard Ellmann (New York, 1958), p. 17.

9. Kenner, *Dublin's Joyce*, p. 113.

10. The phrase is not Stephen's, as was once thought, but has been traced by James Atherton in his edition of the *Portrait* (1963) to Hugh Miller's *Testimony of the Rocks* (Edinburgh, 1869).

11. Stanislaus Joyce has reported that it is an actual early poem of Joyce's and "belonged to one or other of the earlier collections" (*My Brother's Keeper*, p. 151).

12. See Robert Scholes, "Stephen Dedalus, Poet or Esthete?" *PMLA* 79 (September 1964): 484–89.

13. Kenner, *Dublin's Joyce*, p. 123. See also Bernard Benstock, "A Light from Some Other World: Symbolic Structure in *A Portrait of the Artist*," in *Approaches to Joyce's Portrait*, ed. Thomas F. Staley and Bernard Benstock (Pittsburgh, Pa., 1976), p. 205; and Baruch Hochman, "Joyce's *Portrait* as Portrait," *The Literary Review* 22 (Fall 1978): 37.

14. Scholes, "Poet or Esthete?" p. 485.

Free Fall: The Bursting of the Door

1. *Free Fall* (London, 1959). All subsequent references are to this first edition of the novel.

2. Golding's own comments in an interview are relevant here. Jack I. Biles reports him as saying: "it seems to me that we do live in two worlds. There is this physical one, which is coherent, and there is a spiritual one. To the average man . . . that world is very often incoherent. But nevertheless, as a matter of experience, for *me* and I suspect for millions of other people, this experience of having two worlds to live in all the time—or not all the time, [but] occasionally—is a vital one and is what living is like. And that is why *Free Fall* is important to me, because I've tried to put those two worlds into it, as a matter of daily experience" (*Talk: Conversations with William Golding* [New York, 1970], p. 79).

3. Mark Kinkead-Weekes and Ian Gregor draw an analogy between the narrative technique and the procedures of an artillery officer ranging his guns on a target: "After three necessary sighting shots, the target area is pinpointed" (*William Golding: A Critical Study* [London, 1967], p. 187).

4. Biles, *Talk: Conversations with William Golding*, pp. 81–82.

5. Virginia Tiger reports that Golding intended a contrast between the Beatrice of *Free Fall* and Dante's Beatrice. She says that, in a "conversation with Peter Green," Golding traced the source of the ironic contrast to Dante's "coherent cosmos" as opposed to "Sammy's confused cosmos" (*William Golding: The Dark Fields of Discovery* [London, 1974], p. 156).

Mark Kinkead-Weekes and Ian Gregor comment illuminatingly on attitudes to the two Beatrices: "This is Sammy's *Vita Nuova*, acridly rewriting Dante's experience of the revolution of Love. Sammy's Beatrice, first manifested to him . . . in the art-room, is as much a showing-forth of another world as Dante's, a miraculous Being, equally unattainable. But Sammy sets out to attain her . . . The basis of his tragedy is that he confuses, as Dante never did, sharing in that Being with possession of the body that manifests it" (*William Golding: A Critical Study*, pp. 174, 177).

6. Howard S. Babb believes that Sammy *is* ready to betray his comrades, though his view of a further significance of the cry is similar to mine: "The primary narrative sense . . . is that Sammy has reached the end of his resistance and seeks release from the cell to confess what he knows about his fellow prisoners . . . however tortured he feels at the prospect of betraying his comrades. But simultaneously the paragraphs display Sammy arriving at the boundaries of the self and recognizing his limitations as a guilty human in his call for help. The change . . . which has been produced by 'the very act of crying' would indicate an incipient acknowledgment on Sammy's part of some power that transcends the self to which he has been enslaved" (*The Novels of William Golding* [Columbus, Ohio, 1970], pp. 108–9).

See also James R. Baker: "It is a stark outcry to something beyond the self, beyond the world of the finite consciousness, and the moment it is uttered the door bursts open on the forgotten world of the spirit" (*William Golding: A Critical Study* [New York, 1965], pp. 65–66).

7. To some critics, the conjunction of the end of the novel with the passage that describes the bursting of the door seems to make for an unresolved ambiguity. See Frank Kermode, who says that "at the height of his agony [Sammy] bursts out (or is let out) of the cell, forgiven" ("William Golding," in *Puzzles and Epiphanies* [New York, 1962], p. 212).

8. Howard S. Babb approaches the question differently, but he makes a similar point about Sammy's self-imprisonment: He says that Sammy's "local terror at the blackness of the cell . . . turns out to be engendered by his guilt, for it finally becomes clear that the decisive cell confining Sammy is his own self" (*The Novels of William Golding*, p. 107).

Aphrodite of the Foam and *The Ladybird* Tales

1. Page references are to the Penguin edition of *The Ladybird* (Harmondsworth, 1960).

2. Compare Julian Moynahan's statement: "Henry's act is not a murder. It is an inspired and creative deed" (*The Deed of Life: The Novels and Tales of D. H. Lawrence* [Princeton, New Jersey, 1963], p. 199).

3. See F. R. Leavis's chapter on "The Captain's Doll" in *D. H. Lawrence: Novelist* (London, 1955), pp. 197–224.

Hardy's Reluctant Heroines

1. Page references to *Far from the Madding Crowd* are to the Penguin English Library edition, ed. Ronald Blythe (Harmondsworth, 1978). All subsequent references are to the Penguin text, which is based on that of the Wessex edition of 1912.

2. The history of the composition of *The Woodlanders* suggests that in some ways it is a reworking of *Far from the Madding Crowd*. Hardy started writing *The Woodlanders* in 1874, in the same year that the former novel was published, that is, but then put it aside until he returned to it more than ten years later. See Florence Emily Hardy, *The Life of Thomas Hardy* (London, 1962), pp. 102, 168.

3. Page references to *The Woodlanders* are to the New Wessex (paperback) edition (London, 1974), which is based on that of the Wessex edition of 1912.

4. Thomas Hardy to J. T. Grein and C. W. Jarvis, 19 July 1889, *The Collected Letters of Thomas Hardy*, ed. Richard Little Purdy and Michael Millgate, vol. 1, *1840–1892* (Oxford, 1978), p. 195.

5. See Mary Jacobus, "Sue the Obscure," *Essays in Criticism* 25 (July 1975): 304–28.

6. Page references to *Jude the Obscure* are to the Penguin English Library edition, ed. C. H. Sisson (Harmondsworth, 1978), which is based on that of the Wessex edition of 1912.

7. Hardy to Edmund Gosse, 20 November 1895, *Collected Letters*, vol. 2, *1893–1901* (Oxford, 1980), p. 99.

Alan Sillitoe: The Novelist as Map-Maker

1. In the absence of a standard edition of Sillitoe's novels, references are to chapters, or to parts and chapters. The following is a chronological list of the novels referred to: *Saturday Night and Sunday Morning* (1958); *The General* (1960); *Key to the Door* (1961); *The Death of William Posters* (1965); *A Tree on Fire* (1967); *A Start in Life* (1970); *Travels in Nihilon* (1971); *Raw Material* (1972); *The Flame of Life* (1974); *The Widower's Son* (1976); and *The Storyteller* (1979).

2. Stanley S. Atherton, *Alan Sillitoe: A Critical Assessment* (London, 1979), p. 45.

3. John Coleman, "The Unthinkables," *New Statesman* 62 (27 October 1961): 610.

Postscript: The Univocal and the Equivocal

1. Paul de Man, *Blindness and Insight: Essays in the Rhetoric of Contemporary Criticism* (New York, 1971), p. 29.

2. See J. Hillis Miller's chapter on *Henry Esmond* in his *Fiction and Repetition: Seven English Novels* (Cambridge, Mass., 1982), pp. 73–115.

3. J. Hillis Miller, "Theory and Practice: Response to Vincent Leitch," *Critical Inquiry* 6 (Summer 1980): 610.

4. Geoffrey Hartman, preface to Harold Bloom, et al., *Deconstruction and Criticism* (New York, 1979), p. vii.

5. Paul de Man, *Blindness and Insight*, pp. 17, 133, 136.

6. J. Hillis Miller, "The Critic as Host," in *Deconstruction and Criticism*, p. 230.

7. The essay was originally published as a rejoinder to strictures on Deconstruction by Wayne Booth and M. H. Abrams, and appeared together with their articles in *Critical Inquiry* 3 (Spring 1977).

8. The word "host" in the sense of "an animal or plant having a parasite . . . habitually living in or upon it" comes from the Latin *hospes* (*hospitem*; host, guest). The word "host" in the sense of "an armed multitude of men; an army" comes from the Latin *hostis* (*hostem*; stranger, enemy). Definitions and derivations are from *The Shorter Oxford English Dictionary*.

9. J. Hillis Miller, "Stevens' Rock and Criticism as Cure," *The Georgia Review* 30 (Spring 1976): 10–11.

10. Shlomith Rimmon, *The Concept of Ambiguity—the Example of James* (Chicago and London, 1977), p. 10. Rimmon (later Rimmon-Kenan) herself points out that "Miller replaces the narrow notion of ambiguity as a feature of some texts by the broad notion of unreadability as a characteristic of all texts" ("Deconstructive Reflections on Deconstruction: In Reply to Hillis Miller," *Poetics Today* 2 [1b, 1980–81]: 187).

11. J. Hillis Miller, "The Fiction of Realism: *Sketches by Boz, Oliver Twist*, and Cruikshank's Illustrations," in *Dickens Centennial Essays*, ed. Ada Nisbet and Blake Nevius (Berkeley, Los Angeles and London, 1971), p. 116.

12. Miller, *Fiction and Repetition*, p. 97.

13. Jacques Derrida, "Living On • Border Lines," in *Deconstruction and Criticism*, p. 79.

14. Derrida talks, apropos of problems of translation, of "impoverishment by univocality" (*Deconstruction and Criticism*, p. 90); and de Man says that "we no longer take for granted that a literary text can be reduced to a finite meaning or set of meanings, but see the act of reading as an endless process in which truth and falsehood are inextricably intertwined" (foreword to *Blindness and Insight*, p. ix).

15. Miller, *Fiction and Repetition*, p. 21.

INDEX